I0836973

PROBLEMS

OF

LIFE AND MIND.

BY

GEORGE HENRY LEWES.

First Series.

THE FOUNDATIONS OF A CREED.

VOL. I.

BOSTON:
JAMES R. OSGOOD AND COMPANY,
LATE TICKNOR & FIELDS, AND FIELDS, OSGOOD, & CO.
1874.

AUTHOR'S EDITION.

From Advance Sheets.

University Press: Welch, Bigelow, & Co.,
Cambridge.

PREFACE.

THE work, of which this is the first volume, has been many years in preparation; indeed, its origin may be said to go so far back as 1836, when with the rashness of ambitious youth I planned a treatise on the Philosophy of the Mind in which the doctrines of Reid, Stewart, and Brown were to be physiologically interpreted. In 1837 I gave a course of lectures on the subject in Fox's Chapel, Finsbury. The scheme was abandoned, partly because of a growing dissatisfaction with the doctrines of the Scotch School, and partly perhaps from a misgiving as to my physiological knowledge. Other studies and other labors occupied me until 1860, when I believed that my researches into the nervous system had placed in my hands a clew through the labyrinth of mental phenomena; and, misled by the plausible supposition that the complex phenomena in Man might be better interpreted by approaching them through the simpler phenomena in Animals, I began to collect materials for a work on Animal Psychology. This also proved to be premature. Rightly to understand the mental condition of Animals, we must first gain a clear vision of the fundamental processes in Man; since, obviously, it is only through our knowledge of the processes in ourselves that we can interpret the manifestations of similar processes in them; and here we are hampered by the anthropomorphic tendency which leads us to assign exclusively human motives to animal actions.

In 1862 I began the investigation of the physiological mechanism of Feeling and Thought, and from that time forward have sought assistance in a wide range of research. Anatomy, Physiology, Pathology, Insanity, and the Science of Language, have supplied facts and suggestions to enlarge and direct my own meditations, and to confirm and correct the many valuable indications furnished by previous psychological investigators. Let me not be thought ungrateful to my predecessors, some of whose contributions are of imperishable value, if, while acknowledging the illumination I have received from their labors, I declare my conviction that, in spite of all they have achieved, Psychology is still without the fundamental data necessary to its *constitution* as a science; it is very much in the condition of Chemistry before Lavoisier, or of Biology before Bichat. Isolated discoveries, however valuable, do not suffice. A science is constituted — that is, has received its definitive construction and place in the hierarchy of Philosophy — when its object is circumscribed, its phenomena defined, its Method settled, and its fundamental principles established, so that henceforward the development is progressive, the discovery of to-day enlarging and not overturning the conception of yesterday, each worker bringing his contribution to a common fund, not presenting it as a reversal of all that predecessors had done.

To note a deficiency is one thing, another to remedy that deficiency. Clearly as the want of fundamental principles appeared to me, I was under no illusion as to my being in possession of the necessary inductions; and I therefore only contemplated working at special questions, without reference to their common connections. A varied set of detached investigations had grown into a huge mass of heterogeneous MS. before any central light appeared to shape the chaos into a system. When I began to organize these materials into a book, I only intended it to be a series of essays treating certain problems of Life and Mind. But out of this arose two results, little contemplated.

The first result was such a mutual illumination from the various principles arrived at separately that I began to feel confident of having something like a clear vision of the fundamental inductions necessary to the constitution of Psychology; hence, although I do not propose to write a complete treatise, I hope to establish a firm groundwork for future labors.

The second result, which was independent of the first, arose thus: Finding the exposition obstructed by the existence of unsolved metaphysical problems, and by the too frequent employment of the metaphysical Method, and knowing that there was no chance of general recognition of the scientific Method and its inductions while the rival Method was tolerated, and the conceptions of Force, Cause, Matter, Mind, were vacillating and contradictory, I imagined that it would be practicable in an introductory chapter, not indeed to clear the path of these obstacles, but at least to give such precise indications of the principles adopted throughout the exposition as would enable the reader to follow it untroubled by metaphysical difficulties. That introductory chapter has grown insensibly into a substantive work; and the two volumes of which it consists are but a portion of what has been written. Not only has the chapter grown into a work, the work itself has grown into a systematic introduction to the philosophy of Science; and what was intended merely as a preparation for a Psychology discloses itself as the *Foundations of a Creed.*

This brief sketch of its history may not only explain and partly justify the somewhat ambitious pretensions of this work, it will also explain and partly justify certain defects in its composition. Having grown up heterogeneously, its structure is heterogeneous. Sections now brought together have been wrought out at the distance of years, and without reference to each other; while during repeated revisions and remodifications many repetitions and cross-references have been inserted, and sentences bearing the obvious trace of 1872 or 1873 appear in pages originally written perhaps eight or ten years previously. The reader is also sometimes called upon to accept results for which the evidence can only be produced in subsequent chapters or volumes. I have so far guarded against this evil that in such cases I have only asked for provisional assent.

The Foundations of a Creed ought to have sufficient standing-room for antagonistic schools. The general consideration that every philosophical opinion must have some truth sustaining it, is here adopted; and therefore due weight is attempted to be assigned to adverse arguments, — for example, those which affirm and those which deny the possibility of Metaphysics, or the existence of Innate Ideas; the facts which favor, and the facts which exclude, the spiritualist hypothesis and the materialist hypothesis. While cordially agreeing with those philosophers who reject both Spiritualism and Materialism, I do not agree with them in their conclusion that we know nothing whatever of Mind or Matter. I hold with their antagonists that we know a great deal of both. I cannot agree that Philosophy gains any refuge from difficulties by invoking the Unknowable; though it may admit the existence of the Unknowable, this admission is transcendental, and leaves all the purposes of Philosophy unaffected. Deeply as we may feel the mystery of this universe and the limitations of our faculties, the *Foundations of a Creed* can only rest upon the Known and Knowable.

The second volume, completing this First Series, is now under final revision.

THE PRIORY, *September*, 1873.

CONTENTS.

INTRODUCTION.

PART I.—THE METHOD OF SCIENCE AND ITS APPLICATION TO METAPHYSICS.

PROBLEM I.—THE LIMITATIONS OF KNOWLEDGE.

CHAPTER I.

CHAPTER II.

CHAPTER III.

CHAPTER IV.

CHAPTER V.

CHAPTER VI.

CHAPTER VII.

CHAPTER VIII.

CHAPTER IX.

CHAPTER X.

CHAPTER XI.

CHAPTER XII.

CHAPTER XIII.

CHAPTER XIV.

CHAPTER XV.

CHAPTER XVI.

INTRODUCTION.

PART I.

THE METHOD OF SCIENCE AND ITS APPLICATION TO METAPHYSICS.

PART II.

THE RULES OF PHILOSOPHIZING.

"England's thinkers are again beginning to see, what they had only temporarily forgotten, that the difficulties of Metaphysics lie at the root of all Science; that those difficulties can only be quieted by being resolved, and that until they are resolved, positively whenever possible, but at any rate negatively, we are never assured that any knowledge, even physical, stands on solid foundations."

STUART MILL.

"Ich erkühne mich zu sagen, dass nicht eine einzige metaphysische Aufgabe sein müsse, die hier nicht aufgelöst, oder zu deren Auflösung nicht wenigstens der Schlüssel dargereicht worden."

KANT.

INTRODUCTION.

PART I.

THE METHOD OF SCIENCE AND ITS APPLICATION TO METAPHYSICS.

CHAPTER I.

THE CONFLICT OF OPINION AND THE ISSUE.

1. No one meditating on the present condition of the intellectual world can fail to be arrested by the evidences of its deep-seated unrest. Yeast is working everywhere. Ancient formulas and time-honored creeds are yielding as much to internal pressure as to external assault. The expansion of knowledge is loosening the very earth clutched by the roots of creeds and churches. Rejoice over this or deplore it, the fact is unmistakable. Sects and parties, in the endeavor to sustain their positions, and to preserve at least their watchwords and the outward semblance of their creeds, nowadays snatch eagerly at compromises which a few years ago would have been scouted as heresies. Science is penetrating everywhere, and slowly changing men's conception of the world and of man's destiny. Doctrines which once were damnable are now fashionable, and heresies are appropriated as aids to faith. Ours is no longer the age described by Carlyle, "destitute of faith, yet terrified at scepticism." It is an age clamorous for faith, and only dissatisfied with scepti-

cism when scepticism is a resting-place instead of a starting-point, a result instead of a preliminary caution. The purely negative attitude of Unbelief, once regarded as philosophical, is now generally understood to be only laudable in the face of the demonstrably incredible.

2. The great desire of this age is for a Doctrine which may serve to condense our knowledge, guide our researches, and shape our lives, so that Conduct may really be the consequence of Belief. We are growing impatient of futile compromises and half-beliefs; we see that it will not do to believe, or pretend to believe, one theory of the universe, yet show, in every way wherein confidence can show itself, that our lives are ruled by another theory. In consequence of this desire, while thinking men appear, on a superficial view, to be daily separating wider and wider from each other, they are, on a deeper view, seen to be drawing closer together, — differing in opinion, they are approximating in spirit and purpose.

There is a conspicuous effort to reconcile the aims and claims of Religion and Science, — the two mightiest antagonists. The many and piteous complaints, old as Religion itself, against the growing infidelity of the age, might be disregarded were they not confirmed on all sides by the evidence that Religion is rapidly tending to one of two issues, — either towards extinction or towards transformation. Some considerable thinkers regard the former alternative as the probable and desirable issue. They argue that Religion has played its part in the evolution of Humanity, — a noble part, yet only that of a provisional organ, which, in the course of development, must be displaced by a final organ. Other thinkers — and I follow these — consider that Religion will continue to regulate the evolution; but that to do this in the coming ages, it must occupy a position similar to the one it occupied in the past, and express the highest thought of the time, as that thought widens with the ever-growing experience. It must not attempt to imprison the mind in formulas which no longer contain the whole of positive knowledge. It must not attempt to force on our acceptance, as explanations of the universe, dogmas which were originally the childish guesses at truth made by barbarian tribes. It must no longer present a conception of the world and physical laws, or of man and moral laws, which has any other basis than that of scientific induction. It must no longer put forward principles which are unintelligible and incredible, nor make their very unintelligibility a source of glory, and a belief in them a higher virtue than belief in demonstration. In a word, this transformed Religion must cease to accept for its tests and sanctions such tests as would be foolishness in Science, and such sanctions as would be selfishness in Life. Instead of proclaiming the nothingness of this life, the worthlessness of human love, and the imbecility of the human mind, it will proclaim the supreme importance of this life, the supreme value of human love, and the grandeur of human intellect. Those who entertain this hope, and this view of a Religion founded on Science expressing at each stage what is known of the world and of man, believe — and I share the belief — that the present antagonism will rapidly merge in an energetic co-operation. The internecine warfare which has so long disturbed Religion and obstructed Science will give place to a Doctrine which will respect the claims of both, and satisfy the needs of both.

3. This future may be undetermined, but it will come. It will not come without contention. The ground will be contested inch by inch. The pathway of Progress will still, as of old, bear traces of martyrdom; but the advance is inevitable. The signs of the advent are not few. Looking at them with some closeness, one observes that

Science itself is also in travail. Assuredly some mighty new birth is at hand. Solid as the ground appears, and fixed as are our present landmarks, we cannot but feel the strange tremors of subterranean agitation which must erelong be followed by upheavals disturbing those landmarks. Not only do we see Physics on the eve of a reconstruction through Molecular Dynamics, we also see Metaphysics strangely agitated, and showing symptoms of a reawakened life. After a long period of neglect and contempt, its problems are once more reasserting their claims. And whatever we may think of those claims, we have only to reflect on the important part played by Metaphysics in sustaining and developing religious conceptions, no less than in thwarting and misdirecting scientific conceptions, to feel assured that before Religion and Science can be reconciled by the reduction of their principles to a common Method, it will be necessary to transform Metaphysics, or to stamp it out of existence. There is but this alternative. At present Metaphysics is an obstacle in our path: it must be crushed into dust, and our chariot-wheels must pass over it; or its forces of resistance must be converted into motive powers, and what is an obstacle become an impulse.

4. It is towards the transformation of Metaphysics by reduction to the Method of Science that these pages tend. Their object is to show that the Method which has hitherto achieved such splendid success in Science needs only to be properly interpreted and applied, and by it the inductions and deductions from experience will furnish solutions to every metaphysical problem that can be rationally stated; whereas *no* problem, metaphysical or scientific, which is irrationally stated, can receive a rational solution. I propose to show that metaphysical problems have, rationally, no other difficulties than those which beset all problems; and, when scientifically treated,

they are capable of solutions not less satisfactory and certain than those of physics.

To one class of readers this announcement will perhaps seem extravagant, and the attempt absurd; to another class the limitation to scientific Method will seem narrow and insufficient. But if I succeed in showing the first that solutions *can* thus be reached, and in showing the second that *only* thus can any solution be reached, the gain will be obvious; not only will a vast region of speculative disorder be reduced to order, not only will one obstacle to the reconciliation between Religion and Science be removed, but we shall be in possession of a Method which will make Religion also the expression of Experience, and thus dissipate the clouds of mystery and incredibility which have so long concealed the clear heavens.

5. Should these pages fall into the hands of readers who on former occasions have given me their attention, they will doubtless feel some surprise at this announcement of my present aim. I may here seem to be unsaying what it has been the chief purpose of my labors to enforce. But it is not really so. I have indeed incessantly, for some thirty years, tried to dissuade men from wasting precious energies on insoluble problems; that purpose still animates my efforts. But, although formerly I regarded problems as insoluble which I now hold to be soluble, there has been no other change than this, that I now see how problems which were insoluble by the Method then in use, are soluble by the Method of Science. This is not a retreat, but a change of front. Throughout my polemic against Metaphysics, the attacks were directed against the irrational Method, as one by which *all* problems whatever must be insoluble.

6. Descartes opened Modern Philosophy by his famous "Discourse on Method." It was a brilliant effort, but the

consecration of experience has been wanting to it. History proves that it was not really capable of furnishing any satisfactory solutions.

Auguste Comte opened the new era by his great conception of Method, namely, the extension to *all* inquiries — even morals and politics — of those inductive principles which alone have been found fruitful in any inquiries. I shall not be supposed to underrate the value of the Positive Philosophy, as conceived by Comte, in pointing out a defect of that scheme which has often been pointed out by its opponents, namely, that it displays no effort to apply the positive Method to one great branch of speculation, — that of Metaphysics. He peremptorily excluded all research whatever in this direction, declaring metaphysical problems to be essentially insoluble, consequently idle and mischievous. Nor can there be any dispute that the speculations he had in view are inane, when pursued on the Method traditionally followed; but an extension of the principles of positivism may legitimately include even these speculations; and Scientific Method, rightly interpreted, will find its employment there. It is surely more philosophical to bring metaphysical problems under the same speculative conditions as all other problems, than to exclude them altogether, since our ignoring them will not extirpate them. The problems exist, and form obstacles to Research. Speculative minds cannot resist the fascination of Metaphysics, even when forced to admit that its inquiries are hopeless. This fact must be taken into account, since it makes refutation powerless. Indeed, one may say, generally, that no deeply rooted tendency was ever extirpated by adverse argument. Not having originally been founded on argument, it cannot be destroyed by logic. The very mind which admits your evidence to be unanswerable will swing back to its old position the instant that the pressure of evidence abates;

and the opponent whom you left yesterday seemingly converted, is found to-day no less confident than of old. Contempt, ridicule, argument, are all vain against tendencies towards metaphysical speculation. There is but one effective mode of displacing an error, and that is to replace it by a conception which, while readily adjusting itself to conceptions firmly held on other points, is seen to explain the facts more completely. The one permanent victory over a false Method is by philosophizing better. The disciples of Descartes were not drawn over to the side of Newton by arguments exposing the imperfections of their system, but by examples of the greater sweep and efficiency of the Newtonian system, interpreted on principles common to Descartes and Newton: the hypothesis of vortices gradually sank into neglect when the law of gravitation was seen to be equally consistent with the mathematical principles advocated by Descartes, and more competent to explain the phenomena.

7. No array of argument, no accumulation of contempt, no historical exhibition of the fruitlessness of its effort, has sufficed to extirpate the tendency towards metaphysical speculation. Although its doctrines have become a scoff (except among the valiant few), its Method still survives, still prompts to renewed research, and still misleads some men of science. In vain History points to the unequivocal failure of twenty centuries: the metaphysician admits the fact, but appeals to History in proof of the persistent passion which no failure can dismay; and hence draws confidence in ultimate success. A cause which is vigorous after centuries of defeat is a cause baffled but not hopeless, beaten but not subdued. The ranks of its army may be thinned, its banners torn and mud-stained; but the indomitable energy breaks out anew, and the fight is continued. Nay, — instructive fact! — even some great captains of Science, while standing on triumphal cars in

the presence of applauding crowds, are ever and anon seen to cast lingering glances at those dark avenues of forbidden research, and are stung by secret misgivings lest after all those avenues should not be issueless, but might some day open on a grander plain. They are not quite at ease in the suspicion that other minds confessedly of splendid powers can deliberately relinquish the certain glories of scientific labor for the nebulous splendors of Metaphysics. They are not quite at ease lest what to their unaided vision now appears a nebula may not one day by aided vision resolve itself into stars. This hesitation is comprehensible: it is due in some measure to an imperfect appreciation of the limits and possibilities of Research, and in many cases due to the fact that many minds well trained in Science are imperfectly trained in Philosophy; hence a want of harmony in their conceptions leads them to follow implicitly in one direction the principles which they peremptorily reject in another.

8. Few researches can be conducted in any one line of inquiry without sooner or later abutting on some metaphysical problem, were it only that of Force, Matter, or Cause; and since Science will not, and Metaphysics cannot solve it, the result is a patchwork of demonstration and speculation very pitiable to contemplate. Look where we will, unless we choose to overlook all that we do not understand, we are mostly confronted with a meshwork of fact and fiction, observation curiously precise beside traditions painfully absurd, a compound of sunlight and mist. Thus in various writings we come upon Laws which compel phenomena to obey their prescription, — Plans and Archetypal Ideas which shape the course of events, and give forms and functions to organisms, — Forces playing about like sprites amid Atoms that are at once contradictorily indivisible and infinitely divisible, — Bodies acting where they are not, and Non-

Being (pure space) endowed with physical properties, among others that of resistance (since Forces in spite of their alleged independence of Matter are supposed to be diminished by the spaces they traverse); — these and many analogous phantoms, more or less credited, too frequently hover amid phenomena, and convert speculation into what Hegel in another connection sarcastically calls a "true witches' circle." *

9. Why is this? Mainly because men of science are generally trained either to ignore all metaphysical questions, or to regard them as "mysteries which must be accepted." Some of the first have their confidence shaken by the steadfast faith of the metaphysician that the mysteries can be unveiled. Some of the second are found expressing decided opinions on those very mysteries declared to lie beyond human ken. Both argue from metaphysical assumptions and traditions as from acceptable data. Both resemble those theologians who solemnly affirm God to be unknowable, yet nevertheless have no hesitation in assigning attributes to his nature, and purposes to his creations.

The continuance of metaphysical inquiry is, for the present at least, inevitable. The continuance of the metaphysical Method is a serious evil, and is evitable. It sustains and fortifies those theological conceptions which would be seen to be preposterous, were it not for the dialectical dexterity which presents them in a light assuredly no less rational than that in which many metaphysical conceptions are presented. It is this which causes the adhesion of so many eminent men of science

* "In der That befindet man sich in einer Art von Hexenkreise worin Bestimmungen des Daseyns und Bestimmungen der Reflexion, Grund und Begründetes, Phænomene und Phantome in unausgeschiedener Gesellschaft durch einander laufen und gleichen Rang mit einander geniessen." — *Logik*, II. 93.

to theological dogmas flagrantly at variance with their positive knowledge. Renouncing all hope of a rational solution, yet unable to release their minds from the pressure of certain problems, they fly to Faith for refuge. One of the sincerest of men and one of the most cautious of investigators, — Faraday, — when asked by a friend how he could believe the astounding propositions current in the religious sect to which he belonged, replied: "I prostrate my reason in this matter; for if I applied the same process of reasoning which I use in matters of science I should be an unbeliever." It was in a less philosophical spirit that Pascal wrote: "Je trouve bien qu'on n'approfondisse pas le système de Copernic." Pascal carried even into Science his theological terror at the possible consequences of reasoning when a dogma seemed in peril; Faraday kept the two provinces and their two Methods distinct. It is remarkable that both these great men were not reassured by the certainty that no truth in one direction can really contradict another; and Faraday might have been told that the legitimate application of those tests and sanctions which he regarded as sufficient in physical research, might, if applied to metaphysical or theological questions, make him an unbeliever in the doctrines of his sect, but not an unbeliever in the truths which replaced them.

10. It may be noted that Metaphysics refusing to adopt the Method of Science has received the protection of Theology, but only such protection as is accorded to a vassal, and which is changed into hostility whenever their conclusions clash, or whenever argument threatens to disturb the secular slumber of dogma. Treated as a vassal by Theology, it is treated by Science as a visionary. Is there no escape from this equivocal position?

We have two cardinal facts to consider: first, that certain problems, though incessantly grappled with, have yielded no permanently accepted solutions; secondly, that in spite of constant failure they press on our attention with ever-renewed solicitation. Here, then, is ample justification for the attempt to create a doctrine capable of embracing all that Metaphysics rationally may seek and all that Science finds, by the reduction of both to common principles and common tests. One Method, one Logic, one canon of Truth and Demonstration, must be applied to both. Which must it be? Not the one hitherto employed in Metaphysics: its incompetence is manifest in the unprogressive nature of its results. There is, therefore, only the alternative of prolonging this uncertainty, or of adopting the Method which has been uniformly successful wherever rightly employed.

CHAPTER II.

THE CONDITIONS STATED.

11. WHAT is here proclaimed is the possibility of finding rational solutions to questions which have hitherto baffled effort. And this will be effected by invoking those principles only which are invoked in physical research. The probabilities which guide us, and the certainties on which we rest in Science, will guide us here. In such an attempt, precisely because it is a first attempt, there will assuredly be much imperfection; but the reader's agreement is far less claimed in respect of any particular solutions here offered, than in respect of the conditions of the search. No one thinks of discrediting scientific Method because the particular conclusions of the physicist or biologist are often debatable and sometimes false. All I claim is a recognition of the legitimacy of the attempt to apply the rational procedure of Science to every question which may rationally be asked. This is founded on the conception that under the two cardinal points of view — *what* is to be known, and *how* it can be known — the object and the logic — there is the same accordance between Metaphysics and Physics as between any two branches of inquiry, — Mathematics and Biology, for example. What is known, what is knowable, and what is unknowable in the one, and *why* these are so, having their counterparts in the other. The several sciences differ amongst each other by reason of the differences in their sensible data, and the complexity of

the phenomena they investigate. With these differences necessarily arise different means of investigation, different tests, and different degrees of certainty. Each science has thus its special logic. The means and tests which suffice in Mathematics are no longer sufficiently comprehensive for Physics; the logic of Biology is, in special characters, unlike that of Chemistry. Yet one Method, one Logic, rules throughout; and this general Method may be applied to problems — social or metaphysical — which have hitherto been investigated in a quite different spirit, and under different tests. When so applied, it will reach results having scientific certainty, because conforming to the conditions of Science. More cannot lawfully be claimed. If after all efforts there still loom in the distance vast stretches of untrodden ground, and beyond these a region inaccessible to man, — this is equally true of all research. I do not claim a wider reach nor a higher validity for metaphysical conceptions than for scientific conceptions; but I claim one equivalent reach and validity. To many minds this holds out promise of but a meagre result: impatient to pass beyond the limits of Experience, they will reject a solution which confines them within the human horizon. That which fascinates them is the hope of passing beyond this horizon. It will, therefore, be incumbent on me to show that such a hope is futile; and *per contra* that every question which can be stated in terms of Experience is capable of an answer on the Experimental Method.

12. Not unfrequently in recent times have men professed to apply the Inductive Method to Metaphysics, and proclaimed that they were guided by it in their speculations. Nay, even the very pretension of deducing metaphysical conclusions from the data of Experience has not been wanting. But to the best of my knowledge all such pretensions have been illusory, partly because the

writers imperfectly understood the Method of Science, and mainly because they did not consistently apply it. The idea of applying such a procedure is one thing; *how* it can be applied, is another. At this present moment I have a conviction that the Differential Calculus *could* be applied to Psychology, and will be in some future time; but I have no distinct vision of how to make the beginning, because I cannot yet determine the co-ordinates, cannot put the questions in a calculable shape. It has been thus with philosophers who talked of applying Scientific Method to Metaphysics. Unless I deceive myself these pages will show how the problems may be presented in a soluble shape; how they may be affiliated to all other soluble problems.

13. By way of preliminary I will ask permission to coin a term that will clearly designate the aspect of Metaphysics which renders the inquiry objectionable to scientific thinkers, no less than to ordinary minds, because it implies a disregard of experience; by isolating this aspect in a technical term we may rescue the other aspect which is acceptable to all. The word Metaphysics is a very old one, and in the course of its history has indicated many very different things. To the vulgar it now stands for whatever is speculative, subtle, abstract, remote from ordinary apprehension; and the pursuit of its inquiries is secretly regarded as an eccentricity, or even a mild form of insanity. To the cultivated it sometimes means Scholastic Ontology, sometimes Psychology, pursued independently of Biology, and sometimes, though more rarely, the highest generalizations of Physics. In spite of this laxity in its use, the term is so good a term, and has had godfathers so illustrious, that if possible it ought to be preserved. And it may be preserved if we separate it from its Method, and understand it in its primitive sense as τὰ μετὰ τὰ φυσικὰ, that which comes *after* Physics, and

embraces the ultimate generalizations of Research. It thus becomes a term for the science of the most general conceptions. This is the Aristotelian view of it, adapted to modern thought. It is also in accordance with the scheme of Bacon, which represents Philosophy as a pyramid, having the history of Nature for its basis, an account of the powers and principles which operate in Nature (Physics) for its second stage, and an apex of formal and final causes (Metaphysics) for the third stage.* Let us only modify the Baconian conception by substituting "the highest generalization of Research," in lieu of the "formal and final causes," and we have a grand province to bear the ancient name.

14. But what is implied in this arrangement? That since we are to rise to Metaphysics through Science, we must never forsake the Method of Science; and further that, if in conformity with inductive principles we are never to invoke aid from any higher source than Experience, we must perforce discard all inquiries whatever which transcend the ascertained or ascertainable data of Experience. Hence the necessity for a new word which will clearly designate this discarded remainder, — a word which must characterize the nature of the inquiries rejected. If then the *Empirical* designates the province we include within the range of Science, the province we exclude may fitly be styled the *Metempirical.*

The terms Empiricism, Empiricist, Empirical, although commonly employed by metaphysicians with contempt, to mark a mode of investigation which admits no higher source than Experience (by them often unwarrantably restricted to Sensation), may be accepted without demur, since even the flavor of contempt only serves to emphasize the distinction. There will perhaps be an equivalent

* Compare the passage, too long for extract, in SECCHI, *L'unità delle Forze Fisiche*, p. 470. Rome, 1864.

contempt in the minds of positive thinkers attaching to the term Metempirical; but since this term is the exact correlative of Empirical, and designates whatever lies beyond the limits of possible Experience, it characterizes inquiries which one class regards as vain and futile, another as exalted above mere scientific procedure. Nor is this the only advantage of the term; it also detaches from Metaphysics a vast range of insoluble problems, leaving behind it only such as are soluble.

15. Thus whatever conceptions can be reached through *logical extensions of experience,* and can be shown to be *conformable with it,* are legitimate products, capable of being used as principles for further research. On the contrary, whatever lies beyond the limits of Experience, and claims another origin than that of Induction and Deduction from established data, is illegitimate. It can never become a principle of research, but only an object of infertile debate. The metempirical region is the void where Speculation roams unchecked, where Sense has no footing, where Experiment can exercise no control and where Calculation ends in Impossible Quantities. In short, Physics and Metaphysics deal with things and their relations, as these are known to us, and as they are believed to exist in our universe; Metempirics sweeps out of this region in search of the *otherness* of things: seeking to behold things, not as they are in our universe,—not as they are to us,—it substitutes for the ideal constructions of Science the ideal constructions of Imagination.

16. The reader may here ask how it is that great metaphysicians, like Descartes, Leibnitz, and Kant, who were also great scientific thinkers, failed to perceive that the Method they followed in Mathematics and Physics was equally applicable in Metaphysics? The answer is simple. The traditional influence of metempirical conceptions, and the potency of certain prejudices, which Science

confessed its inability to justify or eradicate, prevented these philosophers from even conceiving the possibility of excluding metempirical data. Kant who, in his exposition of the relativity of knowledge, came so near a true conception of Method, not only missed the truth, and fell back upon the traditional prejudice of Innate Ideas, or *à priori* Forms of Thought, as the source of knowledge, but expressly declared that "the fountain of Metaphysic can in no sense be empirical, its axioms and principles must never be drawn from Experience, either inward or outward," * — a declaration which ceases to be even plausible when his unwarrantable restriction of Experience to mere sensation is set aside. Nor is this all. Granting that Metaphysic could dispense with the inductions of Experience, all that it could effect for Philosophy would be the superfluous explanation of phenomena which lie outside the circle of Experience; whereas Philosophy aims at an explanation of the world in which we have our being. Consider this: If abstract Science, which obtains its principles through concrete phenomena, is confessedly incapable of explaining concrete phenomena, but only capable of guiding us to their explanation, how much less hope can there be of an explanation of concrete phenomena from principles that do not pretend to an empirical basis! Kant displayed great ingenuity in proving that, the empirical and metempirical worlds (by him called the phenomenal and noumenal) having nothing in common, no conclusions formed respecting the one could have any validity when extended to the other. Why, then, did he continue to coquet with Metempirics, after having struck such blows at its foundation? I believe it was partly

* KANT, *Prolegomena zu jeder künftigen Metaphysik*, § 1. It is true that by Metaphysic he sometimes only means the inquiry into the limits of knowledge; but at others he means what is usually meant by the word, namely, metempirical inquiry.

the consequence of the traditional conception that metempirical knowledge was possible; and partly the want of any clear conception of how the Method of Science could be applied to questions which insisted on an answer.

17. Hegel, on the other hand, is urgent for treating Metaphysics and Science on the same Method. Unhappily he has a very erroneous view of the conditions of inquiry; and in point of fact reverses the principle I am here proclaiming, and instead of treating Metaphysics by the Method of Science, treats Science by the Method of Metaphysics. He separates the philosophical sciences into empirical and speculative. The empirical embrace those which furnish axioms, laws, theories, — the thought of what is *actual*. So far he seems to be arguing on our side; but he adds, "However satisfactory this knowledge may be in its own field, there are other subjects which it does not include, — Freedom, Mind, God." * And elsewhere (§ 37) he characterizes the tendency to prove everything by finite consideration as "Empiricism, which, instead of seeking truth in Thought itself, seeks it in groping amid Experience inward and outward"; adding that consequent Empiricism excludes all knowledge whatever of the Suprasensible. It is unnecessary to pause and consider under what aspects Hegel's view coincides with the strictly positive conception of Research; all we have here to note is the retention of those very metem-

* "Wir heissen jene Wissenschaften, welche Philosophie gennant worden sind, *empirische* Wissenschaften, von dem Ausgangspunkte den sie nehmen. Aber das Wesentliche das sie bezwecken und hervorschaffen sind Gesetze, allgemeine sätze, eine Theorie; die Gedanken des Vorhandenen. . . . . So befriedigend zunächst diese Erkenntniss in ihren Felde ist, so zeigt sich fürs erste noch ein anderer Kreis von Gegenständen die darin nicht befasst sind — Freiheit, Geist, Gott. Sie sind auf jenem Boden nicht darum zu finden weil sie der Erfahrung nicht angehören sollten." — HEGEL, *Encyklopädie der Philos. Wissenschaften*, §§ 7, 8.

pirical elements, which it is the aim of Science to exclude. In point of fact, when we see Hegel at work we find that the metempirical is not kept apart from the empirical, but dominates it; and his inquiries in Physics no less than in Psychology are all vitiated by this.

18. Thus while metaphysicians have never really applied scientific Method, because they have never relinquished their faith in the Metempirical, men of science have never thought that their Method could be applied to Metaphysics, because they imagined that Metaphysics was inseparable from Metempirics. It is this misapprehension we must rectify by showing that the problems rightly stated are empirical precisely in the degree that physical problems are so, and that both are in an equal degree metempirical when improperly stated. Scientific thinkers, viewing certain questions solely in the light in which metaphysicians were accustomed to place them, and seeing that to these no application of ordinary tests was applicable, declared — and the declaration rapidly became a dogma — that "all such questions relate to mysteries beyond human ken." With this magisterial phrase they justified their neglect of problems they were unable to solve.

19. Such lavish humility is far from admirable. Such readiness to admit mysteries is misleading. We have no right by self-abasement to abase Humanity, and thus present our own incompetence as the standard of power. Particularly objectionable are these professions of humility when accompanied, and they often are, by exaggerated pretensions, so that the man who considers it almost a religious duty humbly to avow his eternal ignorance of Cause, Force, Mind, and the like, has no hesitation in expressing decided and precise opinions respecting their nature and modes of operation. It is thereby manifest that the ignorance on which he eloquently insists is *your*

ignorance rather than his. Nay, even when this is not so, and he avows his ignorance sincerely, he is too apt to regard the avowal as an act of piety, — a confession of his "nothingness."

Philosophy, thus boasting of its own impotence, is a tradition of that theological spirit which, terrified at the free exercise of Doubt, yet conscious of the necessity of Doubt for the activity of Reason, excommunicated the Intellect as an heresiarch, after having vilified this life as a theatre for Satan. There was a time when all knowledge was considered dangerous, except for theologians and lawyers; for others it was of the nature of Magic. The tradition still lingers, and a vague horror hangs over all "prying into the mysteries of the universe." It may be noticed influencing audiences at almost every scientific lecture not addressed to students. Ludicrous, were it not painful, would be the eagerness of delight with which every acknowledgment of ignorance and incompetence is saluted by the listeners. Although they are seated there to learn what has been discovered respecting the processes of Nature, they are never so well pleased as when told that what has been discovered is nothing compared with the undiscoverable. Let but the lecturer say, — and he must often say it, — "Here Science pauses. Beyond this we cannot go. Beyond this lie mysteries before which the wisest philosopher is no better than a child," — immediately a round of applause bursts forth; numerous feet stamp approval; flattered Ignorance feels at ease, and shakes its head significantly. "Ah! you see, Science is vain *there.* In spite of its proud boasts, there are mysteries it cannot penetrate!"

Now surely it is no matter of exhilaration, but rather of deep regret, that we find ourselves in a universe of mystery, compelled to grope our way amid shadows, with terrible penalties affixed to each false step. To resign ourselves to this condition is one thing; another to exult in it, and claim the exultation as an act of piety. Among the many strange servilities mistaken for pieties, one of the least lovely is that which hopes to flatter God by despising the world and vilifying human nature.*

20. There is no intention here of applauding the unthinking confidence which leads many minds to pursue inquiries beyond their powers, nor of underrating the lessons which dissuade us from such efforts. It is of supreme importance that we should ascertain the limits of Research. But these limits must be ascertained, not arbitrarily assigned. Before declaring any subject inaccessible, to others no less than to ourselves, we must clearly see the grounds why it is so; and before attempting to reach one that is accessible, we must have some vision of the path by which it may be reached.† Inaccessibility is relative, and science has answered questions which, to minds unfamiliar with its data and procedures, might seem hopelessly beyond human power; which indeed, in the absence of such data and procedures, would be beyond it. What, for example, could be more absurd than for one of the laity to attempt to measure and weigh stars many millions of millions of miles removed from his grasp, or to ascertain the velocity of Light, or of the translation of our solar system towards the constellation of Hercules? Yet Geometry, Trigonometry, and Dynamics render these things possible. We believe the statements that the sensation of violet is produced by the striking of the ethereal waves against the retina more

* The Author of Creation is the only author who is supposed to be flattered by our lavish assurance that his works are imbecile.

† The padre Secchi, noticing the readiness with which men conclude that nothing is known on certain subjects, quietly remarks that this is a conclusion "che se onora il filosofo ove manchi fondamento alla deduzione, lo degrada ove derivi dal non saper intendere il linguaggio della Natura." — *L'Unità delle Forze Fisiche*, p. 51. 1864.

than seven hundred billions of times in a second, and that our sun and its planets are moving through space with a velocity of many millions of miles in a year; but these statements are accepted on trust by us who know that there are thinkers for whom they are irresistible conclusions; the facts belong to mysteries penetrable only through a mathematical initiation.

21. It is thus also with Metaphysics. Its problems are inaccessible, and must remain so to minds which will not approach them through the only accessible path. But there is a path through which they may be accessible; all depends on our selecting it. A few years since it would have been preposterous to speculate on the present chemical constitution of the sun's atmosphere; it would have been one of the mysteries which no astronomer would consider investigable. Why? Simply because there were no accessible data. The question was one wholly beyond the known paths. It was so obviously metempirical that even metaphysicians abstained from speculating on it. Suddenly the discovery of spectrum analysis placed an instrument in our hands by which the presence of gases and vapors in the sun's atmosphere could be ascertained as rigorously as their presence in our laboratories. The mystery submitted to demonstration. Newton's feat of interpreting celestial Mechanics by the laws of motion detected on our planet (with the consequent reflected improvement in the definition of those very laws) was supplemented by the identification of the chemistry of the stars with that of our planet, and the consequent revelation of new substances in our earths and waters, which might otherwise have remained unsuspected. In like manner one may hope that the application of scientific Method to problems hitherto inaccessible may reflect light on questions of Science otherwise hopelessly obscure. (Compare § 62 *a*.)

22. In saying that all depends on the selection of the right path, I may appear to be uttering a truism, the very difficulty being precisely this selection. It is, however, only a truism to those who believe such a path may be found. The majority do not believe it, but insist that Metaphysics is essentially removed from any access through Experience. There is something gained, then, if we gain the admission that a pathway through Experience is possible. To effect this it may be requisite to show that unless some stringent proof be advanced in support of the assumption that the human mind is endowed with a special organ for the perception of met-empirical relations, there must be either a total abandonment of metaphysical Speculation or an adoption of the empirical Method. And I hope to show that there is no such special organ. Meanwhile let us here consider two favorite arguments for the continuance of the old speculations, with which metaphysicians vindicate their neglect of science.

23. First, it is said that "a noble impulse moves the soul to rise above the sordid aims of Science, which is mainly anxious to satisfy our vulgar needs." This ascription of a nobler aim must be rejected, not only because of its unwarrantable self-complacency,* but because of its misrepresentation of the true position of Science, which — as will hereafter appear (Prob. I. Chap. V.) — is purely that of an Ideal Construction. Science is

* It is in this sense that Hegel likens a people without Metaphysic to a temple without its Holy of Holies. "These be brave 'orts," as Sir Hugh Evans would say; and would be justified if the pretensions of Metaphysic were justified; but when we examine these we come to Trendelenburg's conclusion respecting the Hegelian procedure: "Man fragt nicht mehr was *mit menschlichen Mitteln geschehen kann*, sondern was nach höheren Ideal geschehen sollte. Man nimmt die Absicht der Dialektik für die That. Aber weil sie hoch greift, hat sie nicht das Höhe ergriffen; und weil sie mehr verspricht, ist das Versprochene noch nicht da." — *Logische Untersuchungen*, I. 105. 1862.

an idealist, moving amid the world of realities as if *they* were but fleeting shadows, and as if the only permanent existences were Abstractions. But were this otherwise, and were the satisfaction of our commonest needs the only aim, the objection would be none the less misplaced. There is no greater vulgarity than that of despising the common needs of life as vulgar. It is the greatness of Science, that, while satisfying the spiritual thirst for knowledge, it satisfies the pressing desire for guidance in action; not only painting a picture of the wondrous labyrinth of Nature, but placing in our hands the Ariadne-thread to lead us through the labyrinth.

24. The second plea urges that, granting the study to be doomed to failure, the mere energy it evokes is so strengthening and ennobling that Metempirics must always be an admirable course of intellectual gymnastics. The answer to this is simple. Without denying that intellectual athletes may find in it an arena for the exercise and display of their powers, we may urge that there are other and nobler arenas than the Gymnasium, where the greatest powers may not only be freely exercised, but exercised for the welfare of mankind. The measureless region of scientific Research is not only capable of calling out every intellectual faculty, but is one in which no exercise is sterile.* Incapable of application to concrete phenomena and the practical needs, incapable of demonstration because incapable of verification, the most splendid achievements in the metempirical arena are sterile displays.

25. Although it is true that only those problems which are capable of solution can profitably employ mankind, the common assertion that metaphysical problems are incapable of solution is true when there is a tacit assumption that they can only be investigated on the Metaphysical Method. But the whole subject changes

* Compare on this subject COMTE, *Politique Positive*, III. 13, 14.

its aspect directly we institute the distinction between Metaphysics and Metempirics. Unless this distinction be clearly maintained, *all* problems whatever become hopeless, and we are incapable of explaining the simplest phenomenon; *with* this distinction, all problems whatever become capable of solution, under empirical limits.

26. The objection will doubtless be raised that such a procedure as that of excluding all metempirical data, and rejecting all metempirical inquiry, is an obliteration of the characteristic peculiarity of Metaphysics, and an evasion of the difficulty. It will be urged that an empirical answer to speculative questions can never satisfy the mind yearning for insight into the world of things *behind* phenomena,—for knowledge of the *otherness of things,*—for glimpses of "the light that *never was* on sea or shore." This is so. But we must remember that whatever speculative curiosity may prompt, our real and lasting interest is in ascertaining the order of the things we know. A sublime aspiration after the otherness of things is sublimely irrational. To know things as they are to us, is all we need to know, all that is possible to be known: a knowledge of the Suprasensible, were it gained, would, by the very fact of coming under the conditions of knowledge, only be knowledge of its relations to us; the knowledge would still be relative, phenomenal.*

* What Professor Tait says of Quaternions may here be made to illustrate the distinction between the empiricist and metempiricist, if we allow the pure mathematician to stand for the latter: "In the eyes of the pure mathematician Quaternions have one grand and fatal defect. They cannot be applied to space of n dimensions; they are contented to deal with those three poor dimensions in which mere mortals are doomed to dwell. From the physical point of view this, instead of being regarded as a defect, is the greatest possible recommendation. It shows, in fact, Quaternions to be a special instrument so constructed for application to the Actual as to have thrown overboard everything which is not absolutely necessary, without the slightest consideration whether or not it was thereby being rendered useless for application to the Inconceivable."—*Address before the Mathematical Section of the British Association*, 1871.

CHAPTER III.

THE METHOD.

27. A MOMENT'S reflection will show that the Experiential Method is by no means restricted to that enumeration of particulars and classification of sensations which is assumed to be its scope by those philosophers who vilify it under the name of Empiricism, and those rhetors who declaim against it as dealing with nothing but what can be seen and felt. It is the methodizing of what is known. The range of the known embraces much more than the sensible. (See Prob. I., Ch. IV.) Not only the direct presentations to Sense, but the indirect representations, — the verifiable Inferences from Sense, — constitute its elements. Not only the individual experiences, slowly acquired, but the accumulated Experience of the race, organized in Language, condensed in Instruments and Axioms, and in what may be called the *inherited Intuitions,* — these form the multiple unity which is expressed in the abstract term Experience. This being stated once for all by way of forestalling hasty criticism, let us now proceed with our exposition.

28. Whether the object of research be Nature, Man, or Society in general, or some special group of their phenomena, we always find it presenting three aspects: 1°, the *positive* or known; 2°, the *speculative* or unknown though knowable; 3°, the *unknowable.* The two first are empirical; the third is metempirical. The two first rest

either, 1°, on direct Sensation and verified Inference,* or, 2°, on Intuition and logical deductions from Intuition, which are verifiable by direct or indirect reduction to Sensation. The third rests on no such bases, and is therefore distinguishable from the two former in kind, not simply in degree.

29. By way of illustration, suppose the object investigated is the motion of the heavenly bodies. The first step is to determine the positive, or known, elements of the question, namely, that all the planets move round the sun in the same direction and in nearly the same plane, and that, inasmuch as their orbits are nearly circular, they describe paths which are parallel. This general plane of circulation is very nearly the plane of the sun's equator. The same facts are ascertained respecting the motion of the satellites round their planets, although their equators have various inclinations to the plane of the sun's equator. This leads to the inference that the two circulations of planets and satellites, although independent as facts, depend on the same principle, and have a common origin. What is that? This question brings forward the speculative aspect. The principle sought cannot be seen, it must be deduced. Speculation is seeing with the mind's eye what is not present to Sense or to Intuition. It is ideal construction, and begins with conjecture, — too often, alas! ending where it began.

* "In the experimental department," says Professor Challis, "a law is a grouping of observed facts; in the theoretical, the law is shown to be the consequence of certain primary facts. Every fact and every law which experiment makes known is a problem for the theorist to solve by mathematical reasoning," — aided by Conjecture, let us add. Thus Kepler discovered the fact that the radius vector of each planet describes round the sun equal areas in equal times, and conjectured that each planet tended continuously towards the sun, — in consequence, he thought, of a magnetic power; this was a conjecture supporting a conjecture. Newton grasping the fact observed, and the fact conjectured, solved the problem by mathematical reasoning which dispensed with the hypothetical magnetic power and disclosed the law.

The satellites present also another remarkable law, their rotation on their own axes being executed in the same time as their rotation round their planets (hence we always see the same face of the moon). This law is positive; it is the observed order. But the cause, i. e. that it depends on tidal friction in the satellite while it was still in motion, is at present speculative.

Suppose now the astronomer, after expounding the positive and speculative aspects of the planetary motions, is led to expound his conception of the *purpose* which these laws were intended to fulfil in creation, and his estimate of the wisdom and benevolence in so disposing them, and not otherwise, — is it not obvious that in this teleological explanation he quits the ground of Experience to enter on that region where all sensible data and all verifiable inferences vanish? His conjectures on this point may be approximately right or absurdly wrong; no possible means of determining whether they are right or wrong exist. If he regard them as no more than subjective fancies wherewith to satisfy his own feelings, we cannot object. But if he regard them as in any degree entering into astronomical science, and if he permit any deductions from them to modify the positive and speculative data or in any way to modify the course of astronomical thought, he violates the first principle of Method, by suffering the empirical to be controlled by the metempirical, and allowing the unknowable to distort the known.

30. Having thus sharply defined the three aspects which every question may present, and which every one would always present had not men long ago quietly set aside the metempirical aspect in most questions of practical aim and most questions of scientific research, I need scarcely insist that in dealing with the speculative we ought to follow the same canons as in dealing with the

positive, except that we are forced to substitute analogies for perceptions, forced to employ hypotheses and rely on inferences. When a platinum wire is raised gradually to a white heat, we see a succession of combinations of more and more of the primitive colors, but we do not see the motions of the wire which successively determine these colors, nor the tremors of the optic tract which are determined by these motions and produce these colors. We only see the changing colors. We infer the rest. But these inferences have been verified a thousand times, and are but reproductions of analogical experiences. Our mental vision is a reproduction of the past and application to the present. It is Experience — our own or that of others — on which we rest. We are not at liberty to *invent* Experience, nor to infer anything *contrary* to it, only to extend it analogically. Speculation to be valid must be simply the extension of Experience by the analogies of experiences.*

31. The speculative begins where the positive ends; and where the speculative quits the ground of Sense and Verification, the region of the Metempirical begins. It is possible to move securely on the ground of Speculation so long as we carefully pick our way, and consider each position insecure till what was merely probable becomes

* "From a starting-point furnished by his own researches, or those of others, the investigator proceeds by combining intuition and verification. He ponders the knowledge he possesses, and tries to push it further; he guesses, and checks his guess; he conjectures, and confirms or explodes his conjecture. These guesses are by no means leaps in the dark; for knowledge once gained casts a faint light beyond its own immediate boundaries. . . . . The profoundest minds know best that Nature's ways are not at all times their ways, and that the brightest flashes in the world of thought are incomplete until they have been proved to have their counterparts in the world of fact. Thus the vocation of the true experimentalist may be defined as the continued exercise of spiritual insight, and its incessant correction and realization." — TYNDALL, *Fragments of Science*, p. 110. 1871.

proven. But in the metempirical region we have not even probability as a guide; it is a morass of uncertainty where all footing yields and all tests fail. In this region, conjectures, however fantastic, are as valid as conceptions which seem rational. They maintain their ascendency over the mind which has once admitted them, because being, by the nature of the case, incapable of proof, they are incapable of refutation; they never approach *near* enough to the truths of Experience for us to show how widely they diverge from or contradict it.

32. Whenever a question is couched in terms that ignore Experience, reject known truths, and invoke inaccessible data, — i. e. data inaccessible through our present means, or through any conceivable extension of those means, — it is metempirical, and Philosophy can have nothing to do with it. We need not trouble ourselves with it, until in possession of the requisite means; it is *adjourned*, not suppressed. Perilous it may be to set bounds to human possibilities, and to forejudge what future inquiries may disclose; but there is no peril in standing inflexibly by the rule which declares all questions to be unanswerable when the means of answering them are not at hand. He who propounds an answer is called upon to show that he has the requisite means. What is invisible to the naked eye may be made visible by microscope or telescope. Let these be produced, and their powers demonstrated. No assertion, however confident, will suffice; no "inner vision" which dispenses with verification. Roger Bacon passionately declared that he *could* construct an instrument which would make objects visible at a distance of many miles; and because such instruments have been constructed, he is believed to have anticipated the discovery, whereas, in point of fact, he not only made no such discovery, but showed, in his very statement of the conception he had formed, that he

had not mastered the elementary principles which were requisite. The theories of many speculators are in this not unlike the telescope of Roger Bacon.

33. While no question which cannot be couched in terms of Experience, and answered on its data, ought for a moment to be entertained, *any* question which can be so asked and answered is admissible. In Science this has long been understood; in Metaphysics it is ignored. No geologist, no biologist, would listen patiently if asked, What is the succession of strata in Sirius? What are the leading characters of the flora and fauna of Saturn? Yet metaphysicians patiently listen to questions of equal irrelevance; nay, confidently give answers to them.

Without travelling so far as Sirius, suppose we present a new substance to the chemist, and ask him what are its properties, and what reactions it will exhibit under given conditions. He will decline to answer until he has sufficiently examined the substance and classed it among substances already known; because he is aware that any guess he may make before trial must be valueless unless guided by analogy; in as far as it is like known substances he will infer that it has like properties. Guessing is only fertile in proportion to the fertility of the experiences it reproduces. If a man knows little, he can infer but little. All knowledge is reproduction of experiences, the direct or indirect assimilation (making *like*) of the new phenomena to phenomena resembling them, formerly experimented on. Ask the profoundest analyst to resolve an equation numerically, and he is silent unless the values of the coefficients are assigned; nor can the child tell the result of multiplying 5 by 5, until he has learned the multiplication-table.

34. Must not this be equally true in Metaphysics? To ask the metaphysician to answer questions respecting things *per se* (or what is usually understood by them),

and to tell us their nature and properties, is asking him to resolve equations numerically without assigning their several values to the coefficients. Nay more, these values *cannot* be assigned, for the symbols profess to be symbols of what was never presented in Experience. But if instead of this irrational procedure we give the metaphysician verifiable data, he can deal with them as the physicist and chemist deal with theirs; and his answers will be as valid as theirs, if his data and method be like theirs.

35. Hitherto metaphysicians have asked, What is Matter? What is Force? What is Cause? And these words are symbols of an imaginary class of Noumena, *Dinge-an-sich*, Things as they *are* and underlying the Things which *appear*, — a world behind phenomena, incapable of being sensibly grasped, but supposed to have a more perfect reality than the phenomenal world. Because questions thus irrationally put are found to yield no rational answers, one class of thinkers hurries to the conclusion that this impotence proves all metaphysical inquiries to be idle; another class infers that knowledge of this superior world must be gained through another source than that relied on in the investigation of phenomena. But we may urge that all inquiries are not idle because some are improperly conceived; nor is any special organ needed for the interpretation of questions rationally put. Since it is a fact that we have ideas of Matter, Force, Cause, etc., and that these words are symbols of sensible experiences, the genesis of such ideas and the interpretation of such symbols are not less legitimate objects of inquiry than the genesis and interpretation of our ideas of Animal, Plant, Planet, or Cosmos. I shall hereafter endeavor to make clear that these abstract ideas are integrant parts of what I call the Logic of Feeling, before they are raised into terms of the Logic of Signs. They are threads

woven into the web of Experience; and because they have this warp and woof they are capable of being raised into the tissue of Abstraction, — they are experiences before they are signs. The Method which enables us to unravel the complex threads in the one case will aid us in the other.

36. As already hinted, the chief source of perplexity is the irrationality of the terms in which the questions are propounded. But although this defect is specially flagrant in the case of Metaphysics, it is frequently noticeable in Physics. Take, for example, the puzzle concerning the communication of motion from one body to another, either through impact or "action at a distance." This communication is accepted as a fact, and declared to be beyond our comprehension. The inconceivability of the statement is not allowed to suggest a doubt respecting its certainty. But the inconceivability, when closely examined, will be found to rest entirely on the irrational mode of expressing the fact observed; instead of stating what is observed in simple terms, the statement is made in terms of an hypothesis which cannot be steadily conceived. What is observed is that one body in motion — that is to say, in changing space relations — is succeeded by changes in the space relations of another, and that there is a constancy in this sequence. This not being held sufficient, there is invented a hypothetical Motion (not an abstract symbol, but a physical entity), which is passed from one body to another like so much milk poured from one jug into another; and to complete the hypothesis, this Motion is imagined under the control of the body moving, — since this body *divides its quantity* of Motion, keeping one portion to itself and *communicating* the other portion to the other body! Is it strange that having travestied the observed phenomena in this way, and accepted our metaphorical language as exact, we marvel that the entity

thus created is beyond comprehension? Instead of throwing the onus on human incompetence, suppose we ask whether it may not rest on the illusory statement. Analyze the real data, and it will then be seen that the "communication of Motion" is one of those metaphorical phrases which (as Lagrange remarks, on a somewhat similar occasion*) are supposed to reveal the essence of Nature's laws, and which can "par quelque vertu secrète ériger en causes finales, de simples résultats des lois connues de la mécanique." We first raise a dust and then exclaim, "Impossible to see through it!"

37. Of a similar kind is the puzzle respecting Force inherent in Matter. Neither abstraction is reduced to its concretes, neither term accurately defined; and then such questions as the following are asked (which I cite from a distinguished mathematician and physicist, Maupertius): "Qu'est-ce que cette force impulsive? comment réside-t-elle dans les corps? qui eût pu deviner qu'elle y réside avant que d'avoir vu des corps se choquer? La résidence des autres propriétés n'est pas plus claire. Comment l'impénétrabilité et les autres propriétés viennent elles se joindre à l'étendue?"†

When such questions are detached from a work and seriously considered, it seems difficult to understand how any thinking mind could have propounded them. Yet, having puzzled himself with irrational questions, Maupertius evades them with the customary formula: "These must ever remain mysteries for us." Mysteries no doubt; but mysteries quite needlessly fabricated.

38. Examples need not be multiplied; enough if we understand that every problem is mysterious when irrationally stated; but, when rationally stated, there is no greater mystery in the existence of an external world, or

* LAGRANGE, *Mécanique Analytique*, I. 245. 1811.

† MAUPERTIUS, *Sur les figures des astres; Œuvres*, p. 65. Dresden, 1752.

the relation between Object and Subject, than in the relation between activity and waste in the tissues, the relation between heat and expansion, or the relation between an arc and its chord. The successful interrogation of Nature mainly depends on the selection of the question to be put, and the ability with which it is expressed in terms that admit of an answer. Hence the first operation in dealing with any metaphysical problem must be this: —

> To disengage the metempirical elements, and proceed to treat the empirical elements with the view of deducing from them the unknown elements, if that be practicable, or, if the deduction be impracticable, of registering the unknown elements as transcendental.

This procedure seems very simple. It is the ordinary procedure of the analyst, whose first operation is to disengage the unknown quantity, — and of the physicist, who always seeks to eliminate whatever is irrelevant or indeterminate, replacing it by exact data, so that nothing finally remains for exploration but what is expressible in calculable terms. Yet simple as the procedure may seem, it has rarely been adopted by metaphysicians; and never, I believe, avowedly stated as a principle of research. On the contrary, there has been a confused mingling of empirical and metempirical elements, sensations and abstractions, inferences and traditions, exact quantitative data, and imaginary unquantitative data, facts and phrases, phenomena and phantoms, — and then it is thought marvellous that such a network of cordage and cobweb should let everything run through!

39. Our first operation must be to disengage the unknown quantity, and endeavor to ascertain whether it is knowable or unknowable; and this will determine whether it is empirical or metempirical.

In every question, from that presented by the growth of a blade of grass to that presented in the evolution of a social organism, from the chemical union of two gases to the formation of ideal types, there must necessarily be certain transcendental elements, not determinable by us, *unexplored remainders* after the most exhaustive exploration. These may be grouped under three heads: —

1°. Elements known to be present in the phenomena, but not yet quantitatively appreciable, and therefore now incalculable;

2°. Elements not certainly known to be present, but assumed hypothetically for the sake of provisional explanation;

3°. Elements which, lying beyond all possible appreciation, because incapable of being brought within the range of Sense and Inference, are to be set aside, and not allowed in any way to enter into the explanation.

40. An illustration or two may here be useful. Geometers agree that the exact ratio of the circumference of a circle to its diameter cannot be accurately expressed in ordinary finite numbers, although the real value may be approached as nearly as we please.* They indicate this

* The impossibility of squaring the circle is the attempt to find a straight line the square on which shall be exactly equal to a given circle.

The impossibility of expressing the ratio of diameter and circumference in finite numbers was first demonstrated by Lambert in 1761, according to De Morgan. I imagined from Euler's language that the use of the symbol π was proposed by himself (*Introd. à l'Analyse des infiniments petits*, Chap. VIII. Traduit par Pezzi. Strasbourg, 1786), but a friend informs me that this is not the case. Euler gives 128 decimal places; subsequently Vega carried the expression as far as 140 places. Now, when it is considered that the first decimal involves only a defect of hundreds, and ten decimals a defect less than one inch compared with the circumference of the whole earth, we may say with Leslie that Vega's was the "luxury of calculation, and, though superfluous, might convince any judicious person of the impossibility of stating the ratio in finite terms."

ratio by the sign π, — a sign which dispenses with a long series of figures and an *unexplored remainder*. This sign, although entering into the expression of the *quantities* compared, does not enter into the expression of their *ratios*, but vanishes from the final equation. Thus the surface of a sphere, and the surface of a great circle of that sphere, are two quantities which cannot be accurately expressed in numbers, because π enters into both, and this π containing an *unexplored remainder* must remain transcendental. Nevertheless the presence of this transcendental element produces *no* disturbance in the calculation; for we are certain that the first quantity is exactly the quadruple of the second, whatever values these may have. Thus the transcendental element, which exists in both quantities, disappears from the ratio of the one to the other.

We thus lay down the important formula: —

> *The existence of an unknown quantity does not necessarily disturb the accuracy of calculations founded on the known functions of that quantity.**

41. If in Mathematics we can thus deal with transcendentals without peril to the exactness of our deduc-

* Thus, although we may be wholly unable to answer the question, "What is the result of adding $5x$ to $7x$?" so long as x remains without an assigned or assignable value, we are absolutely certain that the sum will be $12x$, *whatever* value x may have.

On this point let Euler be cited. "On rencontre quelquefois des fonctions algébriques dont on ne peut donner une valeur absolue et dégagée. Z est une fonction de cette nature de z, si Z se trouve dans une équation de ce genre $Z^5 = azzZ^3 - bz^4 Z^2 + cz^3 Z - 1$; mais quoi qu'on ne puisse pas résoudre cette équation, il est clair cependant que Z est égal à une certaine expression de z mêlée de constantes, et que ainsi Z est une fonction de z. Quant aux fonctions transcendantes il est à remarquer qu'une fonction est de cette nature lorsque non seulement l'opération transcendante y entre, mais qu'elle affecte encore la variable; car si les opérations transcendantes appartinment aux seules constantes la fonction n'en sera pas moin algébriques." — *Introd. à l'Analyse des infiniments petits*, p. 4.

tions, the question arises whether in other sciences and even in Metaphysics the same procedure may not be adopted with similar effect. My purpose is to show that this procedure can be followed; and that in all inquiries, *unexplored remainders* must be eliminated, and our deductions be confined to the known functions of these unknown quantities. The profitless discussions upon Space and Time have been profitless, because of the non-recognition of the transcendental elements and their consequent separation from the positive elements. What is Time? This philosopher holds it to be an objective existence, which must be accepted as ultimate. Another holds it to be a purely subjective Form of Sense. A third says it is a Form of Sense because it is a Form of Things. Others are fascinated by Lagrange's definition of it, "a fourth dimension of Space." Mathematicians are content with Newton's conception of it as a fluent which has no variable fluxion, the only independent variable which "flows equally without regard to anything external and by another name is called Duration." *

Without pausing to choose between these conceptions, or to trace the genesis of the abstraction and its relations to the concretes it expresses, we simply note that each conception leaves something indeterminate, none accurately conveys all that is meant by Time. A mystery always remains unexplained, unexplorable. Let this be granted, let the presence of a transcendent element be insisted on, how you will, the truth is, that in the only use we ever make of the conception of Time — i. e. in its known functions, the *measurement of intervals* — this

* NEWTON, *Principia; Scholium to the Definitions.* "This conception of time as the one absolute and independent variable is undoubtedly one of the most splendid and fruitful in the history of human thought." — PROFESSOR ROBERTSON SMITH, *On Hegel and the Metaphysics of the Fluxional Calculus.* (Transactions of the Royal Society of Edinburgh, XXV. 495.)

transcendent disappears, the mystery vanishes. Whatever Time may be, the intervals, which are all we deal with, are equal or unequal, and our equations are rigorously exact.

42. It is the same with Space. Whether we are to regard it as an entity or an abstraction, is a question for Psychology. What Space *is* may be left undetermined. The vulgar imagine it to be pure Nothing, — which nevertheless does mysteriously contain all things, holding them like a vessel. They speak of it as of an infinite air-pump, empty of all contents. They do not ask themselves what need Being has of Non-Being to contain it, what need Existence has for another Existence *in which* to exist. The psychologist may be called upon to explain the genesis of such conceptions, but Science and Practice detach themselves from such puzzles, and without endeavoring to lay hold of the transcendental element in Space, are content to *measure spaces* with rigorous precision.*

43. Matter and Motion, Force and Cause, have also their transcendental elements, and it is the province of Metaphysics to demarcate these from the known and knowable elements. Character, again, involves many incalculable elements, organic, historic, social; yet this does not prevent our comparison of one character with another, or with the different manifestations of one character under different conditions. Vitality, again, presents certain aspects which, if only from their speciality, must always distinguish organic from inorganic existence.

* "Absolute Space in its own nature, without regard to anything external, remains always similar and immovable. Relative Space is some movable dimension or measure of the absolute spaces, which our Senses determine by its position to Bodies. Because the parts of Space cannot be seen or distinguished from one another by our Senses, therefore in their stead we use sensible measures of them." — NEWTON, *Principia; Scholium to the Definitions.*

Although many vital phenomena have been assigned to physical and chemical conditions, there still remain unexplored remainders after all our analysis. These we may assign either to some special Agent, the supposed vital Force, or to some special Agency, some peculiar combination of physical forces, not yet determined. Whichever hypothesis we adopt, the presence of the transcendental need in no way disturb the accuracy of our calculations, if we deal with it properly, and eliminate it from the equations. We may compare one vital phenomenon with another, or with its conditions, as we compare one sphere with another, or any one function of an unknown quantity with another; and the comparison may yield exact results, although we remain eternally ignorant of the excluded elements.

44. The initial defect in transcendental Philosophy and all metempirical inquiry is not the admission of transcendental elements* as facts and mysteries, but

* Kant designates by *transcendental* that which is anterior to all Experience; *transcendent*, that which is beyond all Experience. The words thus respectively stand for *à priori* and metempirical. Denying the transcendence of the mental forms which Kant assumes, I use the words "transcendental" and "transcendent" according to their mathematical analogies. "Toute fonction mathématique," says the philosophical mathematician Cournot, "qui ne se trouve pas comprise dans la définition des fonctions algébriques est réputée transcendante." (*Traité des Fonctions et du Calcul infinitesimal*, I. 24. 1841.) That is to say, whatever cannot be expressed in the terms of the science is transcendental to that science: Biology, containing phenomena not expressible in terms of Physics, is transcendental to Physics; and Sociology is transcendental to Biology on similar grounds. Whatever is Suprasensible cannot be expressed in terms of sensible Experience, and is therefore transcendental to Experience, — metempirical. But whenever, by any means, what is now transcendental becomes expressible in terms of Experience it will thereby cease to be metempirical. The term "transcendental," therefore, designates not only that which can never be brought within the range of Experience, owing to the constitution of things, but also that which cannot at present be so brought, owing to the condition of our knowledge: it is the unexplorable remainder and the unexplored remainder.

the admission of them *among the calculable elements;* and the supposition that by means of guesses and constructions in which these incalculable data enter as components, man can reach a higher truth than is attainable through Experience. It will indeed be urged by metaphysicians that although the transcendental elements are not calculable from data furnished by Sense and Understanding, they are directly knowable and calculable through the so-called *Vernunft,* or Intellectual Intuition, which deals with them as Understanding deals with the data of Sense. I do not pause here to consider this argument which will occupy us further on, but continue my exposition of the Method by which metaphysical problems may be treated without the assumption of any such special faculty for the discernment of the transcendental. If I can succeed in extricating such questions from the confusion which results when two diametrically opposite Methods are employed, and if I can thus confine the metempirical Method to the metempirical aspects of each question, it will then be time to examine the pretensions of the Intellectual Intuition.

45. Our first step then is to state each question in such a way that the "unexplored remainder" is disengaged from the positive and speculative aspects, and carefully kept apart as a transcendental, not allowed to enter into the equations.

The second step is the analysis by which we ascertain whether this unknown quantity is to be accepted as an ultimate fact, a fiction, or a phrase. We inquire, 1°, whether it is ultimate, as in itself beyond analysis, incapable of reduction to some more general fact; 2°, whether it might possibly be analyzed were certain data secured; but, these not being secured, we make a provisional guess, throwing out some hypothesis which, if correct, would link the phenomena into intelligible unity; 3°, or failing even this speculative aid, we adopt a phrase which, although explaining nothing, serves at least to baptize the unknown, and is thus often of advantage (sometimes the reverse) in keeping under one rubric phenomena which have essential points of similarity along with manifold differences.

46. These three modes of dealing with the unknown quantity may be thus exemplified. A biologist having ascertained that organic phenomena always require special combinations of oxygen, carbon, hydrogen, and nitrogen for their basis, and are never found where these are absent, accepts the ultimate fact of Vitality dependent on this combination. It is a fact no more explicable by reduction to some other fact, than why the ratio of $\frac{2}{3}$ is the ratio of $\frac{4}{6}$ or $\frac{8}{12}$. The fact is so, is observed to be so; *why* it is so admits no further answer (for the present) than that whatever is is.

46*a*. The speculative biologist is dissatisfied, and thinks this dependence may be explained by the introduction of an Agent, visible to his speculative eye. He creates the fiction of a Vital Principle, which no one has seen, which no one can connect with positive data; and endows it with whatever properties are needed for the results obsreved. He invents an Imponderable, a Force, which has the power of fashioning the Ponderable, — which can select and combine physical and chemical elements, and can animate lifeless matter.

We see that this is a fiction; but we do not on that account reject it. Fictions are potent; and all are welcome if they can justify themselves by bringing speculative insight within the range of positive vision. What then must be our attitude with respect to this Vital Principle? We must submit it to all the tests by which hypotheses are controlled, — tests which, while allowing the freest scope to the energy of Imagination, prevent that energy from degenerating into license.

This fiction *has* been tested, and has proved a failure: it explains nothing. Nevertheless it has left behind it a convenient phrase; and now positive biologists are quite ready to speak of Vital Force, or the vital forces, as brief ways of designating phenomena. There is indeed always danger in thus appropriating the phrases of rejected fictions, — the danger lest insufficient vigilance allow the phrases to be interpreted in their old meanings; and an immense service to Science would be effected by some notation which would always accompany hypotheses and hypothetic phrases, — a sort of algebraic x, keeping alive our sense of the presence of an unknown quantity.*

47. The metaphysical problems of Matter, Force, Cause, Law, Soul, etc., likewise present elements positively known, elements speculatively knowable, and elements that lie beyond all reduction to Experience, positive or speculative. The novelty of the procedure followed in this work consists in treating these problems on the same Method as that followed in Science, first separating the three aspects, and then seeing how far inductions will carry us.

No one can have studied the history of physical investigation without seeing that progress has been mainly effected by the habit of more or less consciously eliminating from each question the metempirical aspect. It is strikingly manifest in the labors of Galileo and Newton, when compared with those of Kepler and Descartes. But in instituting this comparison we must guard against the common confusion of the speculative with the metempirical point of view, — a confusion explicable enough when no sharp definition of the metempirical had been given. It is a serious error to imagine that the true

* Fontenelle charmingly says: "Il faut être presentement sur ses gardes pour ne pas lui imaginer quelque réalité : on est exposé au péril de croire qu'on l'entend." — *Eloge de Newton.*

scientific spirit is opposed to the speculative, because it is opposed to the metempirical. The error arises partly because the Logic of Speculation has not yet been organized with sufficient precision, — its tests and canons are left undisciplined; hence, because Speculation is conterminous at one side with Metempirics, it has frequently been carried by its ardor over its own lawful boundaries into that nebulous region where all tests fail; and thus the speculative thinker is regarded with distrust by positive thinkers. Nor is the distrust surprising, when we see the discordant mingling of unprovable fictions with provable conjectures in the writings of even such splendid workers as Kepler and Descartes.

48. To confirm our vindication of the speculative procedure, it is enough to glance at the labors of the two supreme positive inquirers, Galileo and Newton. Illustrious judges have declared that Galileo's conception of the laws of Motion is his greatest achievement.* If we examine his famous dialogue we find that it is mainly theoretical; experiment is rarely invoked, though everywhere implied. Let us, he says, conceive the simplest and most perfect rule, and we shall form the most probable hypothesis. If we follow out the consequences of this rule, and express them in mathematical theorems, we may do so without peril. "*Geometry has already studied numerous curves never met with in reality*, and detected in them wonderful properties; and to geometry

* Thus Lagrange, speaking of the discovery of the Composition of Motions, says that although during his lifetime it brought him less celebrity than his astronomical observations, "elle fait aujourd'hui la partie la plus solide et la plus réelle de sa gloire. Les découvertes des satellites de Jupiter, des phases de Vénus, des tâches du soleil, etc., ne demandaient que des télescopes et de l'assiduité; mais il fallait un génie extraordinaire pour démêler ces lois de la nature dans des phénomènes qu'on avait toujours eus sous les yeux, mais dont l'explication avait néanmoins toujours échappé aux recherches des philosophes." — *Mécanique Analytique*, p. 221. 1811.

our conclusion also will belong even if *experiment is unable to confirm them.*" Here there is an explicit announcement of the deepest conception of scientific Method, and the conjunction of the principle of Ideal Construction (on which see Prob. I. Chap. V.) with the principle of Sensible Verification. The separation and co-operation of the speculative and positive points of view could not be more clearly stated. Galileo knew that such a conception as Velocity was ideal; and that the proportionality between the velocity of a falling body and the time of its fall could never be *directly* verified in experiment; but he knew also that it could be *indirectly* verified through consequences accessible to observation and experiment. His laws of Motion would have been speculatively true, like those of geometry, even could they never have received positive verification; and I shall hereafter show that they are only rigorously true in the region of Abstraction, and are not true of *actual* motions.

49. The reader was perhaps somewhat incredulous on finding Newton cited as an example of speculative greatness. The veneration which consecrates the name of Newton has so far failed to dignify his practice, that the simple characterizing of that practice wears the air of paradox. Was he not the ideal of a positive thinker? Did he not protest against Speculation? It is true. But although Newton's language is sometimes directly counter to his practice, and is vitiated by the misplaced alarm which he shared in common with all the reformers of that day, at the chaotic consequences of speculative ingenuity, this was mainly due to the absence of a clear discrimination between speculative and metempirical inquiry. At any rate, it is the fact that Newton's glory is founded quite as much on the purely speculative as on the purely positive part of his labors; while nearly all his popularity, outside the mathematical circle, is due to it.

He who declared that he made no hypotheses — insisting that they could have no place in experimental philosophy — has raised his name out of the very small circle of mathematicians, where he must ever occupy a glorious position, into its leadership among philosophers, by virtue of his splendid speculative insight, the daring keenness of his venturesome imagination in creating hypotheses. It was an hypothesis, and a daring one, by which he instituted the Infinitesimal Calculus, introducing velocities, under the name of Fluxions, whereby the correlative values of two variables were supposed to increase together. The element of Velocity was as pure an hypothesis as the element of Ether in the explanation of Light, or of Electricity or Nervous Fluid in the explanation of Neurility: it was, moreover, an *accessory* hypothesis, — an artifice, not an inference. Again, his identification of celestial and terrestrial motions was an hypothesis; so was the extension of gravitation beyond the solar system; an hypothesis his conception of the attraction exercised by spherical bodies on a point beyond or within their spheres;* an hypothesis his conception of attractive and repulsive forces similar to positive and negative quantities in Algebra, the former vanishing where the latter begin; an hypothesis that Motion is constantly destroyed, and consequently that the universe requires active Principles, "such as the cause of gravity, by which planets and comets keep their orbits, and bodies acquire great motion in falling; and the cause of fermentation by which the heart and blood of animals is kept in constant motion and heat"; an hypothesis that Light consists of corpuscles emitted from the luminous source; an hypothesis that "the Senses are not for enabling the soul to perceive the species of things in its sensorium, but only for conveying them thither"; — these, and several other

* Comp. POINSOT, *Eléments de Statique*, 5th ed. § 66.

queries propounded in the *Optics,* are surely strange contradictions to the often-quoted and much-misunderstood *hypotheses non fingo.*

49 *a.* It may be objected that some of these hypotheses he himself brought so near to demonstration that they have taken place among established truths, and that they were legitimate constructions on mathematical principles. This does not alter their speculative character. And while we know that some of his illustrious contemporaries regarded these hypotheses as revivals of a scholastic spirit, rejecting Attraction because it was an occult quality,* we also know that Science, which has accepted some of the hypotheses, has recognized others as non-verifiable, and some as false, nay, even absurd. Be this as it may, our purpose is simply to recognize the large latitude given by this mighty investigator to the operation of that speculative imagination which he is commonly supposed to have discredited. In this connection it is piquant to observe that in the very passage which follows his famous denunciation of hypotheses, he has no hesitation in propounding a view which in these days must startle the most speculative by its wildness: —

"And now we might add something concerning a most subtle Spirit which pervades and lies hid in all gross bodies; by the force and action of which Spirit the parti-

* Huyghens and Leibnitz, so eminently qualified to comprehend the mathematical theory of attraction, rejected it as unworthy of examination. In writing to Leibnitz, before he had seen the *Principia,* Huyghens says: "I am anxious to see Mr. Newton's book. I am content at his not being a Cartesian, provided always he does not thrust forward such suppositions as that of attraction." After having read the book he says: "The explanation of the cause of reflux of the tides does not in the least satisfy me, nor all those other theories which he founds on his principle of attraction, a principle that seems to me absurd. I am amazed to see any one taking so much trouble and entering into calculations so elaborate founded on such a principle." — See BERTRAND, *Les Fondateurs de l'Astronomie Moderne,* 311.

cles of bodies mutually attract one another at near distances, and cohere if contiguous; and electric bodies operate to greater distances, as well repelling as attracting the neighboring corpuscles; and light is emitted, reflected, refracted, inflected, and heats bodies; and all sensation is excited, and the members of animal bodies move at the command of the will, namely, by the vibrations of this Spirit, mutually propagated along the solid filaments of the nerves from the outward organs of sense to the brain, and from the brain into the muscles. But these are things that cannot be explained in few words, nor are we furnished with that sufficiency of experiments which is required to an accurate determination and demonstration of the laws by which this electric and elastic spirit operates."

50. In presence of evidence like this one may well ask, What meaning is to be attached to the famous *dictum*, and what is the vindication of Newton's practice which so obviously departs from that dictum? The answer is, that Newton had thoroughly grasped scientific Method; and his magisterial superiority is nowhere more lucent than in its clear and careful distinction between the positive and speculative aspects of each question. The positive part of his work always consists of geometrical and dynamical facts and deductions. The precision and reach of this are uncontested, incontestable. Then comes a speculative part, brilliant, seductive, and peculiarly acceptable, because it fulfils the primary condition of affording facilities to calculation. But this part is always questionable, hypothetical. Observe how clearly he separates these very different aspects in the declaration which opens the exposition of the system of the world in Book III.: —

"In the preceding books I have laid down the principles of philosophy, principles not philosophical but mathematical; such, to wit, as we may build our reasonings upon in philosophical inquiries. These principles are the laws and conditions of certain motions and powers or forces, which chiefly have respect to philosophy. But lest they should have appeared of themselves dry and barren, I have illustrated them here and there with some philosophical scholiums, giving an account of such things as are of more general nature, and which philosophy seems chiefly to be founded on."

And towards the close of the general scholium he says: "Hitherto we have explained the phenomena of the heavens and the sea by the power of gravity, but have not yet assigned the cause of this power. . . . . I have not been able to discover the cause of those properties of gravity from phenomena, and I frame no hypotheses. . . . . To us it is enough that gravity does really exist, and act according to the laws which we have explained, and abundantly serves to account for all the motions of our celestial bodies and our sea."

From this alone it would be evident that he did not, as is often said, discourage inquiries into the cause of gravity, but simply discouraged the facile and illusory explanations which were constructed out of arbitrary suppositions, instead of out of observed phenomena. "Physics, beware of Metaphysics," was his warning. He was ready enough to speculate as to the cause of gravity, but well knew that his speculations were mere gropings in the dark, not to be placed beside the positive principles he had so laboriously brought to bear on the facts observed. The cause, whatsoever it might be, he declared was an active Principle, not an occult quality supposed to result from the specific Forms of Things, but one of the "general Laws of Nature" by which the things themselves are formed; "their truth appearing to us by phenomena, though their causes be not yet discovered. For these are manifest qualities, and the causes only are occult. And the Aristotelians gave the name of occult qualities not to manifest qualities, but to such only as they supposed to lie hid in bodies, and to be the unknown causes of manifest effects, — such as would be the causes of Gravity, and of magnetic and electric attractions and of fermentations, if we should suppose that these forces or actions arose from qualities unknown to us, and incapable of being discovered and made manifest. Such occult qualities put a stop to the improvement of natural philosophy, and therefore of late years have been rejected. To tell us that every species of things is endowed with an occult specific quality by which it acts and produces manifest effects, is to tell us nothing. But to derive two or three general Principles of Motion from phenomena, and afterwards to tell us how the properties and actions of all corporeal things follow from these manifest Principles, would be a very great step in philosophy, though their causes were not discovered." *

In the preface to the *Principia* he says: "For all the difficulty of philosophy seems to consist in this, —*from the phenomena of Motion to investigate the forces of Nature, and then from these forces to demonstrate the other phenomena.* And to this end the general propositions in the first and second books are directed. In the third book is given an example in the explanation of the System of the World. For by the propositions mathematically demonstrated in the first book, we there derive from the celestial phenomena the forces of Gravity with which bodies tend to the sun and the several planets. Then from these forces, by other propositions, which are also mathematical, we deduce the motions of the Planets, the Comets, the Moon, and the Sea. *I wish we could derive the rest of*

* *Optics*, Book III., *sub finem.*

the phenomena of Nature by the same kind of reasoning from mathematical principles. For I am induced by many reasons to suspect that they may all depend upon certain forces by which the particles of bodies by some causes hitherto unknown are either mutually impelled towards each other and cohere in regular figures, or are repelled and recede from each other; which forces being unknown, philosophers have hitherto attempted the search in vain. But I hope the principles here laid down will afford some light either to that or some true method of philosophy."

And again, towards the close of the *Optics*, he says: "As in Mathematics, so in Natural Philosophy the investigation of difficult things by the method of analysis ought ever to precede the method of composition. This analysis consists in making experiments and observations, and in drawing general conclusions from them by induction, and admitting of no objections against the conclusions, but such as are taken from experiments or other certain truths. For hypotheses are not to be regarded in experimental philosophy. And although the arguing from experiments and observations by Induction be no demonstration of general conclusions, yet it is the best way of arguing which the nature of things admits of, and may be looked upon as so much the stronger by how much the Induction is more general. And if no exception occur from phenomena, the conclusion may be pronounced generally. But if at any time afterwards any exception shall occur from experiments, it may then begin to be pronounced with such exceptions as occur. By this way of analysis we may proceed from compounds to ingredients, and from motions to the forces producing them; and in general from effects to their causes, and from particular causes to more general ones, till the argument end in the most general."

This, then, was Newton's doctrine, and it was also his practice in general; although he sometimes so far forgot his own principles that he allowed theological and metempirical elements to mingle with the inductions of Experience.

51. The reader has already seized my drift, which is that Metaphysics can be pursued on the Method of Science, provided it accepts all the tests and conditions of that Method, and keeps within the range of Experience. Thus treated, its dangers and difficulties would be no greater than those of Science, its certainties would have the same foundation. In both we have to disengage the known and knowable from the unknown and unknowable; and having disengaged the known quantities, we proceed to operate on them in the detection of the unknown. In every problem we have to determine,—1°, Is there a known Agent or Agency, which will furnish the answer? 2°, By what operations can the presence of this be made manifest? by what tests can we assure ourselves that the Agent is the one which we have assumed, or that this Agency has the requisite law, or order?

52. Now the common error of metaphysicians, and one not uncommon also among men of science, is hastily to assume an *unknown* Agent or Agency, or to assume the presence of one *known*, and then to operate on that assumption as on a solid basis. There is one aspect in which such a procedure is perfectly legitimate, namely, when it is avowedly conducted as a tentative hypothetical mode of establishing an equation, afterwards to be verified when the values are assigned. The procedure is fatal when this artifice is forgotten, and is made to solve the problem without verification of the assumed values. The geometer resolves his problem by deriving the prop-

erties of the figure from those already known and analogous; having before him the laws to which the several parts of the system conform, he deduces from these the quantities sought, and thus constructs his figure. To obtain his equation he assumes the problem to be already solved, and constructs a figure according to the hypothetical state of the known and unknown quantities. Thus, so far from dispensing with Hypothesis, the geometer largely invokes its aid, *only he never forgets the nature of the aid invoked.* He is mostly guided by probabilities, which he intends reducing to certainties; he anticipates by divination what is afterwards to be reached through demonstration. The chief distinction between his probabilities and those of the physicist or biologist lies in the greater simplicity or unequivocalness of his terms, and the consequent greater facility of their verification. Sometimes he finds his construction leads to a nugatory solution, and he here sees that the hypothetical figure does not agree with the question, and that somewhere some contradictory conditions have been introduced. In this case he constructs another, invoking fresh hypothesis, and thus he tries one after the other, until he hits upon that which will *satisfy* the equation.

53. The procedure of the physicist is similar. He constructs a hypothetical scheme of the dependent parts of the phenomenon from those already known, and by processes of Verification ascertains whether this scheme agrees with Observation and Deduction. If he has introduced into the scheme contradictory conditions, or has left out conditions that are co-operant, the discrepancy between Observation and Calculation warns him of his error; and he tries another scheme. Although the task of Verification is usually more arduous and delicate than in Geometry, it is essentially the same. Dealing as the physicist does with data which are more complicated, less

accurately definable, and dependent on minute and numerous observations and inductions, he is more easily led to accept a complex condition for a simple one, and to disregard conditions which seem insignificant because he is not alive to their significance.

54. If the physicist is thus hampered, still more are the biologist, psychologist, and metaphysician hampered, because their data are excessively complex, and their definitions fatally equivocal. Yet their Method should be the same. Could they pursue it with the same rigorous regard to its tests and canons, their results would be as *exact* as those of the physicist and geometer. The common notion of the exclusive superiority of what are called the exact sciences I hold to be an error. There is always an admitted inaccuracy, or incompleteness, in every geometrical solution, except in the region of Abstraction, i. e. ideal construction; and *in* that region the solutions of Biology or Metaphysics may have equal accuracy. In Mathematics, which consists of operations on symbols, the exactness is ideal; when the results thus obtained are applied to reality they are approximately true in as far as the symbols express real terms; but mathematical operations may be equally exact when their symbols are avowedly unreal; and it has been possible to ingenious geometers to construct a non-Euclidian geometry, on the assumption that Euclid's postulate is false. Hence we may conclude that Metaphysics, consisting of operations on symbols of Force, may be equally exact, and their results approximately true in regard to reality, the degree of approximation depending on the reality of the terms. The presence of transcendent elements need not disturb us. Every physical problem involves metempirical elements beside those which are empirical; but Physics sets them aside, and, dealing only with the empirical, reaches conclusions which are exact, within that sphere. No dis-

turbance in the accuracy of calculation follows from the existence, outside the calculation, of elements which are incalculable. The law of gravitation, for example, is exact, although its transcendental aspect — namely, what gravitation is in itself, whether Attraction, Undulation, or Pressure — is not merely left undetermined, but by the majority of physicists is not even sought. The law of Association of Ideas is equally exact, although not quantitatively expressible. The dependence of Sensation upon Stimulus is not less so, and has received a quantitative expression.* The laws of Causation may be formulated with equal precision. And *exact* knowledge of Force, Cause, Matter, ought to be attainable, in spite of their transcendental elements, by the one procedure of eliminating these, and operating solely on the empirical. Hence the conclusion: —

> The scientific canon of excluding from calculation all incalculable data places Metaphysics on the same level with Physics.

* The ratio of the increase of a sensation to the increase of its stimulus is that of a logarithm to its number. (FECHNER, *Psychophysik*, Bd. II. p. 11. 1860.)

CHAPTER IV.

OBJECTIONS TO METAPHYSICS.

55. THE Method just sketched in outline must be exhibited in practice through the subsequent chapters. What has already been said purports only to show that Metaphysics is possible under certain limitations which apply to all Science; and under this programme may be included everything that is rational in the persistent effort of mankind to solve certain problems, while at the same time firm hold is kept of that Method which alone has rewarded effort. "Tout est permis au philosophe," says Maupertius truly, "pourvu qu'il traite tout avec l'esprit philosophique." All problems are open to the metaphysician, provided he treat them on scientific principles. All? Yes, all that can be brought under the conditions and limitations which regulate research. But problems which cannot be so treated are idle and mischievous.

56. There has probably arisen in the minds of some readers a feeling of uneasy distrust, and in others a feeling of surprise, at finding me advocating the study of Metaphysics. "*Timeo Danaos*," will be the remark of the former. "He has relinquished the Positive Philosophy," will be the remark of the latter. The first suspicion I cannot remove. The second may be easily answered. Referring to what was said in § 5, I may add that the exclusion of all metempirical questions, and the rejection of the metempirical Method, is the cardinal position of the Positive Philosophy; which also admits much of

what is here called Metaphysics, namely, the highest generalizations of the several sciences, though it excludes the problems of Matter, Force, Cause, Life, Mind, Object, and Subject. Why does it exclude these? Simply on the ground of their being insoluble, metempirical. But this rejection seems to me somewhat arbitrary, when the state of the case is examined; and injudicious, when we find that it not only irritates those who might be convinced, but irritates them by a misconception. All who put their trust in the Positive Philosophy must regret that it should alienate instead of alluring speculative thinkers, capable of extending its reach; and it alienates them by the supercilious assertion that they are, and have been, wandering on the wrong path; which may be true, *is* true, but which would be better enforced by pointing out their point of divergence from the right path, so that their steps might be retraced. Nor can the appeal to History suffice; at the utmost it can only be somewhat of a *reductio ad absurdum*, — a procedure which even mathematicians now agree to regard as cumbrous,* since it constrains assent in lieu of enlightening conviction, and is therefore inferior to demonstration. Instead of a supercilious negation or unsatisfactory historical refutation, it will surely be a gain if the problems are admitted, and shown to be soluble on the positive Method.

57. The grounds of opposition to metaphysical inquiries may be grouped under two heads: 1°, that they move in a world of Abstraction regardless of concrete realities, — consequently their solutions can never be more than purely subjective constructions without objective validity; 2°, that they seek to penetrate Causes and Essences, which are necessarily unknowable.

There is truth in both objections, as applied to the common practice of metaphysicians; but we have only to

* See DUHAMEL, *Cours d'Analyse*, I. 3. 1841.

rectify that practice by a more rational statement of each question, and the objections fall away. For nothing is more clearly demonstrable than that what is called exact Science is also a purely ideal construction, dealing primarily with abstractions, and not with concrete realities; so that the valid objection against any system of Metaphysics is not that it moves in a world of ideal conceptions, but that its conceptions have been illegitimately constructed or illogically applied. Further, I shall hope to show that the search after Causes, nay, *efficient* Causes, is the aim of Science, and that the aim is attainable. But to understand this it is necessary that we set out with a clear conception of what it is we seek, and how it may be found: the search after Causes is futile or fertile accordingly. In like manner, according to the meaning assigned to the term, there will be a truism or a falsism in the common declaration that the human mind is incapable of knowing the Essences of things. A traditional perversion makes the essence of a thing to consist in the relations of that thing to something unknown, unknowable, rather than in its relations to a known or knowable, i. e. assumes that the thing cannot *be* what it *is* to us and other known things, but must be something "in itself," unrelated, or having quite other relations to other unknowable things. In this contempt of the *actual* in favor of the vaguely imagined *possible*, this neglect of reality in favor of a supposed deeper reality, this disregard of light in the search for a light behind the light, metaphysicians have been led to seek the "thing in itself" beyond the region of Experience. To reflective minds it was early apparent that such a *quæsitum* was a phantom; and because it could not be grasped, they declared, not that *this* phantom-essence was beyond our reach, but that all essences were impenetrable mysteries. With the reality before them they declared it was a phantom, and that the shadow was the reality, the essence!

58. No wonder if questions thus inappropriately conceived were condemned to remain without answers. Were a mathematician asked, What is the essential color of a circle? he would reject the question as not geometrical. *The* circle has no color. But any circular figure may have any color, and that color is essential to *it*. Were a physicist asked, What is the nature of the emotion felt by a mass when undergoing molecular change? he would reject the question as not physical. Emotion does accompany certain molecular changes, but, as far as we know, this is only under very special conditions, and the phenomenon lies wholly beyond the province of Physics. But if such questions can receive no answer, because not put in answerable terms, how much more so the questions which avowedly travel quite beyond all range of Experience, and ask, What *is* the thing in its relations to something unknown? To know a thing is to know its relations; it *is* its relations. Therefore to ask, What are its relations to an unknowable? is absurd.

59. Under this bias men declare, truly enough, that Metaphysics belongs to a condition of culture from which Europe has finally, though with immense difficulty, emerged; a condition in which men, instead of interrogating Nature, please their fancy with trying to discover the general character of Being in the abstract. But although there is truth in the contemptuous phrase designating Metaphysics as the pursuit of ontological chimeras, — and it is the conviction of this which has caused metaphysical study to be abandoned, — there is also truth in the rejoinder that Metaphysics may be fruitful although the efforts of metaphysicians have hitherto been failures; and it is the conviction of this which sustains inquiry among the valiant few.

60. What is our position in this controversy? It is that there is Ontology, and Ontology: *il y a fagots, et fagots.* There is Ontology pursued on the Metempirical Method; and this, like all inquiries so pursued, is necessarily fruitless. There is Ontology pursued on the Empirical Method, and this is Abstract Science, which is occupied with the general laws of Being. A moment's consideration will make this clear. What is the object of each science? It is to detect the general order of Things, as manifested in particular groups of phenomena, i. e. the abstract laws of Being under particular conditions. It is not moving bodies in all their complex relations, but laws of Motion; not living organisms, but laws of Life; not thinking organisms, but laws of Mind; — it is these which are the objects of Science; and the particular substances, plants, and animals which manifest such laws, are used only as stepping-stones to reach those higher points of view. The reproach, if it be a reproach, conveyed in the term "ontological" when applied to Metaphysics, is shared by Science. In both the search is after abstract Being, not after concrete individual fact. Rightly understood, there is truth in saying that a metaphysician may have a knowledge of Being as certain as the mathematician's knowledge of Magnitude, as the chemist's knowledge of Affinity, as the biologist's knowledge of Life, as the sociologist's knowledge of Society; and this knowledge may be gained in the same way.

61. By way of illustration consider the positive science of Crystallography, and presently it appears that the mineralogist is studying the *abstract Crystal,* its geometrical laws and its physical properties. He constructs this abstract conception out of data furnished by many individual minerals; but although these are necessary stepping-stones, they and all their *individual* characters disappear, leaving only the general characters common of

all; from these is obtained the abstract conception, The Crystal. Now, when the mineralogist expounds the principles of his science he is obviously dealing with the laws of abstract Being exemplified under the special conditions of crystallography. It is the same with the biologist; in expounding the laws of Life he is dealing with Ontology. *The* crystal does not exist as a phenomenon, neither does *the* animal; they are ideal creations, and in this light may stand beside the entities of the Schoolmen, or the ὄντως ὄν of the Eleatics; but although the ancient and the modern Ontologies are alike ideal creations, they differ profoundly in their construction: the one is seen to be *incapable of a reduction to sensible experience,* the facts are not resolvable into assignable factors; the other is seen to be only an abbreviated symbolical expression of the *observable order in things.* The constructions of the ancients admitted metempirical elements beside the empirical, and endowed possibilities with the value of realities; they differ from those of positive Science as fallacies and paralogisms differ from facts and syllogisms.

62. There is then a rational and an irrational Ontology, an empirical and a metempirical Metaphysics. It is wholly a question of the manner in which the abstractions are formed, and not of the degree of abstractness. The scientific acceptance of Laws and Properties is quite as metaphysical as the scholastic acceptance of Entities and Quiddities; but the justification of the one set is their objective validity, i. e. their agreement with sensible Experience; the illusoriness of the other is their incapability of being resolved into sensible concretes. So nearly are the two allied that many an incautious scientific speculator treats the Laws precisely as the Schoolmen treated Entities; and thus we so often see a Law supposed to rule the phenomena, as if from the outside; and the Property of a substance is often an ill-

disguised Quiddity. The current notions about Force are as irrational as anything to be found in Scholasticism.

63. With this rectification of the prejudice against Ontology, which is one with that against Metaphysics, we may say that understanding by Ontology the science of the abstract laws of Being, it is the science of those highest generalities which emerge from the study of Things, and there can be no difference between Science and Metaphysics except in the degrees of generality. In other words, every science has its metaphysic; and our definition of empirical Metaphysics (we recognize no other) will be "the science of the most general principles." This definition resembles that of Aristotle in its terms, though of course widely different in its meaning. Thus conceived, Metaphysics holds a position with respect to Science somewhat analogous to the position held by Algebra with respect to Arithmetic. The objects of Arithmetic are quantities; the objects of Algebra are not quantities, but the relations of quantities. In like manner the objects of Science are the laws of sensible phenomena; the objects of Metaphysics are not these, but laws of the laws, — the Calculus of operations. Although dealing with the generalities of general principles, as the Transcendental Analysis deals with relations of equations, the equations having been furnished by Algebra, and the values by Arithmetic, — Metaphysics must not be otherwise detached from the grounds and limitations of Experience. Unless its general principles have been securely established by Science, its operations will be as chimerical as those of a Calculus of imaginary equations; and unless its operations be verifiable, they will be worthless. Its point of departure and its point of arrival must be Reals. All its intermediate positions may be far removed from sensible reality, nay, considered in themselves, they may be impossible as Reals, provided they re-enter the

domain of Reality, and conduct us to our goal; that is all we ask of any operation. When we desire to reach the summit of a mountain whose sides are too steep for ascent, we may quit the firm earth, and trust ourselves to the yielding air, if a balloon be ready to carry us through it. The result justifies the means. Most of our scientific operations have this airy character. But there are others — and all metempirical hypotheses are of this class — which, instead of the balloon furnished by Science, and proved to be effectual, call upon the poet's Hippogriff, and hope by it to be carried through the air. They never reach the summit.

63 *a*. Metaphysics then, as we often say, comes after Physics, does not precede but follows the establishment of relations. From the laws of the Cosmos discovered by Science it elicits certain general relations, which are then visible in phenomena, just as the theory of Gravitation, originated by inductions from terrestrial physics, was confirmed by inductions from celestial physics, and when thus established was afterwards reflected back on terrestrial physics, disclosing unexpected relations there. This reflected light discloses unsuspected equations, and is always regulative of Research. The conception of what is called the Correlations of Force, or more suitably the Transformation of Energy, is a metaphysical conception, and has led to the discovery of unsuspected relations. The relation of Function and Organ, although a biological law, could hardly have been established except as a deduction from the metaphysical conception first gained through Mechanics, and then seen to be universal, — I mean the relation of Dynamic and Static. Thus between Science and Metaphysics there is a constant give and take. And this give and take we find between sensation and idea, induction and deduction, particular experiences and general Experience; and it is itself a luminous example

of the metaphysical Law of Polarity, which we shall hereafter have to consider as the expression of that Twofold Aspect under which all Experience presents itself.

Not to anticipate more than is absolutely needful here, I will content myself with suggesting that Experience has two grand divisions: the Cosmos, or Object-world; and the Consciousness, or Subject-world. Both are subdivided into Static and Dynamic aspects. The Cosmos is conceived as Existence, and as Cause: Existence is the static aspect of Cause; Cause is the dynamic aspect of Existence. The Subject-world is conceived as Organ and Function. The relations of Object and Subject which Psychology discovers are carried up into the region of Metaphysics, as the relations of the Cosmos are; that is to say, they remain strictly matters of Science while restricted to particular divisions, and become matters of Metaphysic when they are extended to several or all divisions. But this point we must discuss in the next chapter.

CHAPTER V.

THE PLACE OF METAPHYSICS AMONG THE SCIENCES.

64. HAVING agreed that Metaphysics, or the science of the highest generalities, is possible, we may now inquire whether it should be detached from the sciences which severally furnish those generalities, and be erected into a separate Discipline (to use the German term), just as there is a separate Discipline of Logic formed out of the several logics; or whether, in conformity with Comte's classification, Metaphysics should not be thus detached, but distributed among the sciences from which its data are drawn.

Mr. Mill has objected to Comte's scheme, in relation to Logic, that while furnishing an organon of Discovery it omits the organon of Proof, so that the ancient Discipline finds no place assigned to it. The answer to this objection is, that in point of fact the organon of Discovery includes the organon of Proof; to discover a process is to prove it; and the several sciences furnish their own methods of Proof. But it may still be urged that Comte's scheme does not exhibit the extraction of these methods and their systematization in a special Discipline. He seems to have had some misgiving on this point when, in his latest work, he proposed to identify Logic (in its restricted sense) with Mathematics; although by Logic in its widest sense he meant all intellectual construction. In the former sense, he identifies it with the Calculus, Geometry, and Mechanics, because the sole existence which is common to all appreciable beings is reducible to the three attributes, — number, extension, and movement.*

65. Let us pause a moment to consider the very different meanings assigned to the word Logic. It commonly stands for: 1°, the art of reasoning; 2°, the theory of reasoning; 3°, Reasoning itself; 4°, the laws of mental operation, irrespective of the symbols operated on (Formal Logic); 5°, the rules of Proof.

The first of these I hold to be absurd. There is no more an art of Reasoning then there is an art of Breathing or Digesting. But so little is this understood that even thoughtful writers will be found declaring that we must learn how to reason, as we learn how to fence or to swim. In consequence of this misconception, certain studies, notably Mathematics, are popularly believed "to strengthen the Faculty," to develop the logical powers, to "invigorate the Judgment." The psychological notions which lie at the basis of such declarations are sadly defective.

The second and third meanings of the word are objectionable because restricting Logic to the process of Ratiocination when the ratios are abstract. This restriction is got rid of in the fourth and fifth meanings, which may be accepted as comprehensive. The fourth designates the universal Logic, it includes all Laws of Grouping (λεγειν means to bind together, to group), and is therefore applicable to Feeling and Thought (in the subjective world), and to Cause (in the objective world).

The fifth has the technical and restricted meaning of a *Codification of the rules of Proof*. In this last sense only can Logic be a separate Discipline. It may be likened to the science of Grammar apart from Language. Thus the speech of men of various nations embodies and exhibits certain general rules, or tendencies, according to which

* COMTE, *Synthèse Subjective*, p. 71.

words are grouped. These tendencies grammarians detach and treat separately as Laws of Speech, Rules of Grammar. Logicians may in like manner detach certain general procedures of the investigating intellect, and treat them apart as the Rules of Rational Inquiry.

66. Having fixed on the meaning Logic may bear when employed for a special Discipline, namely, the Codification of the rules of Proof, we may complete it by assigning to Metaphysics the parallel position of a Codification of the laws of Cause. It will thus occupy very much the place assigned to it by Hegel, namely, that of Objective Logic. The Object and the Subject world have one general Logic, separately viewed as the Logic of Intelligence, and the Logic of the Cosmos. In the Cosmos, viewed objectively, things influence each other and events succeed each other according to invariant tendencies, or laws. When these phenomena are reproduced in Consciousness they are also reproduced according to invariant tendencies; and thus it is that a law of Cause becomes a rule of Proof. Logic in its widest sense is Grouping. The laws of Grouping are the general tendencies of Things and the general tendencies of Thought. The common separation of Thought from the Things thought of is an artifice; but it is one so deeply inwoven with our philosophy and practice that the mind, untutored in such researches, is astonished and distressed at the statement of the identity between Thing and Thought, Object and Subject. With what qualifications this statement has to be received we shall hereafter discuss. Here I am only concerned to define the position of Metaphysics as Objective Logic, — the Codification of the most abstract laws of Cause. The subjective Logic takes no account of the special instruments and processes by which each science reaches Proof, it is occupied solely with the codification of the processes. In like manner the objective Logic dis-

regards special details in the processes of Causation, solely occupied with codifying the most abstract results. Subjective Logic rejects whatever lies beyond the range of Verification, and thus demarcates Reality from Possibility, Fact from Fiction. Objective Logic rejects whatever lies beyond that world of sensibles and extra-sensibles which can come within the range of Experience, and thus demarcates Metaphysics from Metempirics.

67. This distinction between the two aspects of Logic represents the distinction between Knowing and Being; and the identity underlying this diversity is also represented. In one we find the laws of Investigation, the abstract conditions to which all knowledge is subject. In the other we find the laws of the Investigated, the abstract conditions to which the Knowable is subject. Only on the assumption of the invariability of relations objective and subjective is Philosophy possible. In the most abstract of the sciences, that of Number, this identity is manifest. No arithmetical operation would be valid were there not this accord between the internal and external; and the assumption of such an accord runs throughout Science. Indeed, the axioms of Logic and the axioms of Science are the concave and convex aspects of the same curve.*

68. The Positive Philosophy may in one sense be said

* Since this was written Mr. Spencer has propounded a new view of Logic. Starting from the position that the syllogism refers to the dependencies of Things and not of Thoughts, he comes to the conclusion that Logic must be carried over entirely to the Object-world. He therefore places it beside Mathematics, — as it is placed in Comte's latest scheme. He holds that "it formulates the most general laws of correlation among existences considered as objective." Referring the reader to Mr. Spencer's exposition (*Psychology*, II. § 302 et seq.), I will merely here add that my chief divergence from it arises from my inability to accept his conception of there being only a symbolic correspondence between the inner and outer worlds. I hope to make it clear that the correspondence is real.

to absorb Metaphysics, for it claims to be the Codification of the laws of the Cosmos. Nor, except as a matter of special classification, should I have any objection to this, were it not accompanied by the peremptory exclusion of certain questions which can and must be answered. And with respect to the classification there is precisely the same difficulty with Logic. Comte insists that Logic should never be separated from Science: "Car en n'étudiant chaque partie de la méthode inductive qu'avec les doctrines qui l'ont spécialement suscitée, on sent aussitôt que son usage doit être conforme aux notions fondamentales que cette science reçoit de la précédente." * True and valuable as this consideration is, there are nevertheless several considerations which justify the erection of Logic as a special Discipline; and these equally apply to Metaphysics. There are many speculative advantages in having the highest generalizations of Objective and Subjective existence classed together and apart from the sciences which furnish them. When Logic is seen to embrace both, under its twofold aspect, the ancient barrier between Matter and Mind so long regarded as impassable vanishes, to reappear under the intelligible forms of concave and convex. Idealism is vindicated in all that it has of truth, and Realism is rescued. The Inner and Outer forms of Consciousness, the Subjective and Objective forms of Existence, are no longer antagonistic, but homogeneous and differentiated.

69. The identity of Fact and Idea, general Law and general Conception, is more readily appreciated in the higher sphere of Reason than in the lower spheres of Perception, because in the higher sphere the Object seems detached from Sense and is transformed into pure Thought. Thus in investigating the processes of Induction and Deduction we abstract these operations from

* COMTE, *Politique Positive*, I. 518.

their sensible elements, we let drop all the ministrations of Sense and fix attention solely on the mechanism of Thought; by a similar abstraction the mathematician detaches Extension from Matter and Motion from Solidity, although perfectly aware that pure Extension and pure Motion are impossible in the concrete. But no one believes that inductive and deductive processes can go on without at every step involving sensible correspondences. So long as we are observing and calculating the changes in objects, our conception of these changes as taking place in the objects, and *not* in us, is fixed, undisturbed. The objective aspect is the aspect presented to Consciousness. But no sooner do we pass from the observation of the changes to the conception of their Law, than the distinction between Conception and Law begins to fade: we recognize that the Law is not in the facts but in our minds; if we elicited it from the facts we *constructed* it anew, and replaced it among the facts. Whether this construction is to be regarded as an objective Law or a subjective Conception depends on our point of view; it is both, or either.

70. This will seem very unacceptable to those, and they are the majority, who imagine that phenomena are ruled by law in a literal sense, and who think that laws exist in the objective world as general facts which *determine* particular facts. It is thus that, in Pindar's phrase, the very Gods are subject to law, like mortals: —

> Νόμος ὁ πάντων βασιλεὺς
> θνητῶν τε καὶ ἀθανάτων.

And if the Gods, of course the fleeting phenomena. And yet we may hear utterances of this kind: "The comets follow no law in their motions through space," — which simply means that no conception has been *formed* by astronomers of all the determining conditions, and by them *placed* among the facts observed of the planetary courses.

The purely ideal construction of Law will hereafter be expounded (Prob. I. Chap. VI.) ; suffice it here to say that it throws no uncertainty over the results of investigation. The conception we form of a process in Nature may be no less accurate as a symbolical expression of the reality, than the perception we form of an object in Nature is an accurate sensible expression of the reaction of Consciousness under the stimulus of the object, and of what that reaction will be under all similar conditions. Both conception and perception are logical *constructions*, and are verifiable by similar tests.

71. If Laws are simply our Conceptions, and these are the Notations of what Experience has revealed to be the Order in which phenomena coexist and succeed each other, it is clear that Idealism demands a basis in Realism, and that our Conceptions to be valid, when regarded objectively as Laws, must be capable of reduction to a sensible origin, each of their constituent elements must be a real experience, and the order of their combination must be real. If we find among the constituents any element not thus reducible to Sense or to Intuition, that element must be set apart and treated as a transcendental. Thus treated, there need be no misgiving as to its part in the construction, nor as to the certainty of the results reached through that construction. The identification of Law with Conception will by no means warrant the too common procedure of metaphysicians who endeavor to explain *the* Order in Things, by unfolding *an* Order in Thought, and propound theories of the Universe which rest mainly on the "clear ideas" whose genesis is not inductively verifiable. It is quite possible to have very clear ideas which are inexact expressions, and very logical arrangements which do not conform to the Order of Experience. Although Science constantly anticipates Observation by a far-reaching Deduction, and reveals hid-

den facts by simply unfolding the consequences shut up in general conceptions, this is only possible when the general conceptions have been framed from *and express* actual relations, and thus *include* what is deductively *concluded.* Because they are conceptions which were abstracted from realities, they can in turn be applied to all similar realities. Tangents, sines, and cosines are not things found isolated in Nature, but because they are abstractions from realities, they are applicable to Nature. No one observing a curvilinear motion can see in it the double motion in the tangent to the curve and towards the centre of the curve, — no one in watching a beam of light can see the slightest indication of what the geometer finds there (or places there), viz. that the luminous vibrations are perpendicular to the line of propagation; in other words, that each vibration takes place at each instant on the surface of a sphere which has for its centre the point from which the ray diverges. Tangents, centres, vibrations, perpendiculars, — these are constructions of the intellect, not facts of sensible concretes. Yet such constructions are by no means arbitrary, — they are all reducible to Sense and Intuition, they all conform to rigorous objective tests; and because they are so, and because objectively found to reconcile Calculation with Observation, they are *stamped upon phenomena* as laws. Is it necessary to add, that, although every law is a conception, every conception is not to be accepted for a law? It is necessary, because we frequently overlook the distinction, and give out the forms of our own fancies for forms of phenomena. There is an order in our sensations, and an order in our thoughts; but even these orders do not always coincide. There is, further, an order in things on which the order in sensations and thoughts depends. But the dependence is *particular,* — that is to say, the order in our sensations will depend on the momentary order in things, but this may or may not be an order which is *general*. Now it is only the general order in things with which Philosophy is concerned, and which is expressed in laws; particular events are evanescent and only interest the moment; Philosophy seeks to frame conceptions which represent the Order in things, not at one instant and under particular exceptional conditions, but at all times, and under varying conditions. Such conceptions obviously cannot be framed irrespective of particular experiences, but they must nevertheless be abstracted from particulars and represent what is common to all.*

72. What has been already said will perhaps suffice to justify confidence in the recognition of Metaphysics as a possible branch of Science. For what constitutes a science? The co-ordination of facts. By what characters may it be recognized? A science exists, 1°, when it has a clearly defined *object;* 2°, when it has a clearly defined *place* in the region of research, a place not occupied by any other; and, 3°, when it has a clearly defined Method of applying the results of Experience to the extension of experience.

All these characters are recognizable in Metaphysics. Its object is the disengagement of certain most general principles, such as Cause, Force, Life, Mind, etc., from the sciences which usually imply these principles, and the exposition of their constituent elements, — the *facts*, sen-

* "Toute *science* consiste dans la coordination des faits ; si les diverses observations étaient entièrement isolées, il n'y aurait pas de science. On peut même dire généralement que la *science* est essentiellement destinée à dispenser, autant que le comportent les diverses phénomènes, de toute observation directe, en permettant de déduire du plus petit nombre possible de données immédiates, le plus grand nombre possible de résultats. N'est-ce point là l'usage réel, soit dans la spéculation soit dans l'action des *lois* que nous parvenons à découvrir entre les phénomènes naturels ?" — COMTE, *Philosophie Positive*, I. 131.

sible and logical, which these principles involve, and the relations of these principles. Its place, as a special Discipline, is that of an Objective Logic. Its method is that of dealing exclusively with the known functions of unknown quantities, and at every stage of inquiry separating the empirical from the metempirical data.

73. It may be expected that most metaphysicians will accept our premises, but with a reserve which will cause them to reject our conclusion. They will proclaim that what is here called Metempirics is equally the co-ordination of facts; and they will urge that the range of facts to be co-ordinated and the Method of co-ordination are unwarrantably restricted to the facts of Experience and the procedures of positive Science. The facts which we declare to be unknowable, they affirm to be knowable and known. The debate on this point can only be settled by an analysis of Knowledge, and agreement as to its necessary limitations. We shall therefore have to treat this at length.

And with regard to Method they urge that what is usually understood as Science cannot fitly grapple with the highest problems of Metempirics, because, dealing only with the particular and contingent, it cannot rise to universal and necessary truths, — cannot pass into "the field behind phenomena." This also we shall have to debate. Without venturing here to assume that every reader will find me expressing his conclusions on these two deeply interesting points, I am content to rest my case on the indisputable ground occupied by both schools, namely, that whether we have, or have not, a class of facts which transcend Experience, and a special organ — the so-called Intellectual Intuition — by which such facts may be apprehended and co-ordinated into a system, there still remains that marked separation indicated in the terms Metaphysics and Metempirics; and hence I affirm that the only fruitful procedure in the treatment of metaphysical problems is the disengagement of their metempirical elements.

74. Kant tells us that a rational theory of Nature only deserves the name when its laws are *à priori* and cannot be gained through Experience; indeed, only becomes rational in proportion as it admits of mathematical treatment. This is plausible if we accept his unacceptable definition of Experience, his eminently questionable view of *à priori* truths, and his assumption that Mathematics has not an empirical origin. Fichte consistently declared that all natural laws, from the law by which a blade of grass will grow to the law which keeps the planets in their orbits, might be deduced from first principles.* The deduction was attempted; and whoever desires to see with what result, may open Oken or Hegel. Closely connected with this reliance on the *à priori* procedure is the significant fact that every metaphysical thinker, who pretends to bring a contribution towards the explanation of things, has his own personal system, and would be offended by any accusation which implied the contrary. Nay, it is a boast that "Philosophy is not to be learned like Mathematics, or like a trade." Each philosopher holds himself independent of fellow-workers, like an artist expressing his individual conceptions. Hence Fichte can truly say, "the kind of Philosophy which a man chooses depends upon the kind of man." Contrast this with Science. Who would think of choosing his astronomical or biological system? Who would speak of Faraday's Physics or Liebig's Chemistry as he speaks of Kant's Psychology and Hegel's Logic? Absurd as it is, this notion of a personal choice in Philosophy is very common, and finds its analogue in the personal choice of a Religion. Consistently with this there is a demand on

* FICHTE, *Werke*, I. 64, 65.

the part of the public that the philosopher's system should sustain the Theology and Polity of his age and nation. The public, which insists, and rightly insists, on an artist's not outraging the taste and moral convictions of his audience, is consistent in demanding a like conformity to prejudices and doctrines on the part of the philosopher, if that philosopher desires recognition for his system as an individual conception. Schelling was justified in declaring that a system of Philosophy which contradicted the moral feelings could never be a system of Reason but only of Unreason.* But he omitted to add the qualification, namely, that men too readily assume their own personal views to be those which cannot be contradicted without contradiction of the moral consciousness. Unless Philosophy be an Art, and wholly personal, we must agree with Kant that there is something preposterous in demanding enlightenment from it, and at the same time prescribing the opinion it is to enforce.

75. Philosophy, like everything else, is evolved from pre-existing conditions, and the novelty of any valid system should consist in supplying some missing links or in formulating some unformulated evidence, thus extending and systematizing the known. When, therefore, I claim novelty for the conception of applying to Metaphysics the procedures consciously and unconsciously applied by men of science in all successful investigation, I do not mean that the conception is now for the first time originated, but that now for the first time it is definitely expressed in its principles and bearings. Many have thought, and some few have proclaimed, that Metaphysics should be based on facts, and its problems resolved on the principles of Experience. But no one — to my knowledge — has explicitly stated *how* this was to be effected.

* SCHELLING, *Werke*, VII. 413.

After all, the question of originality is of quite minor importance; that of efficiency most concerns us. Convinced that all germinal conceptions are the product of their age rather than of any individual mind, I should look at any conception of mine with extreme suspicion if it wore the air of other novelty than that of added precision or of extension; for, as De Morgan felicitously remarks in tracing the discovery of the Differential Calculus, "A great method is always within the perception of many before it is within the grasp of one."

76. Is it not a justifiable hope that, by applying the Method of Science to *all* questions, England may some day possess a Philosophy, the absence of which during the last two hundred years has been a serious defect in her culture? Science she has had, and Poetry, and Literature, rivalling when not surpassing those of other nations. But a Philosophy she has not had, in spite of philosophic thinkers of epoch-making power: Hobbes, Locke, Berkeley, Hume, have produced essays, not systems. There has been no noteworthy attempt to give a conception of the World, of Man, and of Society, wrought out with systematic harmonizing of principles. There has not been an effort to systematize the scattered labors of isolated thinkers. Mr. Herbert Spencer is now for the first time deliberately making the attempt to found a Philosophy.

While no one can deny that there has been this deficiency, many will declare it to have been an advantage. In some respects it was. So long as the ground was unprepared for a stable edifice, the collection and sifting of the materials was the best work to be done. In other respects the disadvantage has been palpable. Philosophic research has lost itself in out-of-the-way corners. It has never placed itself on a height from which a wide view of the universe could be had. This was inevitable, because its Method isolated it from Science. With our Philosophy, as with our Politics, the parochial point of view has supplanted the cosmopolitan. The same spirit which manages the affairs of the Nation too much through Parish Boards, forgetting that the Nation is an integrant part of the living world, has parcelled out the Universe into "Sections" of a British Association, and from those sections has carefully excluded not only Psychology, Ethics, Metaphysics, and Religion, but anything wearing the aspect of a general doctrine embracing all research.

77. In this respect Germany has had an advantage which has outweighed the serious evils of a radically false Method. The habit of philosophizing — that is, of taking general views, and connecting special truths with them — has become, so to speak, organized in the German mind; and its influence on culture has been highly beneficial. It percolates the soil, and is felt even when metaphysical problems are not directly touched on, — in the treatment of History, Language, Politics, Criticism, etc. No doubt this has its drawbacks. Our parochial system will sometimes be favorably contrasted with the results of their world-system ; sometimes also unfavorably. Our system has kept closer to reality ; theirs has oftener been allured by phantoms. We shook off Scholasticism ; they retained it. But in shaking it off we also shook off the speculative passion for nice accuracy of distinction, and for wide general conceptions ; and they, now that they have learned to look more closely at realities and trust less in logical legerdemain, still retain the old love for systematic and exhaustive treatment. The German Philosophy of recent years has become more and more infused with the scientific spirit.

78. In conclusion, I may here simply state my conviction that the Philosophy in the construction of which the efforts of all nations converge, is that Positive Phi-

losophy which began with Kepler and Galileo, Descartes and Bacon, and was first reduced to a system by Auguste Comte: the Doctrine embracing the World, Man, and Society on one homogeneous Method. The extension and perfection of this Doctrine is the work of the future. The following pages are animated by the desire of extending positive procedures to those outlying questions which hitherto have been either ignored or pronounced incapable of incorporation with the positive doctrine.

Kant asks: "If Metaphysics is a science, how comes it that she cannot boast of the general and enduring approbation bestowed on other sciences? If she is no science, how comes it that she wears this imposing aspect, and fascinates the human understanding with hopes inextinguishable yet never gratified? We must either demonstrate the competency or incompetency; for we cannot longer continue in our present uncertainty."*

The answers to these questions which Kant gave not having been satisfactory, a new attempt, under more favorable conditions, is made in these pages. To render this attempt satisfactory we must first clearly understand the conditions of metaphysical inquiry. The initial condition — that of separating the insoluble from the soluble aspects of each problem — would be accepted by all. But the question would everywhere arise: *What* is insoluble? *How* is this ascertainable? There are problems which are recognized as insoluble because of their conditions. For example, it is impossible to extract the square root of a number which is not made by multiplication of any whole number or fraction by itself. To all eternity this must be impossible. Yet an approximation is possible which may be made near enough for any practical purpose. There are other problems, again, which do not admit of even ap-

* KANT, *Prolegomena zu einer jeden künftigen Metaphysik: Einleitung.*

proximative solutions. No one really tries to solve what he is already convinced is an insoluble problem. But one man thinks the problem soluble which another pronounces not to be soluble. What then is our criterion? We say the metempirical elements must be thrown out of the construction. But what *are* the metempirical elements?

Here we find ourselves fronting the great psychological problems of the Limitations of Knowledge, and the Principles of Certitude. To settle these it will be necessary to examine the pretensions of the *à priori* school. Our first labor, then, will be to examine the principles of positive and speculative research, and then to show that the principles of metempirical research must either be unconditionally rejected, or, if accepted, must be isolated from all departments of Knowledge and restricted solely to the Unknowable.

By way of introduction to these, and to the problems which will succeed, it may be useful to group together in an accessible form the principal Rules of Philosophizing which ought to regulate our efforts.

INTRODUCTION.

PART II.

THE RULES OF PHILOSOPHIZING.

AT the opening of his Third Book, Newton sets forth the Rules of Reasoning in Philosophy, which in England have been generally accepted with an almost unquestioning reverence. Yet Newton himself never professed them to be exhaustive; and indeed, as Whewell remarks, they were obviously constructed with an intentional adaptation to the case with which he had to deal, — namely, the induction of universal gravitation, — and are meant to protect the reasonings before which they stand. It is not strange, therefore, that, when considered under other aspects, these Rules should prove to be defective both in precision and in range. Whewell has criticised them without hesitation. Instead of criticising, or defending them, I here propose certain Rules which, while including those of Newton (with such modifications as may bring them into closer accordance with my views), will serve also by their wider range to protect the reasonings which will follow in the course of this work. There may be some temerity in deviating from Newton, for it is with Newton as with Shakespeare, — the genuine reverence of the Few has become stiffened into the superstition of the Many; and the formalism of superstition is always outraged by a suggestion of dissent. Men who have seldom or never turned over the leaves of the *Principia* are exasperated when they hear that any one who has studied and been strengthened by that work ventures to hint at flaws in it. Never having slaked their own thirst at the Holy Well, they hear with impatience of drinkers who presume to reject the weeds and dead leaves which float in its pure water.

Newton is not, however, directly here in question. What the following Rules profess is no more than certain general results of philosophic reflection on the conduct of Research, which are offered to the attentive meditation of the student.

RULE I. — *No problem to be mooted unless it be presented in terms of Experience, and be capable of empirical investigation.*

REMARK.

The proper statement of a question often carries with it the answer. When the answer is not at once conspicuous, a proper statement limits the field of search by disengagement of the unknown elements, which are then examined in order to determine whether, 1°, they are unknown, and unknowable because metempirical; or, 2°, they are unknown only because the requisite conditions of knowledge lie beyond our present data. In the former case research ceases. In the latter case it proceeds, and is guided by the following rules: —

RULE II. — *Any contradiction of fundamental experiences of Sense or Intuition to be taken as evidence of some flaw either in the data or the calculation.*

REMARK.

This seems a truism, yet it is a rule fatally disregarded, partly owing to impatience, which leads men to accept even logical contradiction rather than remain without an explanation; partly to the conviction that many of the most certain results of science seem in contradiction with ordinary experience. But, in truth, what seems a contradiction proves to be due either to the contradictory mode of statement, or to an erroneous inference from experience; sometimes it is the substitution of a prejudice or tradition for experience.

The Rule simply asserts that since the direct experiences of Sense and Intuition (the perception of objects, and the perception of the relations of objects) have the highest possible validity, and form the basis and the test of all Demonstration, they cannot be contradicted by any real deduction from them; so that, whenever our deductions or hypotheses involve this logical inconsistency, it is the indication of something somewhere wrong. Does the error lie in our assuming that the experience we declare to be fundamental is *direct*, whereas it proves by analysis to be *indirect*, derivative, and possibly imperfect? Critical examination must decide. The question must be reduced to its components. Thus the old opinion respecting the sun's revolution round the earth seemed to be a fundamental experience which Copernicus contradicted. It was nothing of the kind. It was an inference from experience; and what the Copernican hypothesis contradicted was not the visible fact, but the inference respecting the invisible cause of that visible fact. Although we believe that the earth revolves round the sun, and that this motion has the effect of making the sun seem to describe the circle, yet what we *see* is not the motion of the earth, and for most practical purposes the old hypothesis is still employed.

The application of this Rule requires great tact and accurate knowledge. It is violated in many theories which have gained a wide acceptance, and its value is great in keeping the mind open to new evidence, and warning us that any conclusion which violates it must be wrong. The notion of "action at a distance," which still finds energetic defenders, could never have gained acceptance had this Rule been clearly recognized.

RULE III.—"*The qualities of bodies which admit neither of intension nor remission of degrees, and which are found to belong to all bodies within the reach of our experiments, are to be esteemed the universal qualities of all bodies.*"

REMARK.

This is Newton's Third Rule. On it he remarks: "For since the qualities of bodies are only known to us by experiments, we are to hold for universal all such as universally agree with experiments, and such as are not liable to diminution can never be quite taken away. We are certainly not to relinquish the evidence of experiments for the sake of dreams and vain fictions of our own devising; nor are we to recede from the analogy of Nature, which uses to be simple and always consonant to itself. . . . . We no otherways know the extension of bodies than by our senses, nor do these reach it in all bodies; but because we perceive extension in all that is sensible, therefore we ascribe it to all others also. And this is the foundation of all philosophy."

Professor Challis calls this a golden rule. Whewell speaks slightingly of it; and indeed it accords ill with his system. To me it seems absolute, if taken with the qualification involved in Rule X. When we generalize experience, and conclude what *will be* from what *has been*, it is obvious that our justification rests on the assumed homogeneity of the terms: the event predicted must be of the same nature as the event observed, otherwise the Rule cannot be fitly applied.

RULE IV. — *No Agent to be admitted unless it have a sensible basis; nor any Agency unless it be verifiable or calculable.*

REMARK.

This relates chiefly to Hypothesis. It permits the adoption of any conjecture as to Agent or Agency, provided such conjecture facilitates calculation. But so long as the verifiable nature of either is uncertain, the conjecture must be kept *apart* from all the positively ascertained data, and rigorously shut out from the final conclusion. In other words, the solution of an equation must always express the unknown quantity in terms of the known quantities; and every interpretation of a phenomenon must be the interpretation of it in terms of Feeling.

RULE V. — "*We are to admit no more causes of natural things than such as are both true, and sufficient to explain the appearances.*"

REMARK.

This is Newton's First Rule; and, though not expressed with perfect precision, is pregnant with wisdom. The objection may be raised that, inasmuch as causes avowedly not true can gain no acceptance, the whole question turns on the validity of the causes invoked. What *is* a *vera causa?* Newton obviously means by it an Agent or Agency already known to exist, and seen to be sufficient to account for the phenomena if its presence be admitted. Whewell objects that if we never look for a cause except among those already familiar, we shall never become acquainted with any new cause. This objection misses its mark. New Agents or Agencies, when discovered, may be seen to be the causes of phenomena hitherto unexplained; but to attempt to explain by unknown causes is futile; and the Rule is directed against this very futility.

Curiously enough, Newton himself in his remark on the Rule violates it: "To this purpose the philosophers say that Nature does nothing in vain, and more is vain when less will serve; for Nature is pleased with simplicity, and affects not the pomp of superfluous causes." Now who shall say that Nature doing nothing in vain is a "true cause," or that Nature's "pleasure" can be known?

The Rule is important by its exclusion of unknown causes, and by its correction of the tendency to multiply causes. We often find philosophers dissatisfied with an explanation which is *sufficient*, and seeking additional causes among data that are not given but assumed for the purpose. They fail to recognize that when we have discovered the law of a series, the *form* of a function, we have reached the limit of research.

RULE VI.—*Each cause must always and everywhere have the same effect; and never more than this.*

REMARK.

This will be much disputed, owing to the wavering interpretation assigned to the idea of cause. We often hear that different effects arise from the same cause, and that every cause has many effects: in this way Indigestion is said to be the effect of overwork of the brain or the effect of eating raw apples. This is utterly unscientific. Owing to the current laxity of conception even Newton has expressed himself timidly on this point in his enunciation of the Rule: "Therefore to the same natural effects we must as far as possible assign the same causes."

The unalterable rigor of the canon is necessary to the integrity of the conception of every phenomenon every process, every law. All experience, all science, would be a mere sand-heap without it. If the same cause could have different effects, or even slightly varying amounts of the same effect, prevision would be impossible. What we call the different effects, are the differences resulting from new combinations of causes. When I come to treat in detail the Problem of Cause, it will be made clear that whether we speak of complex or of simple phenomena there must necessarily be at least two factors for every product; hence, if we sum up the factors in the term Cause, and name the product Effect, it is obvious that the Effect is always the *Procession of its Cause: the dynamical aspect of the statical conditions.*

Not to enlarge on this point here, let us only remark that the Rule reminds us that no verified fact can be contradicted by any other fact: each has its own intrinsic validity. When two observations seem contradictory, or when the same facts present two different aspects to two observers, this is an indication of some alteration in the conditions, either of the fact itself, or of the observer's position. Under the same conditions phenomena are unalterable.

We may also see that no process can destroy another, although it may be so compounded with it that the resultant of the two will present a different aspect from that of either of the components. Causes, like motions, may be superposed, each acting independently; or combined, each acting as a factor: but whether superposed or fused, each cause is *invariant;* it is only the phenomena that are *variable.* Hence

RULE VII. — *No proof can be valid beyond the range of its data; no conclusion is exact which shuts in what is not included in its premises.*

REMARK.

The violation of this is seen when conclusions reached in one department of phenomena are extended to departments wherein their premises are not the only premises. Although each science throws its light on every other, owing to the interdependence of phenomena and the community of Consciousness, yet no science can be controlled by the results of another, and this because phenomena are *in*dependent not less than *inter*dependent. Mathematics cannot receive laws from Chemistry, nor Physics from Biology; the phenomena studied in each are special. But underneath the special differences there are interdependencies, communities, whereby mathematical laws enter into chemical and biological explanations, physical laws into chemical, and chemical into biological. These laws are absolute at their points of intersection, but not beyond. That is to say, the mathematical law is absolute for the mathematical relations of the physical, chemical, or biological phenomenon, but not beyond; and so of the others. The validity of each vanishes with its limit. In the development of an ovum, for instance, it is demonstrable that physical and chemical laws are involved, and that these are absolute in their order; but more than these are involved, since by none of the laws hitherto detected in operation among inorganic phenomena is it possible to explain the biological laws of Nutrition, Evolution, Reproduction, and Decay. Should Molecular Dynamics one day be in a position to furnish such a deduction (which is probable), there would still remain the speciality of organic phenomena dependent on a speciality of concurrent causes, which would continue to separate biological from physical and chemical laws.

RULE VIII. — *Because the significance of a phenomenon lies wholly in its relation to other phenomena we must never isolate it from this relativity, and draw conclusions respecting it* per se.

REMARK.

It is the constant error of metaphysical speculation to attempt a real distinction corresponding with the analytical distinction of a thing from its relations. The thing is its relations, and although analytically we may separate them, attending now to this relation, now to that, we must never imagine the separation to be real.

RULE IX. — *We are not to conclude the properties of elements from the properties of the groups they form; nor* vice versa.

REMARK.

This, which is the direct consequence of Rule VIII., although obvious enough in many cases, often requires delicate tact in application. No one commits the mistake of supposing that either of the elements of water has when separate the properties of water; no one supposes that the properties of each element combined in water could be deduced from the observed properties of the combination; no one supposes that from the observed properties of oxygen and hydrogen, separately considered, the properties of water could be deduced. Yet analogous mistakes are often committed. Many philosophers assume that atoms, or the ultimate elements of Matter, must have the properties observed in masses; and still more assume that the properties of an object belong to it apart from the subject, not as elements of the combined object-subject, but as qualities of the thing *per se;* while still greater is the number of those who assign to one factor in a causation the character noted in a result due to several factors.

Every mathematician knows that there are numberless theorems true of integers which are not true of the fractions, the properties of the fractions often widely differing from the properties of the integers.

The mistake here pointed out often arises from not discriminating between component *parts* and constituent *elements.* What is true of the mass is generally true of any part of that mass, the difference being only quantitative. A molecule of water has the properties of a gallon of water. But even this is true only of those properties not directly dependent on quantity; for experiments on finely divided substances show that many a substance begins to lose its molar properties in becoming molecular, since some of the effects which depend on the individual molecules, and which in the mass were mutually balanced, then begin to manifest themselves, the balance being disturbed.

The distinction here indicated between Components and Constituents, or between Parts and Elements, will be seen hereafter to have its importance. All quantitative relations are componental; all qualitative relations elemental. The combinations of the first issue in Resultants, which may be analytically displayed; the combinations of the other issue in Emergents, which cannot be seen in the elements, nor deduced from them. A number is seen to be the sum of its units; a direction of movement is seen to be the line which would be occupied by the body if each of the incident forces had successively acted on it during an infinitesimal time; but a chemical or vital product is a combination of elements which cannot be seen in the elements. It emerges from them as a new phenomenon.

RULE X. — *The validity of conclusions rests on the preservation of homogeneity in the terms and the identity of their ratios.*

REMARK.

This extremely important Rule we shall often have to invoke. It will be brought prominently forward in the discussion of Necessary Truths. One of the commonest sources of error is that of unconsciously changing the terms of a proposition without at the same time making the corresponding change in the ratios. Valid generalization can only be effected by extending to *many* or to *all* what is positively true of *some,* it being therein assumed, or proved, that the *many,* or *all,* do not differ from the *some* in the characters ascribed. For example, when we generalize from masses to molecules, it is like passing from large numbers to small numbers, so long as the molecules are assumed, or proved, to possess all the characters known of masses; but if we observe — and we often do observe — that the masses tend to lose their homogeneity in becoming molecular (which is the passage to their heterogeneity in becoming resolved into their constituent elements), our conclusions respecting their properties tend to become more and more uncertain. We cannot deduce the relative movements *in* a system from our observation of the movements of that system, — the movements of animals from the movement of the earth, — the rotation of the earth from the movement of the solar system; or, *vice versa,* the orbital movements of the earth from the relative movements of its bodies. Each problem has its *equation of condition;* and it is only by generalizing this, that is to say, preserving the homogeneity of its terms and ratios, that any conclusion can be established beyond the particular case.

RULE XI. — *Science is built up from Abstractions, and these are built up from Concretes. No Abstraction must contain more than is warranted by its Concretes.*

REMARK.

When the Abstraction expresses more than is given in the Concretes, it must be understood as the geometer understands a transcendent; however useful in preserving the symmetry of expressions, it must never enter into the final equation. We may employ the abstraction Life to express all the concrete phenomena observed, and the unexplored remainder; but it is only the former that we must admit into our theoretical explanation: the unexplored remainder must not be treated as if it had been explored and mastered. We may employ a fourth co-ordinate to facilitate calculation, but must never allow this symbol to be mistaken for the sign of a concrete reality.

RULE XII. — *Carefully to discriminate between the abstract or analytical point of view and the concrete or synthetical point of view.*

REMARK.

Experience is the registration of feelings and the relations of their correlative objects. Science is the explanation of these feelings, the analysis of these objects into their components and constituents, which are then held to be the factors of the facts. These factors are of various kinds, real and ideal, concrete and abstract, appreciable by Sense, and appreciable by Intuition.

Considered subjectively, the real is what is either *felt or perceived;* the ideal is what is either *imaged* — that is to say, the feeling reproduced in the absence of its external object — or *conceived*, i. e. the feeling represented in a symbol. The real is what is actually given in Feeling. The ideal is what is virtually given, when Inference anticipates what would be Feeling, were the objective causes in direct relation with Sense. Thus the direct experience of the one is supplemented by the indirect experience of the other: vision is completed by prevision: real observation by ideal construction. No sooner has the construction been verified, all its inferences reduced to sensations, all its inductions to deductions, and its deductions to intuitions (by a process we shall hereafter consider), than ideal factors take the place of real factors, prevision of vision, and the truths of ideal relations are recognized as having the same validity as the truths of real relations, for the ideas are virtual feelings. But the process of verification is both complex and delicate, so that whenever an ideal relation is inconsistent with the corresponding real relation, and prevision contradicts vision, the error must lie on the side of the ideal construction.

The starting-point is always Feeling, and Feeling is the final goal and test. Knowledge begins with indefinite Feeling, which is gradually rendered more and more definite as the chaos is condensed into objects, effected through a rudimentary analysis determined by the fundamental Signatures (Qualities) of Feeling, namely, Tension, Intension, Extension, Duration, Likeness, Unlikeness.

Each object is by a subsequent analysis resolved into its components; these again are resolved into their constituents; and these in turn into their constituents, if the regressive analysis be practicable or serviceable. Thus water is a real object, a concrete fact of our experience. We learn its properties, and we also learn that it is a mass of molecules, each molecule having the properties of water, and that the weight or force of the mass is the sum of the molecules. Analysis of this mass will resolve each of the molecules into its constituent elements, oxygen and hydrogen gas: these have their properties, not the properties of water, and they have their movements, which are not the movements of the molecules. Analysis is still within the region of the sensible, for the water is only the molecule "writ large"; but now it takes a further regressive step, and decomposes each molecule of the gases into constituent atoms, or ultimate elements. These are purely ideal. They cannot be presented to Sense, but are presented to Intuition, and are seen by the mind, not as reals, but as logical postulates, symbols to assist calculation. Thus a curve is a real, but the infinitesimal straight lines into which it is ideally analyzed are symbols only, not reals.

Analysis is *descriptive* when it deals with components and *genetic* when it deals with constituents. The one is proximate, sensible, and generally certain; the other remote, extra-sensible, and liable to error: it is always an attempt to explain the known by the less known, sometimes by the unknown but hypothetical, consequently it must always have less validity than the synthesis it is invoked to explain. I mean that a fact must always be more certain than the factors by which we elucidate its origin.

Analysis always requires the verification of synthesis. Having taken an object to pieces, we cannot be sure that we have in the pieces all the components or constituents unless we can, really or ideally, build up again the object from those pieces. The failure to rebuild indicates the oversight of one or more of the constituents.

RULE XIII. — *Philosophy, being the harmony between the concrete and abstract, the synthetic and its explanatory analytic, demands that everywhere the abstract be subordinate to the concrete in respect to validity, though it is superior in point of dignity.*

REMARK.

This is insisting on the subordination of means to ends. The purpose of knowledge being the guidance of primitive Impulses for the satisfaction of Desires, obviously Speculation must be subordinated to the Practice which it is intended to serve; and all conceptions of Reason, however lofty, must have perception and action for their final aim: they are intermediates between the feeling which is an impulse and the feeling which is the result of that impulse in action.

But although the end is more important than the means, and although Feeling is final, and Thought has only validity in accordance with Feeling, in point of dignity (that is, of *governing* value) Thought is supreme, and abstract conceptions are of far higher moment than concrete perceptions. The animal life is higher in dignity than the vegetal; the social life is higher than the individual. Yet the animal functions depend on the vegetal, the social on the animal. Theories which embody multitudes of relations are more dignified than facts which embody particular relations; but the theories are subordinate to the facts. The Nation is of more importance than any one Family, and the Family than one of its members; nevertheless the dependence of the Family on its members, and of the Nation on its Families, is absolute.

Hence the fallacy must be guarded against which assumes that general laws, or axioms, because of their superior dignity, have a deeper validity than particular truths. Connected with this is the fallacy that laws *rule* phenomena, *determine* them; whereas they only *express* the phenomena in a formula.

One consequence of this fallacy, which has many, is the error of deducing from averages conclusions which are not of average but of particular relations, — e. g. when the average amount of food consumed by a hundred men is taken as the guide for the rations of the individuals, each man being taken as if he were a unit of the average; whereas, in fact, each man is markedly different from every other, and the average eliminates the differences.

On the other hand, the Law, or abstract formula of the concretes, is valid when once verified; any contradiction to such a law must be assigned either to a misinterpretation of its terms, or to a misapplication of it to the case in point. An example of misinterpretation is the common opposition to Mr. Buckle's statement that the number of marriages in a community is regulated by the price of corn, and not at all by the inclinations of the sexes. He has expressed this law so unguardedly that readers in general have rejected it with indignation. But if we reflect that the inclinations of the sexes are constant factors which would determine the marriage of all men and women, were their inclinations left unopposed, and if we recognize among the grounds of opposition none at once so general and so imperative as the need of sufficient food, we see that food must be the variable factor determining the variation in the number of the unmarried, which variation it is that the statistical law formulates. Mr. Buckle was injudicious and wrong in saying that the inclinations have nothing to do with marriage; what they have nothing to do with is the variable number of the unmarried, a number expressive of the perturbations to which sexual unions are subjected.

RULE XIV. — "*In experimental philosophy we are to look upon propositions collected by general induction from phenomena as accurately or very nearly true, notwithstanding any contrary hypotheses that may be imagined, till such time as other phenomena occur by which they may be made more accurate or liable to exceptions.*"

REMARK.

This is Newton's Fourth Rule, and he remarks that we must follow it in order that the argument of induction may not be invaded by hypothesis; in other words, without too confidently relying on the universality of an induction, we must always prefer it to any reasoning not founded on an inductive basis.

RULE XV. — "*Always to prefer the simplest hypothesis compatible with all the observed facts.*"

REMARK.

This is Comte's first law of Primary Philosophy; and however self-evident it may appear, is very frequently disregarded, because the scientific use of Hypothesis is so little understood.

That many more rules might be added is indisputable; but these fifteen are all that I deem necessary for my present purpose. They will be implied throughout the following investigations, and from time to time specially invoked.

PSYCHOLOGICAL PRINCIPLES.

ALSO bestimmt die Gestalt die Lebensweise des Thieres ;
Und die Weise zu leben sie wirkt auf alle Gestalten
Mächtig zurück. So zeiget sich fest die geordnete Bildung
Welche zum Wechsel sich neigt durch äusserlich wirkende Wesen.

GOETHE, *Die Metamorphose der Thiere.*

Entre l'Homme et le Monde il faut l'Humanité.

AUGUSTE COMTE.

NOTE.

Although the arguments set forth in the following pages ought to carry with them their own evidence, it may not be without advantage to them if I here set down the Principles adopted from previous writers or arrived at in my own researches, and give a general sketch of what it is proposed to establish in several of the Problems to be successively treated. A systematic treatise on Psychology seems to me premature until there is something like general agreement on many questions of fundamental importance, these being partly metaphysical and partly biological. Instead, therefore, of a treatise, I have here sketched the programme of Psychology; and in the ensuing pages have undertaken the examination at some length of those questions which seemed most pressing.

What is here set down must be accepted as a programme only. I do not pause to prove the positions; in many cases I do not even illustrate them. The reader is not called upon to assent to them; he is only asked to consider that they are the positions on which I have founded my arguments. They may, perhaps, also be accepted as suggestions to further inquiry.

PSYCHOLOGICAL PRINCIPLES.

1. MAN is not simply an Animal Organism, he is also a unit in a Social Organism. He leads an individual life, which is also part of a collective life. Hence two classes of Motors: the personal and the sympathetic,— the egoistic and the altruistic. From these chiefly issue the Animal sentient life, and the Human intellectual and moral life.

Human Psychology, therefore, the science of psychical phenomena, has to seek its data in Biology and in Sociology. The great mistake hitherto has been either that of metaphysicians, seeking the data solely in introspective analysis of Consciousness; or that of biologists, seeking the data in the combination of such analysis with interpretation of nervous phenomena.

2. The biologist who is true to scientific Method accepts Vitality as an ultimate fact, of which he only seeks the factors, i. e. its conditions, and its laws of manifestation. He leaves to metaphysicians the ulterior task of settling, if they can, what Life is, apart from these, or in the general system of things. The mathematician does not concern himself with what Quantity, Space, and Time are; nor the physicist with what Force is; nor the biologist with what Life is.

The psychologist likewise must accept Consciousness, or, to speak more precisely, Sensibility, as an ultimate fact, of which he only studies the factors,— its conditions and laws.

The analogy of Life and Mind is the closest of all analogies, if indeed the latter is anything more than a special form of the other. Hence what is known of Life will be the best guide to what is knowable of Mind. Both are processes, or, under another aspect, functional products. Neither is a substance; neither is a force. To speak of Vitality as a substance, would shock all our ideas; but many speak of it as a force. They might with equal propriety hold Mortality to be a force. What, then, is meant by Vitality, or vital forces? If the abstraction be resolved into its concretes, it will be seen that a certain process, or group of processes, is condensed into a simple expression, and the final result of this process is transposed from a resultant into an initial condition, the name given to the whole group of phenomena becomes the personification of the phenomena, and the *product* is supposed to have been the *producer.* In lieu of regarding vital actions as the dynamical results of their statical conditions, the actions are personified, and the personification comes to be regarded as indicating something independent of and antecedent to the concrete facts it expresses. The vital force manifested by an Organism may be likened to the mechanical force manifested by a Machine. No one really tries to reach and modify the mechanical force (which is a pure abstraction); he only tries to reach and modify the mechanical conditions (which are reals), certain that if he lessen the friction of the parts he will increase the mechanical product. In like manner, no philosophic biologist now tries to reach and modify a vital force, but only to reach and modify those biostatical conditions which, when considering them as causes, and condensing them all into a single expression, he calls Vitality or the Vital Forces. When we speak of electrical force, cohesive force, attractive force, and the like, we are using abstractions which condense a vast amount of concrete observation; but it is not on these abstractions that our experiments lay hold, it is on the concrete phenomena themselves.

The same is true of Sensibility. Vitality and Sensibility, Life and Consciousness, are abstractions having real concretes. They are compendious expressions of functional processes conceived in their totality, and not at any single stage. A function is the activity of an organ. And since Function is a conception which is in its very nature distinguished from the material conditions, obviously both Life and Mind are terms which designate phenomena that are immaterial, the two conceptions of Matter and Motion, although correlative, being mutually exclusive. In so regarding them, however, we are not to conclude that this exclusion justifies the spiritual hypothesis of Life and Mind. This hypothesis is simply a reintroduction of an unknown kind of Matter to serve as the Substance, in lieu of the known Matter which is presented by the Organism. Who does not see the contradiction of requiring a substance for that which by its definition is not substantial at all, but pure dynamism?

3. We cannot be sufficiently on our guard in the use of abstractions, and especially against our tendency to confound ideal separations with real separations. It is this tendency which keeps up the tradition of Mind existing apart from Life, and following other laws. We separate, for convenience, mental phenomena from other vital phenomena, and then again separate mental phenomena from neural phenomena; this done, we overlook the real identity, and do not see that every mental phenomenon has its corresponding neural phenomenon (the two being as the convex and concave surfaces of the same

sphere, distinguishable yet identical), and that *every neural phenomenon involves the whole Organism;* by which alone the influence of the body on the mind, and of the mind on the body, can be explained.

Among the broad distinctions of phenomena those of Physical, Chemical, and Vital must be maintained, expressing as they do the characteristic motions of *propulsion,* motions of *combination,* and motions of *evolution.* A chemical combination, even if finally reducible to physical laws, is markedly distinguished by presenting new structural relations. A still broader demarcation is given in the vital phenomenon of Evolution (characterized by Nutrition, Development, and Decay, through serial changes), distinguishable from the chemical combinations out of which it emerges. Not only is it impossible to deduce the phenomenon of Evolution from the phenomena of chemical combination, not only is it impossible to explain Nutrition by Chemistry, unless we replace the Laboratory by the Organism, and thus introduce the special evolutive conditions, namely, the presence of organic substance formed into histological elements (cells, fibres, tubes); but it is *à priori* evident that a phenomenon differing so widely from all chemical phenomena must be due to widely different conditions. We may never know all these conditions; but that analysis will ever resolve them into simple chemical conditions irrespective of the speciality of their theatre, may confidently be denied. It is an old remark that Life escapes under the scalpel, leaving only a dead "subject" for dissection. Life equally vanishes under chemical analysis.

A similar mistake perverts the efforts of most psychologists. They do not keep in view the speciality of the psychological theatre, nor allow for the continual presence of those *sentient conditions* implied in the general term Soul. The spiritualists are prone to split up the sentient organism into independent Faculties, dividing it into Sense, Understanding, Reason, Volition, etc. The materialists split it up into independent Organs. Thus both schools — the school which affirms the unity of the Soul in its spiritual substance, and the school which affirms the dependence of the Soul on its cerebral substance — practically deny their principle when they come to treat mental phenomena in detail.

And in both cases the source of the error is the exclusive employment of Analysis without the due regard to its needful correction by Synthesis. Theoretically taking the Organism to pieces to understand its separate parts, we fall into the error of supposing that the Organism is a mere assemblage of organs, like a machine which is put together by juxtaposition of different parts. But this is radically to misunderstand its essential nature and the universal solidarity of its parts. The Organism is not made, not put together, but *evolved;* its parts are not juxtaposed, but differentiated; its organs are groups of minor organisms, all sharing in a common life, i. e. all sharing in a common substance constructed through a common process of simultaneous and continuous molecular composition and decomposition; precisely as the great Social Organism is a group of societies, each of which is a group of families, all sharing in a common life, — every family having at once its individual independence and its social dependence through connection with every other. In a machine the parts are all different, and have mechanical significance only in relation to the whole. In an Organism the parts are all identical in fundamental characters, and diverse only in their superadded differentiations: each has its independence, although all cooperate. The synthetical point of view, which should never drop out of sight, however the necessities of investigation may throw us upon analysis, is well expressed by

Aristotle somewhere to the effect that all collective life depends on the separation of offices and the concurrence of efforts. In a vital organism every force is the resultant of *all* the forces; it is a disturbance of equilibrium, and equilibrium is the equivalence of convergent forces. When we speak of Intelligence as a force which determines actions, we ought always to bear in mind that the efficacity of Intelligence depends on the organs which co-operate and are determined: it is not pure Thought which moves a muscle, neither is it the abstraction Contractility, but the muscle, which moves a limb.

To those who, having relinquished the spiritualist hypothesis, have adopted the view that Mind is only one of the forms of Life, and that Life is not an entity but an abstraction expressing the generalities of organic phenomena, it is obvious that Psychology must endeavor to ascertain the conditions of these phenomena, both general and special. These may be classed (by a serviceable extension of the term statics) under the heads of Biostatics and Psychostatics.

BIOSTATICS.

4. Owing to the necessary abstraction which characterizes all analytical investigation, we are too prone to neglect that *restitution* of the omitted elements which is needful when we would complete the analysis by a real explanation. It is thus that we separate each organ or function from its complications with all the others, and forget that it is really only a part of a living whole, and explicable only through the whole Organism. It is thus that we consider only one factor in studying a product, and forget that every product necessarily has at least two factors each equally indispensable. When, therefore, we define an Organism it should always be with clear vision of its relation to a Medium; and when we define a func-

tion as the activity of an organ, we should always distinctly recognize the fact that this activity does not take place *in vacuo*, but involves the co-operation both of that which is acted on and of that which acts. The function of an organ is as rigorously determined by the stimulus which excites it as by the structure which is excited; unless this unification of the two factors takes place there is no product at all, — the organ is not active because not adequately stimulated.

I shall repeatedly have occasion to invoke this principle, and here simply invoke it in reference to the nutrition of the Organism, the structure of which is built up from materials originally drawn from the external Medium, but proximately drawn from its internal Medium, or plasma. Between the *reception* of this external material and the *assimilation* of it by the tissues (of plant or animal), there is always an intermediate stage passed through, the inorganic, unvitalized material becoming there transformed into organizable, vitalized material. What this special change is we do not know; we only know that until it has taken place the inorganic material is not assimilable; it must enter as a constituent of the *Bioplasm* to form part of what Claude Bernard calls the Physiological Medium, before it can become a constituent of the tissues. The supposition that plants are nourished *directly* by inorganic substances drawn from the soil and atmosphere, is now proved to be erroneous: the Nutrition of plants takes place through processes similar to those in animals. The inorganic has in both to pass through the organizable stage, and form proximate principles, before it can become organized into elements of tissue.

5. Among the most important laws of Biostatics may be named the following: —

I. *The Law of Correlated Development.* — There is a marked tendency in organic substance to vary under varying excitations, which results in the individualization of the parts, so that growth is accompanied by a greater or less differentiation of structure. Were this tendency uncontrolled, there would be no organic unity: the organism would then be simply an assemblage of organs. But owing to the solidarity which underlies all differentiation, the parts are not only individualized into tissues and organs, but are all connected. Thus each new modification of structure is secured, each organ is independent yet subordinated to the whole; and instead of being an obstacle, this independence becomes, through the consensus and co-operation of each, a source of enhanced power in the organism. In organic, as in social life, the indispensable condition of perfect action is the co-operation of independent agents, — the Freedom which is subordinated to Law, and the Law which secures Freedom.

II. *The Law of Adaptation.* — Although an organ can only respond to a stimulus according to its own modes, which depend on its structure, and which vary with the variations of structure, yet the very reaction itself tends to establish a modification which will alter subsequent reactions. It is in this sense, and this alone, that we must understand the statement that organs are created by functions. What is exact in the statement is that by the exercise of an organ its structure becomes differentiated, and each modification renders it fitted for more energetic reaction and for new modes of reaction.* But we must

* How important this principle is in the evolution of our moral no less than our intellectual aptitudes may be seen in the growth of the sympathetic tendencies. "Telle est la douceur naturelle des bons sentiments que, de quelques excitations que provienne leur éveil, ils tendent à se développer par leur propre charme, quand ils ont une fois surgi, même d'après un motif personnel, trop souvent indispensable à leur torpeur primitive." — COMTE, *Politique Positive*, II. 119. Unhappily our bad sentiments follow the same law, and become intensified by exercise.

never lose sight of the absolute principle that Function is the action of Organ, and can never be dynamically other than what its statical conditions permit.

III. *The Law of Heredity.* — The modifications of structure acquired through Adaptation tend to become transmitted to offspring, and would always in effect be transmitted were it not for perturbations of the result owing to the action of external forces during the embryonic development, and to the influence of the other parent.

PSYCHOSTATICS.

6. Let us now pass from Life to Mind. The vital organism we have seen to be evolved from the Bioplasm, and we may now see how the psychical organism is evolved from what may be analogically called the Psychoplasm. The Bioplasm is characterized by a continuous and simultaneous movement of molecular composition and decomposition; and out of these arises the whole mechanism, which is also sustained and differentiated by them. If, instead of considering the whole vital organism, we consider solely its sensitive aspects, and confine ourselves to the Nervous System, we may represent the molecular movements of the Bioplasm by the neural tremors of the Psychoplasm: these tremors are what I term *neural units:* the raw material of Consciousness; the several *neural groups* formed by these units represent the organized elements of tissues, the tissues, and the combination of tissues into organs, and of organs into apparatus. The movements of the Bioplasm constitute Vitality; the movements of the Psychoplasm constitute Sensibility. The forces of the cosmical medium which are transformed in the physiological medium build up the organic struct-

Herein lies the supreme importance of an Education which is directed towards the development of aptitudes by their effective exercise, rather than by the inculcation of rules.

ture, which in the various stages of its evolution reacts according to its statical conditions, themselves the results of preceding reactions. It is the same with what may be called the mental organism. Here also every phenomenon is the product of two factors, external and internal, impersonal and personal, objective and subjective. Viewing the internal factor solely in the light of Feeling, we may say that the *sentient material* out of which all the forms of Consciousness are evolved is the Psychoplasm incessantly fluctuating, incessantly renewed. Viewing this on the physiological side, it is the succession of neural tremors, variously combining into neural groups.

7. An organism lives only in relation to its medium. What Growth is, in the physical sense, that is Experience in the psychical sense, namely, *organic registration of assimilated material.* The direct relation of the organism is to the internal medium, the indirect relation is to the cosmical medium. The Bioplasm is constituted out of the fluids which bathe the tissues, and from which each tissue derives its nourishment, molecule by molecule. It is necessarily liquid because in a tissue liquidity is requisite for chemical action. Hence Claude Bernard suggestively notes that the cellular elements of the tissues are veritable aquatic organisms. The internal medium is incessantly fluctuating, — a point to which especial attention must be given. Materials are incessantly absorbed from without, and are there elaborated, made fit for assimilation. Materials are also incessantly thrown into it as products of waste of tissue, and have to be excreted. Thus does the Bioplasm contain the materials of Yesterday, the materials of To-day, and the materials of To-morrow. Nutrition may, to speak mathematically, be designated a function of three variables, namely, tissue, internal medium, and cosmic medium. A little more heat or a little less of carbonic acid, or of oxygen, press-

ure, etc., in the external, will accelerate or retard the evolutions of Nutrition by its effects on the internal medium. But no variation in the cosmic medium which does not affect the internal medium will have any modifying influence on the organism. This also it is important to bear in mind. The direct relation is between the organism and the internal medium : these two factors therefore comprise the Biostatical conditions ; and the influence of the external medium is through these. Food is not *food*, nor is poison *poison*, until it has passed into the Bioplasm.

8. The reader sees at once how this applies to the sentient organism. We have already spoken, metaphorically, of the Psychoplasm, or sentient material forming the psychological medium from which the Soul derives its structure and its powers. It is the mass of potential Feeling derived from all the sensitive affections of the organism, not only of the individual, but, through Heredity, of the ancestral organisms. All sensations, perceptions, emotions, volitions, are partly connate, partly acquired : partly the evolved products of the accumulated experiences of ancestors, and partly of the accumulated experiences of the individual, when each of these have left *residua* in the modifications of the structure.

Thus Vitality and Sensibility may be said to rest on seriated Change. If the changes were simply movements, propulsive or combined, physical or chemical, they would not present the phenomena of Life or of Consciousness. The changes must be serial, and what we term organized, to present the phenomena of Evolution. That Life is Change, and that Consciousness is Change, has always been affirmed. We have only to add that the changes are serial, and convergent through a consensus determined by essential community of structure, and we have characterized the speciality of organic change, demarcated Life and Mind from all inorganic change.

9. Corresponding with the Biostatical laws previously formulated there are three Psychostatical laws.

I. *The Law of Interest.* — It has long been observed that we only *see* what interests us, only know what is sufficiently like former experiences to become, so to speak, incorporated with them, — assimilated by them. The satisfaction of desire is that which both impels and quiets mental movement. Were it not for this controlling effect of the established pathways, every excitation would be indefinitely irradiated throughout the whole organism; but a pathway once established is the ready issue for any new excitation. The evolution of Mind is the establishment of definite paths: this is the mental organization, fitting it for the reception of definite impressions, and their co-ordination with past feelings.

II. *The Law of Signature.* — Every feeling being a group of neural units, and varying with the varying units, or varying groups of such groups, has its particular signature, or mark in Consciousness, in consequence of which it acquires its objective Localization, i. e., its place in the organism or in the cosmos.

III. *The Law of Experience.* — This is only the mental side of the laws of Heredity and Adaptation. *Experience is the registration of Feeling.* Through their registered modifications, feelings once produced are capable of reproduction; and must always be reproduced, more or less completely, whenever the new excitation is discharged along the old channels.

The laws just formulated are special forms of the primary law, which in Biology is expressed in the formula: *Every vital phenomenon is the product of two factors, the Organism and its Medium;* and in Psychology is expressed in the equivalent formula: *Every psychical phenomenon is the product of two factors, the Subject and the Object.* The importance of keeping these steadily before us in all detailed investigation, and the frequent mistakes which arise from overlooking them, will appear in the course of this work. Note, in passing, that the latter formula replaces the old Dualism, in which Subject and Object were two *independent* and unallied existences, by a Monism, in which only one existence, under different forms, is conceived. The old conception was of Life in *conflict* with the External; the new conception recognizes their *identity;* and founds this recognition on the demonstrable fact that so far from the external forces tending to destroy Life (according to Bichat's view), they are the very materials out of which Life emerges, and by which it is sustained and developed.

10. There are of course several other derivative laws, but these three are the principal, and are all that need be noted here. A glance at them suffices to discredit the old idea that the Senses directly apprehend — or *mirror* — external things. It is equally mistaken to suppose that sensitive impressions are the *immediate* motors. Each excitation has to be *assimilated,* — taken up into the psychological medium and transformed into a sensation or perception, — a process that will depend upon the psychostatical conditions at the time being. The different ways in which the same external stimulus affects different organisms, or the same organism at different times, are thus explicable. Think of the diversities of feeling produced by the image of a sheep on the retina of a man and a wolf, or of an artist and a grazier. Think of the dissimilar effects produced by the same musical intervals on the organism of an Asiatic and on that of a European. Or, take an example from Insanity: A visceral disturbance, especially in the digestive or the generative organs, will cause a perversion of Sensibility from which will arise abnormal sensation, hallucination,

moods, melancholy, depression, etc. These prompt the intellect to explanation. External causes are imagined; and the wildest hypotheses of persecution, divine or diabolic communication, are invented. As the disturbance spreads and the organism becomes more and more abnormal, the ideas become more and more incoherent, till Dementia supervenes.

This influence of the psychostatical conditions in determining the character of every psychical phenomenon suggests an important distinction which must be established between Animal Consciousness and Human Consciousness, one far greater than any other distinction to be established between Animals and Man. It is formulated by Auguste Comte in that phrase which is placed as an epigraph to this chapter, although the phrase was not by him understood precisely in the sense here assigned. We have seen how between the Cosmos and the Consciousness there is interposed a psychological medium, briefly designated by the term Experience. This applies both to animals and to man. But in man we must recognize another medium, one from which his moral and intellectual life is mainly drawn, one which separates him from all animals by the broadest line: this is the Social Medium, — the collective accumulations of centuries, condensed in knowledge, beliefs, prejudices, institutions, and tendencies; and forming another kind of Psychoplasm to which the animal is a stranger. The animal feels the Cosmos, and adapts himself to it. Man feels the Cosmos, but he also *thinks* it; again he feels the Social world, and thinks it. His feelings and his thoughts of both are powerfully modified by *residua*. Hence the very Cosmos is to him greatly different from what it is to the animal; for just as what is organized in the individual becomes transmitted to offspring, and determines the mode in which the offspring will react on stimulus, so what is registered in the Social Organism determines the mode in which succeeding generations will feel and think. By Tools and Instruments, by Creeds and Institutions, by Literature, Art, and Science, the Social Organism acquires and develops its powers; and how even simple perceptions are modified by social influences will strikingly appear in a subsequent part of this work, wherein it will be shown that all perceptions are the results of slow evolution, as the organic forms are; and not only will it be shown that many thousands of years passed before even man was able to *perceive* the color blue for instance (though of course he felt a difference between a blue object and a brown one), it will be shown that no animal can possibly perceive blue as we perceive it; and the reason in both cases is not to be sought in physiological processes of Vision, but in psychological processes of Thought. The possibility of this perception is due to Language; and Language exists only as a social function.

THE METHOD OF PSYCHOLOGY.

11. Here we may briefly indicate the Method to be pursued. The mental life of man has two sources: 1°, the animal organism, and 2°, the social organism. Man apart from Society is simply an animal organism; restore him to his real position as a social unit, and the problem changes. It is in the development of Civilization that we trace the real development of Humanity. The soul of man has thus a double root, a double history. It passes quite out of the range of animal life; and no explanation of mental phenomena can be valid which does not allow for this extension of range. Nevertheless I believe this necessity of extending the survey is now for the first time placed on its true footing; nor was it, indeed, even recognized, until Comte, in his second great work, insti-

tuted his *théorie de l'âme* by the combination of the biological and the sociological points of view.*

12. For a very long period philosophers deemed it enough to study Mind with little reference to its dependence on the Organism; the introspection of Consciousness was supposed to be sufficient. Nay, even when Physiology began to furnish indications of the connection between vital and psychical phenomena, and to exhibit the dependence of mental states on neural states, the psychologists pointed to the fact that Consciousness told us nothing of such dependence; and hence they concluded that Psychology, occupied solely with Consciousness and its changes, need not concern itself with Physiology and its laws. Rightly interpreted, this very fact that Consciousness tells us nothing of its physiological conditions would have been recognized as fatal to the pretensions of the introspective Method. Indeed, Psychology without illumination from Biology is something like the Astronomy of the Chaldeans without the aid

* In the present brief indication of my scheme I cannot pause to assign to each philosopher the conceptions adopted from him, nor will the well-read student need such references; but, as Comte's *Politique Positive* will be known to few of my readers, justice demands a summary statement of the fundamental agreement and difference between his conception and my own. They agree in regarding Science as a social product stimulated by social needs, and constructed by the co-operation of successive generations, so that civilization and Humanity are developed *pari passu*. They agree in subordinating individual introspection to the study of the collective evolution. "Quand j'eus fondé la sociologie," says Comte, "je compris enfin que le génie de Gall n'avait pu construire une véritable physiologie du cerveau faute de connaître les lois de l'évolution collective qui seule en doit fournir à la fois le principe et le but." (I. 729. Compare III. 45, 46.) But they differ primarily in this: he holds that Humanity develops no attribute, intellectual or moral, which is not also to be found in Animality (I. 624), whereas I hold that the attributes of Intellect and Conscience are special products of the Social Organism, and that although animals possess in common with man the Logic of Feeling, they are wholly deficient in the Logic of Signs, which is a social, not an animal function.

of Mathematics; watching the stars however patiently would no more disclose the laws of their movement than watching the changes in Consciousness would disclose their laws. Not only were centuries of such observation inadequate, but we now know that some of the elementary facts escaped notice, and must forever have escaped it unless otherwise aided.

This need not be insisted on, however, since there is now an almost universal agreement respecting the necessity of studying the organism; and many psychological treatises are avowedly based on the Physiology of the Nervous System, while all largely invoke physiological aid. We may observe, indeed, in most of these a disposition to translate psychological observations into physiological language, and to accept this as biological illumination; which not unjustifiably excites the scorn of the pure psychologist. One example of this translation may be given here: some anatomists having conceived the infelicitous idea of distinguishing nerve-cells into sensory, motor, and sympathetic, this nomenclature, so misleading even when it is not profoundly unphysiological, is adopted by several writers, who first establish the illusory distinctions of sensational cells, ideational cells, and emotional cells, and then proceed to explain the mental mechanism by these imaginary cells.

The early chemists paid no attention to the part played by the air in Combustion; nay, it was long before the fact of its materiality was vividly realized, and a century after Torricelli it was first recognized as an agent in Combustion. No wonder, therefore, if for a long while Biology paid insufficient attention to the Medium as a necessary co-operant, and directed its study mainly to the Organism. This mistake has been rectified, and now the true relation is always recognized. There must be a parallel rectification in Psychology; the co-operation of

Object and Subject must never for a moment be lost sight of.

Yet even this will only furnish one-half of the necessary data. Let us suppose the student equipped with all the aid which the science of the day will supply, not only respecting the normal actions of the nervous system, but also respecting its abnormal actions, especially in Insanity, he will still need to invoke another aid, for he will only have what may be called biological data, and will still need the equally important sociological data. Having studied the Organism in relation to its Medium, he has only studied the Animal side of the problem; there still remains the Human side, and he has to study the Organism in relation to the Social Medium, in which man lives no less than in the Cosmical Medium. If there is a valid objection against the functions of the brain being investigated in the cabinets of metaphysicians, there is an equally valid objection against intellectual and moral processes being sought in the laboratories of physiologists. To understand the Human Mind we must study it under its normal conditions, and these are social conditions.

And it may be observed that the psychologist, moralist, and politician often disregard a fundamental truth which is never disregarded by the physicist, — the truth that it is vain to expect a result in the absence of its necessary conditions. The politician who will cordially admit the axiom that "Constitutions are not made but grow," will nevertheless daily be found endeavoring to remedy social evils by legislative enactments, which leave the conditions unchanged. The moralist will be found passionately arguing that the conduct of men, which is simply the expression of their impulses and habits, can be at once altered by giving them new ideas of right conduct. The psychologist, accustomed to consider the Mind as something apart from the Organism, individual and collective, is peculiarly liable to this error of overlooking the fact that all mental manifestations are simply the resultants of the conditions external and internal.

THE BIOLOGICAL DATA.

13. In its relations to the Cosmos, and under what may be called the purely biological aspect, the Organism presents two points of study: the biostatical and the biodynamical, — i. e. the consideration of the structure *ready to act*, and the consideration of the structure *acting*.

14. The statical aspect of the Organism is that of the balance of its nutritive forces developed in the molecular movements of composition and decomposition. The balance itself is incessantly fluctuating; for the Organism, although a mechanism, is specially distinguished from every other kind of mechanism by the instability of its materials. A watch wound up to-day is the same as it was yesterday, and will be to-morrow. No Organism is so, for it is living, growing, changing. The structure and actions of the watch are unaffected by the surrounding changes, unless these changes have a direct relation to it. It is unaffected by a snow-storm, a dog in the room, a political crisis; all of which affect the Organism, or may affect it. Moreover, the Organism is affected by its own internal changes, by the food it has eaten, the feelings it has felt, the dreams that have varied its sleep, etc.

15. The force stored up in the tissues through nutritive changes is liberated by stimuli internal and external. This is the biodynamical aspect, including the physiological *properties* of the tissues. From various combinations of the tissues result organs; from various combinations of the properties result functions. (It is of supreme importance to bear in mind the distinction between the

property of a tissue, and the function of an organ, or group of organs.)

16. The Organism exhibits three fundamental modes: Assimilation, Sensibility, and Motility. From the first of these issue the general laws of Nutrition, — whence Growth, Development, and Reproduction. From the second issue the general laws of Feeling, using that term in its widest sense, including Sensation, Perception, Emotion, Volition, and Intelligence, and also Instinct (which is Impulse and organized Intelligence.)* From the third issue the general laws of Action, including Impulse, Automatic Movement, Reflex Movement, and Voluntary Movement.

17. This separation must be understood as purely analytical. In reality the three modes are inseparable. Assimilation *may* perhaps take place without the intervention of Sensibility, — at least in Plant organisms, — but it is certain that the processes of Growth, Development, and Reproduction are in the Animal very much determined by the reactions of Sensibility; while it is obvious that they require Movement, molecular and molar.

Sensibility, in turn, requires the incessant co-operation of Assimilation, from which is drawn the *material* of the sensitive structure and the *force* expended in its function. Motility, again, requires both the stimulus and the guidance of Sensibility. The animal must feed to live; it must move its organs to get and eat the food; it must feel the stimulus of hunger to impel its movements, and

* Dr. Johnson, on being asked whether there was not Imagination in a certain poem, answered, "No, sir, there is what was Imagination once." In like manner we may say that in Instinct there is not Intelligence, but what was once Intelligence; the specially intelligent character has disappeared in the fixed tendency. The action which formerly was tentative, discriminative, has now become automatic and irresistible. But the impulse is always *guided* by feeling. See farther on, § 30.

the satisfaction of desire to determine its selection of food; in this Discrimination lies the germ of Intelligence.

18. All sensitive affections have the quality of Pleasure, or its correlative Pain. These qualities tend to fade into relative indistinctness with the decrease in energy consequent on ease of neural discharge, consequent on frequency of *repetition* at brief intervals.

19. All sensitive reactions have their *Signatures*. In proportion as their intensity and massiveness decrease they become more and more *Signs*, and thus become fitted to enter into intellectual operations which are purely symbolical. The least *sensible* of the Senses, if the expression may be allowed, is Sight, and therefore it is the most intellectual. It is the most *impersonal*, — that which draws with it the least amount of feeling. In looking at an object, it is the object out of us which most calls upon the attention. Only when we touch, taste, or smell the moving object, does it seem to enter into personal feeling. On the other hand, a more subjective feeling, say of sound or taste, becomes objective so soon as it is connected with a sight or a touch.

20. Sensations are usually, but improperly, restricted to the reactions of what are called the Five Senses, and which are commonly spoken of as *the* Senses. This is doubly wrong. A sensation is not a simple excitation of the sensory organ, but a compound of that with the consequent excitation of a Perceptive Centre. The excitation of the sense organ is only one element in a complex process. Divide the optic nerve before its entrance into the optic ganglion, and no excitation of the retina will produce a luminous sensation; cut off an animal's leg and stimulate the sciatic nerve, the leg will move, but no sensation will have been produced. Nor is this all. Unless the excitation is *assimilated* by the psychological me-

dium it does not become *sentient;* and unless it becomes sentient it cannot become a sensation.

Quitting the analytical point of view, we at once recognize the fact that every perception, instead of being the reaction of a single organ, is the resultant of the combined reactions of the whole Organism; the only question in each case being the relative proportions of the parts involved, and how far the irradiation has been restricted to certain channels. The several Senses are no more vicarious than the several Secretions; and when we see an apple we do not in the visual sensation include the sensations of taste, fragrance, resistance, etc., which are all included in the perception of an apple, because all more or less excited by the irradiation of the optical stimulus. It is the non-recognition of this which originates many of the difficulties touching the theory of Vision. The organic seat of Vision is too often assumed to be the retina; whereas that is only the seat of the visual excitation, which in the Perceptive Centre is blended with the residua of other excitations.

21. The same is true of all sensations, the Systemic no less than those of the special Senses. And this leads me to the second error just referred to, the restriction of Sensation to the reactions of the Five Senses. Physiology teaches us that there is another and indeed far more important class of sensations, arising from what I have proposed to call the Systemic Senses, because distributed through the system at large, instead of being localized in eye, ear, tongue, etc. Although not so easily and definitely assigned to special organs, they may be classified as the Nutritive, Respiratory, Generative, and Muscular Senses. The feelings accompanying secretion, excretion, hunger, thirst, etc., belong to the first. The feelings of suffocation, oppression, lightness, etc., belong to the second. The sexual and maternal feeelings belong to the

third; while those of the fourth enter as elements into all the others.

The Systemic Sensations not only blend with those of the Five Senses to produce Desires, Emotions, Instincts, etc., they make up the greater part of that continuous stream of Sentience, on which each external stimulus raises a ripple.

22. One aim of Psychology is to reduce sentient facts to physiological facts. Consciousness precedes Science. We learn slowly to assign certain feelings to the Five Senses because the stimuli of these Senses are objectively appreciable, — we can see the object we have touched, and taste the object we have seen. Not so with the Systemic feelings. Their stimuli, because internal, cannot be alternately submitted to various Senses. Still further removed from such objective appreciation are the central processes of Judgment, Memory, Imagination, etc.; and hence the disposition to regard these feelings as due to another source: it is even paradoxical to speak of such processes belonging to Feeling, and to affirm that the Laws of Thought are identical with the Laws of Sensation, differing not as operations, but only in the materials operated on. The paradox disappears when we learn to consider psychical phenomena in the true synthetic way (§ 3).

23. The sensations of the Five Senses are more impersonal than those of the Systemic Senses; hence their greater importance in the construction of objective knowledge. They are pre-eminently intellectual, not only on this ground, but also because of their inferior massiveness and diffusiveness, and of their greater capability of definite *localization;* hence they are fitted to become *signs.* The systemic sensations have, however, great importance, and their immense superiority as *motors* has been singularly overlooked. They make up by far

the larger portion of our sentient material, since from them mainly issue the Emotions, Sentiments, etc., combined indeed with the objective sensations, but subordinating these as means to their ends, inasmuch as we only see what interests us.

Note here, in passing, the error which arises from not viewing the organism synthetically, but detaching the Intellect, and treating it independently. Having separated it from the Feelings, philosophers have been led to pay exclusive attention to the Five Senses, overlooking the necessary subordination of these to the more fundamental and energetic Systemic Senses. Hamann picturesquely expresses the general error when he says: "The Five Senses are the five loaves with which Jesus fed the multitude." I hope to show in detail that it is *not* these which supply our highest spiritual food; and that the doctrine of the Sensational School is wholly untenable, partly because our highest knowledge is *not* gained through the Senses in any such way, but is gained through psychological evolution of sociological material; and partly also because, if we isolate the Animal from the Social Organism, the Senses furnish only a small quota to the mass of human Experience.

PSYCHODYNAMICS.

24. From the biological stand-point our first division of the Organism is into Affective and Active, which division represents the reception of stimulus and the discharge of force, — sensation and movement.

The physiological fact, first enunciated by me, and now adopted by some teachers of great eminence (Vulpian, Gavarret, etc.) that *nervous tissue is identical throughout in Property as in Structure*, has extremely important consequences.* For if the Property be everywhere the same,

* The only psychologist whom I can cite as having adopted this physio-

all the Functions, into which that property enters, must have a common identity; differing quantitatively among themselves only so far as neural processes are concerned, they will of course differ qualitatively in so far as other elements enter into the functions: thus the Neurility which stimulates a muscle is identical with the Neurility which stimulates a gland, but the functions of Locomotion and Secretion, involving different organs, are qualitatively different.

The great problem of Psychology as a section of Biology is, in pursuance of this conception, to develop all the psychical phenomena from one fundamental process in one vital tissue. The tissue is the nervous; the process is a Grouping of neural units. A neural unit is a tremor. Several units are grouped into a higher unity, or neural process, which is a fusion of tremors, as a sound is a fusion of aerial pulses; and each process may in turn be grouped with others, and thus, from this grouping of groups, all the varieties emerge. What on the physiological side is simply a neural process, is on the psychological side a sentient process. We may liken Sentience to Combustion, and then the neural units will stand for the oscillating molecules. Sentience may manifest itself under the form of Consciousness, or under that of Sub-Conciousness, — which may be compared to Combustion manifesting itself in Flame and in Heat.

25. The grouping, or active aspect of the affective or sentient state, is what may analytically be called the Logical element. Logic we have already seen may comprise all the laws of grouping, subjective and objective (*Introd.*, § 65). I institute a marked division into the Logic of

logical principle, and extensively applied it in the investigation of mental phenomena, is Adolf Horwicz, whose *Psychologische Analysen auf physiologischer Grundlage* (Halle, 1872) may be recommended to the attentive study of all interested in this subject.

Feeling and the Logic of Signs; ranging under the first all the laws of grouping manifested in Sensation, Perception, Emotion, Instinct, with a further subdivision into the Logic of Images, which is intermediate between that of Feeling and that of Signs; under the second head, all the laws of Conception, or what is specially termed Thought. It is necessary to distinguish Conception, or the formation of symbols expressing general ideas, from Perception, or the formation of particular ideas by synthesis of sensations. Conceptions are no more *like* real objects than algebraic formulæ are like the numbers whose relations they symbolize. Our perception of an animal or a flower is the synthesis of all the sensations we have had of the object in relation to our several senses; and it is always an individual object represented by an individual idea: it is *this* animal or *this* flower. But our conception of an animal or flower is always a general idea, not only embracing all that is known or thought of the class in all its relations, but abstracted from all individual characteristics, and is not *this* animal or *this* flower, but any one of the class; just as a and b in Algebra are not quantities and magnitudes, but their symbols. Perceptions are concerned directly with the *terms* of Feeling; Conceptions with the *ratios* of those terms. Hence the real nature of the one, and the symbolical nature of the other.

26. Another biological principle teaches that an Organism, being a structure in relation to a Medium, is determined to action by a stimuli, both external and internal, and therefore its most general characteristic is that of Reflex action, — the issue of an excitation in a movement. A stimulus is reflected from one part of a tissue to another, and (owing to the continuity of the tissues) from one organ to another, till it terminates in a movement which may either be the movement of some special

organ or of some component part of an organ; in every case the motion which originally came from the external Medium is restored to it again, and, so far as the Organism is concerned, it there comes to an end.

27. This REFLEX is a process of Grouping underlying all psychical phenomena. Its *summa genera* are FEELING and ACTION.

The Organism is stimulated to action by Sensation, and guided by Intelligence, — the affective becomes active, not in the sense in which one phenomenon is succeeded by a different phenomenon, but in the sense in which *vis tensionis* passes into *vis viva.* The determinations of this process are *logical,* even in the simplest and most rudimentary cases; for the neural units must be grouped, if a sensation is to result.

Intelligence, which in its rudimentary form is simply Discrimination in Feeling, becomes, in its highest forms, the Discrimination of *remote means towards desired ends.* In what is called pure Thought, the means are so remote from the ends that the ends are scarcely recognizable; these means then become ends for the Intellect.

28. The popular classification which condenses one large group of phenomena under Feeling, and another under Intellect, — the one eminently personal, the other impersonal, — would have been more serviceable had it not been hampered by two misconceptions, — one respecting the assumed independence and autonomy of the Intellect, the other respecting its superior energy and importance. Although it is pretty generally acknowledged that ideas have their origin in sensations, it is rarely acknowledged, and is often expressly denied, that all the Feelings, whether those of the Five Senses, specially styled sensations, or those prompted by the Systemic Senses, and more often called impulses, emotions, desires, etc., are the real Motors, and that it is they, not ideas, which determine actions.

The Intellect, even at its highest, is a guide, not an impulse, — it shows the way, it does not cut the way.

29. Whenever the mental phenomena are considered as wholly within the Organism, they are Sensation, Emotion, Impulse; when passing out of the Organism, they are Perception, Ideation, Volition.

The Feeling which is Sensation or Emotion has little or no reference to any object causing the feeling; whereas Perception, or Ideation, passes beyond the personal circle, *projects* the Feeling outside as an object. The infant feels a sweet taste or a soft surface, and feels anger or terror, long before it has assigned sweetness and softness to objects as qualities, or learned to form any idea of objects. Such discriminations are the germs of Intelligence, and when Intelligence itself becomes developed by the large accumulations of such discriminations, it reacts on the feelings, guiding them more and more, and converting blind Impulse into clear Volition.

30. Actions are the energies of organs, and the synergies of groups of organs. They are of two kinds, — 1°, the Fixed, or directly reflex; and, 2°, the Facultative, or indirectly reflex, spontaneous. The Fixed Actions are those which uniformly result from excitation of their organs, — such are the energies of the Senses, and the actions classed under Impulses, Habit, etc. The Facultative Actions are those which, although ultimately dependent on the energies of the organs, are yet neither inevitably nor uniformly produced when the organs are stimulated, but, owing to the play of forces at work, take sometimes one issue and sometimes another. No organ has a power of control; but the Organism will control an organ. The individual man is powerless against Society; but Society can, and does, compel the individual. This does not prevent the individual from initiating a change, which may be passed on from one to another like yeast-

cells growing in a fermenting mass; and in this sense Society is of course affected by the actions of individuals, since, indeed, it is itself only the sum of individuals. We may note as one broad characteristic of the social organism, that it is constituted by organs which are independent, and which voluntarily co-operate, the strength of each residing in the measure of its co-operation. A man, although powerless *against* Society, becomes a power *with* Society.

31. Although all actions are prompted and really guided by Feeling, many of them have so little accompaniment of what is usually designated Consciousness that they are said to be insensible. Many of these are called *automatic*, they are the inevitable activities of the energies or synergies; many of them are called *involuntary*, and are supposed to be the precursors of the *voluntary*.

These conceptions need modifying. It can be shown that Sentience is involved in all actions, even the automatic and involuntary; and that the actions which are now involuntary were originally voluntary, if by voluntary we understand the presence of Intelligence. I mean that all such distinctions are psycho*logical*, not psycho-*genetical*. They mark differences which now exist, but they do not mark differences in the genesis of the phenomena. The facts of congenital Instincts and of acquired Habits, which operate so rapidly and so securely that all the intermediate stages between impression and motion escape notice, has led to the denial of these stages. Thus the uniformity of the earth's movement causes us to consider it at rest; we know the movement only through indirect sources. By indirect methods we may also learn that when involuntary or instinctive acts are slackened or thwarted their sentient and selective characters appear. Knowing how actions which were once slow and laborious become rapid and easy, and how what cost us painful efforts to learn is now performed without sensible effort, we understand how the voluntary lapses into the involuntary and we may be sure that, however easy and rapid the process may become, it must necessarily pass through the stages originally followed, though without the *irradiation* of nascent impulses in other directions.

32. This question of Instinct will occupy us more fully when we come to treat of the origin of knowledge (Prob., I. § 21). Enough here to define it as *lapsed* or *undiscursive Intelligence,* — the fixed action of an acquired organization, transmitted from ancestors who acquired it through Adaptation, whereby what was facultative became fixed, what was voluntary became involuntary.

The objection will doubtless be raised that Instinct is wholly destitute of the characteristic of Intelligence in that it has no choice; its operation is fixed, fatal. The reply is twofold: in the first place, the objection, so far as it has validity, applies equally to Judgment, where, given the premises, the conclusion is fatal, no alternative being open. Axioms, in this sense, are logical instincts. Thus the highest intellectual process is on a level with this process said to be its opposite.

And in the second place, the element of choice always does enter into Instinct; although the intelligent discrimination of means to ends may be *almost* absent, it never is *entirely*. The guiding sensation which directs the impulse is always selective. If we restrict Intelligence to the Logic of Signs, — to ideas, — there cannot of course be anything intelligent in Instinct; but if we extend it — as we must — to the Logic of Feeling, the dispute will cease.

33. Neural processes which formerly were accompanied by Consciousness sink into Sub-Consciousness, and on occasion re-emerge into distinct light of day. But even

in the sub-conscious stage they are always *sentient.* The practice, too frequent, of speaking of actions as *un*conscious, is more than a contradiction in terms. "Unfelt feelings" are altogether inadmissible. On the other hand, to speak of Consciousness (meaning thereby a particular aspect) as the *substance* of Mind, the universal condition of psychical phenomena, is also misleading. What is universal is the neural process, which on the subjective side is the sentient process. Sentience may assume the form of Consciousness, or the form of Sub-Consciousness; as Vision may take place when the central point of the retina is impressed, and then the effect is most distinct, or when any point of the area of the retina is impressed, and then the effect is less and less distinct as it is farther from the centre. Sentience is always sentient, as Vision is always visual.

34. The region of Sub-Consciousness is much the larger region. There is more heat than flame. The difference between them depends on the greater or less *irradiation* of an excitation.

Here we may note two Psychodynamic laws,— 1°, of Irradiation, and, 2°, of Restriction. Although Anatomy, for its purposes, divides the nervous system into several different organs, this division is only an artifice, and must not permit us to overlook the cardinal fact that the nervous tissue is one, and has one general Property,— Neurility,— and one general Function,— Reflexion. No stimulus can excite a single part of this whole without indirectly exciting all the other parts. Hence the law of Irradiation: every excitation must be propagated; it cannot cease with itself, for this would violate the first law of motion. But the *directions* in which it will be propagated (the law of Restriction here emerges) are determined by the structural conditions at the time being. It is probable that irradiation is vague so long as it takes place through *neuroglia,** and becomes definite conduction when it is restricted in its course by the cells and fibres. Be this as it may, we must understand that while, according to the abstract law of Irradiation, every excitation is diffused throughout the tissue, terminating only in a muscular excitation, this diffusion is in effect always controlled by the law of Restriction, and the pathway of discharge becomes more or less defined. The concrete facts of excitation no more agree with the abstract law, than the actual motions of bodies agree with the abstract law of uniform rectilinear Motion. Every real excitation is subject to the statical conditions of the Organism at the time being; that is to say, what are the lines of least resistance along which a motion will be propagated must necessarily be determined by the state of the structure at the time being; any paths which have formerly been traversed by an impulse will be more ready to yield an issue to the new impulse. These formed paths therefore restrict the irradiation, which would otherwise be indefinite.

35. Many obscure facts receive their explanation through this law of Irradiation. Two only need here be specified for illustration: the fact that Extension is felt as a *continuum*, although the feeling arises from the excitations of discrete nerve-fibrils and discrete pulses on those fibrils, has greatly puzzled some investigators, most of whom have been led to invent an extra-neural agency to explain it. Irradiation suffices, since by it there is a necessary blending of the discrete points, a fusion of the similar tremors.

The second fact may be the obverse of this. It was

* *Neuroglia* is the name given by Virchow to the interstitial substance connecting the nervous elements, — *nerve-cement*. It is peculiarly interesting from its close resemblance to other connective tissues, since it is the link, so to speak, which enables us to understand how nerve-tissue arises.

noticed by Aristotle that knowledge begins with vague conceptions, and increases with increasing definiteness in the conceptions. All impressions must at first be irradiated, and produce a chaos of vague sentience; as these irradiations gradually become restricted, the processes are grouped, the paths are defined, distinctions are established.

It is conceivable how differentiations in the tissue arise from differentiations of the pathways of discharge; how the nerve cells and fibres, the magazines of conductible energy and the channels of conduction, arise amid the neuroglia; and how old age or disease increasing the relative proportions of neuroglia and nerve elements reduces the mental functions to infantile or imbecile states; finally, how the tendency of Restriction is, as old age advances, to prevent new acquisitions, and resist new combinations.

36. Although when viewed synthetically every sensation, every perception, every conception, is a unit, viewed analytically and genetically, it is a compound. There is no single sensation which is an element, i. e. irreducible.

This is to be considered in reference to the disputes respecting the unity of Consciousness, the simplicity of the Ego. Every act of Consciousness is *one;* every Ego is a unity. But analysis, which resolves a sensation into its constituent neural elements, resolves Consciousness into its constituent processes, and the Ego into a consensus of psychical activities. The demonstration that thinking is *seriation,* and that a series involves Time, disproves the notions of ultimate unity and simplicity assigned to a Thinking Principle. In any positive meaning of the term, that Principle is not an antecedent but a resultant, not an entity but a convergence of manifold activities.

37. This convergence is a necessary consequence of the synergy of the organs dependent on Irradiation. The seriation depends on the law of Reinstatement or Reproduction, by which one neural process tends to re-excite

those processes which formerly were excited in conjunction with it, or which are anatomically linked with it. Those pathways of discharge which were once determined by the combined action of the stimulus and reaction of the Organism are the pathways which will be statically connected, and hence they will form the lines of least resistance along which any fresh excitation will pass.

38. But this law of Reinstatement whereby one feeling calls up associated feelings, is itself only the expression of the statical conditions. We are not therefore to expect that a given stimulus will always re-excite a given group of feelings; we can only formulate the general *tendency*,* in virtue of which a sensible stimulus draws with it fainter feelings of previous impressions, so that they are grouped into a judgment or perception. This group is, in turn, the element of some wider group, whenever it is not directly reflected in discharge on some organ. But in all cases an action of some kind results; directly or indirectly, every sensation is *completed* in an action; and thus Action is the pole-star of even the most wide-wandering Speculation.

39. Thus the three terms of the progression from Stimulus to Reflex, are respectively, Feeling, Logic, and Action; or Impulse, Guidance, and Result.

Let me again remind the reader that he is by no means called upon to adopt the foregoing conclusions until he has had laid before him in detail the anatomical, physiological, and psychological evidence. There is much that will no doubt seem inadmissible, much questionable. He is only asked to accept whatever he can, and to suspend his judgment on the rest.

* *Tendency* is the ideal summation of the statical conditions which tend to a dynamical result; or, to express it less technically, it is one gathering up into a picture of all the events which *we foresee* will succeed each other when the organism is set going, and of the final result.

I will now state a principle which hereafter will be extensively applied. It wears so paradoxical an air, that I should not venture to bring it forward until the evidence had been duly exhibited, but that the explicit announcement here will protect me against a possible anticipation on the part of some other writer. While lingering over the execution of the present work, I have more than once had the mingled pleasure and pain of finding results I had laboriously reached, arrived at by other writers; and as I believe that the Psychological Spectrum is physiologically demonstrable, the possibility of some one else discovering it is worth taking into account.

THE PSYCHOLOGICAL SPECTRUM.

40. Briefly, then, the principle may thus be formulated. The optical spectrum is constituted by three fundamental colors, red, green, and violet, which are due to three modes of vibration affecting the rods and cones of the retina, or perhaps to three different sets of rods and cones; and each sensation of an individual color depends on the *proportions* in which these modes — the number of pulses in a second — affect the retina. Each color also contains all the characteristic vibrations of the others, and consequently each color owes its individuality, not to vibrations which the others want, but to a *predominance* in a certain order of vibration. Thus there is a special rapidity in the pulses on the retina in the waves producing red; but in every red there are waves of fainter rapidity such as produce green and violet when they are dominant. In the color green, there are likewise the red and violet waves; in the color violet, there are red and green waves.

41. The analogy of Vision and Consciousness, so usefully employed by many writers, may justify my use of the term the Psychological Spectrum, which likewise is

constituted by three fundamental modes of excitation, namely, Sensation, Thought, and Motion. I shall show that these three orders of nervo-muscular excitation are involved in every sensation, perception, image, or conception; and of course also in every emotion, desire, volition, etc. In other words, the psychical process is everywhere a triple process. Every psychical fact is a product of sense-work, brain-work, and muscle-work. Each sentient phenomenon (perception, emotion, conception, or volition) is individualized by, and receives its specific character from, the *predominance*, of one of the three orders; and one feeling is distinguished from another of the same kind by quantitative differences in their constituent units. All varieties among the several mental states are due to the varying degrees of energy with which Sensation, Thought, and Motion co-operate. Each mental state is thus *a function of three variables.**

42. Leaving this to the reader's meditation, I now pass to the consideration of another result of the law of Reinstatement, which law is another aspect of the law of Registration. A sensation or perception, once produced, may of course be reproduced by a recurrence of the original conditions; but it may also be reproduced with fainter energy, as an *image*, when the original objective conditions are absent, and only the subjective conditions are present in the modification of structure. That is to say, the original feeling is registered in the organism as a modification, and whenever this neural tract which was

* Combining this conception with Fechner's law of the proportionality of sensation to stimulus, the reader may perhaps seize my meaning when I said (Introd., § 12) that the Differential Calculus might some day be applied to Psychology. Another indication is furnished by Helmholtz, when he assumes that the local feelings derived from the different points in the retina more closely resemble each other the closer the points are, so that the kind of local feeling is a continuous function of the co-ordinates of the retinal points." — *Physiol. Optik*, p. 800.

originally in action, is again excited, the old feeling will be reinstated. The sight of an orange thus recalls the associated feelings of taste and smell, and perhaps of the person who gave the first orange, or the plate on which it was handed. In this series the visual sensation is *directly* reproduced under conditions closely resembling its original production; therefore the energy of this feeling is incomparably greater than that of the *indirectly* reproduced feelings of smell, taste, etc. Whatever antecedent may stimulate the neural tracts, any one of these may re-excite the others. Thus the mere name of the person or the place, the sight or sound of the word "orange," will suffice.

43. All sentient acts are acts of Presentation or of Re-Presentation, usually called Sensation and Idea. The Germans distinguish the directly excited feeling as "the feeling in us," — *Empfindung;* and the indirectly excited feeling as "the placing before us," — *Vorstellung.* We have no such happy terms, but Sensation and Image, or Idea, serve pretty well.

The sensation, or presentation, is fitly considered *real,* because it has objective reality (*res*) for its antecedent stimulus. The *re*-presentation, whether image or symbol, is *ideal,* because its antecedent is a subjective state. Reality always indicates *that* antecedent which excites sensation when in direct relation with the censory organism. Hence we say that a feeling is real when it is felt, ideal when it is only thought, not felt. To feel cold, and to think of cold, are two markedly different states.

44. An image, therefore, — being a representation, a Vorstellung, an indirectly excited feeling, — may be called the ideal form of a sensation. It is a transition between the pure real and the pure ideal, i. e. between sensation and symbol. Because of its connection with sensation, it passes into pure sensation when the energy of its tremors is greatly increased; as in Hallucination,

wherein the feeling, although excited by internal stimuli, having its antecedent in a subjective state and not in some objective *res*, does assume all the energy of a sensation objectively excited. We may consider the gradations of Sensation, After-sensation, Imagination,* and Hallucination, as the varying energies of the same neural tracts.

Owing to the indirect, representative origin of Imagination and its ideal character, there are important differences between it and Sensation, and After-sensation; one of these being that Images are facultative, and are thereby capable of entering into intellectual constructions.

45. Sensation, Perception, and Imagination, all involve the co-operation of the Logical or Grouping element, whence Judgment, and of the Motor element, whence Action (§ 41).

By including under these rubrics the phenomena of Cognition and Conation, and treating in due order the Appetites, Emotions, and Volitions, we shall exhaust the Biological Data of Psychology, if to this examination of the structure and functions of the Animal Organism in detail we add a consideration of it as a Whole. From this point of view we must consider certain general results.

46. Of these general results perhaps the most perplexing, as it assuredly is the most interesting, is Consciousness, which may be pictured as the mass of *stationary waves*† formed out of the individual waves of neural

* This word must be understood literally, i. e. as the image-forming process; not metaphorically, as the poet's fantasy.

† Stationary waves play a great part in the speculations of modern physicists. They may be thus illustrated: If the surface of a lake is set in motion by the various streams which enter it from various points, each stream diffuses waves over the surface, and these finally reach the shores, whence they are reflected back towards the centre of the lake. The reflected waves meet with new incoming waves, and the product of the two is a stationary wave, forming, so to speak, a pattern on the surface. This

tremors. Next comes what may be called the *psychical mood* or attitude. Each individual feeling has its special *signature*, so likewise the resultant general feeling has its signature; and we are at each moment conscious of a vague massive feeling of comfort or discomfort, exhilaration or despondency, joy or grief, fear, rage, kindness, etc. There is also a *logical attitude* which is called Attention, itself the product of feeling, and one of the necessary factors in Perception.

47. When this survey has been completed we have the final task of exhibiting how the sentient phenomena may be explained by neural phenomena. The structure and action of the Organism have to be psychologically interpreted. This will require a new anatomy of the nervous system. What now exists, although of immense value, is defective in many respects. Not only must each function be traced to its special organ, and the part played by each constituent assigned to it; not only must the connection of the parts be displayed, but there must be taken into account the very important element of Vascular Irrigation. The distribution of the arteries is an essential element in the biostatical estimate. Arterial territories have to be defined. Many individual variations in mental character depend on the variations in the calibre of the cerebral and carotid trunks; and many variations in the intellectual, emotive, and active tendencies depend on the *relative* importance of the

pattern is of course a fluctuating figure depending on the concurrent waves. Now when a *fresh* stream enters the lake its waves will at first pass *over* this pattern of stationary waves, neither disturbing nor disturbed; but after reaching the shore they will in turn be reflected back towards the centre, and there mingling with incoming waves from the same source, they will, according to circumstances, either markedly alter the pattern of the stationary waves, or modify it but slightly: analogically, in the one case there will be an appreciable change in Consciousness, in the other none.

cerebral and carotid trunks. The *energy* of the Brain depends mainly on the *calibre* of its arteries; the special *directions* of that energy depend on the *territorial distribution.*

48. But when this programme is thoroughly worked out, it will only present one half of Psychology. It will embrace the Logic of Feeling, common to animals and to man, but it will still leave undeciphered that which constitutes the wonder and glory of man, — his intellectual and moral life. Rising out of the Logic of Feeling there is the Logic of Signs, which is to the former what Algebra is to Arithmetic (§ 25). Rising out of the Animal Organism there is the Social Organism, the collective life of all the individual lives; and if we desire to decipher Human Psychology we must study the Human Organism in its relations to the Social Medium as well as in its relations to the Cosmos.

THE SOCIOLOGICAL DATA.

49. It is now almost universally admitted that animals and men having similar structures must have similar functions; and further, that the mental manifestations being determined by organic structures, the mental functions of animals and men must be essentially similar. That animals have sensations, appetites, emotions, instincts, and intelligence, — that they exhibit memory, expectation, judgment, hope, fear, joy, — that they learn by experience, and invent new modes of satisfying their desires, no philosopher now denies. And yet the gap between animal and human intelligence is so wide that Philosophy is sorely puzzled to reconcile the undeniable facts. When it was customary to attribute to Instinct all the manifestations of Intelligence in animals, and to Reason all the similar manifestations in men, this difficulty was not felt. A phrase did duty for an explana-

tion. To say that man was endowed with a Rational Soul, inhabiting the organism yet independent of it, and altogether distinct from the Vegetative Soul which ruled the body, seemed an easy way of accounting for all the observed facts.

50. Untenable as this hypothesis is, I am disposed to regard it with more favor, in some respects, than the crude materialist hypothesis; for I, too, hold that the superiority of human Intelligence is due to the presence of an important factor, one wholly wanting in the animal. Instead of regarding the differences between man and animal simply as differences of degree, I hold that by no conceivable extension of animal faculties, *unaided* by this important factor, could the highest of the animals be raised into that moral and intellectual world which is the habitual medium of the civilized human soul. Believing, as I believe, in the evolution of the higher from the lower, and disbelieving therefore in any abrupt break in the continuity of evolution, I still say that in so far as we are justified in classing phenomena into distinct groups, and thus distinguishing the products of complex factors from the products of simpler factors, the group recognized under the class "Human Intelligence" is so different from the group "Animal Intelligence" that it requires for its analytical interpretation different factors of corresponding importance. The circle and the ellipse are different figures, the former having but one centre with all its radii equal, the latter having two foci and unequal radii. Circles differ from circles in degree; they differ from ellipses in kind. Whether large or small the circle has the same properties, and these are different from the properties of the ellipse. It is true that by insensible gradations the circle may flatten into an ellipse, or the two foci of the ellipse may blend into one, and form a circle. But so long as there are two foci, the ellipse has its characteristic

properties. In like manner the boundaries of the animal and human may be found insensibly blending at certain points; but whenever the "animal circle" has become transformed into the "human ellipse," by the introduction of a second centre, the difference ceases to be one of degree, and becomes one of kind, the germ of infinite variations.

The question arises: What are these respective foci? What are the respective centres of animal and human Intelligence? I answer: The Logic of Feeling and the Logic of Signs; or, in more familiar terms, Feeling and Thought: the one belonging to the Animal Organism, the other rising out of this and out of the Social Organism.

51. The answers hitherto propounded have been either founded on the spiritualist hypothesis, endowing man with a Soul of spiritual structure; or on the biological hypothesis (materialist or not), deducing all the mental phenomena from the *animal* functions in adaptation to the Cosmos.

Eminent thinkers still cling to some form or other of the spiritualist hypothesis, repelled from the biological hypothesis by their sense of its inadequacy. They admit that all our bodily functions depend on bodily organs. They admit that among these functions are those of Feeling with its varieties and complications. But they also know that animals having organs closely resembling our own, and feelings closely resembling our own, have little or nothing of the highest order of mental activity: Animals are intelligent, but have no Intellect; they are sympathetic, but have no Ethics; they are emotive, but have no Conscience.

When it is said that Animals however intelligent have no Intellect, the meaning is that they have perceptions and judgments, but no conceptions, no general ideas, no symbols for logical operations. They are intelligent, for we see them guided to action by Judgment; they adapt their actions by means of guiding sensations, and adapt things to their ends. Their mechanism is a sentient, intelligent mechanism. But they have not Conception, or what we specially designate as Thought, — i. e. that logical function which deals with generalities, ratios, symbols, as Feeling deals with particulars and objects, — *a function sustained by and subservient to impersonal, social ends.* Taking Intelligence in general as the discrimination of means to ends, — the guidance of the Organism towards the satisfaction of its impulses, — we particularize Intellect as a highly differentiated mode of this function, namely, as the discrimination of symbols. This differs from the rudimentary mode, out of which it is nevertheless an evolution, as European Commerce differs from the rudimentary Barter of primitive tribes. Commerce is impossible except under complex social conditions out of which it springs; and its operations are mainly carried on by means of symbols which take the place of objects: the bill of invoice represents the cargo; the merchant's signature represents the payment. In like manner Intellect is impossible until animal development has reached the human social stage; and it is at all periods the index of that development; its operations are likewise carried on by means of symbols (Language) which represent real objects, and can at any time be translated into feelings.

52. It is obvious that the biological data can only resolve one half of the psychological problem, only present one of the foci of the ellipse, since by no derivation from the purely statical considerations of man's animal organism can we reach the higher dynamical products. Isolate man from the social state, and we have an animal; set going his organism simply in relation to the Cosmos, without involving any relations to other men, and we can get no Intellect, no Conscience. Whence are these derived?

The organism of the anthropoid apes is very little differenced from ours; their sensory organs, nay, even their brain (the so-called "organ" of the mind), can be distinguished from ours only by trifling deviations; but with this external structural resemblance, what an infinite mental disparity! Biology forces us to seek for a *status* corresponding to this diversity. Between the various types of vertebrate structure there are gradations; but between the vertebrate and invertebrate there is a gap. The internal skeleton characteristic of the Vertebrate is approached in the Cephalopoda; the symmetrical arrangement of nerve-centres is seen in the Articulata; but in spite of these and other indications of a general resemblance, the marked types, Vertebrate and Invertebrate, stand out distinct. So between the extremes of human Intelligence — say a Tasmanian and a Shakespeare — there are infinitesimal gradations, enabling us to follow the development of the one into the other, without the introduction of any essentially new factor. But between animal and human Intelligence there is a gap, which can only be bridged over by an addition from without. That bridge is the Language of symbols, at once the cause and effect of Civilization.

53. The absurdity of supposing that any ape could under any normal circumstances construct a scientific theory, analyze a fact into its component factors, frame to himself a picture of the life led by his ancestors, or consciously regulate his conduct with a view to the welfare of remote descendants, is so glaring, that we need not wonder at profoundly meditative minds having been led to reject with scorn the hypothesis which seeks for an explanation of human Intelligence in the functions of the bodily organism common to man and animals, and having had recourse to the hypothesis of a spiritual agent superadded to the organism.

54. Yet the spiritual hypothesis is scientifically unten-

able. It is an imaginary hypothesis, and has not only the defect of being incapable of verification, it has the more serious defect of being incapable of extending our insight: it gives a name to the facts observed, it throws no light on them, connecting them with others; nor does it enable us to discover unsuspected relations. Further, it is the introduction of an *unknown* to take the place of a *knowable.* The spirit is proposed as an agent; yet of *its* nature and agency we know absolutely nothing.

And if, for the sake of argument, we grant the existence of a spirit, and accept it as the agent, the same objection rises against it which rose against the materialist hypothesis, namely, that it fails to cover the facts. Man, possessing this spirit but isolated from Society, could no more manifest the activities classed under Intellect and Morality than the animal could. He would still require that his Spiritual Organism should be in relation to the Social Medium. For one thing he would be without the mighty instrument Language, which we shall prove to be *indispensable* to the creation of abstract Thought. He would only have perceptions, and the Logic of Feeling; he would be without conceptions, and the Logic of Signs. Then, again, he would have none of the many needs which arise from social relations; nor the *accumulation of experiences* which form the material of scientific evolutions. This is demonstrable from many sides. Here we simply note the fact that our intellectual wealth is not only *capitalized Experience,* but is always in strict accord with social development; so that the savage is not less incompetent than the animal to originate or even understand a philosophical conception; the peasant would be little better than the ape in presence of the problems of abstract science; and it would be hopeless to expect either of them to weigh the stars, or to understand the equations of curves of double curvature. Nor are the moral conceptions of the savage much higher than those of the animal. His language is without terms for Justice, Sin, Crime; he has not the ideas. He understands generosity, pity, and love little better than the dog or the horse does. His intelligence is mainly confined to perceptions and sentiments. His aims are almost all immediate and practical, rarely remote, never theoretical. The most intelligent inhabitants of Guiana, though far removed from primitive savagery, could not believe that Humboldt had left his own country and come to theirs "to be devoured by mosquitoes for the sake of measuring lands which were not his own."

There is a further ground, still more decisive, against the spiritualist hypothesis, namely, that we have no need of an imaginary agent to explain what can be perfectly explained by a real agent, — the Social Organism. Not having this conception, the spiritualists imagine that to deny the existence of the Spirit is to deny the existence of the Soul. It is no more a denial of the Soul, than the rejection of the old hypothesis of a nervous fluid was a denial of nervous physiology. All the facts of Consciousness, all the marvels of Thought, remain, whatever changes may take place in our theories respecting them. It is scarcely necessary to add that biologists may quietly disregard the common rhetorical objection against their "mechanical views," as if such views were self-condemned. No sooner does any philosopher attempt to substitute clear conceptions of the processes of Nature, for vague speculations incapable of verification, than the framers of such speculations and the acceptors of them with one accord exclaim, "This is degrading human nature!" as if to leave men in ignorance were to sustain them in their dignity.

55. If man is a social animal, which is undeniable, the unit in a living whole, just as any one organ is the unit

of an organism, obviously his functions will be determined not only by his individual structure, but also by the structure of the Collective Organism. The functions of the liver or of the kidneys are determined partly by their structure, partly by influences from the other organs. Man's individual functions arise in relations to the Cosmos; his general functions arise in relations to the Social Medium; thence Moral Life emerges. All the animal Impulses become blended with human Emotions. In the process of evolution, starting from the merely animal appetite of sexuality, we arrive at the purest and most far-reaching tenderness; from the merely animal property of Sensibility we arrive at the noblest heights of Speculation. The Social Instincts, which are the analogues of the individual Instincts, tend more and more to make Sociality dominate Animality, and thus subordinate Personality to Humanity.

56. All the attempts to explain Mind without taking the social factors into account have been signal failures; but especially mistaken have been the estimates vainly founded on anatomical data, and above all on the measurements of crania, and the weighing of brains. The spiritualists were more philosophical in demanding another agent and another test. The anatomical estimates proceed on three assumptions generally regarded as axioms, — 1°, that the brain is the "organ of the Mind"; 2°, that the mental diversities observable between men and animals, and between different races of men, are due solely to differences of cerebral mass; 3°, that these diversities can be approximately estimated by estimates of volume and weight.

We must reject all three. The first, because to seek for *an* organ of the Mind is not less preposterous than to seek for *an* organ of the Life. Nor is this difficulty avoided by those who regard the brain simply as the organ of the Intellect; for the Intellect is also an abstraction, and if we reduce the abstraction to its concretes we have acts which involve sensory and motor organs, and groupings of their reactions. The brain may be the organ in which sensory processes are finally grouped before they are reflected on other organs; but it is only in artificial analysis that we can consider the process of grouping independently of the materials grouped. Let us, however, for a moment grant that the brain is the organ of the Mind; this will not justify the second assumption. No one will suppose that I deny the cerebral structure to be one of the determinants in all mental manifestations; but the same scientific evidence which necessitates this conclusion, necessitates the rejection of that precipitate conclusion which assigns the whole product to one of its factors. The co-operation of the Medium is not less indispensable than that of the Organism; and, in the case of man, the Medium is constituted by the education of the race and of the individual; so that the state of social evolution which has been reached at any given time in any given place, will be one of the necessary determinants in every individual mind. I shall recur to this presently; here it is enough to point out that, admitting the general mental resemblances, dependent on community of structure and of the general Medium, we cannot assign the diversities of the mental *manifestations* of such common powers to structural differences alone. Every organism has not only an inherited and gradually modified structure which is one of the determinants of its history, it has also a history of incident, that is of transient conditions, which may lead two similar organisms along divergent paths, and determine them to different manifestations.

And this leads me to the third assumption. The differences of cerebral structure which are evolved in the education of the race, and which are necessary conditions of the observed diversities in mental manifestation, can no more be estimated by measurements of volume and mass, than the skill of a Joachim, as distinguished from that of an old crowder playing a popular jig, could be estimated by taking the size and weight of his arms and fingers.

57. We return then to our position that Mind cannot be explained without constant recognition of the statico-dynamical relations of Organism and Social Medium.

To understand the first we must regard it physiologically and anatomically. It is not a passive recipient of external impressions, but an active co-operant. It has not only its own laws of action, but brings with it that very elementary condition of Consciousness which most theorists attempt to derive *ab extra*. I mean that the sensitive mechanism is not a simple mechanism, and as such constant, but a variable mechanism, which has a *history*. What the Senses inscribe on it, are not merely the changes of the external world; but these characters are commingled with the characters of preceding inscriptions. The sensitive subject is no *tabula rasa;* it is not a blank sheet of paper, but a palimpsest. The sensational school was strangely blind to the very conditions of the results it intended to explain. It treated Thought as "transformed Sensation," without seeing that the presence of the grouping faculty, on which Thought depends, was necessary both for the Sensation and for the transformation. Not aware of the fact that the Organism is an evolution, bringing with it, in its structure, evolved modes of action inherited from ancestors, these writers overlooked the fact that the Organism brings with it inherited Experience, i. e. a mode of reaction antecedent to all direct relation with external influences, which necessarily determines the results of individual Experience. There is thus what may be called an *à priori* condition in all

Sensation, and in all Ideation. But this is *historical,* not *transcendental;* it is itself the product of Experience, though not of the individual. Our perceptions are evolutions; and, having necessarily a history at their back, it is clear that all perceptions are modified by pre-perceptions, all conceptions by pre-conceptions. Hence mental diversities.

58. We are not, however, to conclude that this *à priori* condition is metempirical. It is an inheritance of acquired modification. It may, analytically, be separated from the *à posteriori* experiences, as the Organism may, analytically, be separated from its functions; and in this way we may accept Kant's position that the *à priori* Forms of Sense and Understanding render Experience possible. But this is only saying that function is determined by structure; and we must wholly reject his position that these Forms are transcendental, and are not only antecedent to and independent of all Experience whatever, ancestral and individual, but are sources of a higher truth than can be gained through individual experiences. They are congenital modifications, and are *à priori* because congenital.

59. It is important here to remark, that while function is necessarily determined by structure, — being nothing but the structure in action co-operating with the medium, — the transmission from generation to generation is confined to the structural *modification,* not including the *incidents* which caused that modification, nor any of the special actions which were the *products* of that modification in combination with special incidents. What we inherit is the modified structure, and, with that, the aptitude to act in a certain way under certain stimuli; but the inheritance of the historical result is not the inheritance of the incidents which severally converged to that result, nor of the consequences which is-

sued from the result under special conditions. Thus the tissue of the lungs subjected to certain influences becomes so modified that tubercle is formed. The child may inherit a tuberculous diathesis, but cannot inherit the causes which originated the tubercle, nor the peculiar mental experiences which resulted from the influence of tubercle in the parent organism; these being due to a complex of conditions never recurring in the child's experience.

In discussions on Heredity it has not been sufficiently recognized that only results can be inherited, and that every modification of structure is the issue of many complex experiences. Could one experience be isolated from prior and posterior experiences, it might be transmitted from parent to child; but each experience is not only complicated by prior experiences, its transmission is complicated by the influence of the other parent. A musical *aptitude* will be inherited, but no particular melody. The aptitude represents a modification of structure whereby the response to auditory stimuli takes a melodic form; but any particular melody is the form which this general aptitude takes under very special and complex conditions. In other words, the inherited organism is predisposed to play tunes of a certain character, but the music it will give forth must depend on the player. Here once more we see the necessity of allowing for the objective factor no less than for the subjective factor. Certain external influences co-operating with the organism have modified the structure of that organism, and produced what may be called a musical instrument; could the external influences which were originally grouped into a definite melodic form be repeated, the result would be repeated, and the musician's child would again create *de novo* the melody created by his parent. The chances are infinite against such a recurrence in the *order* of the stimuli. But there are, in other regions, necessary recurrences in the order, so that every mind rediscovers the most general truths for itself, because every mind has presented to it the same phenomena in the same order.

60. This is a biological doctrine of Innate Ideas, which we shall have presently to consider at length. Here we must be content with saying that in the old meaning the doctrine is untenable. There are no innate ideas, no innate truths, no thoughts having a metempirical source, — simply innate *tendencies*, congenital *aptitudes*, which cause us to respond in certain ways to certain stimuli; but if the stimuli differ in kind, or in degree, or in their *order* of presentation, the responses must proportionately differ.

In this sense we have Moral and Intellectual Instincts, — the action of congenital arrangements in the mechanism when set going under appropriate stimuli. Thus defined, it is clear that we are born with Logical Instincts. Strictly speaking, we no more learn to reason than we learn to see. In one sense we learn both, since Experience (the action and reaction of Organism and Medium) is requisite for both; and in both we have to *acquire* what is but partially *given* at birth, namely, the structure capable of co-ordinating impressions. *What* we learn, *what* we acquire, both in reasoning and vision, is the result of the aptitudes evolved through external influences acting on a primitive arrangement of nervous tissue. If any one contemplating the infant, so obviously incapable of seeing or of reasoning, should demur to our presentation of Reason as congenital, he must equally demur to the universal acceptance of the sexual instinct as congenital; all three functions are only congenital in the sense in which the oak is said to lie ready in the acorn. The oak will not be developed unless under the appropriate conditions, and every variation in the soil or atmosphere will impress corresponding variations on the structure of the developed product. But the acorn inherits certain structural *tendencies*, which will manifest themselves in definite forms. The nervous organism also inherits certain tendencies, and whether these are early or late in evolution is quite a subsidiary consideration.

61. Our activities are of two classes, — the personal and impersonal. The personal comprise Sensation, Perception, Imagination, Judgment, Volition, — all directed to the satisfaction of egoistic impulses or primary needs: the need of Food, of Exercise (with its correlative, Repose), of Expression, and of Reproduction. The impersonal are directed to the satisfaction of sympathetic impulses, — the need of Affection, and the need of Knowledge. Intelligence, in the one case, is the conquest of means for immediate ends; Intellect, in the other, is the conquest of means for remote ends.

The animal has sympathy, and is moved by sympathetic impulses, but these are never altruistic; the ends are never remote. Moral life is based on sympathy: it is feeling for others, working for others, aiding others, quite irrespective of any personal good beyond the satisfaction of the social impulse. Enlightened by the intuition of our community of weakness, we share ideally the universal sorrows. Suffering humanizes. Feeling the need of mutual help, we are prompted by it to labor for others. The egoistic impulses are directed towards objects simply so far as these are the *means* of satisfying a desire. The altruistic impulses, on the contrary, have greater need of Intelligence to understand the object itself in all its relations. Hence so much immorality is sheer stupidity.

62. Thus it is that we are to seek in the Social Organism for all the main conditions of the higher functions, and in the Social Medium of beliefs, opinions,

institutions, etc., for the atmosphere breathed by the Intellect. Man is no longer to be considered simply as an assemblage of organs, but also as an organ in a Collective Organism. From the former he derives his sensations, judgments, primary impulses; from the latter his conceptions, theories, and virtues. This is very clear when we learn how the Intellect draws both its inspiration and its instrument from the social needs. All the materials of intellect are images and symbols, all its processes are operations on images and symbols. Language — which is wholly a social product for a social need — is the chief vehicle of symbolical operation, and the only means by which Abstraction is effected. Without Language there can be no meditation, no theory, no Thought, in the special meaning of that term. A perception condenses many feelings into one, and is so far knowledge. A word — the symbol of a conception — condenses many perceptions into one; and is thus not only knowledge of a wider range, but is a knowledge which is *facultative*, and capable of transmission and preservation.

63. Language is the creator and sustainer of that Ideal World in which the noblest part of human activity finds a theatre, the world of Thought and Spiritual Insight, of Knowledge and Duty, loftily elevated above that of Sense and Appetite. Into this Ideal World man absorbs the universe as in a Transfiguration. It is here that he shapes the programme of his existence; and to that programme he makes the Real World conform. It is here he forms his highest rules of Conduct. It is here he plants his hopes and joys. It is here he finds his dignity and power. The Ideal World becomes to him the supreme Reality. It multiplies his pleasures and his pains. Its phantoms haunt him, — filling life with infinite misery, such as never troubles less gifted creatures; setting tribe against tribe, brother against brother, father

against son, spreading bitter hate and the intolerable tyrannies of Superstition. Its fantasies animate him,—filling life with infinite and subtle joy, and in many ways aggrandizing his capacities and aims. This is man's spiritual being; who would renounce it for the comparative calm of the most fortunate brute?

64. An animal suffers from a physical calamity, seeks to escape from it, but never seeks to understand and modify its causes. The savage also suffers, and seeks to escape. But he wonders, speculates on the causes, hopes to master them by invocations or incantations. The civilized man tries to understand the causes that he may modify them when they are modifiable, and resign himself to them when they are unmodifiable. The animal has only the Logic of Feeling to guide his actions. He observes and concludes, never explains. The man has besides this, the Logic of Signs: he observes, and explains the visible series by an invisible series. The one has only knowledge of particular facts; the other a knowledge of general facts. The knowledge of the one is fixed, that of the other facultative.

Between the Logic of Feeling and the Logic of Signs we must intercalate the Logic of Images, since the passage from Perception to Conception is effected through Imagination. Images, although reproductions of perceptions, possess a property not possessed by perceptions, namely, that of facultative reproduction, which enables them to be abstracted from the sensible order of presentation, and combined and recombined anew. Animal Imagination is reproductive but not plastic; it never constructs.

65. It is in Imagination that must be sought the first impulse towards Explanation; and therefore all primitive explanations are so markedly imaginative. Images being the ideal forms of Sensation, the Logic of Images is the

first stage of intellectual activity; and is therefore predominant in the early history of individuals and of nations. The first attempts to explain a phenomenon must be to combine the images of past sensations with the sensations now felt, so as to form a series. In the next stage, words, representative of abstractions, take the places both of images and objects. Thus the Logic of Signs replaces the Logic of Images, as the Logic of Images replaced the Logic of Sensation. Imagination precedes Science; Poetry precedes Prose; Ornament precedes Comfort.

66. The Logic of Signs is a higher development of the Logic of Feeling, but its processes are similar. The differences do not spring from the laws of neural grouping, but from the groups that are grouped. Sensations are groups of neural tremors; perceptions are groups of sensations; therefore Perception may be styled *construction in the sphere of Sense.* Intuitions are perceptions of relations, — ideal observation. Conceptions are groups of intuitions symbolized in words. Conception therefore may be styled *construction in the sphere of symbols.*

But symbols are representatives of values; it is only by their possible reduction to Reals — i. e. to feelings — that their employment can be justified. A bank-note is a symbol representing so much gold, which in turn represents so much food or labor. But it is always assumed that the bank is solvent, and that gold is a current article of exchange. A forged note, or a note issued by an insolvent bank, may pass from hand to hand, but its final object is not accomplished. Thus all our reasonings by means of symbols proceed on the assumption that the symbols can at any time have their values assigned, and that they represent Reals, which will excite feelings. Our perceptions proceed on the assumption that the qualities not felt, but inferred to be coexistent with those now felt, do really coexist as *virtual* feelings, to become *actual* feelings when the object is brought into direct relation with the respective Senses.

67. The Real is that which is felt. An object *is* to us what it is felt or thought by us. Knowledge is virtual Feeling: it is pre-vision of what will be vision, under sensible conditions, because it, or something like it, once was vision. Theory is virtual Experience, reproducing past experiences, and anticipating the effects of real presentation.

Sensation and Intuition always carry Belief. Inference is Expectation, or qualified Belief. We cannot resist belief in a sensation, though we may doubt any of the inferences it awakens. We cannot resist belief in an intuition, though we may doubt whether the relations intuited be real or not. In the act of intuiting, our feeling of security is undisturbed.

The distinction between Observation and Inference is the distinction between the real and ideal, the actual and virtual. But in point of fact pure Observation — i. e. sensation wholly unmingled with Inference — is impossible; it is so by the Laws of Reinstatement. Pure Theory — i. e. logical combination of relations unmingled with related terms — is also impossible.

68. The purpose of Intelligence being to direct our impulses towards their satisfaction, and the purpose of the Intellect being to accomplish this through a wider survey of means and possibilities, we learn how on the one hand all Intelligence must have its final test in Reality, and on the other how the Intellect, which is the highly developed form of Intelligence, has erected *means* into *ends*, and now pursues these proximate ends in oblivion of the ultimate end, and will even substitute fictions in place of facts, abstract types for concrete things. The direct object of the Intellect is not Reality; that, how-

ever, is its ultimate object. The progress of development is an ever-increasing tendency towards more and more remote conceptions and indirect methods, detaching the mind more and more from sensible observation. It may be illustrated by the stages of numerical calculation. Man begins by counting things, grouping *them* visibly. He then learns to count simply the numbers, in the absence of the things, using his fingers and toes for symbols. He then substitutes abstract signs, and Arithmetic begins. From this he passes to Algebra, the signs of which are not only abstract but general; and now he calculates numerical relations, not numbers. From this he passes to the higher calculus of relations of relations.

It is the same with the development of Commerce. Men begin by exchanging things. They pass to the exchange of values. First money, then notes or bills, is the symbol of value. Finally, men simply debit and credit each other, so that immense transactions are affected by means of this equation of equations. The complicated processes of sowing, reaping, collecting, shipping, and delivering a quantity of wheat are condensed into the entry of a few words in a ledger.

69. In consequence of this development of Intellect — i. e. of the interest in remote means substituted for direct ends — man acquires his immense superiority over animals in achieving the final end. It is thus, and thus only, that he is enabled to modify the course of events. It is thus that Sentience becomes Science, facts are condensed into laws, and direct vision is multiplied and magnified by remote pre-vision.

But while insisting on the claim of Intellect to pursue its ideal objects, and to be uncontrolled in its prosecution of even the remotest research, we must never forget that its ideal ends are only sanctified by the final end, — by that correspondence with Reality which was its starting-point and must be its goal. No speculation, however wide of actual experience, can be valueless, if, in any way, it enlarge our vision of the Real, but this is its final test. If with mighty span of wing it soar above the sphere of the Real, it must not keep hovering there, but must at some point re-enter the sphere. Ideal construction is unlimited in freedom, on the understanding that it must always submit to real verification, and have values assigned to its symbols.

70. Thus the human Intellect emerges from animal Intelligence, and develops a vast independent creation, having the whole Cosmos and Humanity for its material. Concurrently with this, the Moral Intelligence develops its system. Both Intellect and Conscience are products of the animal impulses and social impulses acting and reacting. While the Intellect is mainly occupied with the relations of the Cosmos and its History, having the ultimate aim of making these subservient to practical needs, the Conscience or Moral Intelligence is mainly occupied with the relations of Humanity, — human needs and human actions, — having the ultimate aim of conforming our conduct to those relations, harmonizing our impulses with the impulses of others, thus aiding others and gratifying ourselves.

The Intellect, although under sympathetic conditions, — since it depends on others for its activity, and for the means by which the activity may be guided, and since, moreover, its results are achieved for all, — is not so directly sympathetic as the Conscience. Could we suppose a man born with his inherited aptitudes, left solitary on an island, before having had access to any of the stores of knowledge accumulated by the race, he might acquire a rudimentary knowledge of cosmical relations, although without Language, or any accessible store of the experience of others on which to proceed, this would necessarily be little above that of an animal. But of Moral Intelligence there would not be a trace. There cannot be moral relations apart from Society.

71. Hence two noticeable facts: the part played by Sentiment in Philosophy is of immense importance in so far as the problems involve elements of social relations; but is simply perturbing and obstructive in problems of cosmical relations. We ought not to deny the admission of Sentiment, but we must definitely assign its sphere. A social theory which omitted it would be as defective as a cosmical theory which admitted it. If Evangelical Geology or High Church Chemistry would be absurd, equally so would be an exclusively physical theory of Marriage, or of the filial and parental relation.

72. The Intellect and the Conscience are social functions, and their special manifestations are rigorously determined by Social Statics, — i. e. the state of the Social Organism at the time being, — which they in their turn determine. The Language we think in and the conceptions we employ, the attitude of our minds and the means of investigation, are social products determined by the activities of the Collective Life. The laws of intellectual progress are to be read in History, not in the individual experience. We breathe the social air; since what we think, greatly depends on what others have thought. The paradox of to-day becomes the commonplace of to-morrow. The truths which required many generations to discover and establish are now declared to be innate. Even discovery has its law, and is only an individual product, inasmuch as the individual voice articulates what has been more or less inarticulate in the general thought. The great thinker is the secretary of his age. If his quick-glancing mind outrun the swiftest of his contemporaries, he will not be listened to; the prophet must find disciples. If he outrun the majority of his contempora-

ries, he will have but a small circle of influence, for all originality is estrangement.

Not recognizing the social influence, men seldom appreciate the true point of view in discussions respecting ancient and modern Literature. It is undeniable that Sophocles, Plato, Aristotle, Hipparchus, and Galen were not less splendidly endowed than Shakespeare, Bacon, Newton, Comte, or Helmholtz, — their intellectual lineaments may have been as grandly drawn, but it is absurd to pretend that the products of the ancient and the products of the modern mind are of anything like equal *value.*

73. Some of our Impulses are simply organic activities, others are Instincts. There is no Instinct to breathe, to digest, to secrete, etc., for there never was a time when an alternative action was possible with these organs under their appropriate stimuli, — the actions were necessarily determined in one way only. But food is selected by Instinct; the bird flies, and the mammal walks by Instinct: these actions are tentative, and guided by discerning Feeling. The sexual instinct is obviously an impulse guided by Discernment.

Directly connected with the Nutritive Instinct are three egoistic Impulses, offensive and defensive, which may be characterized as the Aggressive Instincts. The animal must destroy, or it could not feed. A rival threatening to take some of this food rouses Anger, the emotion of a thwarted impulse. The thwarted sexual impulse calls out the same feeling. Derived from this will be in the higher imaginative animals the love of Domination; the desire to make others afraid of, or subservient to us. Where food is abundant, and accessible, there is little development of these tendencies; as may be observed in the herbivora, who rarely fight unprompted by the sexual impulse. Tigers would be sociable were animal food as abundant and accessible as vegetable food. War is the outcome of this tendency. In Trade we see the war spirit animated by the desire for Property.

The so-called instinct of Self-preservation is a fiction. The only impulse at work there is the shrinking from Pain; and this in the matured experience leads to the intelligent act of self-preservation.

As the Aggressive Instinct springs from the Nutritive, so the Sexual Instinct springs from the Reproductive. It is the first of the sympathetic tendencies, the germ of Altruism. Love, which is the social motor, has this origin. Thus modified, the tendency to Domination becomes the love of Approbation; it is the sympathetic form of the egoistic impulse. The love of wife and children extends to relatives and friends, to the tribe, to the nation, to Humanity.

How intimately the social and religious emotions are connected with this primary fact of the mutual dependence of two human beings, and how from it slowly emerge all the marvels of Art and Science, must be exhibited in detail.

REASONED REALISM.

74. Having briefly indicated the Psychological Principles, I will now indicate what is their outcome with respect to the great metaphysical question touching an external reality. It will be argued at length in a separate Problem; but as the publication of this Problem is distant, and as its conclusions will everywhere be implied, I take this opportunity of clearly marking my position.

The doctrine of this work, then, may be called Reasoned Realism. It is distinguished from the Natural Realism, the Hypothetic Realism, and the Symbolical or Transfigured Realism of modern thinkers, no less than from the unhesitating Realism of unreflecting minds. It is a doctrine which endeavors to rectify the natural illusion of Reason when Reason attempts to rectify the supposed illusion of Sense. I call it Realism, because it affirms the reality of what is given in Feeling; and Reasoned Realism, because it justifies that affirmation through an investigation of the grounds and processes of Philosophy, when Philosophy explains the facts given in Feeling.

75. The reality of an external existence, a Not-self, is a fact of Feeling so indissolubly woven into Consciousness, that the very terms in which Idealism seeks to disprove it are themselves derived from it. Now this fact, because it is a fact of Feeling, and ultimate, can neither be got rid of nor explained by interpretation of it into terms of some more general fact. Why then has Philosophy persisted in the attempt to explain it? Simply because Philosophy, being in its very nature Explanation, persists in attempting to explain even the inexplicable; dissatisfied with ultimates, it is prone to ask what is their ultimate? This search for light behind the light is the natural illusion of Reason, the will-o'-wisp of Philosophy; and this can only be rectified by showing what are the grounds and what the limitations of Knowledge.

76. The facts of feeling are directly given. All the phenomena constituting the external reality to us are presented discontinuously; and it is the office of Philosophy so to connect them that their actual continuity be discerned; and we thus not only have the separate feelings, but also a feeling of the relations of these feelings. The Logic of Feeling, which is primary, has to be supplemented by the Logic of Signs, which is derivative. Analysis attempts to display, in symbols, what has been implicit in sensation. But — and this is the point too commonly overlooked — all interpretation must finally be a reduction into terms of Feeling, all the symbols must signify sensations. Feeling is the starting-point

and goal of investigation. All that we can know of the external is what we have felt or might feel.

77. This being the ground, what is the limit of Knowledge? The limit is attained when we have attained what in Algebra is called the "form of a function." In Mathematics a "function" is the quantity which varies when some other quantity varies. When observation of two phenomena discloses that the one — say the density of a gas — varies with another, — say its pressure, — the density is said to be a function of the pressure; when vital activity is observed to be exalted or depressed with increase or decrease of respiration, the activity is said to be a function of the respiration. Such knowledge of a function is valuable, but it is obviously not final. What is still needed is the form of the function, — the manner in which the two quantities are combined. When this is reached the limit is reached. When the law of a series is found, nothing remains to be sought. When we know the *how*, it is idle to ask the *why*. The fact is what it is, and what its factors are: if we know the fact and the factors, to ask for more is to ask *why* $2 \times 2 = 4$. The gas *presses* against the sides of the containing vessel, because the gas is composed of movable molecules dashing about in all directions with various velocities, and the amount of this pressure must of course increase in proportion to the diminution of the space in which these motions take effect, since on every inch of surface there will then be a proportionately greater dashing of molecules. Thus the smaller the vessel becomes, the greater must be the density of the gas contained in it, since the gas fills the vessel; and the greater the density, the greater will be the pressure excited by the gas. Now if it be true that the gas molecules in their movements repel each other inversely as the fifth power of the distance (or, indeed, if any other law of repulsion can be

established), we shall then be in possession of the form of the function, and the final result of analysis will be reached. To go beyond this, and to ask *why* the molecules repel according to this law, is irrational, because travelling beyond the real limits and conditions.

78. Now it may seem a very bold thing to say, but I hope to justify the assertion, that with respect to the world-old debate on the relation of Object and Subject we have not only a knowledge of the function, but of the form of the function; or, to put it in more familiar language, we not only know that an external Not-self exists, — know it with the same assurance that we know an internal Self to exist, — but we also know the manner in which the two are combined in Feeling and Thought.

Fully aware of the paradoxical aspect this statement must present to almost every reader, I only ask him to suspend his judgment on it until he has accompanied me through all the evidence which this work will offer. Having made my statement, I will here say no more, but call attention to the unsatisfactory nature of the position commonly held. The ordinary man believes that the objects he sees, touches, and tastes do veritably exist, and exist *as* they are seen, touched, tasted. They *have* the qualities he feels in them. The philosopher, dissatisfied with the facts directly given in Feeling, though he, no more than the ordinary man, doubts that these qualities *are* felt, endeavors to explain *why* it is that they are so. To explain a fact is to interpret it by its factors, to analyze it into its constituents; which again means to interpret a feeling in terms of feeling. This need for an explanation is exclusively human. No animal explains; he feels, and his action is the direct consequence. But man desires to understand what he feels, in order that he may modify the course of events, by rearranging their separate factors. To do this he must take the complex whole to pieces, and see of what it is composed. The speculative intellect carries out in the remote regions of knowledge, what the practical intellect daily performs in the familiar regions of Practice; it takes the object to pieces.

79. Great and beneficent as the results of this analytic tendency have been, there have also been attendant drawbacks. By cultivating this tendency to look *away* from the given reality, in search of its prior conditions or its presumed factors, men have learned to slight the plain indubitable facts of Feeling, in favor of the obscure and doubtful representations of these facts in Thought, — that is to say, replacing perceptions by conceptions, facts by theories and hypotheses, men have come to distrust the Logic of Feeling, even within its own domain, and to rely on the Logic of Signs, even when it contradicts that of Feeling. Accustomed to attach exclusive importance to symbols irrespective of the realities, they have forgotten that ideas can be valid only as representative of sensations, and symbols can be useful only when capable of interpretation. For what was the starting-point of every theory? An observation. And what is the test of the theory? A reduction of its inferences to sensations. The theory started to explain a fact; the inferences were intended to re-present what would be presented in Feeling, were the *inferred* facts, facts *perceived.* Obviously, therefore, every theory must be a failure which ends in denying, or ignoring, the original fact. Yet this assuredly is the case with the current theories of Perception, idealistic and realistic. The original fact given to all, is that of an external reality present in Feeling; the fact that a Not-self exists, that objects affect us by their presence, and have *qualities* variously felt by us, — this, I say, may possibly be explained, interpreted in other terms of Feeling, and classed with other

facts, but cannot be ignored, or denied, without violation of first principles.

80. Yet this is done by metaphysicians under various forms. What they have to explain is not the fact which is ultimate, but the factors of the fact, i. e. the indirect conditions of this direct reality, the invisible constituents, objective and subjective, of this visible phenomenon. That is to say, to exhibit in analysis what was given in a synthesis ; to reach if possible the "form of the function." How have they proceeded on this quest ? From of old they made the false step of proclaiming the natural illusion of Sense ; founded on a precipitate conclusion from practical mistakes, this notion of the Senses as sources of deception led to the conclusion that Reason was the only ground of security. If Sense deceived us, Reason corrected the false reports. Reason henceforward became authoritative, final. This, which may in turn be called the natural illusion of Reason, can only be dispelled by a thorough investigation of the genesis of Reason ; and since that genesis exhibits it in the light of a derivative form the primary facts of Feeling, — the virtual representation of what would be actual presentation, — we cannot hesitate to assign a lower validity to its symbolical constructions than to the primary facts which those constructions render intelligible. It is surely obvious that no theory of Perception can have the certainty that belongs to the Perception itself ; no explanation of a conclusion can be valid which ignores the very facts concluded, *shut up* in the starting-point.

81. It was to explain the perception of an external reality that Philosophy started on its quest. The Idealist schools find the explanation to be, — that there is really nothing to explain except the illusion that an external reality exists. The Realist schools, while admitting that an external reality veritably exists, declare that it can

never be known by us *as* it exists, but only under some form in which *we* clothe it; there is, therefore, still a touch of the old illusion lingering in it, and our surest knowledge is after all phantasmal.

82. The Reasoned Realism of this work denies altogether the assumed distinction between noumenon and phenomenon, — except as a convenient artifice of classification by which the *unknowable otherness of relations* is distinguished from the *knowable relations:* that is to say, noumena standing for things in their relations to other forms of Sentience (if there are such) than our own; and phenomena standing for things in any conceivable relations to Sentience like our own. Getting rid of the *Ding an sich,* or noumenon, as a phantasm that has no existence for us, consequently cannot come within our perceptions, nor within any theory of perception, and is therefore altogether banished from the sphere of Knowledge, we are led through our psychological analysis back to the synthetic starting-point, — namely, that the external world exists, and *among* the modes of its existence is the one we perceive. Rationally interpreted, we may accept the ordinary belief that color is a quality of the object seen, that heat is in the fire, roughness is in the rough surface, etc.; and at the same time we may accept the philosopher's assertion, that all these qualities in objects are feelings in us. Psychogeny will show us that color, heat, etc., are, from one point of view, both in the objects and in us; from another point of view, they are in neither.

83. Let me explain. When first men began to analyze their perceptions, they were so greatly impressed by the importance of the subjective aspect, and the dependence of Feeling on the state of the sentient organism, the same object producing such various sensations at different times, that they reversed their primary and in-

stinctive judgment, and instead of saying, "qualities belong to objects," they now said, "it is we who invest objects with the qualities of our feelings." From that time the subjective aspect has so predominated that Psychology has almost lost its hold of the objective world; and in many treatises resembles an Astronomy which should record the laws of planetary movement, ignoring the existence of planets and perturbations; or a Biology which should explain Life by processes of composition and decomposition, denying that there were any organisms in relation to a medium to manifest these.

84. Kant boldly carried out this reversal of the primary judgment of Feeling. The external phenomena were to him only "objects" in virtue of the Mental Forms imposed on the noumenon. I do not discuss the question here; but only say that the doctrine of this work stands by the primary judgment of Feeling, and is a Reasoned Realism because it does so. The external world must be at first simply a confused chaos, without shape or order, when reflected in a Sentience which has not acquired shaping reactions. But as the sentient Organism develops, the external Order emerges; not because this Order is the creation of the Organism, *stamped upon* the chaos, but because this Order is *assimilated* by the Organism, — selected, according to its shaping reactions, from the larger Order of the Real. The undifferentiated animal substance slowly develops into highly differentiated tissues and organs, through the action on it of the external agencies, which leave their traces in a modified structure and capability of reacting: the pulpy mass of the brain acquires, through manifold experiences, a structure more and more variously definite, with corresponding reactions; and as Feeling becomes differentiated and defined, Qualities arise in the Felt. It is thus that the nebula of the external is condensed into objective phenomena, and

the confused irradiation of Sensibility is grouped into feelings.

85. Is this figured Cosmos figured in Feeling through the *adaptation* of the sentient organism to the external Real, or is it simply a *subjective construction* — the figuration of Sensibility — which we illusively project outwards and receive back again in reflection? Do we see objects colored because objects colorably affect the retina? or do we see them colored because the retina casts its tints upon them? Do we acquire our modes of sentient reaction through modifications impressed by the actions of the external? or do we bring with us, and from another source, the Mental Forms in which the unshaped external takes shape?

These different statements of the same fundamental problem suggest somewhat different answers. Between Realism and Idealism, I should say that the question must be rendered more definite by a preliminary settlement as to whether we ask a question of Psychogeny or a question of Psychology. If it is the genesis of our modes of sentient reaction, and their relation to the external, which we consider, then the answer will take the realistic form; since Psychogeny, tracing the evolution of Sensibility in the organic world, must conclude that it is the External Order which *determines* the Internal Order, by determining the organic structure of which Sensibility is the property: the evolution of perceptions, instincts, volitions, conceptions, is through successive adaptations of the successively modified structure; precisely as the evolution of all the vital phenomena is through successive adaptations.* But if the question be not one of genesis, if it assume the existence of the organized structure with its developed aptitudes, the answer will be a sort of compromise between the realistic and idealistic

* This has been shown in a masterly manner by Mr. Herbert Spencer.

answers. Psychology accepting the developed Organism, as one of the factors in the fact of Perception, estimates the influence of this co-operant, and concludes that since the Organism necessarily reacts according to its modes, it may be said to color objects, although this mode of reaction is itself a mode *originally* due to the action of objects. It is Light which fashions the retina to luminous responses. Not that the external Real which stimulates the retina can be supposed to be itself luminous: it is only one factor of the luminous product. Nor can the retina, apart from stimulation, be luminous: it also is only one factor. But Light — the Object — *is* both factors: thus the object is necessarily object-subject; and subject is equally subject-object. I do not agree with those realists who conceive the thing represented in Perception, in the way mathematicians regard an algebraic function as represented by a curve, — object and subject forming a Dualism having something of a pre-established harmony, but no real union. I would rather liken the Thing represented in Perception, to the weight of the atmosphere represented by the height of the mercury in the barometer; while the differences between weight and height, and between atmosphere and mercury, are wide, both rest on a common identity of pressure. The pressure of the atmosphere *is* the pressure exerted on the mercurial column, and the barometrical expression of this pressure is, in one sense, no more *like* the object expressed, than a feeling is like the vibrations it expresses; yet, in another sense, the barometrical expression *is* what it expresses, and the feeling is what it expresses.

86. It seems to me a grave objection to Idealism that there is no possibility of separating Object from Subject, or Subject from Object, in Feeling, but only in Reflection; and Reflection is not primary, but derivative. Nay, even here it soon appears that the distinction is simply that of

aspects. We declare the existence of a Real apart from Feeling, and of events linked together by other ties than those of our modes of conceiving them; because if we assume such an existence it enables us to explain the phenomena which agree with, and the phenomena which contradict our previsions. Granting this assumption to see what are its consequences, we find that, having through successive adaptations acquired an order in our feelings corresponding with the order in things, we can from it predict what will be the order of events on a future occasion; and this prediction is verified, not simply in respect of the events following the order *we* have prefigured, but the order which will appear the same to others who have no such prefiguration of it, and cannot therefore be supposed to have introduced their subjective constructions into it. A chemist, suppose, has learned the order of events by which salts are produced. He can produce a salt where there is no salt. If his conception of the real order were a subjective construction without objective correspondence, he could only *see* what he had *foreseen*, and the salt would inevitably appear to him. But on proceeding to realize his conception he sometimes stumbles on a contradiction: no salt is produced: he sees what he had not foreseen. Why? Because he had assumed that the order of real events would be that of his ideal scheme; whereas in reality there has been some other order, some events not included in his construction, and he has to seek these out, reform his construction, and then proceed to verify it when thus reformed.

87. But while Idealism tries to get rid of the primary fact that Not-self is the correlative of Self, and in no wise a product or *projection* of Self, but a given factor in Consciousness, having the same validity as Self, all the schemes of Realism with which I am familiar err on the side of neglecting the one factor or the other.

The ordinary man, undisturbed by philosophic speculation, accepts a Dualism of Mind and Matter, and imagines the External Order to be something wholly independent of the Internal Order, imagines Things to exist precisely *as* they are felt and thought, even when there is no sentient subject to feel and think them. But the philosophic realist also more or less avowedly accepts a Dualism; since, although he may reject the crude distinction of Mind and Matter, he keeps to the wide distinction of Motion and Feeling, with its correlative distinction of Object and Subject, as two parallel existences which can never approach each other, much less unite. The Subject is conceived under the likeness of a kaleidoscope; every external force will disturb its arrangement of colors, and the rearrangement will accurately represent the amount and direction of the external force, but will have no other similarity or point of community with it. In this view our perceptions are symbols of the external reals, but have no more *likeness* to the reals, no more community of kind, than a numerical figure has to the figures of the numbered objects.

88. This view has advocates so eminent that I must decline the discussion of it until the fitting occasion arrives for treating it exhaustively. Here, where I am avowedly indicating my own position, and not endeavoring to prove it, the statement must suffice that I regard the Subject in no such alienation from the Object; and regard Perception as the assimilation of the Object by the Subject, in the same way that Nutrition is the assimilation of the Medium by the Organism. Out of the general web of Existence certain threads may be detached and rewoven into a special group, — the Subject, — and this sentient group will in so far be different from the larger group, — the Object; but whatever different arrangement the threads may take on, they are always

threads of the original web, they are not different threads. The elements of the sentient Organism are the elements detached from the larger group; the motions of the sentient Organism are the motions of these elements. We do not suppose that when what is called the physical motions of molecules are grouped into what is called the chemical actions, and surprisingly novel phenomena emerge, there has been anything essentially superadded to the primitive molecules and their forces. Nor do biologists now suppose that when physical and chemical actions are specially grouped and vital phenomena emerge, anything essential has been superadded to the primitive threads of objective existence. The chemical phenomenon is new, the vital phenomenon is new; but the novelty is one of special grouping of the old material and the old energy. In like manner, when the psychical phenomenon emerges from the vital, and the social phenomenon from the psychical, there is a regrouping, not the introduction of new material, above all, not a casting away of the old. The Subject is inseparable from the Object, in any real sense; is only separable ideally. As the flower which comes into existence through the action of the sun incorporates the energy of the sun, and grows by what it takes from the sun, so the sentient Organism incorporates the energy of the External, and *re*produces all that produced it.

89. To those who have accepted the view of Life being an emergent, not due to a *conflict* between the external and internal, but to their *co-operation*, the extension of the view to Perception lies near at hand. To those who have accepted the view of Mind drawing material from the Social Medium, and who admit that the human being lives, feels, and thinks by the continual assimilation of such material, the following question may be submitted: When the mind perceives any social fact, and apprehends

its social significance, is the fact real, or not? Let the fact be a religious service performed in a cathedral, or a political service performed in a legislative assembly. The sensible phenomena are of course perceived through sensible channels, and are interpreted with more or less accuracy according to the registered experiences of the observer; precisely as any cosmical fact will be perceived and interpreted. In both cases there is a synthesis of sensible impressions, feelings reproducing former feelings; and if these are interpreted, it is by an ideal construction which is determined by previous constructions. By an animal, or a stranger, the sensible phenomena which the religious service presents would be very differently interpreted; but the sensible phenomena presented in any cosmical process would also be differently interpreted by them; since interpretation means mental assimilation, the significance of the phenomena must depend upon the pre-perceptions and pre-conceptions which they arouse. Nevertheless, wide as the gap may be between the interpretation of the savage and the interpretation of the citizen, the reality of the religious service is unaffected: it is to each what they *feel* it to be, and it is to each what they *think* it to be; in other words, they have been sensibly impressed by certain reals, and have interpreted these impressions by means of certain symbols. From these subjective differences it has been concluded that there is an objective existence independent of all, and *unlike* each; I hold, on the contrary, that the objective existence *is* to each what it is felt to be.

We have already (§ 25) briefly indicated what must hereafter be exhibited in detail, that whatever is *felt* is necessarily real, since Reality and Feeling are correlative. Feeling only arises in the sensible excitation of the Organism by something acting on it, whereas whatever is *thought*, conceived, is necessarily symbolical, since conceptions are not perceptions but symbols: they are not the sensations themselves in a synthesis, but general signs indicating such synthesis; as algebraic letters are not the numbers and magnitudes themselves, but symbols of their relations. This, which is obvious enough in the case of general conceptions, — Life, Cause, Nation, Virtue, etc., — is perhaps less obvious yet equally demonstrable in the case of less general conceptions, — Flower, Horse, River, etc., which are markedly distinguishable from the perceptions of a Flower, a Horse, or a River, which are always syntheses of feelings, and are *real* because both the elements (the sensations) and the synthesis are the actual and direct products of the external and internal factors; whereas the conceptions formed out of these perceptions, although they have only validity in so far as they accurately represent real syntheses, are in themselves indirect products, mere symbols. The conception of Virtue, for example, is altogether unlike the concrete actions which it signifies; unlike in its elements, unlike in its synthesis. It is not a real, i. e. an external agent capable of exciting a corresponding perception, but an abstraction, a symbol expressing the many feelings which the concrete actions are capable of producing; and is comparable to the algebraic symbols, which, though utterly unlike the quantities they represent, do nevertheless stand for those quantities, and are operated on with equal facility. In some of our conceptions and in some of our pictorial symbols, there is a sensible suggestion of likeness between the sign and the thing signified; in the conception of Flower — or in the symbol of a Lion representing the kingly attributes of a Chief — there can be traced some perceptive suggestion. But in other conceptions and symbols no resemblance, no perceptive suggestion, is traceable; if there were originally a suggestion, it has long since faded from the view; and in all cases the symbol is constructed out of different elements in different ways, so that it is really unlike what it stands for, is different from what it signifies.

This contrast between Conception and Perception, between the Symbolical and the Real, which is a fundamental point in Psychology, renders intelligible what was said (§ 63) respecting the Ideal World absorbing the universe in a Transfiguration; and at the same time marks my dissent from the theory of Transfigured Realism, upheld by Helmholtz and Spencer; for that theory professes to be a theory of Perception, and declares Perception to be symbolical; whereas, according to the principles here expounded, Perception being the resultant of the two factors, internal and external, the conclusion deduced is that the object thus felt exists precisely *as* it is felt; existing for us only in Feeling, its reality is what we feel. The great thinkers whom I am here opposing fully admit the premises of this conclusion, with this reservation: they hold that since the internal factor is a necessary co-operant, it must alter by its co-operation the character of the external, and the product of the two will be unlike either. Having for many years maintained this position, I am not insensible to its significance. I shall endeavor, however, to reconcile the differences, and to show that Perception, because it is a resultant, not a symbol, does not alter the Real: on the contrary, an object only *is* to us what we feel it to be, — it exists in that relation. This does not, of course, exclude the possibility of the external factor having *another* existence in relation to *other* factors; all that can legitimately be affirmed is that this particular thing in this particular relation is what it is in this relation, i. e. what it is felt to be. What we mean by saying that a thing is real simply amounts to this: it will always in such or such relations have such or such modes of existence, and in all similar relations similar modes.

This conclusion is as absolute as that two multiplied by two will always be four, and that two multiplied by three will always be six.

This question of the reality of an external world will have to be treated at length in a separate problem; I here indicate simply the principal lines of the conclusion to which I have been led. Neither crude Realism nor any form of Idealism satisfies all the conditions of the problem. The world conceived by us, the world in Thought, is demonstrably not a picture of the Existence lying outside of us and unrelated to us: it is a Transfiguration effected by the ideal construction of real presentations in Feeling. Were this External, such as we conceive it, existing objectively, Science would not have been in travail for centuries; the objective existence would have been plain to Sense, needing no Science to make its order plain. On the other hand, were this External a purely subjective creation, the projection of an ideal order, it would have needed no study to understand it, for it would have spontaneously unfolded its mysteries before our gaze. The necessity of long-continued observation and reasoning, the necessity of analytical operations to make clear the sequences of observed events, the changes in our knowledge, and the slow evolution of our conception of the External Order, disprove both Realism and Idealism. The psychological facts that Existence is directly perceived and indirectly conceived, that what is felt is real, and what is thought is symbolical of what is felt, suffice to justify the theory of Reasoned Realism.

90. No little confusion arises from an almost inevitable ambiguity. We apply the term Object to the Not-self. This Not-self may be either the objective aspect of the world felt and thought, i. e. of the External in actual and virtual relation to Sentience; or the universe of existence,

conceived in its totality, including that smaller section of it which is grouped by a Subject. When we say that there is identity of Object and Subject, the meaning ought to be that in respect of Existence in its relation to Consciousness, Object and Subject may abstractedly be considered under different aspects, but they are one and the same phenomenon.

> "Nichts ist drinnen, Nichts ist draussen,
> Denn was innen, das ist aussen,
> So ergreifet ohne Säumniss,
> Heilig öffentlich Geheimniss."

But this can no longer be said of the Universe considered as the totality of Existence, under which aspect the Object is not the *other side* of the Subject, but the *larger circle* which includes it. This is, however, a topic which must be discussed hereafter.

Reasoned Realism not only justifies the primary judgment of Feeling, but gets rid of the notion that because Knowledge is necessarily relative therefore it cannot be real. I hope to show that instead of invoking an Unknowable as the dark Dynamis to which all researches point, — instead of concluding that knowledge of things as they are is impossible, and that our most certain results are only symbols of an unknown reality, — the conclusion will be, that although the region of the Unknowable may be infinite, within the region of the Knowable we do know things as they are, know them absolutely, comprehensively, — in any rational sense to which the term Knowledge ever was applied.

This chapter may be fitly closed with the words of Auguste Comte : "Le but le plus difficile et le plus important de notre existence intellectuelle consiste à transformer le cerveau humain en un miroir exact de l'ordre extérieur. C'est seulement ainsi qu'elle peut devenir la source directe de notre unité totale, en liant la vie affective et la vie active à leur commune destination. La possibilité d'une telle transformation repose sur la part nécessaire de l'ordre extérieur dans notre propre exercice mental, dont il fournit toujours les premiers matériaux. Outre cette alimentation élémentaire, il y influe aussi comme stimulant, et même comme régulateur, ainsi qu'envers toutes les autres fonctions vitales, végétatives ou animales." *

* *Politique Positive,* II. 382.

PROBLEM I.

THE LIMITATIONS OF KNOWLEDGE.

"It is the very essence of Philosophy to rest upon the foundation of common perceptions, and by reasoning from these to account for phenomena."

PROF. CHALLIS, *Philosophical Magazine*, XXVI. 285.

"Alles ist in der Empfindung und, wenn man will, Alles was im geistigen Bewusstsein und in der Vernunft hervortritt, hat seine Quelle und Ursprung in denselben; denn Quelle und Ursprung heisst nichts anders als die Erste unmittelbarste Weise in der etwas erscheint."

HEGEL, *Encyklopædie*, § 400.

THE LIMITATIONS OF KNOWLEDGE.

CHAPTER I.

THE PRINCIPLE OF RELATIVITY.

1. HODGE, who has never left his native village, knows little of this wondrous planet, and less of the wondrous universe of planets; yet something of it he does know, and this knowledge is real, if narrow, nor would it be made more real by a wider horizon. The cattle grazing in the meadow, the pigs foraging through the quiet street, the apple-blossoms brightening the orchard, the rooks cawing among the squire's elms, the children at his hearth, the neighbors in the parlor of the *King's Arms*, the parson, the doctor, the squire, — these, and the other objects of his world, are realities, not phantasms; nor are Hodge's affections and duties illusions. His world is bounded by a not very distant horizon. Visitors passing through his village now and then bring news from the larger towns. Newspapers carry to him murmurs of the far-off roar of things. These tell him that *his* world is not the whole world; and the death of those dear to him tells dimly of a world of mystery surrounding all he knows. But these intimations of a larger life do but intensify the reality of his village life.

Hodge has a brother, who early left home, travelled far, learned something of other villages, cities, continents; passed into strange lands where alien faces and unfamiliar voices obtruded on his notice. His conception of the world widened. The details of external nature acquired new significance for him. Things passed from the commonplace into the grandiose. The sun no longer pleasantly warmed, it scorched; the wind became a whirlwind; the rain a deluge; woods were forests, hills mountains, cats tigers. In the moral world the changes were equally great. That which in one place was duty, in another place was sin, in a third was indifferent; what inspired honor here was held as infamy elsewhere. Yet under all these varieties there came to him no deepened sense of reality; *more* relations of things were learned, but Life still remained at once the old revelation and the old mystery.

Hodge is the common man; his brother a philosopher. The parochial conception of the world formed from the experience of the one is different from the provincial conception of the other; but neither conception embraces the whole Universe, though both conceptions are real, and relatively true.

2. The principle of the Relativity of Knowledge, which is indicated in these sentences, is sometimes resisted on the ground of its leading to universal scepticism. The fact, however, is otherwise, and may be shown to be so by the teachings of Psychology and the examples of History. The certainty of knowledge is not affected by its circumscription. The principle of Relativity furnishes a Criterium which is coextensive with the domain of intelligence. The opposing principle is productive of scepticism, because it has no Criterium. It remains fluctuating, because its data are personal, and cannot be communicated. Those who, affecting to despise the certainty attainable through Science, because it can never transcend the relative sphere, yearn for a knowledge which is not relative, cheat themselves with phrases; and were it not so, we might still fall back on the position that relative

knowledge is all we need. The aim of Science is prevision, — the guidance and regulation of action. Our ancestors guided their course by the stars, without knowing much about the stars; the ascertainment of a few relative positions sufficed. Their successors constructed an elaborate science of Astronomy without inquiring into the nature of gravity, contented with the ascertainment of its law. And so throughout. What is positive may be absolutely certain and available, although it is but a small section of the circle swept by Speculation.

3. The world is to each man as it affects him; to each a different world. Fifty spectators see fifty different rainbows in the sky, and all believe they see the same one. Nor is this unanimity delusive; for "the same" here means the similarity in their states of consciousness. Whether we affirm the objective existence of something distinct from the affection of consciousness, or affirm that this object is simply a reflection from consciousness, in either case we declare that the objective world is to each man the sum of his visionary experience, — an existence bounded on all sides by what he feels and thinks, — a form shaped by the reactions of his organism. The world is the sum total of phenomena, and *phenomena are affections of consciousness with external signs.*

4. We may for the present set aside the questions whether there is one Existence (Matter), and another Existence in every way contrasted with it (Mind); or only one Existence, Matter *or* Mind; enough if we recognize the fact that among phenomena there are two classes broadly distinguishable, — the material and the psychical. These classes require corresponding names, even should we finally regard them as only different aspects of a common reality, and with Fechner regard material and psychical as the convex and concave of the same curve.*

* FECHNER, *Zendavesta*, II. 340. 1851.

At the outset, therefore, we declare the limitations of Research to be fixed by the natural limits of Consciousness. A truism, no doubt, but not to be despised. We can determine what problems are inaccessible (as distinguished from those which are simply unapproached) by ascertaining the conditions under which objects do affect, or could affect us; and we can determine what elements in every problem are unapproachable, by ascertaining if they lie outside the sphere of Experience .

Nor would this position be disputed, in its first clause at least, even by those who believe in the possibility of a knowledge of things transcending Experience; for they claim their *à priori* organ as a "fact of consciousness"; and they affirm that because it is *à priori* its verdicts have a higher validity than those of inductive reasoning. In presence of such a school we must be careful not to affix limits to the reach of Investigation, which this school would reject. It would be absurd to exclude an organ so important as that named Intellectual Intuition (or its equivalent fund of Innate Ideas, Fundamental Truths, *à priori* Forms of Thought), unless we could show either that this faculty does not exist, or, granting its existence, that its products must be so removed from all Verification as to be of no avail in Research. The former alternative — that no such faculty exists — cannot be demonstrated; since its assumed range of operation lies beyond the sphere of demonstration ; the latter alternative — that it lies beyond the sphere of Verification — is implied in the very statement of its pretensions. Philosophy, therefore, is not called upon to take any account of it, since for all the purposes of Research it is non-existent.* It is a musician playing on a violin without

* Hegel sarcastically says of this Intellectual Intuition : "Es ist die bequemste Manier die Erkenntniss darauf zu setzen — auf das was einem einfällt." — *Gesch. d. Phil.*, III. 655.

strings, in the halls of a castle in the air. Fancy may endow this musician with superhuman skill, since Fancy has created him; but the melodies are too subtle for human ears.

5. Rejecting, as I think we must, the notion of a possible source of Knowledge transcending Experience, we may admit that the notion has had some justification in the great imperfection of the psychological analysis put forward by the Sensational School. Striking as have been the merits of that school, which explain its survival in the face of violent opposition and virulent criticism, and its gradual extension over the convictions even of opponents, these merits have not sufficed to displace altogether the doctrine of its opponents; and very eminent thinkers still reject with scorn the conception of Knowledge being limited by Experience. This implies one of two things: either the doctrine itself is imperfect, or there is a radical imperfection in the statement of its principles and canons. I think both causes operate in keeping up the fundamental discordance between the empirical and metempirical schools. Let us first glance at the difficulties which beset not only the investigation but the exposition of metaphysical questions, difficulties not found in science.

6. Suppose we have to ascertain the changes in Sensibility produced by some modification of a nerve-centre, or the introduction of some poison into the blood. Complex as the question is (how complex only those can appreciate who have made the experiment), it is at any rate free from doubts overhanging the very instruments we employ, and the laws by which the effects are measured. If in physical research we use a thermometer, or a thermo-electric pile, we have no need to pause and investigate the theory of the instrument, or to prove that its indications are quantitatively exact. We accept from

the chemist the reagents we employ, and the ascertained laws of their properties. We never need argue respecting the accuracy of chronometer or hygrometer. All the primary physical facts are ready to hand, and have not now first to be established. Quite otherwise is it with Metaphysics. There every problem, besides its own obscurities, is overshadowed by the uncertainties hovering round its data. We cannot, for instance, accept Force as the cause of motion unless Cause and Motion have already been clearly defined; and they are as obscure as the Force they are employed to render intelligible. We cannot stir a step in the exposition of the relation of Object and Subject without presupposing to be already settled fundamental points of Psychology which are still under discussion. No explanation can be given of Matter which does not involve a conception of Force. Thus the inter-connections which are potent aids in physical inquiry are so many obstacles in metaphysical research.

7. Over and above these difficulties there is the special difficulty arising from the misleading influence of language. The sciences have each their technical terms, terms which, however arbitrary, are exact, terms which mean always the same thing, and not various things. Exaggerated as Condillac's notion was of Science being simply *une langue bien faite*,* — a notion which reappears in the writings of those who hold that Mathematics is founded solely on its definitions (as if the objective relations thus defined were not real), — there is an important truth in it; and no one can doubt that the superior exactness of Mathematics would vanish if the language in which its operations are expressed were tainted with the laxity so common in Metaphysics. No equations could be successfully treated if 5 were sometimes the

* CONDILLAC, *Langue des Calculs*, p. 7.

symbol of 4 + 1, sometimes of 4 + 3, and sometimes 2 + 1. Yet such variation in the values is trifling compared with the variation in many metaphysical terms. Probably no two men mean precisely the same thing by the word Sensation, or Thought, or Cause, or Force. If these terms agree pretty well in their *denotations*, they differ greatly in their *connotations*. Thus the proposition that thought is a transformed sensation, may appear preposterous, or indisputable, according to the meaning assigned to the terms. We often hear a dispute dismissed as "a dispute about terms." In Metaphysics, a dispute about terms is frequently the whole of the question: that once settled, Logic takes its course, and all differences disappear. I have already compared a metaphysician to the algebraist who does not assign arithmetical values to his symbols; and it is obvious that the chief difficulty in Metaphysics, as in Algebra, is finding the value of the unknown quantity which will satisfy the equation.

8. The great dispute respecting the origin of knowledge is a very striking example of this laxity in the use of terms; and as the question is fundamental, we must pause here to consider it with some attention. Each school has seized one aspect of the truth; and a reconciliation may be effected if we can point out the common ground of agreement, and their points of divergence. In attempting such a reconciliation I am not unaware of the position which a mediator between contending schools must necessarily seem to occupy; mediation always carries with it an air of superiority which is resented by both the antagonists; nor will any disclaimer of such an assumption allay the irritation. On the other hand, the first lesson in controversy is to unlearn our native tendency to treat our adversaries as fools. If we learn this lesson, and try to seize the aspect of the truth

which presents itself to their minds, we may find that this aspect which represents their experience also represents our own, and that the points of difference are reducible to differences in the data, leading to errors of interpretation.

CHAPTER II.

THE SENSATIONAL AND À PRIORI HYPOTHESES.

9. THE school of Locke maintains that "there is nothing in the Intellect which was not previously in Sense; all the differences between our thoughts and our sensations are due, not to differences of origin, but to differences of combination." The rival school of Leibnitz says: "Besides the *materials* furnished by Sense there must be taken into account the *forms* furnished by the Intellect."

So far the two schools are but little opposed. The point of separation is in the assumption of a *special* source of knowledge in the *Intellectus ipse,* — an entity, or faculty, which has no community with Sense, and which not only furnishes Sense with *forms,* but also furnishes *material,* namely, certain Innate Ideas, or Fundamental Truths, which relate to existences *beyond* the range of Sense.

Instead of simplifying the question by thus stating their common ground, and their point of separation, the two schools have been fighting on the supposition that the question was, "Is there *anything* in the Intellect which cannot be traced to Sense?" Such a question could not be answered unless a distinct understanding of its terms was arrived at. This was not done. The answers were consequently acceptable, or absurd, according to the meanings each school assigned to the terms.

10. The sensational hypothesis is acceptable if by Sense we understand *Sensibility and its laws of operation.* This, indeed, which includes all the Biostatical and Biodynam-

ical conditions, external and internal, is an extension of the term, and obliterates the very distinction insisted on by the other school; but since it includes all psychical phenomena under the rubric of Sensibility, it enables psychological analysis to be consistent and exhaustive. Although such was obviously the dim meaning of the sensational school, one must admit that their language very imperfectly expressed it, and to some extent justified their adversaries in supposing them to mean by Sense simply the Five Senses; and *thus* interpreted, the reduction of all knowledge to a sensuous origin is absurd.

11. The hypothesis of the *à priori* school is acceptable if by Intellect be meant the *process* by which many different sensations are grouped together, thus forming products unlike any of the several components; and since this process of grouping may be extended from the elements to the groups, the products will, after successive evolutions, be so far removed from all resemblance to the original sensations as to appear due to a different source. This is only another and a better way of expressing the sensational doctrine. It demarcates the process of grouping from the elements grouped; the operation from the symbols: a convenient demarcation, but liable to mislead the unwary into the belief that the separation is real, and that Intellect is a special faculty having no community with Sensibility and its laws. Once detached from Sensibility, it is easily imagined to be capable of operating on symbols that have no sensible values; transcending the range of Sensibility, it can deal with transcendentals, as Sense deals with sensibles.

The error of both schools will be more fully exemplified when, in a future problem, we come to examine the relations of Feeling and Thought, and see reason to conclude that Sense and Intellect so thoroughly interpenetrate each other that it is no less impossible to conceive

Sensation which does not embody the *logical* processes supposed to be peculiar to Thought, than to conceive Thought which does not embody the *neural* processes specially named Feeling. Meanwhile let us remark that both schools fall into the error of confounding a question of Psychogeny with a question of Psychology, — an error similar to that frequently occurring in Biology, where questions of Anatomy are confounded with questions of Morphology. Thus the point at issue is, what is the *genesis* of mental products, their origin and evolution? Instead of retracing this genesis by analysis, the debaters fix their attention on the full-statured mind,— or at any rate on some stage far removed from the embryonic, — and the *constituent forms* there discovered are accepted as *initial phases:* the results which have been evolved through successive experiences are accepted as the primary conditions of all Experience; the inductions are made to precede the particulars from which they were generalized.

12. Before entering on an examination of this question it may be well to state here briefly the leading conclusions which will guide us throughout our criticism of the two schools. The main question must remain nebulous so long as we are without a precise definition of Experience. The term is very variously and very laxly used. I have defined it "the Registration of Feeling." And what is Feeling? It is the reaction of the sentient Organism under stimulus. Observe, it is not the reaction of an organ, but of the Organism, — a most important distinction, and rarely recognized. This reaction is a resultant of two factors, — one factor being the Organism and the other being the Stimulus. We are not to accept every response of an organ as a feeling; nor every feeling as an experience. The secretion of a gland is a response physiologically similar to the response of the eye or ear; but it is not a feeling, although entering as an element into the mass of

Systemic Sensation. Nor will the response of a sensory organ, even when a feeling (through its combination with other sentient responses), be an *experience,* unless it be *registered* in a modification of structure, and thus be *revivable,* because a statical condition is requisite for a dynamical manifestation. Rigorously speaking, of course there is no body that can be acted on without being modified: every sunbeam that beats against the wall alters the structure of that wall; every breath of air that cools the brow alters the state of the organism. But such minute alterations are inappreciable for the most part by any means in our possession, and are not here taken into account, because, being annulled by subsequent alterations, they do not become *registered* in the structure. We see many sights, read many books, hear many wise remarks, but, although each of these has insensibly affected us, changed our mental structure, so that "we are a part of all that we have met," yet the registered result, the *residuum,* has perhaps been very small. While therefore no excitation of Feeling is really without some corresponding modification of Structure, it is only the excitations which produce permanent modifications that can be included under Experience. A feeling passed away, and incapable of revival, would never be called an experience by any strict writer. But the feelings registered are psycho-statical elements, so that henceforward when the Organism is stimulated it must react along these lines, and the product will be a feeling more or less resembling the feeling formerly excited. The two biological principles — that an Organism is evolved through successive modifications, each of which is a reaction on stimulus, and that the dynamical effect is necessarily determined by its statical conditions, the function by the organ — assure us that what the Organism is at any stage determines what will be the kind of sentient reactions it is capable of.

Such being our view of Experience, the conclusion lies near at hand that every Organism must bring with it, involved in its structure, the statical conditions of those dynamical results traceable in all Perception, Judgment, Instinct, etc. In other words, the Laws of Thought, or, more accurately, the Mental Forms, are connate, and so far *à priori*. But they are as much part and parcel of Experience as any individual perception, judgment, or acquired ability can be. All that can be said to difference them is that, for the most part, they are parts of the Experience of ancestors, — the feelings registered in modifications of structure which have been transmitted from parent to child, so that

> "All experience past became
> Consolidate in mind and frame."

How much of any one mental manifestation is due to ancestral feelings registered in the modified structure inherited, and how much is due to the individual feelings and their modifications acquired through the direct relation of the Organism to its stimuli, cannot accurately be determined. It is like the wealth which a merchant acquires through his own efforts, by employing the accumulated results of the efforts of previous generations. But when the argument turns solely on the empirical or metempirical origin of knowledge, there is no need to determine this; if we can show that all our knowledge arises from, and is limited to, the reactions of the Organism under stimulus, the question reduces itself to the point whether over and above the Organism known as a complex of physical, chemical, and vital conditions, there is also a Spiritual Organism interfused through this, and bringing spiritual properties to co-operate with vital properties. The vital Organism we believe to have been evolved through a succession of modifications due to its adaptations to the external Medium; consequently, we believe all its functions or manifestations to have been evolved through Experience. If, however, the spiritualist hypothesis be accepted, all this argument founded on Evolution comes to naught; or it will come to naught if, instead of relying on the spiritualist hypothesis, we accept the creative hypothesis, and declare that the Organism was created from the first that which we see it now, equipped with all its aptitudes and modes of reacting. It is one of these two hypotheses which underlies the argument of the *à priori* school. Nor can they be directly refuted. Indirectly, however, they may be discredited by showing that while they are wholly without positive evidence, they are imagined only to explain the existence of those very aptitudes, connate tendencies, Laws of Thought, etc., which can be explained without such imaginary data, namely, as the necessary consequences of Experience.

13. Descending from these preliminaries, we see that the true question Psychology has to determine concerning the origin of knowledge is, whether over and above the recognized avenues of Sensibility there are other avenues, in no one respect allied to them, through which Consciousness may be affected, and thus revelations reach the mind which, having no sensible origin, are not amenable to the canons of sensible Experience. But the dispute *seems* to turn on the very different question, whether the material furnished by Sense constitutes the whole product of Mind. The battle has been bloodless and endless, simply because the adversaries have never actually met on a common ground. The empirical proclamation, *Nihil in intellectu nisi prius in sensu,* was answered by the counterblast *Nisi ipse intellectus.* But this was no assault on the empirical position, simply because the assertion, that the Intellect existed, left wholly untouched the question as to *how* that Intellect could be reached, and on what material it could operate.

Both schools rested on the traditional assumption of the existence of a Mind endowed with certain Faculties. This Mind was supposed to be called into activity, and made to exercise its Faculties of Perception, Imagination, Memory, Attention, Reasoning, etc., by the influence of external objects (according to one school), — by the influence of external objects *and* native forms (according to the other). Now, it was obviously no answer to the sensationalists to proclaim what they never denied, — the existence of Mind. What was required was to show that this Mind is furnished with conceptions not in any way reducible to sensible experiences or combinations of such experiences; to show, in fact, that there were innate ideas and truths, whose origin *transcended* Experience. On this point the argumentation of Locke is so triumphant that the doctrine of innate ideas has long been given up, — or rather has become transformed into a doctrine, which, while seeming to occupy the old position, does in truth relinquish it, but brings into prominence a truth never sufficiently allowed for by the school of Locke, — I mean the part played by the Organism and its inherited modes of reaction.

14. The psychologist finds among the phenomena classed under Mind two very distinct groups: perceptions and conceptions, — images of concrete objects, and abstract symbols from which all trace of an image has escaped. He calls the one the products of Sense, and the other the products of Intellect. Not understanding their genesis, and impressed by their disparity, unable to detect any common measure between them, and persuaded that very many of our most important ideas cannot be analyzed into mere affections of Sense, the *à priori* philosopher takes his stand on this evidence of the speciality of Intellect, and impatiently rejects the empirical hypothesis. It is clear that out of mere sensations as affections of the

organism we cannot get negative conceptions and abstract notions. What is the sensible representative of our idea of Mind? What is that of Life? Granting these, and all other abstractions, to have originally had sensible concretes, it is still indisputable that these objects of Thought never could have been objects of Sense. Whence are they derived? If Sensation be restricted to the passive affections of Sense from which the co-operation of the logical processes is excluded, there is a radical defect in the sensational hypothesis. But the *à priori* hypothesis only cloaks this defect by a phrase; it does not explain the phenomena. When Kant says that in order to render any sensible phenomenon *intelligible,* the Understanding must add the notion of Substance, a notion which cannot be given through Sense, the statement really amounts to this: *before a phenomenon can be raised into the logical sphere it must submit to logical conditions*; before the *sensible* can become *intelligible* it must assume intelligible characters. No one would dispute the position. No one would deny that there are logical processes which may be called Laws of Thought, the operation of which is as indispensable in the formation of judgments, as the laws of Geometry in the construction of figures. The question of vital importance is: What are these Laws, and whence their origin? Kant declared that they were antecedent to all Experience, and made Experience possible; he would not allow them to be innate ideas, but he refrained from specifying what they were, except that they were native elements of Mind.* The modern biological school of psychologists

* His language is so confused and contradictory that by turns he is seen espousing the sensational and *à priori* hypotheses. Emphatically declaring against innate ideas, he is yet frequently found employing *à priori* concepts; on the one hand declaring that we have only connate aptitudes, on the other that we have concepts antecedent to all Experience. Herbart's criticism on Kant's distinction between the Faculty of Representation and its products is unanswerable. Herbart peremp-

fully admitting the operation of logical processes, and the wide differences between such processes and passive affections of Sense, endeavors to trace the genesis of these, their organic evolution, and their identity throughout psychical phenomena, from the simplest perception up to the most complex conception. It admits that the Mind, considered psychostatically, in the developed state, has certain endowments, or modes of operation, which determine the forms and products of its thinking; and these are general laws which determine *à priori*, so to speak, even particular opinions, as general laws of Motion determine particular motions. It further admits that these endowments, these Laws of Thought, and the conceptions which are their products when combined with sensible experiences, are assuredly not reducible to any individual experience, but to the evolved Experience of the race.

15. These large admissions, rightly interpreted, give no support to the *à priori* school. In interpreting them it is necessary to guard against the illusion incident to Abstraction, and the illusion incident to Metaphor. The Mind is commonly spoken of in oblivion of the fact that it is an abstract term expressing the sum of mental phenomena (with, or without, an *unexplored remainder*, according to the point of view); as an abstraction it comes to be regarded in the light of an entity, or separate *source* of the phenomena which *constitute it*. A thought, which as a product is simply an *embodied process*, comes to be regarded in the light of something distinct from the process; and thus two aspects of one and the same phenomenon are held to be two distinct phenomena. Because we

torily rejects the notion of a Faculty which fashions sensations as a potter fashions clay. The Faculty and its Product are one thing, not two things. "We have no Sensibility (although we have sense organs) *before* the sensible feelings, no Memory *before* the stored-up material, no Understanding *before* the concepts, etc." — *Aphorismen zur Psychologie*, *Werke*, VII. 611.

abstract the material of an object from its form, considering each apart, we get into the habit of treating form as if it were in reality separable from material. By a similar illusion we come to regard the process (of thinking) apart from the product (thought), and, generalizing the process, we call it Mind, or Intellect, which then means no longer the mental phenomena condensed into a term, but the *source* of these phenomena. This illusion is further strengthened by the metaphors in which it is commonly expressed. We speak of the Mind being furnished with material by Sense; or we liken it to a loom which weaves the threads of Experience into a wondrous web. But if we substitute for these metaphors another more nearly resembling the fact, and instead of a machine take the vital organism for comparison, we may parallel the aphorism: "Nothing in the Intellect not previously in Sense," by the aphorism: "Nothing in the Organism not previously in Food." On hearing this latter statement, a biologist who had no conception of the evolution of an organism, individual and ancestral, might patiently ask: "But whence came this organism? whence its power of fashioning the food? I see no trace of the organism and its functions in the nutritive materials; hence I conclude that these pre-exist, and because they are pre-existent there is the possibility of nutritive materials becoming food." It is thus the *à priori* psychologist asks: Whence the Mind and its Forms of Thought? Whence those conditions which render it possible for sensitive impressions to become Experience?

The answers to such questions must depend on whether we are considering the *functions*, or their *genesis*. It is indisputable that every particular man comes into the world with a heritage of organized forms and definite tendencies, which will determine his feeling and thinking in certain definite ways, whenever the suitable conditions are present. And all who believe in evolution believe that these forms and tendencies represent ancestral experiences and adaptations; believe that not only is the pointer born with an organized tendency to point, the setter to set, the beaver to build, and the bird to fly, but that the man is born with a tendency to think in images and symbols according to given relations and sequences which constitute logical laws, and that *what* he thinks is the necessary product of his organism and the external conditions. This organism itself is a product of its history; it *is* what it has *become;* it is a part of the history of the human race, and in so far resembles that of other members of the race; it is also specially individualized by the particular personal conditions which have distinguished him from his fellow-men. Thus resembling all men in general characters he will in general feel as they feel, think as they think; and differing from all men in special characters, he will have personal differences of feeling and shades of feeling, thought and combinations of thought. All this is equally true of the organism and its food. The body is built up out of elements furnished in the food, and this not simply by a juxtaposition of the elements, but by their selection, combination, recombination, and *assimilation* (or making like); and this assimilation is rigorously determined, 1°, by the special properties of the elements themselves in these relations; and, 2°, by the special properties of the tissues which assimilate them; and these latter are determined by inherited tendencies of the organism. Thus only those elements in the food supplied which admit of being assimilated under these conditions are incorporated in the organism, and help the growth and preservation of the organism; the other elements are rejected, and are, so to speak, non-existent for the organism.

The case is parallel in mental assimilation. The reactions of Feeling are determined by the general laws of Sensibility and the special modes of the individual. The Mind is built up out of assimilated experiences, its perceptions being shaped by its pre-perceptions, its conceptions by its pre-conceptions. Like the body, the Mind is shaped through its history.* It is in this sense — and this only — that we ought to speak of Intellect as a process apart from its products, and continue the metaphor of sensations being the food of the Intellect. Food, regarded objectively, is something not belonging to the organism; although, strictly, a substance never *is* food except in becoming part of an organism. In like manner Sensation is held to imply an element foreign to Mind, in contradistinction to Thought, which like the air we breathe seems part of ourselves. It is reflection and experiment which convince us that the air is a material object capable of being weighed and measured. It is reflection and experiment which convince us that Thought is an embodied process, which has its conditions in the history of the race no less than in that of the individual.

16. Thus explained the doctrine of the sensationalists may be accepted; all ideas may have a sensible origin assigned them when Sensation itself is understood to involve the primary condition of *an organized structure*

* George Eliot in *The Spanish Gypsy* expresses a profound truth in saying: —

> "What! shall the trick of nostrils and of lips
> Descend through generations, and the soul,
> That moves within our frame like God in worlds,
> Imprint no record, leave no documents
> Of her great history? Shall men bequeath
> The fancies of their palates to their sons,
> And shall the shudder of restraining awe,
> The slow-wept tears of contrite memory,
> Faith's prayerful labor, and the food divine
> Of fasts ecstatic, — shall these pass away
> Like wind upon the waters tracklessly?"

whose function is logical * (i. e. constituted by the grouping of neural units) and whose aptitudes are inherited Experiences. And, thus explained, the doctrine may be reconciled with all that is valid in the *à priori* hypothesis, namely, that which insists on the necessary co-operation of logical processes with organized aptitudes. The crude sensational doctrine is equivalent to the crude statement that the Organism and its functions are given in the food. Whether any reputable thinker ever really maintained this doctrine, may reasonably be doubted; many writers have seemed to maintain it, owing to the imperfect precision of their language; yet all would admit that no analysis of food, irrespective of the Organism and its assimilative processes, would yield an explanation even of food, much less of vital phenomena; nor would analysis of external stimuli, irrespective of the sensitive mechanism, yield an explanation of Sensation, much less of higher phenomena. The resistance of the *à priori* school to such crude explanations has been of decided utility.

Respecting the so-called Mental Forms both schools are right, though standing at different points of view. The *psychological* fact tells us that the Forms are connate, therefore *à priori*; the *psychogenetical* fact tells us that the Forms are products of ancestral Experience, and therefore *à posteriori*. But the vital question is not whether we have modes of feeling and thinking which determine the nature of our feelings and thoughts, but whether we can have any knowledge of things which have not been felt, i. e. whether there is a sensible basis and sensible test requisite for every conception, or whether a Supra-sensible is knowable.

17. The transformations which hypotheses undergo have

* To be fully explained in the Problem on Feeling and Thought. Meanwhile see *Psychological Principles*, §§ 24, 25.

been instructively illustrated by Whewell. "When a prevalent theory is found to be untenable, and consequently is succeeded by a different or even by an opposite one, the change is not made suddenly or completed at once, at least in the minds of the most tenacious adherents of the earlier doctrine; but is effected by a transformation or series of transformations of the earlier hypothesis, by means of which it is gradually brought nearer and nearer to the second; and thus the defenders of the ancient doctrine are able to go on as if still asserting their first opinions, and continue to press their points of advantage, if they have any, against the new theory. They borrow or imitate, and in some way accommodate to their original hypothesis the new explanation which the new theory gives of the observed facts; and thus they preserve a sort of verbal consistency; till the original hypothesis becomes inextricably confused, or breaks down under the weight of the auxiliary hypotheses thus fastened upon it in order to make it consistent with the facts." * Such has been the case with the hypothesis respecting the origin of knowledge. Each school has modified its views to include what is valid in the doctrine of its opponent. When the arguments of Gassendi and Hobbes made Descartes aware of the manifest impropriety of supposing that the infant came into the world ready furnished with ideas of objects which could only be presented to Sense, and of ideas which could only be furnished by combinations and abstractions from sensations, — with ideas of Geometry before there had been sensible experiences of Extension, etc., — the philosopher declared that his meaning had been misinterpreted. He declared that he never conceived that the infant had more than an innate faculty of acquiring such ideas under suitable conditions. His admirers and followers have been at some pains to show

* WHEWELL, *Philosophy of Discovery*, p. 493.

that this was his meaning. Thus interpreted, the doctrine of innate ideas amounts to the evident proposition that the native construction of the human mind is such that when given conditions are present given results must follow; when objects are apprehended there will be certain ideas formed, and when certain propositions expressive of the relations of such ideas are stated, the truth of such propositions is seen at once. No sensationalist would demur to this.

18. Let us for a moment glance at the statement of this doctrine by two illustrious defenders of it. Schelling argues thus: All knowledge in as far as it is the product of the Ego is *à priori;* but in as far as it is unconsciously produced it is *à posteriori.* There are therefore *à priori* concepts, without there being innate concepts. The concepts are not innate; but our nature and its mechanism is innate.* Leibnitz is equally explicit: "*Philalèthe.* S'il y a des vérités innées ne faut il pas qu'il y ait des pensées innées? *Théophile.* Point du tout, car les pensées sont des actions, et les connaissances ou les vérités, en tant qu'elles sont en nous quand même on n'y pense point, sont des habitudes ou des dispositions."

In this statement of the doctrine the absurdity is escaped; but at the same time its significance vanishes. We have only to open Locke to see that in this form he frankly accepted it. "I imagine," he says, "any one will easily grant that it would be impertinent to suppose ideas of colors innate in a creature to whom God hath given sight and a power to receive them by the eyes from external objects: and no less unreasonable would it be to attribute several truths to the impressions of nature and

* SCHELLING, *System des Trans. Idealismus,* pp. 316–318. And elsewhere in the *Erster Entwurf eines Systems der Naturphilosophie,* p. 15, he says: "Sobald ich die Einsicht in die innere Nothwendigkeit eines Erfahrungsatzes erlange, wird er ein Satz *à priori.*" —Comp. Hegel in his critique on Locke, *Gesch. Der. Phil.* III. 421.

innate characters when we may observe in ourselves faculties fit to attain as easy and certain knowledge of them as if they were originally imprinted on the mind." Indeed the very distinction on which stress is laid, between capacity and knowledge, is thus expressed by Locke: "The capacity they say is innate; the knowledge acquired. But then to what end such contest for certain innate maxims?"

19. This is the real point: the "capacity to acquire" must be presupposed in the case of maxims avowedly the products of Experience, no less than of maxims declared to be anterior to Experience; on the other hand, "the knowledge acquired" must be the product of Experience in both cases. Leibnitz says that when a man at fifty learns the proposition of the square of the hypothenuse "he acquires an innate idea"; and thus all the truths of Geometry are innate, though millions of men never acquire them. This position, which was reproduced by Whewell in his controversy on the subject with Mr. Mill and myself,* simply amounts to asserting that the mind is so constituted as inevitably to form certain conclusions under certain conditions. Who ever doubted this? It is wholly irrelevant. We are so constituted that under certain conditions inevitably we have sensations of color, sound, taste, etc.; yet no one considers the ideas of color, sound, and taste to be innate. The mind is so constituted as inevitably to conclude (until better instructed) that the sun turns round the earth, moving from east to west, but no one would admit this conclusion to be innate. It is with the functions of our intellectual organs as with the functions of our vital organs, — when the organ is mature, is healthy, and is stimulated, its action is irresistible; and when similar organs in various organisms are stimulated under similar conditions, the action is in each case similar.

* Compare his *Philosophy of Discovery*, p. 530.

20. That all men should form the same conceptions, — mathematical or metaphysical, — under conditions that are universal, is not surprising; but it is surprising, at first, to observe the strange yet identical conceptions formed by lunatics under external circumstances of the widest dissimilarity; and the surprise only ceases when we discover the cause of this identity to be the similarity of cerebral conditions. In the course of my observations in English and German asylums I have been forcibly impressed with the fact, abundantly illustrated in the records of Insanity, that patients belonging to very different classes of society and to different nations have precisely similar hallucinations, which they express in terms so closely alike, that the one might have been a free translation of the other. The pauper lunatic in England will often have the same illusion as the insane German merchant; and the insane soldier in Bohemia will seem to be repeating the absurdities of the insane farmer in Sussex. Not only does the fact of cerebral congestion determine hallucination in the Englishman as in the German, but determines the precise form which that hallucination will take. Twenty different patients of both sexes and of different age, country, and status, will be found having similar morbid sensations; and will all form a similar hypothesis to explain what they feel. Not only will they agree in attributing their distressing sensations to the malevolent action of invisible enemies, but will also agree in describing *how* these enemies molest them; even when such imaginary explanations take peculiar shapes, — for example, that the enemy blows poisonous vapors through the keyhole, or chinks in the wall, strikes them with galvanic batteries hidden under the table, roars and threatens them from underground cellars, etc. To hear in Germany a narrative which one has already heard in England, gravely particularizing the same preposterous details, almost as

if the thoughts of the one were the echo of the thoughts of the other, has a startling effect. I do not refer simply to the well-known general types of hallucination in which patients fancy themselves emperors, Christs, great actors, or great statesmen, or fancy themselves doomed to perdition, made of glass and liable to break in pieces if they move, — I refer to the singular resemblance noticeable in the expression of these forms, so that one patient has the same irrational conceptions as another.* This identity of conception rests on identity of cerebral congestion. Remove the congestion and the hallucination vanishes.

INSTINCT.

21. And here I will digress a little on the subject of Instinct, which, because it is so frequently cited to prove the doctrine of Innate Ideas, may best serve to illustrate the doctrine of evolution. The marvel and mystery of Instinct naturally render it a favorite topic in the writings of those who oppose the experiential School. Instinct is often regarded as so superior to Intelligence in the certainty of its action, that nothing except Creative Wisdom is admitted in explanation of it; while from other sides it is regarded as so removed from all community with Intelligence, that it is declared to be the blind action of a mechanism, not the operation of a rational Soul.

Psychogenesis seems to me to teach the direct contrary of all this. It teaches that Instinct is organized Experience: i. e. *undiscursive* Intelligence; that is to say, while the neural and logical processes are the same in

* "On ne veut pas s'apercevoir que les mêmes sens, les mêmes opérations, et les mêmes circonstances doivent produire partout les mêmes effets. On veut absolument avoir recours à quelque chose d'innée ou de naturel qui précède l'action des sens, l'exercise des opérations de l'âme, et les circonstances communes." — CONDILLAC, *L'Art de Penser*, Chap. V. p. 47.

both, the operations in what is specially termed Intelligence are facultative, and involve the element of choice in the selection of means to ends; Intelligence is therefore discursive; whereas in Instinct the operations are fixed, uniform, with no hesitation in the selection of means.

That Instinct, although in the individual it precedes Experience, is a product of what was Experience in the ancestral organisms from which the individual has inherited his structure, may best be shown by tracing its genesis from actions that at first were tentative, in other words intelligent. We have already (*Psychological Principles*, § 52) established the needful distinction between Intelligence and Intellect, and characterized the former as the discrimination of means to ends, — the guidance of the Organism towards the satisfaction of its impulses; and (Ibid., § 30 and § 74) we have distinguished Instincts from Impulses solely on the ground of the former being guided by discernment of relations. So that the three orders of phenomena may be thus characterized: in cases where there never was an alternative open to an action, the action being the necessary activity of the stimulated organ, — as in Secretion, Respiration, etc., — the action is impulsive; in cases where there was once an alternative, and when the action may still be controlled or modified in consequence, and is always guided by *discernment* of relations, the action is instinctive: however fixed now, it was not always so, and will vary with variations in the conditions; in cases where there are alternatives which may determine the action, the means being various and those that are selected in one case being rejected in another, the action is intelligent, discursive. Thus the nutritive Impulse which urges an animal in search of food is to be distinguished from the Instinct which causes it to select only one kind of food from out of several kinds accessible, all of which would be nutritious, or causes it to procure that one kind only in the ways followed by its ancestors, though many other ways are really open to it. The peculiarity of Instinct is that although guided by discernment of relations which is intelligent, it is restricted in its pathway and rendered undiscursive by an organized tendency of structure resulting from ancestral restrictions. The character of uniformity so often insisted on arises naturally from the success of the means chosen; the Impulse having been satisfied by the object selected, no other object is sought, and the choice once made is made forever. But that the object *was* chosen is proved by the fact that when, under other conditions, it no longer satisfies the impulse, it is rejected, and another sought; moreover, not only is the old object rejected when it ceases to satisfy the Impulse, but a new object will be selected in preference if it gratifies the Impulse. Thus we see insects in our conservatories select their food and nidus among tropical plants which could not live in the open air which these insects were born and bred in; thus indigenous plants which have formed the nidus and the food for generation after generation, are neglected in favor of the new plants which the insects now first discover. Every one who has watched birds knows that they always select the best materials for their nests, and will leave untouched material they and their kind have been accustomed to select, if softer material is at hand. The fact of choice is further confirmed by the fact that Instincts *are subject to illusions as Reason is.* I shall hereafter have occasion to specify many striking examples.

The daily facts of Habit show how easily tendencies become organized, how the actions which at first were tentative, laborious, slow, become inevitable, easy, rapid; and the notorious facts of Heredity show how habits once organized may become transmitted to descendants, so that the unnatural action of "begging," when a dog is taught to perform it, may become a natural action in its descendants, requiring no teaching. Nay, this very process underlies all development. The voluntary actions become involuntary, the involuntary become automatic, the intelligent become habitual, and the habitual become instinctive. It is the same in the higher regions of Intellect: the slow acquisitions of centuries of research become condensed into axioms which are intuitions.

However undiscursive Instinct may be it has always the intelligent character of discernment of relations and consequent control. For example, the instinct in an angry man to strike the offender, or in a dog to bite, is not, as Bossuet* and other writers suppose, a blind impulse unprescient of means and end; on the contrary, the man, however angry, will not strike an offender before whom he stands in awe, or for whose weakness he has pity; nor will the dog bite his master. It is instructive to observe a dog whose tail is pinched by one he loves; the pain excites the impulse to bite, the mouth is rapidly brought down upon the offending fingers, but the biting impulse is restrained, and the teeth do not close on the fingers; whereas if it is a stranger's fingers that have caused the pain, the biting instinct has free play.

21*a*. The general notion that voluntary movements arise out of involuntary movements is only acceptable when by Volition is meant the determination of an impulse by a guiding idea: but if we disengage it from this place in the intellectual region, and restore it to its primary position in the Logic of Feeling, — and otherwise we must deny Volition to animals and infants, — it seems to

* "Un arc bandé ne tend pas plus à tirer que le corps d'un homme en colère à frapper l'ennemi. . . . . La seule impression de l'objèt opère en nous cette action. . . . . Les actions animales s'opèrent par la seule force de l'objet même plus sûrement qu'elles ne feraient si la réflexion venait s'y mêler." — BOSSUET, *De la Connaissance de Dieu*, Chap. III. § 2, Chap. V. § 3.

me demonstrable that the movements now involuntary were originally voluntary, precisely as the instinctive actions were originally intelligent, the undiscursive discursive (*Psychol. Principles,* § 31). One illustration may suffice. The movements of the eye are generally acknowledged to be involuntary; that they are originally voluntary, and have still their guidance in discriminative sensation, and their pole-star in the external object, will be evident to any one who studies their mechanism.*

Now since we know that many Instincts which are manifested as soon as the organisms have acquired the requisite development and are appropriately stimulated, were originally acquired in ancestral experiences, — a striking example being that of the instinctive terror of man felt by animals, a terror which was organized in their immediate ancestors, and was absent from their remote ancestors, — since we know that Instincts like many Diseases are due to registered modifications of structure, transmitted by Heredity, and since these registrations are themselves acquired results, the conclusion that all Instincts are acquired becomes irresistible. Indeed we have only to remember that every mental manifestation is simply the activity of an organized structure, and is rigorously determined by that structure, to see that if the present structure is acquired through successive modifications of pre-existent structures, the present manifestation must have been acquired. It is forgetfulness of this cardinal principle, of the necessary dependence of the dynamical effect on the statical conditions, which renders the interpretation of some familiar facts so uncertain. Thus when the helplessness of the human infant is contrasted with the helpfulness of the young animal, so that what requires a long initiation of experience in the one is seen to be present from the first in the other, and the

* See HELMHOLTZ, *Physiol. Optik.*, pp. 473, 474, and 772.

necessity which the infant is under of learning to walk, learning to see, learning to localize its sensations, is not observable in the rabbit or the bird, it is concluded that these actions have a different genesis in each. Hence one party holds that our perception of Space is innate, because the bird manifests it on quitting the shell; another party holds that our perception of Space is acquired, because the infant has to learn how to see, and how to estimate positions. The truth seems to be that the bird quits the shell in a far more developed condition than the infant on entering the world, — has its organism and its visual organs more ready to enter upon their normal activities, and therefore more quickly manifests what the infant will only manifest when a corresponding development has taken place. On the other hand, in observing how the infant slowly acquires the perception of Space we learn what has been the process of registration in the development of the bird-structure. The state of the infant organism, before it has been modified by the registration of changes produced by reactions on external stimuli, represents what was the state of the ancestral organism before it had been so modified. Embryology teaches us that the embryonic phases of the higher animals repeat the phases of development at which the lower animals are arrested. It is because the immature brain of the infant represents a stage when the Experience was immature, that the infant cannot manifest aptitudes which depend on subsequent Experience; and it is because the stages of subsequent development will take place under similar conditions to those which have occasioned the development of the parents, that the functions of the infant will in time come to resemble the functions of the parents. Let the infant be developed under dissimilar conditions, and it will proportionately deviate in structure, consequently in functions, from the parents. A child born blind will bring with it the requisite conditions for subsequently acquiring the perception of tactual Space, but will obviously never acquire the perception of optical Space. A child born deaf and dumb will bring with it the conditions requisite for the acquisition of visible and tactual symbols, but not for the acquisition of verbal symbols. To these organic conditions let us now add the external conditions. A child born with eyes, but kept in constant darkness, or with only intermittent and brief excitations of light, or born with vocal and auditory organs, but in a society of deaf and dumb companions, rarely hearing the speech of man, — this child will never acquire the perception of visible space, nor the use of verbal symbols which characterize ordinary men. What the child brings with it into the world is an immature organism which under similar conditions will develop into an organism similar to that of other men.

21*b*. How intimately the functions depend upon the organism may be illustrated in this striking example: The tadpole of the salamander is a vegetable feeder; although it is *also* an animal feeder, it is not exclusively nor mainly this; but in its mature phase, when it has acquired its distinctive structure as a salamander, it is wholly an animal feeder, and cannot be induced to take vegetable food, even when starving. There is one kind of salamander (*salamandra atra*) which is peculiarly interesting from the fact that it is *born* a salamander, and not a tadpole, — passing through its tadpole metamorphoses while still in its mother's womb. Now no one will dispute that the selection of food is an Instinct, and that one animal is herbivorous, another carnivorous, just as one animal is aquatic, another amphibious, and a third terrestrial, in accordance with its Instinct. Well, this salamander which is instinctively carnivorous, is in its tadpole stage instinctively herbivorous and carnivorous. I found that if it were taken from the womb while still a tadpole, it would live in water, and feed on vegetable and animal substances. Let it complete its metamorphoses, within the womb, or without, and no sooner does it acquire the organization of the salamander than it acquires the carnivorous Instinct. Again: a pigeon has the Instinct to preen its feathers, and to sleep with the beak under its wing. It does not manifest these tendencies from the first, but always acquires them sooner or later; when once acquired, these actions are performed even after its cerebral lobes have been removed; but it never acquires them if the cerebral lobes be removed before the mechanism has been established. Here we have Instincts manifestly acquired, just as the child *acquires* the Instinct to scratch itself when it itches; being for a long while unable to localize its sensations, and consequently unable to scratch itself however it may itch, it does nevertheless inevitably, in the course of time, acquire the Instinct. But compare this with the same Instinct congenital in animals who are able to scratch themselves from the first. So indubitably is this tendency an organized inherited tendency that it is manifested even when some congenital imperfection prevents its perfect realization. Thus Gudden had a rabbit born with paralysis of the hinder legs, incapable therefore of scratching, and this rabbit which had never scratched itself would, when tickled, turn its head to and fro towards the motionless hinder legs; thus in part realizing the inherited tendency which it was incapable of completely carrying into effect.*

These, and multitudes of other examples which might be cited, prove, what is evident theoretically, that the manifestations, whether under the form of perceptions or instincts, are rigorously determined by the state of the Organism. Indeed the Organism is an *ensemble* of stati-

* See *Archiv für Psychiatrie*, II. 697. 1870.

cal conditions, and its dynamical tendencies vary with these. It is thus that we see temporary states successively manifesting tendencies which are classed as Instincts; and the epileptic patient may be observed passing successively through phases which manifest homicidal, kleptomaniacal, and pyromaniacal Instincts, which are temporary if their statical conditions are temporary. Or, since this illustration may be disputed, consider the periodicity of the sexual Instinct in animals, which is assuredly due to a periodicity in the statical conditions. But although the sexual Instinct is less disputable than those fleeting manifestations observable in Insanity, I adduce the evidence of the latter for the sake of illustrating the position that Experience depends on the registration of Feeling, and exists only so long as the registrations, i. e. modifications, exist. For many of these passing states of Insanity, however violent their manifestations, are forgotten like the visions of a dream, when the abnormal conditions give place to normal conditions, and the over-excited brain resumes its former state. If the statical modification become permanent, there is registration of the feelings, and the patient is permanently insane; if they are fleeting there is no registration, and the patient returned to his normal state has no Experience of all that occurred during his abnormal state.

22. We do not usually class any of the fleeting manifestations under the general term Instinct, though obviously some of the Instincts are but temporary manifestations of temporary states, nor do we class any manifestations that are peculiar to individuals as Instincts, but rather as Idiosyncrasies. Only those manifestations that are common to the species, and are responses to external stimuli of common recurrence, are classed among the Instincts. There are certain statical conditions which are invariable, — such are those dynamically represented

in Space, Time, Causation, etc., which may be set apart, and considered, on this account, as specially entitled to the character of *à priori* Mental Forms, not indeed in the Kantian sense, but in the sense in which Biology understands organized forms. What concerns us here, however, is not the psychological but the psychogenetical interpretation, — not whether man comes into the world with an organized structure the activities of which necessarily lead to the *perceptions* of Extension, Duration, Causation, etc., and also to the *conceptions* of Space, Time, Cause, etc., but whether these perceptions and conceptions have any higher source and deeper validity than the perceptions and conceptions which arise from individual experiences. Neither observation nor reflection warrants the supposition that the infant, in spite of inheritance, has on entering the world innate ideas of Space, Time, Causation; what is innate, or connate, is the structure which will react under stimulus in certain definite ways, and these reactions will depend on the degree of development which the structure has acquired. The infant whose optical organs are imperfect will never react on the stimulus of light in the same way as another infant whose organs are more developed. At birth no child *sees*. It usually takes several days before the child makes any movement of the head towards the light, and four or five weeks before he learns to converge the axes of both eyes.* But, could the infant see at birth, this would not indicate that the perception of Space or of external objects was innate; only that the structure was ready for its function; and how that structure came to be formed would still remain a question. And there is

* There are great varieties in this, and indeed, in all other points of development at birth. Thus Donders, whose authority on such a matter is supreme, records a case in which he observed an infant distinctly converge the eyes and follow an object only a few minutes after birth. — *Archiv für Opthalm.*, XVII. 34. 1871.

one argument which is decisive. Even if we assume, with the advocates of creation, that the structure was not evolved through modifications impressed on organic substance by successive adaptations of the Organism to the external Medium, — that the eye, for example, was created, and not evolved by the action of light upon the sensitive surface, — created with all the powers which it is known to manifest, — still there would remain the necessity of this eye being brought into the appropriate relation with the external object; and in the absence of this, in the absence of light to call the energy of the eye into existence, there would be no visual perception, much less an idea of Space. Nor would this be denied; certainly not by Kant. Yet its admission is an admission of the cardinal principle of the Empirical doctrine, that all perception, consequently all conception, is the product of the reactions of the Organism stimulated by the Cosmos; which is saying in other words that all our knowledge has its origin in Experience, — the registration of such reactions. And this is further confirmed by the fact that on the one hand the development of the Organism has its prescribed course, any interference with the series of successive stages causing another form of structure to result, while on the other hand any interference with the normal course of experience will correspondingly affect the result, so that even results which have the fixed character of Instincts may be frustrated by an interruption of the prescribed *course* of evolution. Many examples might be given, but it will suffice to mention the Instinct of sucking, which is manifested by all mammals very soon after birth. Here is a structure ready for reaction in a particular way directly the appropriate stimulus is felt. But (the observation had not escaped Harvey) if, instead of being put to the breast, the child be fed from a spoon, in a few days it loses the power of sucking the breast, and can only feed from the spoon. Obviously the explanation of this is that the Organism, having been induced to react in a way unlike the normal way, becomes in consequence so modified that it will no longer react in the normal way even when the normal stimulus is applied.*

23. This digression has been made to fix our notion of what is really valid in the doctrine of Mental Forms, as organized tendencies acquired through successive experiences; and to disprove the conclusion that the existence of such Mental Forms indicates metempirical sources of knowledge. When we admit the existence of *à priori* tendencies, we do not admit the existence of *à priori* truths, i. e. conceptions of sensible facts irrespective of Experience, or of supra-sensible facts which no Experience could furnish. When we admit that there are in the organism statical conditions which must determine the directions of its manifestations, so that every Mind must necessarily feel in certain ways and think in certain ways, we do not admit that the feelings, and the truths

* Since this was in the printer's hands, some ingenious and instructive experiments have been published by Mr. Spalding (*Macmillan's Magazine*, February, 1873; compare also the discussions in *Nature* during the months of March, April, and May), which strikingly confirm what is said in the text respecting the variation of Instincts under varying conditions, and on the effects of any interruption of the normal experiences. Mr. Spalding also tells me of a friend of his who reared a gosling in the kitchen away from all water; when this bird was some months old, and was taken to a pond, it not only refused to go into the water, but when thrown in scrambled out again as a hen would have done. Here was an instinct entirely suppressed. What I have said about the instinctive selection of food is also confirmed by the following observation: "Every chicken, as far as my observations go, has to learn not to eat its own excrement. They made this mistake invariably; but they did not repeat it oftener than once or twice. Many times they arrested themselves when in the very act, and went off shaking their heads in disgust, though they had not actually touched the obnoxious matter."

which are their results, are engraven on the Mind, and require no excitations from the external world to elicit them; still less that they can reveal to us a world which never was presented in Experience. The Forms of Sense and the Forms of Thought are evolved, as the branches and foliage of an oak are evolved from the acorn. No one now supposes that the oak *is* ready formed in the acorn, lying there in miniature. The oak is quite as much in the atmosphere and soil; it really is in neither, but will be evolved from both. Given the two factors, — an Organism and its Medium, — and the product will necessarily be evolved; and will be according as they are. Thus the seed of the poplar and the seed of the chestnut are different structures, and will evolve into different trees.

We learn by individual experiences, registrations of feeling, rendered possible by ancestral experiences. The individual structural evolution, in its embryonic phases, rapidly runs through all the grades of vertebrate development. The individual mental evolution in its early phases likewise runs rapidly through all the general experiences of the race; and youth acquires ideas, the products of such experiences, by going through similar successions of feeling. What marvel is there that constant conditions acting upon structures which are similar should produce similar results? It is in this sense that the paradox of Leibnitz is true, and we can be said "to acquire an innate idea"; only the idea is not acquired independently of Experience, but through the process of Experience similar to that which originally produced it. The truth that a straight line is the shortest line between two points, is one which millions of men pass to their graves without acquiring; yet it is a truth which may justly be called innate in so far as it lies involved in the sensible experiences from which Philosophy extricates it, — I mean, it is necessarily given in the Logic of Feeling, before Psychology recognizes it as an Intuition.* The *rational* instinct which makes a man infer a cause wherever he observes a change, is in one sense connate, in another acquired, — it is the acquired result of a connate tendency, quite as much as the sexual Instinct, which seeks the gratification of desires by union with another, is the acquired result of a connate tendency: both are developed some time after birth, the development of both requiring a special state of the Organism, and a special excitation of that state. The infant has no more the idea of Causality, than it has the feeling of sexuality. I shall hereafter show that Causality is an inwoven law of Feeling, not primarily an Induction: it may be said to precede Feeling, and render Experience possible, in so far as it is an organized tendency of Feeling to connect a consequent with an antecedent; it may be called an Intuition in so far as it is the perception of the relation of equivalence; and it may be called an Induction in so far as this perception is raised into a conception, and extended from the particular to the general, raised from a fact of Feeling into an universal Law of Nature.

24. With this view of the genesis of *à priori* truths it is obvious that the ordinary argument which relies on these for an extra-experiential origin and a deeper validity cannot be accepted. True it may be that conceptions which demanded centuries of research are no sooner reached than they are seen to be axiomatic, irresistible; but the fact that they required this research is sufficiently instructive respecting their origin; and if their presence in the primary conditions of Feeling be detected, so that we discover them to be inwoven with our earliest experiences, this does not give them a higher validity than Feeling.

It is Kant's fundamental mistake, which will be eluci-

* If bees had the Logic of Signs they would *know* the geometry which they *feel* in constructing their cells.

dated farther on, to treat the *à priori conditions* of Knowledge as evidence of our possessing *Knowledge* which is itself *à priori* and metempirical,—to assume that because knowledge is rendered possible by organic conditions, and these are not present in the external causes of excitation, therefore there is a Knowledge which is anterior to all excitation, independent of all Experience. But if we get rid of this view we may reasonably admit that there must be *à priori* conditions which render Knowledge possible; and we may also conveniently establish a distinction between *à priori* and *à posteriori* knowledge,—not that either of them can be supposed to have originated independently of Experience, ancestral and individual, or to be founded on different processes, but that the one embraces conceptions which must inevitably and always be formed, because their conditions—psychical and cosmical—are constant, whereas the others are contingent, depending on variable conditions. In illustration take Mathematics and Biology. The former is an *à priori* science, not that it is in any sense independent of Experience (see Chap. XIII.), but that its data and results are invariable: the logical conditions and the external conditions are constants: what is seen to be true of one circle is seen to be true of every circle; therefore the knowledge of one includes *à priori* the knowledge of all, and there is no need of experiment or comparison to determine whether each new case is identical with the known cases. Not so with Biology,—except when its abstract propositions are dealt with. The state of our scientific experience is here a variable factor, and the external conditions are likewise variable. We can imagine a variety of hypotheses to explain every unexplained phenomenon, and it is only by successive tentatives that we reach any reliable explanation. More than this, the most accurate knowledge of any one phenomenon does not enable us *à priori* to conclude respecting every other that may resemble it; each fact demands *à posteriori* verification of its explanation, since we cannot always be sure that it resembles in all respects those which it is seen to resemble in some respects.

Kant erred, I think, in two ways: first, in accepting the traditional Dualism which regarded Mind in the light of a separate entity, having its inherent Forms, or Laws, which had no community with the Laws of the Cosmos; secondly, in limiting the number of these Forms, and not seeing that as evolved products they were necessarily enlarged by increasing Experience. With this rectification, we may accept the position that there are *à priori* Forms of Sensibility necessarily inherent in the organized structure; and these, which may be classed under Forms of Feeling and Forms of Thought, are correctly said to be connate, in precisely the same way that the vertebrate form, or the special forms of the several organs, are connate. Since the manifestations of the organism must be determined by its modes of reaction, obviously the experience of each individual will be rendered possible by the connate Forms; and if we constructively *anticipate* what must necessarily result when this organism is placed under stimulus, we may say that the resulting experience, or knowledge, is connate. In *this* sense it is true that man brings with him into the world the potential knowledge that a straight line is the shortest line between two points, and that every effect must have a cause, just as he brings with him the potential knowledge that sugar is sweet and roses are red; but in no other sense.

The Mental Forms are general and special, i. e. common to an entire group of feelings, and particular to special groups. The *αἰσθητὰ κοινὰ*, or analytical Forms of Feeling, are Extensity, Intensity, Pleasure (and its correlative Pain), Duration, Motion, Difference. There is no sensation which does not involve magnitude, degree, a pleasurable or painful quality, a motor quality, a duration, and a discrimination separating it from other sensations. From these are abstracted the *νοητὰ κοινὰ*, or analytical Forms of Thought, such as Quantity, Relation, Change, Coexistence, Succession, etc., which are raised from the Logic of Feeling into the Logic of Signs. What may be called the particular Forms are those of the Special Senses, such as Color, Odor, Taste, etc.

But these Mental Forms, like the so-called Laws of Nature, are not to be conceived as antecedent and independent realities *ruling* mental and cosmical phenomena. They are only *à priori* in our theoretical constructions. They are not properly speaking conditions which *precede* the phenomena, but modalities under which the phenomena appear, and which Analysis separates, and then assigns them logical priority.

25. We may here bring this discussion to a close in the hope that it has exhibited the promised reconciliation between the experiential and *à priori* schools, by elucidating what is valid in both, and rectifying what is erroneous in both. Although I have argued the question in my own way, it is proper to add that the point of view here advanced is historically to be assigned to the labors of Gall, some modern physiologists, and above all Mr. Herbert Spencer. In Gall's system it is a vital point that our various aptitudes, instincts, and faculties are connate. He particularly distinguishes it from the hypothesis of innate ideas and innate principles, on the one hand, and from that of mere passive capacities on the other, — as if the organism were a block of marble ready to be shaped according to the fancy of the sculptor.*

* "J'entends par dispositions innées, des aptitudes industrielles, des instincts, des penchants déterminés, des facultés, des talens déterminés.

But Gall's analysis, apart from many imperfections, is simply psychological, whereas Mr. Spencer's is psycho-genetical. He not only recognizes the existence of the modalities, he explains their genesis; and by showing that the constant experiences of the race become *organized tendencies* which are transmitted as a heritage, he shows that even such *à priori* forms as those of Space, Time, Causality, etc., which must have arisen in Experience, because of the constancy and universality of the external relations, are necessarily connate. Just as the optical structure of the eye has been, so to speak, fashioned by the external influences incessantly modifying the primitive tissues, and thereby rendering possible and inevitable the functional reaction of that organ, so the cerebral structure has been fashioned by the necessities of internal adaptation to external influences, and thus the constant relations of Space, etc., organized in us.

Such is one of the many profound conceptions with which this great thinker has enriched Philosophy; and it ought to have finally closed the debate between the *à priori* and the experiential schools in so far as both admit a common ground of biological interpretation; though of course it leaves the metempirical hypothesis untouched. The metempiricist not only maintains that there is a something in the mind over and above the mere capacity to know, something not belonging at all to the Organism, but he concludes that we have evidence of this

J'entends que chaque organe cérébral est empreint d'une tendance déterminée ; que chaque organe jouit d'un aperçu intérieur, d'une force, d'une faculté d'une impulsion, d'un penchant, d'un sentiment particuliers. Ici rien n'est vague et incertain, ni d'une influence extérieure, ni d'une abstraction intérieure. Aussitôt que les organes relatifs ont acquis leur parfait développement et leur entière activité, les fonctions qui en resultent, sont aussi déterminées que les dispositions elle mêmes dont ces organes sont les dépositants." — GALL, *Sur les fonctions du cerveau*, I. 63. 1822. Comp. also pp. 66-70.

in a higher source of knowledge than can be gained through Experience of the individual or the race. He maintains that a mark exists by which this can be recognized; and that mark is the twofold character of Universality and Necessity. I shall hereafter devote a chapter to the discussion of this point. Here I can only notice its bearing on the question respecting innate ideas. Obviously since the experiential doctrine admits the universality and necessity of mathematical truths (though Mr. Mill and some others would restrict even these), this character will not of itself suffice to prove the *à priori* position. The origin of these truths still remains a question. Both schools agree that the mind is so constituted as irresistibly to form these conclusions when experience presents the sensible occasions; both schools agree that until such sensible occasions are presented no such conclusions can be formed. The *à priori* school maintains that, although Experience may be necessary to call the latent truths into emergent consciousness, it only calls them out, it does not originate them, for Experience itself is only rendered possible by their pre-existence.

Let us view this hypothesis in a parallel case. Chlorine is so constituted that whenever it combines with hydrogen there is formed hydrochloric acid. From this a metempirical chemist might deduce that hydrochloric acid is innate in chlorine, since chlorine has within it something which shapes the hydrochloric acid into — hydrochloric acid. This something is itself neither chlorine nor hydrogen, nor is it a combined result of the two, but a something which renders the combination possible. The positive chemist is aghast at such a deduction; yet if we replace the terms hydrochloric acid and chlorine and hydrogen by the terms Experience and sensible perception, the argument will be that of the *à priori* school. That school affirms that there *is* a something independent of the chlorine and the hydrogen, namely Affinity, and it is this which combines the two gases in hydrochloric acid. Affinity is neither the gases nor their product, but a *power* which renders the product possible.

25*a*. I do not pretend in this place to discuss the arguments on which the *à priori* school defends its thesis; anything I might have to say on such a subject would be necessarily based upon psychological analysis which can only be attempted at a later stage. What I am here concerned with is to break down the barriers which have so long prevented the two schools from meeting on a common ground. This is effected when the admission is gained that all ideas are the products of two factors, the Subject and the Object, and that no ideas belong exclusively to one of the factors. Whether by Subject we understand the Mind and its connate aptitudes, or the Organism and its organized tendencies, matters nothing in the present question; the admission required is that there is a predisposition to act in certain necessary ways whenever sensible stimuli call the mind into activity. Descartes and Leibnitz, as also Kant and his followers, expressly declare that no truths, not even *à priori* truths, are seen (emerge in consciousness), unless the relations formulated are presented in Experience. The co-operation of the Object is therefore demanded. What they insist upon is that the mind brings with it at birth a structure which renders certain conclusions *necessary*. This admitted, there arises the further question: why is the proposition that acids redden vegetable blues of inferior validity to the proposition "two parallel lines cannot enclose space"? The first is said to be gathered from Experience, and therefore of inferior validity to the second, which is shown not to belong to Experience because of its universal validity. This is an interesting question, which will hereafter occupy us; meanwhile observe that the answer cannot properly rest on an assumed predisposition of the mind, since *that* is common to both examples, the mind having a native predisposition towards *all* the results of Experience, when the terms of those results are presented. The body has likewise a native predisposition to move in *any* direction which is free from obstacles; it is the existence of obstacles, together with the direction of the impulse, which determine what shall be the direction taken by the body. In like manner the presence of external relations impresses certain directions on the course of thought, and this course is determined by the disposition and predisposition of the mind.

Since, then, the character by which certain truths are distinguished from others cannot lie in the structure of the Mind itself, it must lie in the nature of the relations presented: in the Necessity and Universality of the relations formulated. And this is the character fixed upon. Now without here assuming, what will hereafter be proved, that the celebrated distinction of Necessary and Contingent Truths conceals a fallacy, we may remark that even an admission of the distinction by no means justifies the deduction: and for these reasons, 1°, the character of Necessity cannot be assigned as a special mark of native predisposition, innate capacity, but only as a mark of a particular class of objective relations; 2°, the only intelligible meaning of innate capacity by which these ideas are said to be formed is one which irresistibly extends to *all* faculties and to all ideas. Truths, whether universal or particular, necessary or contingent, are still truths evolved in and through Experience, and are subject to all the conditions of Experience.

CHAPTER III.

THE SENSIBLE, THE EXTRA-SENSIBLE, AND THE SUPRA-SENSIBLE.

26. THE discussion of the origin of Knowledge which has just occupied us is chiefly important in reference to the possible range and validity of Knowledge; although primarily a question of Pyschogeny, and therefore interesting only to special students, it is secondarily the vital question of Philosophy, since on it rests the whole of philosophical Method. All that has been written on Method is imperilled if there can be any valid evidence for the existence of an avenue through which knowledge may be reached without recourse to Experience. The metempirical school explicitly, or implicitly, affirms that there is such an avenue, and that it is revealed in Consciousness. Now Psychology being the science of Consciousness, and receiving all its material from Biology and Sociology, we may reduce this great question to something like definiteness by asking whether in the data furnished by Biology, or in the data furnished by Sociology, there is the evidence of a metempirical factor? In the biological phenomena there is assuredly no trace of it. The animal may indeed be said to have Knowledge; though that is often denied, because of an unwarrantable restriction of the term. But although he has knowledge, i. e. such registrations of Experience as suffice to guide his actions in the satisfaction of immediate impulses, the Animal is not supposed to have speculative knowledge, certainly nothing resembling Science. For him, and for

the infant and the rudest savage, Knowledge consists of the synthesis of the feelings produced by external objects. For him the Supra-sensible does not exist, even in Thought. The world for him is simply a *felt* world; and his Knowledge never ranges beyond Feeling.

We must seek then in sociological phenomena, if anywhere, for the metempirical data. And we shall seek in vain. Neither in Social Statics, nor in Social Dynamics, is there a trace of the Supra-sensible; but there *is* a very clear indication of the genesis of its conception, and its position in the world of Thought. If we interrogate History and Science we learn, indeed, that the conception of a Supra-sensible very early arose in the visionary schemes by which men attempted to explain the order of phenomena; but we also learn that this conception, which was at first only a subtilized expression of Sensible experience, became indeed less and less like sensibles as the refinements of Abstraction assumed the character of independent entities, then everywhere gradually vanished before advancing Science, so that the progress of each science was accompanied by the inevitable elimination of every metempirical idea. Nothing can be plainer than the teaching of History on this point. Both animals and men have to *learn* the facts of the External Order with which they come into relation, and to *control* these facts, as far as possible, adapting them to their needs, and adapting themselves to the facts. But man alone endeavors to *explain* the facts, that he may the better control them; he alone constructs Instruments in consequence of his Knowledge, and greatly enlarges Knowledge by the construction of Instruments. The history of Science, and indeed of Social Development, is the history of this perpetual action and reaction of the creation of Instruments and the enlargement of Knowledge. History records but little of Primitive Man, and nothing of the state of his theories of the External Order; but it records distinct evidence that in the remote periods which preceded the earliest known form of civilization there were rude stone implements,* and some means of producing fire. The period between the age of flint axes and the age of steam-engines, vast though it is, will one day be recognized as a slow evolution of continuous growth, through the successive modifications of Instruments by Knowledge, and of Knowledge by Instruments. For, indeed, Knowledge itself is only an Instrument. That the Primitive Man did endeavor to understand phenomena, at least so far as to enable him to modify them, is obvious. The changes he wrought by his instruments became facts that were known, facts that led him to foresee consequences; and his powers grew with his knowledge. But at each step he only knew what he had seen, and could foresee. At no stage could he see the invisible, or modify the intangible. He might imagine the presence of invisible Agents, and attempt to control them by invocations and incantations; but this imagination was visionary, and never served the office of Knowledge, except in so far as it reproduced Experience; nor were any changes wrought in the external visible order by invocations of the invisible Agents. Slowly the conviction emerged that man's power over the external order is limited to his knowledge of its sensible conditions, and of the means by which such conditions could be rearranged. It is this conviction which has animated Science.

But although in the evolution of history we see the supernatural explanations giving place to the metaphysi-

* It is an interesting fact that the stone is the first approach to an instrument which may be seen in the animal kingdom. Montagu observes that the thrush breaks the shells of the univalves on which it feeds by knocking them against a stone; and many readers must have seen monkeys breaking with a stone the nuts too hard to be cracked with their teeth.

cal, and the Metaphysical to the scientific (according to Comte's law). we do not at any stage see that Knowledge was more than a systematization of Feeling, or that Feeling was more than the reaction of the Organism according to its modes, when stimulated by external forces. There is no trace of a Supra-sensible stimulus, either in our perceptions of the external world, or in those of the social world. I am far from implying that a Supra-sensible does not exist. I only affirm that it does not exist *for us* as an object of positive knowledge, though forced upon us as a negative conception; since it could only be knowable by first becoming sensible: it must be positively felt, before it could be positively thought. To know anything is to assign properties to it, and properties involve the co-operation of the subjective factor. Once within the range of Feeling, an object otherwise Supra-sensible comes within the range of Experience.

We have thus prepared the way for the application of Rule I., and this will be more evident when we recognize that the main defect in the sensational hypothesis, and the mainstay of its opponents, lies in the seeming discrepancy between the notorious fact that knowledge does extend far beyond the reach of Perception and the range of sense; while on the other hand Psychogeny, seeming to contradict this, sustains the axiom that all knowledge has its origin in Sense, its limits being the limits of the Sensible. This discrepancy disappears if we divide the field of Speculation into the Sensible World, the Extra-sensible World, and the Supra-sensible World: a division corresponding with our previous distribution of positive, speculative, and metempirical.

27. The Sensible World, or total of sensible phenomena, comprises the *direct* reactions of Sensibility in contact with the External Order. Phenomena I have already defined as the affections of Consciousness with exter-

nal signs. That we only know things in their effects on us, and through the reactions of our Sensibility, may now be taken for granted. Nevertheless it is indisputable that in our conceptions of external things there are elements which cannot be reduced to mere sensation, elements which never were presented to Sense.

The Sensible comprises but a small portion of that External Order which is believed to exist. There is therefore an Extra-sensible existence; and it is revealed through various indications. An examination of the sensitive process discloses that we only receive definite sensations, i. e. groups capable of becoming elements of Consciousness, when the impressions exciting the neural process are of a definite quantity. The neural units which form the elements of such a process are severally non-existent for Consciousness; they must first be grouped under definite conditions. As a matter of fact, we know that the external must incessantly be impressing the organism; nevertheless the reactions of the organism in Feeling only take place under definite conditions of mass, intensity, and duration. The sensory organ needs to be impressed with a certain energy, and for a certain time; neither too small an energy nor too great an energy, otherwise there is not the reaction which is specifically a sensation. There must be a disturbance of nervous tension. The vibrations of the Ether when they disturb the tension of the retina, and this disturbance is propagated to the optic centre, produce the sensation of light. But we know that at one end of the spectrum there are vibrations not visible because the pulses are too rapid and the waves too short. At the other end of the spectrum there are also vibrations which are invisible because they are too slow and their waves too long. Retinal tension is undisturbed by both these agents. This example shows that among the myriads of impressions to which the retina is subjected only some of them are responded to as Feeling; hence the range of Feeling is *quantitatively* determined. Artificial aids may, and do, extend that range, but the quantitative law remains.

28. And what is true of the eye is true of all the other senses. When a note is sounded by one chord it will set vibrating any other chords which are in sympathy with it, and only those. It is thus also external voices awaken sympathetic tones in us. The eyes of animals may possibly be susceptible to vibrations which awaken no response in man.* It is probable that the antennæ of insects respond to stimuli which leave us insensible, while stimuli which affect us leave them undisturbed. Their sensations may begin at that point in the scale where ours end. Be this as it may, the range of Sense in them, as in us, is demonstrably too limited to embrace the objective totality, nay, even to embrace that small portion of it which is in contact with the organism. And if we supplement the deficiency of one sense by the efficiency of another, — as when the air which is invisible can yet be weighed, taken to pieces, and used to stuff cushions or propel machines, — the limits are soon reached. We know there are a thousand tremors in the air which beat upon our ears unheard; and if more sensitive organs are capable of hearing some of these, there must be tremors which no organism can feel.†

* This statement needs qualification. Since it was written the experiments of M. Bert have shown that the tiny crustaceans common in ponds and popularly called water-fleas (*Daphnia*) are susceptible to the same luminous vibrations as men and the higher animals, and only to these. The parts of the spectrum most vividly luminous to us are so to them, and those parts that are invisible to us are invisible to them. *Archives de Physiologie*, p. 548. 1869. It is nevertheless certain that even among men some retinas are not susceptible to the same vibrations as other retinas; and sounds become inaudible to some ears while still audible to others.

† "Nothing can be more surprising," says Herschel, "than to see

29. The Relativity of Feeling — the basis of the Relativity of Knowledge — must also be taken into account. Thus when a weight, say of three pounds, presses on the hand, a distinct sensation is produced; but no increase in that sensation follows an addition to that weight, if the addition be *less* than one pound. Although the pressure of half a pound, nay, half an ounce, will be distinctly felt by itself, any quantity less than one pound when added to three pounds will fail to produce the slightest change in the sensation. This important principle, which has been experimentally verified in the case of each sense, will occupy us hereafter; it is here mentioned in illustration of the Relativity of Feeling.

Hence may be seen the truth of the old proposition, that it is we who create our own world. Diminish the avenues of Sensation, or restrict the varieties of stimuli, and to that extent our world becomes impoverished; increase the avenues, or enlarge their range, — either by Instruments or the Mental Instruments called Hypothesis, Induction, etc., — and to that extent the world becomes enriched. We thus formulate a law which lies at the basis of Rule I., namely: —

> The sphere of Knowledge is limited, 1°, by Sensible Impressions, i. e. definite Sensations; 2°, by Inferences, which are the reproductions and recombinations of such Impressions.

The second clause extricates the sensational doctrine from its seeming discrepancy with observation. By it knowledge is carried beyond the range of Sense into the

two persons, neither of them deaf, the one complaining of the penetrating shrillness of a sound, while the other maintains there is no sound at all. Thus while the person mentioned by Wollaston could but just hear the note four octaves above the middle E of the piano, others have a distinct perception of sounds full two octaves higher. The chirrup of a sparrow is about the former limit, the cry of the bat about an octave above it, and that of some insects probably another octave."

vast Extra-sensible; and the limitations of Feeling give place to the inexhaustible varieties of Thought. Let us therefore pause a moment to consider the nature of Inference.

30. It is perfectly familiar that the feeling originally due to the objective presence of the stimulus may be revived in the objective absence of that stimulus, by the excitation of the neural process through one or more of the feelings associated with it. The object is a group of sensibles; any one of these is capable of reviving the feeling of the others. Inference thus lies at the very root of mental life, for the very combination of present feelings with past feelings, and the consequent inference that what was formerly felt in conjunction with one group of feelings will again be felt if the conditions are reinstated, — that the sweetness and fragrance formerly experienced in conjunction with the color and form of the apple are again to be revived when the organs of Taste and Smell are brought into relation with this colored object, — this act of inference is necessary to the perception of the object "apple," and is like in kind to all other judgments. Inference is "seeing with the mind's eye," — reinstating what has been, but now is not, present to Sense.

Consciousness is admitted to be the only ground of certitude. All Sensation is certain, indisputable.* The test and measure of certitude is therefore in Sensation. To have a feeling is to be incapable of doubting it. The only possible opening for doubt is not respecting the feeling itself, but respecting some inference connected with it. When I say "I see an apple there," I express an indisputable fact of feeling in terms which imply disputa-

* "Sonnenklar ist nur das Sinnliche, nur wo die Sinnlichkeit, anfängt hört aller Zweifel und Streit auf. Das Geheimniss des unmittelbaren Wissens ist die Sinnlichkeit." — FEUERBACH, *Grundsätzen der Philos. der Zukunft.*

ble inferences. The fact is that I am affected now in a way similiar to that in which I was formerly affected when certain colored shapes excited my retina; and this affection reinstates the feelings which accompanied it on those occasions; the whole group of feelings being named apple. I say, "There is an apple." The inference may be erroneous; on proceeding to verify it by reducing it to sensible experiences I find that the colored object is not an apple, i. e. has not the taste, fragrance, etc., which are elements in that complex perception; the color and form which led to the inference are found to belong to a marble or wooden body; or to some other fruit resembling the apple in some respects, differing in others.

31. With Inference begins error. Since in a simple case of direct Perception we are liable to err, it is intelligible how great must be the liability in more complex mental operations. If Perception is mental vision, in which the unapparent sensibles are rendered apparent, — if it is an act of Judgment involving the assumption of homogeneity which everywhere underlies Judgment,* — and if there is even here need of Verification, this is obviously still more urgent in Ratiocination, i. e. that process of mental vision in which ideas are reinstated in their sensible series, and the relations of things are substituted for the things themselves. A chain of reasoning however involved is nothing but a series of inferences, i. e. ideal presentations of objects not actually present to Sense. Could we *realize* all the links in this chain, by reducing conceptions to perceptions, and perceptions to sensibles, — and this would be effected by placing the corresponding objects in their actual order as a sensible series, — our most abstract reasoning would cease to be anything but a succession of sensations. In astronomical phenomena we really see nothing but the directions, sim-

* Compare Rule X.

ultaneous and successive, according to which the mind constructs the form of the motion which the eye cannot embrace. In biological phenomena from a few data we construct a scheme; and this scheme, say that of the evolution of an embryo, represents to the mind the successive stages which might as easily be presented to the eye by a series of embryos at different epochs of development. The only test we have of the validity of our scheme is to translate ideas into sensations. Any point which may be doubtful is tested by ascertaining its sensible basis. We have mentally arranged the facts in one order, assuming that to be the order in which we should see them; and we pronounce this mental order inexact when we find that what is inferred does not correspond with what is seen. Correct reasoning is simply the ideal assemblage of reals. Bad reasoning results from overlooking either some of the reals, or some of their relations. Thus the timid traveller sees a highwayman, where his calmer companion sees only a sign-post in the evening light. Both infer the existence of objects, which if they could be presented in all sensible relations would affect them as a highwayman in the one case, a sign-post in the other. Which inference is correct? Only reduction to Sensation can decide. This reduction effected, the timid traveller finds that he has allowed emotional suggestions to fill up the gap of unapparent details, and from these has constructed his erroneous vision of a highwayman.

THE EXTRA-SENSIBLE WORLD.

32. It is by the aid of Inference that we generalize. Since we have positive proof that the Sensible World comprises only a portion, and an insignificant portion of Existence, we must ascertain how the vast outlying province of the Invisible can be accessible, and how we reconcile our knowledge of it with the principle of a sensible origin.

It has been shown that even our Sensible World, though resting mainly on Sense, and though all certainty respecting it is the *immediateness* of Sensation, also rests on Inference which is *mediate* Sensation; since there can be no Perception of an object, — nothing but vague Feeling, — unless with present sensations there are linked other sensations in ideal reproduction. In like manner the Extra-sensible World, though resting mainly on Inference, or ideal presentation of reals absent from Sense, necessarily implies the presence of a sensible basis. What is now ideal reproduction was once real production: what is now mediate was once immediate. But — and here lies the point of intersection between perception of the Sensible and perception of the Extra-sensible — the reproduction is never a mere *repetition*, it is always and necessarily somewhat different from the original production. The neural units in the two cases are never precisely the same: an image is always quantitatively different from its sensation. When we are said to perceive an existence, or conceive a process, lying beyond the range of actual presentation, one therefore which never could have been given to Sense, the only test of accuracy open to us, the only mark by which it can be discriminated from a mere illusion, fantasy, or illogical conclusion, is the demonstration of its rigorous correspondence with sensible experience.

33. That there is a knowledge of the Extra-sensible, — a mental vision of the sensibly Invisible, — admits of no dispute; the only hesitation permissible is respecting its validity. We do not actually experience through Feeling a tithe of what we firmly believe, and can demonstrate to Intuition. This Invisible is like the snow at the North Pole; no human eye has beheld it, but the mind is assured of its existence; and is moreover convinced that, if the snow exists there, it has the properties found else-

where. Nor is the Invisible confined to objects which have never been presented to Sense, although they may be presented on some future occasion; it also comprises objects beyond even this possible range, beyond all practicable extension of Sense. It presents objects to the mind's eye such as no bodily eye could discern: molecules and waves having their precise measurements and laws, planets and their stages of evolution before man was.* Only one condition is affixed to the inclusion of this region within the circle of Science, namely, that the objects be in such rigorous agreement with sensibles as to be presentable to Intuition with a certainty almost equivalent to that of Sensation. The limit of mental vision is the limit of verification. And what is that? It is the reduction of Inference to Sensation, or to Intuition. This reduction may be direct, or indirect, the final guaranty is the same. We measure the distances and calculate the masses of the heavenly bodies, not indeed with a foot-rule and balance, yet the foot-rule and balance are our guaranties. We infer the existence of sodium in the atmosphere of the sun; we cannot see or handle it, but we know it is there, with a certainty based on grounds similar to those on which we believe in its presence in our laboratories, namely, by its reactions.

34. Whenever an Inference is in agreement with the positive data of Sense, whenever the Invisible is only an extension of the Visible, we pronounce it rationally certain. There is indeed an assumption here of perfect

* "Indeed the domain of the senses in Nature is almost infinitely small in comparison with the vast region accessible to thought which lies beyond them. From a few observations of a comet when it comes within the range of his telescope, an astronomer can calculate its path in regions which no telescope can reach; and in like manner, by means of data furnished in the narrow world of the senses, we make ourselves at home in other and wider worlds, which can be traversed by the intellect alone." — TYNDALL, *Rede Lecture on Radiant Heat.*

homogeneity in the two cases. But this assumption lies at the root of all induction, all generalization. It is on this that Mathematics founds its superior exactness. After calculating a sufficient number of the terms of a series to have seized its law, we do not require to repeat the calculations for all the succeeding terms, but having found that when the law holds for any one term it holds for the next, we have proved it to be general. Such dispensing with calculation is only justifiable, however, on the assumption that the law is universal; and since there is always a possibility that the law will change after a certain number of terms, we have to guard against that possibility whenever the result is important. So long as the Invisible reveals by its *functions* that it is strictly in accordance with the Visible, we can deal with it in confidence, and verification is open to us; when this boundary is passed, we are helpless. In other words, since all Knowledge is the extension of Experience, bringing what was unknown under the rubric of the known, whenever the Extra-sensible is disengaged from conformity with the Sensible, it is no longer an object of Knowledge, but remains metempirical until the conformity can in any way be established. Just as the base line, when accurately measured, gives the indirect yet accurate measure of the otherwise inaccessible side of the triangle, to know the one involving a knowledge of the other, so the phenomenon presented to Sense gives the accurate though indirect measure of its equivalent beyond Sense.

35. The objects of this Extra-sensible World with which Science is chiefly occupied are the objects either of Inference or Abstraction. Since the inference is only a reproduction of sensations formerly felt, or the extension of such to some new yet similar case, its validity can never surpass that of the original experience; and

since the abstraction is a reproduction, in an abridgment, of concrete experiences, its value must always be determined by those concretes. Thus, whether we are dealing with extra-sensible concretes, such as ether, or vibrations, or molecules; or with abstractions, such as Mind, or Cause, or Force, — the process of Verification is equivalent to that with which we prove the reality of a perceived object. To prove that my perception of an apple is no illusion, I have simply to reduce the inferences involved in the perception to their sensibles: the sweetness, fragrance, solidity, etc., which I do not now feel, but infer, are then transformed from inferences into sensations. To prove that my conceptions of an Ether and its vibrations are representatives of objective reals, though more laborious as an effort, is similar as a procedure: the inferences on which the conceptions are founded, the inductions through which the conclusion is reached, must severally be reduced directly or indirectly to sensations or intuitions; that is to say, either to sensibles or to inductions already established on a sensible basis. *An inference, once verified, becomes equally valid with a sensation.* It is henceforward a logical unit; a standard by which we can compare reals and relations otherwise inaccessible. To know that one thing is heavier than another, we need only lift the one after the other at intervals sufficiently brief for memory to retain the sensible impressions; to know how much the one is heavier than another cannot thus be determined: we need a measure; and this involves the inference that if one thing contains the measure more times than the other it will be *so* much the heavier, — an inference which is an intuition and has been verified.

36. These brief indications suffice to show both the vastness and the limitations of the Extra-sensible, the sweep of possible Science, and the conditions under which the imagination may display its energy. After

such an exposition, it will be idle to object to the doctrine of the sensible limitations of knowledge, on the ground that the greater part of the objects known never were, never could be, presented directly to Sense. In a future chapter on the Ideal Constructions of Science this will be more amply carried out; and the reconciliation between the experiential and the *à priori* schools will be effected, in as far as it can be effected by the exhibition of their common ground.

THE SUPRA-SENSIBLE WORLD.

37. The two divisions of Existence which have just been considered comprise all that is accessible to Experience, and consequently all that is admissible in Science. There is, however, a third division claimed by Theology and Metempirics, the region of the Supra-sensible, or Metempirical, which is closed indeed against the Method of Science, but is open to Faith and Intellectual Intuition. Thinkers who believe in such a world of possible knowledge will reject with scorn the inadequate exposition of the genesis and limitation of knowledge set forth in these pages. They hold the soul to be equipped with powers radically independent of any excitation through Sense, anterior even to the very existence of the organism, and exercised on materials that were never given in feeling.* By these powers the soul is said to penetrate far beyond the range of the Sensible and Extra-sensible, and is brought face to face with ultimate Existence, the ground of all Reality. So far from *this* Invisible World being interpretable by the laws of the Visible, it needs a higher reach of Intuition, and Methods of its own. Schelling in the preface to his work *Vom Ich* scornfully

* JACOBI, *Werke*, II. 59. "Wie es eine sinnliche Anschauung giebt eine Anschauung durch den Sinn, so giebt es eine rationale Anschauung durch die Vernunft."

admits that systems which only hover 'twixt heaven and earth without the courage to push onwards to the ultimate goal are less liable to error, but he prefers the system which, taking a bolder flight, will either have the whole truth or none.

38. Even those who refuse to accept the special organ which Schelling calls the Intellectual Intuition, are forced to accept its equivalent, when they maintain the possibility of metempirical knowledge. Whether called Reason, Fundamental Ideas, Innate Ideas, or Forms of Thought, its one characteristic is that it is an organ of the soul having no community with the organs of Experience; and its products are therefore not amenable to the canons of Experience. "Transcendental Philosophy," says Schelling, meaning the only true Philosophy, "must always be accompanied by the Intellectual Intuition; all the presupposed incomprehensibility of such philosophizing rests on no incomprehensibility of the ideas themselves, but on the absence of the requisite organ to grasp them. Without this Intuition there is no substratum to support this Philosophizing. It is what Space is to Geometry." * He declares the Transcendental Philosophy to be like Geometry a science constructed from postulates. But he overlooks the distinction that Geometry is, and his Transcendental Philosophy is not, constructed from sensible postulates, and is thereby applicable to sensible experience.

Metempirical speculators cheerfully admit the claims of Science within its own sphere, and admit that *there* the inaccessible lines can only be measured by the assumed correspondence with lines that are accessible. But they affirm that in Theology and Metaphysics such a procedure is fallacious, because the problems lie wholly boyond the range of Science, and therefore require other

* *Trans. Idealismus*, p. 51.

Methods. This is paralleled by the inventors of perpetual motion who admit that in all machines hitherto constructed the law is absolute which says "what is gained in force must necessarily be lost in velocity"; but this does not deter them from attempting to construct a machine which shall escape the law. They are confident that their sagacity will detect some unknown resource which will extricate the machine from the tyranny of mechanical laws; and as Carnot well says, "Ils se croient d'autant plus sûrs de la rencontrer qu'ils s'éloignent davantage de tout ce qui paroît avoir de la relation avec les machines usitées, parcequ'ils s'imaginent que la théorie établie pour celles ci, ne peut s'étendre à des constructions qui leur semblent n'y avoir aucun rapport." *

39. What can be said to such speculators? Refutation is impossible. They deny the validity of our tests, the applicability of our Methods. To the inventor of a *perpetuum mobile* the mechanician says: "Produce it, and you will prove our arguments erroneous; but till you have produced perpetual motion we shall continue to hold the attempt chimerical." To the metempirical speculator we may say: "All Experience is against you; yet if you have any means of proving the existence of an organ which grasps realities beyond those given through sensible Experience, we shall admit our error; but till this is proved, we must hold your efforts to be misdirected." †

40. There is one thing, however, which is not permitted

* CARNOT, *Principes Fondamentaux de l'Équilibre et du Mouvement*, Preface, xviii. 1803.

† Schelling places us out of court by declaring that "whoever has not the Intellectual Intuition knows not what it is, understands not what is said of it. A negative condition of its possession is the clear and inner vision into the nothingness of all finite knowledge. . . . . As to the pretended fluctuations in Philosophy, they are merely the appearances of change to ignorant minds." — *Vorlesungen über die Methode*, p. 96.

to the metempirical speculator, even on the largest allowance of liberty of speculation, and that is, to control by his results the results of empirical research, — to interpret the positive or speculative teachings of scientific inquiry by doctrines framed on the metempirical Method. If we grant the existence of a Supra-sensible possible to be known, and admit that it is wholly distinct from the Sensible World, we must insist on the two never being confounded; whereas if they are identical they must never be separated. Thus is the Supra-sensible wholly excluded from the field of Research. Whatever conclusions Speculation may reach respecting Existence lying beyond the sphere of sensible phenomena, must be *kept* in that outlying region. If they are brought into the sphere of phenomena, they become amenable to the canons of sensible Experience.

41. Here the reader sees the application of Rule III. adopted from Newton.* He is requested to ponder that Rule and to compare the criticism of a celebrated metaphysician, Herbart; a criticism all the more remarkable because Herbart claims to found Metaphysics on a scientific basis. After quoting passages from Haüy and Biot which are only different expressions of Newton's Rule, he remarks: "We are then to collect and to connect facts as far as possible, and to keep our eyes open that we be not taken by surprise when facts present themselves. Perception must so far precede Thought that both may stand in assured harmony. We have also to ignore all assump-

* Which has also been casually expressed by Descartes, who, however, frequently violated it in his own speculations: "Nec puto quemquam ratione utentem negaturum, quin longè melius sit, ad exemplum eorum quæ in magnis corporibus accidere sensu percipimus, judicare de iis quæ accidunt in minutis corpusculis, ob solam suam parvitatem sensum effugientibus, quam ad hæc explicanda, novas res nescio quas, nullam cum iis quæ sentiuntur similitudinem habentes excogitare." — *Principia*, IV. cci.

tions and forced interpretations. Well and good. Thus far there is no dispute. But I venture to go further and remark that this method ignores an essential element, namely, that Thought must not only harmonize with Perception, but also with itself."*

Now this element, which is said to be ignored in Newton's Rule, and which would indeed be a fatal omission, is really there in the only meaning of it which has a justification, but is not there in the meaning which it may easily be made to bear, and which is the latent poison of all metempirical speculation, namely, the release of Thought from the control of sensible verification. All that Herbart says in his exposition of Method will be accepted by the positive thinker; who will, however, add that the phrase "harmony of Thought with itself" has positive value only when interpreted as the harmony of one induction with another, and the harmony of inference with sensation. A bank-note is only money when convertible into gold, which in turn is convertible into goods; so long as the *pecunia* really represents the *pecus*, there is no need to drive actual cattle into the market; the transference of the money being equivalent to the transference of the cattle which the money will buy. The mistake of the speculative thinker is that he is too apt to interpret the "harmony of Thought with itself" in a more independent way. He is satisfied with a logical harmony; if no logical contradiction presents itself, he relies on there being a corresponding order in things. The note for twenty pounds of which he makes entry in his ledger may have been issued from an insolvent bank, or may be a forgery, and its worthlessness will never appear in his ledger, but only when an attempt is made

* "Das Denken soll nicht bloss mit dem Anschauen, sondern auch mit sich selbst übereinstimmen." — HERBART, *Allgemeine Metaphysik*, *Werke*, IV. 12.

to convert it into gold or goods; the induction which took its logical position in his speculation could only be proved worthless by objective verification. Thus there is no logical contradiction in the existence of a spirit-world in all its features entirely unlike the sensible world. We cannot say that such a world is impossible; we can only say, that, if it exist, it is to us inaccessible, because to become accessible it must pass into the sphere of the Sensible, and in the passage will *cease* to be Supra-sensible.

42. While therefore Herbart's position, in as far as it concurs with Newton's Rule is entirely acceptable, in the only direction of departure from that Rule it is the reintroduction of the metempirical fallacy, that is to say, the release of Thought from the conditions of sensible Experience.

I will add, however, that Newton himself on one remarkable occasion carries his Rule so far as to identify Spirit with Matter with a strict consistency which must be painful to minds accustomed to venerate Newton, and to execrate Matter. The passage has already been quoted (*Introd.*, § 49*a*), and may fitly here be followed by Dr. Thomas Young's attempt to improve on it, while still adhering to the Rule. "We see forms of matter," he says, "differing in subtility and mobility under the names of solids, liquids, and gases; and above these there are semi-material existences which produce the phenomena of electricty and magnetism, and either caloric or an universal ether; higher still perhaps are the cause of gravitation and the immediate agents in attractions of all kinds, which exhibit some phenomena apparently still more remote *from all that is compatible with material bodies;* and of these different orders of beings the more refined and immaterial *appear to pervade freely the grosser.* It seems therefore natural to believe that the *analogy* *may be continued still further* until it rises into existence absolutely immaterial and spiritual." *

43. In reading such a passage, and remembering the greatness of its author as an investigator, one is painfully impressed by the treacherous nature of the "harmony of Thought with itself," — unless one attributes the passage to the influence of tradition. Did Young ever attempt to verify the sensible meaning of *semi-material* existences? Had he done so he must have seen that they could only be either bodies of greater tenuity than those from which they are distinguished, — or bodies one half material, the other half non-material. In the first case they are sensibles, or extra-sensibles, and subject to all the canons of sensible Experience; in the other case they are unthinkables, no definite conception of such hybrids being possible. The popular notion indeed of soul and body united in one organism may seem to render the conception of semi-material bodies intelligible; but this notion, when exact, is of two things, body and soul, not of one thing half and half. In fact semi-material bodies are contradictions; like loud circles, or red tastes, they cannot be united in thought. To pass, as Young does, from material solids to gases, and from gases to bodies that are semi-material, and from these to bodies that are wholly spiritual, is as rational as to pass from one term of a series of numbers to a number which is an integer *plus* blue, and from this blue integer to a pure blue, and thence to no color at all. He professes to be guided by Analogy. But this guidance has its conditions; and Newton would have reminded his great disciple that in passing from one form of Matter to another and subtler form, we must carry with us all the inductions of sensible Experience, and not gradually drop these to replace them "by dreams and vain fictions of our own devising." The only

* YOUNG, *Lectures on Natural Philosophy*, I. 610. 1807.

corrections needed are those suggested in Rules VII. and IX.

44. The following passage written by one of the founders of the experimental doctrine of the Conservation of Force, the Danish physicist, Colding, exhibits the same fallacy: "The first idea I conceived of the relationship between the forces of nature was the following. As these forces are something spiritual and immaterial, entities whereof we are cognizant only by their mastery over Nature, these entities must be, of course, very superior to anything material in this world; and as it is obvious that it is through them only that the wisdom we perceive and admire in Nature expresses itself, these powers must evidently be in relationship to the spiritual and intellectual power itself that guides Nature in her progress; but if such is the case it is quite impossible to conceive these forces as anything naturally mortal or perishable. Surely, therefore, the forces ought to be regarded as absolutely imperishable?" *

Although this is not worse than may be found in hundreds of speculative writings, it is worth holding up as a warning against the practice of "harmonizing Thought with itself," irrespective of any criticism of the ideas harmonized. There is no fault in the logic. An accountant might balance his ledger without rectifying a single entry. But on presenting the bills and checks for payment there would be everywhere the answer, "No effects." Colding begins by an arbitrary distinction, separates one class of phenomena — forces — from Nature, and then assigns to them a mastery over Nature. Grant this, and grant that the forces are spiritual intelligences, and the consequences follow swiftly and surely. Let us propound a musical theory, on a similar method: we class violinists apart from the human nature which is thrilled by

* *Philos. Mag.*, XXVIII. 57. 1864.

their performances; and as these thrilling tones are "evidently related" to the music of the spheres, it follows that violinists are imperishable. How far such a theory will illuminate and advance the art of violin playing, we shall not pause to consider.

45. One more example, and it shall be taken from the writings of one to whom Physics is deeply indebted, J. R. Mayer. The more illustrious the teacher of an error, the more instructive the example. "In Nature," says Mayer, "there are two kinds of causes between which Experience tells us of no intermediate link. The one kind comprises those causes which are ponderable and impenetrable, i. e. Matter. The other kind comprises the causes which are without these properties, i. e. Forces, which are named the Imponderables. Forces are therefore indestructible, variable, imponderable objects." *

The objection to such a separation of Force from Matter is twofold: It misrepresents the fact of both being pure Abstractions; and it transforms a logical into a physical distinction; thus creating two entities, and replunging Speculation into that Scholasticism from which the emergence was so laborious. It reintroduces the old Dualism in which matter is passive, destitute of qualities though capable of receiving Motion, capable of housing qualities, and of becoming the temporary tenement of wandering Forces. In this scheme, qualities are merely superadded, and are consequently capable of being separated. The dream of the Alchemists — and of Francis Bacon also — was to effect this separation. They believed that the transmutation of metals into gold would be easy if they could only hit upon a plan of isolating the Form of gold; and easy it would be, — the difficulty lies in the first step.

* J. R. MAYER, *Die Mecanik der Wärme*, p. 4. 1867. This is a republication of all his essays on Force.

46. Mayer's conception is one which can lead to nothing but confusion. The same must be said of all attempts to give expression to the Supra-sensible. The range of possible knowledge is too wide for man ever to exhaust it; and there is no need to render Research more laborious by impatient rebellion against the inevitable limitations of our faculties. Within the sphere of the Sensible, with its Extra-sensible extensions, there is more than enough to occupy us. To see how Research can effectively be conducted within that sphere, we must examine the various principles it invokes, the Method it employs. That we may do this on a secure foundation, we must first inquire into the nature of Abstraction.

CHAPTER IV.

THE REALITY OF ABSTRACTIONS.

47. No reproach is more frequently urged against metaphysicians than that they confound abstractions with realities, and treat the figments of the mind as objective existences. Nor is it to be denied that the reproach is often deserved, for the error is one to which our native infirmity predisposes all of us. But the gravamen lies not in the "realizing of abstractions," — since that is a process which Science pursues with advantage, — it lies in an imperfect recognition of the nature and validity of the process, and a consequent confusion of the products. Alarmed at the excesses of the Schoolmen and their modern followers, many writers have run into the opposite extreme, and denied all reality to abstractions; whereas the true position is that which assigns to abstractions precisely the degree of reality which pertains to the concretes which have furnished them.

48. The usual explanation of Abstraction limits it to the Logic of Signs. It is said to be "the power which the mind has of attending to one aspect of a complex object, disregarding all the other aspects." Thus, although we have no possible experience of Motion which is not that of a moving something, no experience of Color without Extension, we can and do abstract each from the other, and regard each by itself. There is no objection to this explanation, except its limitation. This process of Abstraction is equally operative in Perception; a fact

which introduces two important considerations into the question. First, it discloses the criterion to be employed in all Abstraction. Secondly, it discloses that the process is not due to a power which the mind *can* employ, by an effort of will, but a process which it *must* follow. Perception, while it groups round a present sensation many absent sensations, never recalls *all* the details previously experienced in conjunction, but always detaches some of these, leaving the rest in twilight vagueness, or complete obscurity. In our perception of a horse, for example, there is not present to consciousness a tithe of the sensations which that object has formerly excited, but only an abstract of these sufficient for recognition. And this by a law of Sensibility: whatever is *out of focus* is necessarily more or less disregarded, since it can only be regarded by being brought into focus. Abstraction is focussing, whether by Sense or Intellect.

49. In an interesting work on modern English Psychology * M. Ribot calls attention to a point seldom clearly apprehended, namely, that Abstraction has its degrees as Number its powers; and that some confusion would be avoided if Philosophy had a precise notation for the ascending degrees of Abstraction, corresponding with the increasing powers of Number, thus exhibiting at a glance whether the abstractions were based on abstractions of a lower degeee, or on concretes. Whiteness, for example, is an abstraction of the first degree, and expresses simply the quality common to all white objects; Extension again is likewise of the first degree; so is soldier, or simply fighting-man. But Army is an abstraction of a higher degree, based on the abstraction soldier; expressing, however, far more than soldiers, because in-

* RIBOT, *La Psychologie Anglaise: École Expérimentale. James Mill, Stuart Mill, Bain, Spencer, Lewes, Bailey, Morell, Murphy.* P. 67. 1871.

cluding elements of military organization. War again is an abstraction still more remote from its concretes, and expressing in an abbreviated form a heterogeneous assemblage of military and political abstractions. Man, Nation, and Humanity are three degrees of Abstraction: the two first being Notations of the concretes given in Experience; the third being not only further removed from all such concretes, but also including the ideal conceptions we form of the capabilities and possibilities of human nature, if it were once freed from present hindrances. It is obvious that the *transcendent* element is involved in each of these abstractions, but in very unequal degrees; the transcendence in Man being not only carried into Nation and Humanity, but being there complicated by the transcendence which is involved in the conception of Nation, which is in turn complicated by that involved in the conception of Humanity.

50. And here we become aware of the paramount danger which besets speculation in dealing with abstraction. It is that of not eliminating the transcendent element, but of introducing it into the calculation, and subsequently personifying the abstraction. Having once detached an aspect, and considered it apart, the mind is prone to assign an objective reality to this separated aspect; and having once transformed a predicate into a subject, the logical tendency is further carried out, and predicates are assigned to this predicate. The danger is slight with abstractions of the first degree. Probably no one ever personified Whiteness, as Virtue and Nature have been personified. Though when we remember that Boundary had its god Terminus, Marriage its god Hymen, and Sleep and Dreaming their gods, it is conceivable that even Whiteness may have passed from a Notation into a Personification. Be this as it may, Rule XI. furnishes a decisive test, by which all abstractions whatever may be

used with license and safety. Remembering that in all cases there is some concrete Feeling with its objective correspondent, and on the other hand that in no case is the whole of the concrete reality expressed in the Notation, we conclude that a careful analysis will reveal the precise degree of reality which pertains to every abstraction; it is only necessary to pass from the symbol to the things symbolized, to re-immerse the abstraction in the concretes out of which it emerged, and we may reduce all that is inferential to pure sensible Experience.

51. Having said so much of the process, let us now say something of the products. The metaphysician who realizes abstractions errs, indeed, when he does not follow Rule XI.; but the man of science is liable to the same error; while some men of science, in alarm at the error, deny all reality whatever to abstractions. The doctrine of a Vital Principle once universal, and still lingering in a few minds, is an example of both mistakes. One school so far realized the abstraction as to believe that a Vital Principle, distinct from and independent of the concrete forces grouped together in an organism, existed objectively, and not simply in the mind as a shorthand expression of the various concretes known to Feeling; while another school, recognizing the subjective creation of this abstraction, denied that it had any objective reality: one transformed a subjective process into an objective entity; the others forgot that objective concretes were expressed by the subjective Notation.

52. When the question of reality is raised, we should first define the term. Is it simply the existence of a group of sensibles indicated by our idea? then the reality of an army is as indisputable as the reality of a soldier; the reality of a river is as positive as that of its constituent molecules. The army is a group, the river is a group; the group has laws not directly deducible from

the laws of its constituents, but belonging to it *as* a group. But there is not an army *and* its soldiers; there is not a river *and* its molecules. There is but one reality which, under different aspects, abstract and concrete, group and constituents, furnishes different conceptions.

CO-ORDINATION.

53. How ready physiologists have been to commit the error with which metaphysicians are reproached, is patent to every well-informed inquirer. Let us select Co-ordination for our example. Certain sets of muscles acting frequently together, as in locomotion, this united action is called their co-ordination. The term expresses compendiously what has been observed and inferred. It is then generalized, extended to all united actions of muscles, or other organs, and the abstract conception of Co-ordination emerges. But now the common tendency towards personification begins to operate, and this abstraction is transformed into a Faculty, almost an Entity. This operation once effected, we must not marvel if we find anatomists eagerly seeking for the *seat* of this Faculty. They soon believe that they have found what they sought. They observe some part of the motor mechanism which, when injured, alters or destroys the Co-ordination; and they rush to the conclusion that this part is the co-ordinating organ. The Cerebellum is the organ most in favor; and such is the laxity of opinion on this subject, that the Cerebellum continues to be credited with this imaginary function of Co-ordination, in spite of the indisputable and varied evidence, both of experiment and pathology, that the Cerebellum may be destroyed, or removed, without the destruction of Co-ordination, and conversely that the "organ" may be intact while this "function" is abolished!

Co-ordination is an abstraction; what are its concretes? Our knowledge of the motor mechanism is our knowledge of its interdependent parts, the nerves, nerve-centres, muscles, ligaments, bones, etc.; each of these parts must co-operate with the others, or the effect will be wanting; when these have been enumerated and their interdependence assigned, there is nothing over and above this mutual interaction in the shape of a *Co-ordination* requiring a special organ: the Co-ordination simply *is* this interdependent action; the co-ordinating organ is this group of organs. In any act of locomotion various stages may be specified. There is first the neural act, — the stimulus of a sensory nerve transmitted to its centre; next a psychical act, the volitional reflex on a motor nerve, an act that may be conscious or unconscious; then a physiological act, the muscular contraction; finally a mechanical act, the movement of the limbs against gravity. Co-ordination is the compendious expression for this mechanism in action. We may for brevity's sake describe the nerve-centre as co-ordinating the various muscles, grouping their several contractions towards one particular end; but this grouping is only possible because the organic mechanism has already been so constituted that the muscles will respond to a given stimulus in this particular manner, — this flexor relaxing when that extensor contracts, and so on. The part played by the centre is doubtless important, — it is the mainspring of the watch; but neither centre, nor main-spring, has anything resembling a "faculty of co-ordination"; and the acceptance of such a faculty is a "realization of abstractions" on a par with any metaphysical chimera.

54. Anatomists endeavoring to detect the *seat* of Co-ordination, not in the whole of the co-operant organs, but in some one organ, may be compared with those who im-

agine they have detected the seat of the Mind in the gray matter of the Cerebrum; though both would laugh to scorn the announcement that the seat of Life was in the mucous membrane of the alimentary canal: a localization which is quite as rational. Co-ordination, Mind, and Life are abstractions; they are realities in the sense of being drawn from real concretes; but they are not realities existing apart from their concretes, otherwise than in our Conception; and to seek their objective substratum we must seek the concrete objects of which they are the symbols.

55. Language is another abstraction which has been personified as a Faculty.* Of late years certain pathological phenomena of great interest, classed under the general term Aphasia, have misled many physiologists into the error of localizing this pretended Faculty in the third convolution of the left anterior lobe of the Cerebrum. I shall hereafter have occasion to discuss this anatomical question; at present I allude to it simply as an example of the loose way in which men of science often deal with abstractions. Theology has explained the phenomena of Language in a characteristic way, which is little less scientific. It assumed Language to be a gift to man direct from the Creator, — handed over to him, in short, as a *thing*. This explanation has been ridiculed by men who see nothing ridiculous in the supposition of Language being a "Faculty," or as some say a "Property of a cerebral convolution." And yet in my judgment the only superiority which the latter can claim over the theological hypothesis is that of directing attention to the physiological mechanism, though only to one part of the

* To what lengths this tendency towards personification may be carried by speculative thinkers is seen in the hypothesis of Becker, reported by Steinthal in his *Abriss der Sprachwissenschaft*, p. 47, 1871, where Becker presents Language as the human Logos incorporating itself in sensuous reality, just as the idea of Life realizes itself in the organism.

mechanism, and thus keeping the hypothesis within the sphere of possible verification.

Language is an abstraction ; its concretes are the articulate sounds of the vocal organs, expressive of emotions and ideas ; and the mechanism is necessarily that of ideation and vocal expression : a very complex mechanism, composed of many parts. It is absurd to confound this with a particular Faculty, or a Property of tissue ; absurd to seek for a particular seat, or tissue, as its "organ."

56. Psychology has long been obscured by a cloud of such personified abstractions, — processes transformed into Faculties. Memory, for example, has not only been made a special Faculty with its special organ, it has even been separated into two Faculties : the one, Reminiscence, a passive retention of images ; the other, Recollection, an active reproduction of images. What wonder if the science is in a backward condition, when such is the Method employed !

57. One point more is worthy of remark. Abstractions, like all other symbols, can only be used safely by those who are careful in assigning the sensible values, whenever reasoning quits the symbolical sphere. Abstractions are words having the values of things only so far as they express sensible concretes. They are counters, and sometimes also counterfeits ; they are Notations of objective experiences, and also of arbitrary combinations. As symbols it is of little consequence if they have no other community with the things symbolized than that of a conventional sign to represent them. The gold coin, ducat or sovereign, which represents the exchangeable value of the thirty or fifty things it will purchase, has no other community with these things ; it is simply an abstract symbol of their concrete values, and as an abstract is perfectly *general*, that is, represents all equivalent values. Virtue is, in like manner, the abstraction of the

moral qualities in human actions. The coin is not only a symbol of value, it is a concrete thing having precise properties. The word Virtue is also a concrete fact, the conception it expresses is a determinate group of neural units, having the properties of neural groups. The coin may be debased by alloy, the word may be perverted by an inclusion of heterogeneous meanings. The coin has to be weighed, the word translated into its concrete meanings, when any doubt arises respecting the exchangeable value of the one, or the objective reality of the other.

CHAPTER V.

IDEAL CONSTRUCTION IN SCIENCE.

58. "No priestly dogmas," says Hume, "invented on purpose to tame and subdue the rebellious reason of mankind, ever shocked common-sense more than the doctrine of the infinite divisibility of extension with its consequences, as they are pompously displayed by all geometricians and metaphysicians with a kind of triumph and exultation. A real quantity infinitely less than any finite quantity containing quantities infinitely less than itself, and so on *in infinitum;* this is an edifice so bold and prodigious that it is too weighty for any pretended demonstration to support because it shocks the clearest and most natural principle of human reason. But what renders the matter more extraordinary is that these seemingly absurd opinions are supported by a chain of reasoning the clearest and most natural; nor is it possible to allow the premises without admitting the consequences."

59. This is an echo of the arguments put forward by Berkeley in his famous *Analyst,* wherein he endeavors to justify the incomprehensible dogmas of Theology by arraigning the not less incomprehensible dogmas accepted in Mathematics. Hume does not intend it simply as a retort, but as an argument to support the sceptical position that Reason is incompetent to solve her own doubts, and that these doubts, which cannot be answered by Philosophy, are nevertheless suppressed by Action. The

fallacy of this argument will appear when we see that the absurdities and incomprehensibilities with which Mathematics are arraigned do not exist. It is true that many fictions and conventions are introduced, but they are never made to take the place of realities; zero is made a quantity, and a curve a straight line, without any misgiving; imaginary quantities and impossible quantities are freely employed; but the question is not whether conventions are made which deviate from common-sense, the question is, What are the uses to which these conventions are applied? Every one admits that the language of Mathematicians is often contradictory and ambiguous; we must also admit that their conceptions are sometimes wanting in the precision which would enable a logical justification to be given for operations which practice justifies. We need a Philosophy of Mathematics to show that an impossible quantity is a possible operation on quantity;* and that infinity, which is indeed inconceivable as a magnitude, all magnitudes having fixed limits, is perfectly intelligible as a *variable* limit, dependent on our will and pleasure. Literally interpreted, nothing can be less conceivable than infinitesimals which are sometimes treated as if they were real quantities, at other times as zeros, "and seem by their equivocal properties to be something between existence and nothing." Mathematically interpreted,

* Thus suppose b is greater than a, and the difference is c, then $a - b$ is an impossible quantity, for you cannot subtract the greater from the less. But $a - b$ is nevertheless a possible operation: it is $a - (a + c)$ which is $a - a - c$, and the result of the operation is $-c$.

"It may seem strange," says Whewell, commenting on Fresnel's application of his formula to the case of internal reflection at the surface of a transparent body, "to those who are not mathematicians, but it is undoubtedly true that in many cases in which the solution of a problem directs impossible arithmetical or algebraical operations to be performed, these directions may be so interpreted as to point out a true solution of the question." — *History of the Inductive Sciences*, II. 337. 1857.

however, they are operations on quantities, which may be made as small as we please without thereby altering the quantities of which we seek the relations.* They are *instruments* of construction, not *elements* of construction: hypotheses, not factors. In interpreting an algebraic operation it is the result, and not the operation, which fixes attention; as in the construction of a palace it is the building itself, and not the scaffolding, which has to be judged.

From this point of view a logical justification may be reached for all the seemingly absurd artifices employed by mathematicians. If the theologian were to imitate the practice of the mathematician, and eliminate from his *results* all that was arbitrary and fictitious in his *operations*, not allowing his incomprehensible data to enter into the final equations, not allowing what was assumed in the premises to be more than an assumption in the conclusion, then indeed Berkeley's argument would be irrefragable.

60. But Hume is more directly concerned with the incompetence of Reason. Reason, no less than Perception and Intuition, is liable to error. The errors of each may be rectified through similar tests. When Perception errs, — when there is what men call an error of Sense, — how is it rectified? Lafontaine charmingly says: —

> "Quand l'eau courbe un baston ma raison le redresse,
> La raison décide en maîtresse,
> Mes yeux moyennant ce secours
> Ne me trompent jamais en men mentant toujours."

And Kant declares the vulgar objection against the veracity of the senses to be the foolishest that can be urged, "not because the senses always judge correctly, but because they never judge at all." † The stick which

* CARNOT, *Métaphysique du Calcul Infinitesimal*, Chap. I.

† KANT, *Anthropologie*, § 10. In the way Kant understands Judgment this is true; but I hold that the logical process technically called

appears bent when seen in the water does not give a false impression of the stick in the water; but the inference that this stick will present this aspect when out of the water is precipitate and false. The falsity is shown by reducing Inference to Sensation, — by removing the stick from the water, and then looking at it. This once done, the memory of it enables Reason on any future occasion to redress, not the error of Sense but the error of Inference.

Intuition, when it errs, may be corrected in the same way. It is mental vision, and is as liable to error as optical vision. Reasoning is also Inference, mental vision, and is corrected by reducing judgments to their sensible elements.

61. Hume did not clearly understand that Science is essentially an ideal construction very far removed from a real transcript of facts. Its most absolute conclusions are formed from abstractions expressing modes of existence which never were, and never could be, real; and are very often at variance with sensible Experience. It not only deals with data that are extra-sensible, but with data avowedly fictitious. The point, the line, and the circle are abstractions; they are elements of ideal, not of sensible space. Nevertheless out of these abstractions a science is constructed which is rigorously exact in itself, and is found to harmonize with that very Experience which it appears to contradict. In the presence of such a fact the question may well arise: How can such abstractions have a positive value, an objective validity, yet metempirical abstractions be rejected? or, to put it in Berkeley's way, Why do you trust the mathematician, and distrust the theologian? The answer to this ques-

Judgment is inseparable from sensation. Aristotle may be interpreted in the same sense : *ἡ μὲν γὰρ αἴσθησις τῶν ἰδίων ἀεί ἀληθὴς, καὶ πᾶσιν ὑπάρχει τοῖς ζῴοις, διανοεῖσθαι δ'ἐνδέχεται καί ψευδῶς, καὶ οὐδενὶ ὑπάρχει ᾧ μὴ καὶ λόγος.* *De Anima*, lib. III. Chap. III. 20.

tion must be postponed till we have examined more closely the procedure of Science, and recognized its essentially ideal construction out of real experience.

62. I say ideal construction, and emphasize it, with the intention of meeting the vulgar objection, iterated from all sides, against the Experiential Method, whose followers are said "to believe only in what they can see and touch"; whereas the truth is that Science mounts on the wings of Imagination into regions of the Invisible and Impalpable, peopling these regions with Fictions more remote from fact than the fantasies of the Arabian Nights are from the daily occurrences in Oxford Street. The fictions of the thinker differ from the fictions of the poet in not being wayward caprices; they are constructed in obedience to rigorous canons, and moulded by the pressures of Reality; two conditions absent in the fictions both of Fairyland and of Metempirics. It is worthy of remark that the two regions of indisputable certainty are the extremes of the mental world, — Sensation and Abstraction. There is no doubt possible in Sensation, whatever doubt may hover round Inference from it. There is no doubt possible in Abstraction, whatever doubt may hover round its concrete reality. The intermediate region of Inference is the sphere of doubt.*

63. Now inferences are hypotheses; and these become

* "Les notions les plus abstraites, celles que le commun des hommes regarde comme les plus inaccessibles, sont souvent celles qui portent avec elles la plus grande lumière : l'obscurité semble s'emparer de nos idées à mesure que nous examinons dans un objet plus de propriétés sensibles ; l'impénétrabilité, ajoutée à l'idée de l'étendue semble nous offrir un mystère de plus ; la nature du mouvement est une énigme pour les philosophes ; en un mot plus ils approfondissent l'idée qu'ils se forment de la matière plus cette idée s'obscurcit et paroît vouloir leur échapper ; plus ils se persuadent que l'existence des objets extérieurs appuyée sur le témoignage équivoque de nos sens est ce que nous connaissons le moins imparfaitement en eux." — D'ALEMBERT, *Traité de Dynamique*, p. ii. 1796.

less and less doubtful in the exact proportion of their reduction to Intuition or Sensation. We shall presently see the part played by Hypothesis ; here let us be content with the significant fact that Science is so truly ideal, without pretence of reflecting real existence, that it avowedly relies on data known *not* to be true, except within its own sphere of Abstraction.*

Note, however this essential point: the abstraction must not have been arbitrarily formed if it is to be subsequently applied to reality: it must have been formed from concretes (*by the substitution of ideal limits for sensibles*) ; and this condition having been fulfilled, the sensible concretes which are its elements not having been capriciously introduced, we may be certain that the abstraction is as true *in its sphere*, as the sensibles were in theirs. A ratio once abstracted from numbers is as true as the numbers from which it was abstracted. In this way an abstraction becomes a truth of Nature, though departing from the phenomena of Nature by its disregard of details.

64. The first law of Motion is an absolute truth. But the supposition that any real body will pursue an uniform movement in a straight line, is flagrantly at variance with all observation, and with what is even physically possible. No such phenomenon was ever seen. No such phenomenon could present itself in an universe like ours, where Motion is always accelerated or retarded, and always more or less divergent from a straight line. The ideal law is absolute within ideal space: it is the identical proposition that no change in velocity or direction can occur unless the factors of such a change are operant. But within real

* "Il importe peu aux géomètres qu'il existe physiquement une sphère parfaite, un plan parfait ; ces figures *ne sont que les limites intellectuelles* des grandeurs matérielles qu'ils considèrent." — MONTUCLA, *Hist. des Mathématiques*, I. 27.

space the requisite conditions are unrealizable: the presence of other bodies in movement must always obstruct the realization of the conditions: the factors of a change are always present.

65. There *is* a real law of Motion, one to which all movements conform without variation; it may be expressed in the formula, *Motion always pursues the line of least resistance.* This formula has the utmost generality. It does not formulate the process as if Motion were necessarily rectilinear; that is quite an arbitrary assumption, and is open to Comte's criticism;* but it says that *whatever* the direction impressed, that, and that only, will be preserved, until another impress modify it.†

66. The ideal law sets aside all resistances. From the Pisgah of *what is,* the mind sees what *will be,* or what *would be,* if all conflicting movements were allowed to neutralize each other. Laws are indeed nothing but general formulæ expressing general facts from which all disturbing particulars are eliminated. They do not describe the path which bodies actually pursue, but the path the bodies tend to take, and would take were the obstacles removed. Thus, to cite the law of the tides,—

* "À l'origine du mouvement il est clair que la trajectoire du corps n'a point encore de caractère géometrique déterminé, et que c'est seulement après que le corps a parcouru un certain espace qu'on peut constater quelle ligne il décrit. Il est evident par la géometrie que le mouvement initial au lieu d'être regardé comme rectiligne pourrait être indifféremment supposé circulaire, parabolique, ou suivant toute autre ligne tangente à la trajectoire effective, en sorte que la même argumentation répétée pour chacune de ces lignes conduirait à une conclusion absolument indéterminée." — COMTE, *Philosophie Positive,* I. 558.

† Compare the celebrated "principle of least action" formulated by Maupertius: "La trajectoire d'un corps soumis à l'action de forces quelconques devait nécessairement être telle que l'intégrale du produit de la vitesse du mobile par l'élément de la courbe décrete fût toujours un *minimum,* relativement à sa valeur dans toute autre courbe."

there never is, in fact, sufficient time for the sea to assume the form towards which it tends, and which it would assume were the period longer; the mathematician disregards this fact, and substitutes his ideal law in its place. If, on this principle, a woman were to argue that her hunchback lover had a form of graceful symmetry, because his back would be straight were there no curvature of the spine, we should point out that she confounded the concrete with the abstract, the real with the ideal. In like manner were any one to declare the law of the tides to be false, because the observed facts did not conform to it, we should point out that laws being ideal constructions are not transcripts of real particulars.

67. Again: the path of a planet is said to be an ellipse. Every one knows that the real orbit is nothing of the kind. The ellipse is not to be found in the heavens, but in the calculations of astronomers. The path would be elliptical *if* there were only one planet moving round the sun; but as, in fact, there are many planets, all acting on each other by forces varying with their varying positions, the planets *cannot* move in exact ellipses. the radius vector of each does *not* pass over equal areas in equal times. The orbit is not only not an ellipse, it is not any regularly formed curve; nor is the *same* curve described in successive revolutions.

Are then Kepler's laws illusions? By no means: they are abstractions; they are Types erected by scientific Imagination, which moulds the elements of concrete observation into abstractions by getting rid of all perturbing particulars. The planet is supposed to move in an ellipse, by assuming the elements of the ellipse to have been perpetually altering. The supposition is a fiction, and is justified by its results. The reader sees at once that by similar fictions Ptolemy and his successors represented the movements of the planets, adding epicycle on cycle to make theory approximate to observation.*

Sir John Herschel reminds us that Kepler's laws are to be regarded as only first approximations to the much more complicated ones which actually prevail, and that "to bring the remote observations into rigorous and mathematical accordance with each other, and at the same time retain the extremely convenient nomenclature and relations of the elliptic system, it becomes necessary to modify to a certain extent our verbal expression of the laws, and to regard the numerical data or *elliptic elements* of the orbits as not absolutely permanent, but subject to a series of slow and almost imperceptible changes. These changes may be neglected when we consider only a few revolutions; but going on from century to century and continually accumulating, they at length produce material departures in the orbits from their original state." †

68. Another fiction is that by which solids are distinguished from fluids; it assigns to the molecules of fluids an independence as respects cohesion, enabling them to move freely among each other. This is needful for calculation, though obviously untrue in reality, many of the observed phenomena of fluids being due

* "Pour représenter le mouvement de la planète les astronomes imaginent un astre fictif qui se meut circulairement autour du soleil dans le plan de l'orbite ; qui part du périhélie au même instant quela planète, et dont la distance angulaire à ce point est toujours égale au premier terme *nt* de la valeur *v*. Le rayon vecteur de cet astre se meut uniformement et fait à chaque instant avec celui de la planète un angle égal à 2 e. sin. *nt*. Cet angle variable s'appelle *l'équation du centre*. Lorsque l'angle *v* est égal à deux ou à quatre angles droits, les deux angles *v* et *nt* sont égaux ; par conséquent l'astre fictif passe à l'aphélie et revient au périhélie en même temps que la planète ; mais dans la première moitié de la révolution la planète précède l'astre, et dans la seconde l'astre précède la planète." — POISSON, *Traité de Mécanique*, I. 369. 1811.

† HERSCHEL, *Astronomy*, Art. 489.

to the cohesion of their molecules, a cohesion less energetic but similar in kind to that in solids; and this fact occasions many discrepancies between theory and practice, notably in the flow of liquids from an orifice. Indeed it is perfectly well understood that all the applications of theory to practice are only approximations. "Take for instance the very simple case of a crow-bar employed to move a heavy mass. The accurate mathematical investigation of the action would involve the simultaneous treatment of the motions of every part of bar, fulcrum, and mass raised; and from our almost complete ignorance of the nature of matter and molecular forces, it is clear that such a treatment of the problem is impossible. It is a result of observation that the particles of the bar, fulcrum, and mass separately retain throughout the process nearly the same relative positions. Hence the idea of solving, instead of the above impossible problem, another in reality quite different, but while infinitely simpler obviously leading to *nearly* the same results as the former. The new form is given at once by the experimental result of the trial. *Imagine* the masses involved to be *perfectly rigid* (i. e. incapable of changing their form or dimensions) and the infinite series of *forces really acting may be left out of consideration;* so that the mathematical investigation deals with a finite (and generally small) number of forces instead of a practically infinite number." *

69. Were the whole circle of the sciences to pass before us, each would in turn display the essentially ideal nature of its construction, and wide departure from reality, either in its abstractions or in its hypotheses. The abstractions necessarily disregard particulars. The laws, usually accepted as absolutely exact (and justly so in the

* THOMSON and TAIT, *Natural Philosophy*, I. 337. 1867.

region of Abstraction), are "only general truths always more or less falsified in every particular case." *

The hypotheses are fictions, provisional guesses. So far from Facts, Perceptions, constituting the material of Science, as is often said or implied, they are simply the elements out of which its material is constructed. Perception gives the naked fact of Sense, isolated, unconnected, merely juxtaposed with other facts, and without far-reaching significance. To the brute simplicity of Sensation must be added the artifice of Construction. Science looks *through* the brute fact, to contemplate the Abstraction which gives it connection, significance. Hence the paradox that we understand the fall of bodies only through the movements of the planets; the growth of a plant only through biological laws. It is through the manifold ideal constructions of the Possible that we learn to appreciate the Actual. Facts are mere letters which have their meaning only in the words they form; and these words again have their meaning, not in themselves alone, but in their positions in the sentence.

The point here insisted on has always been familiar to philosophers in each particular case, but I am not aware of any philosopher having boldly generalized the observation, and proclaimed the introduction of Fiction to be a necessary procedure of Research. The dread lest the admission of Fiction should throw doubt over the certainty of the conclusions reached by its aid, may probably have prevented the generalization; especially when no sharp distinction had been drawn between the fictions of Science and the fictions of Poetry. But perhaps the most deterrent influence has been due to the erroneous conception, almost universal, of the phenomena of Nature being

* "Seulement des vérités générales toujours plus ou moins faussées dans chaque cas particulier." — JAMIN, *Cours de Physique de l'École Polytéchnique*, I. 28.

determined by Law. This must be replaced by the more accurate conception of the *Law being determined by the phenomena.* What we call Laws of Nature are not objective existences, but subjective abstractions, — formulæ in which the multifarious phenomena are stripped of their variety and reduced to unity.

70. Before proceeding to give precision to this perhaps paradoxical view of Law, we may pursue the illustration of the scientific employment of Fiction, especially in the creation of Abstract Types. It has already been shown that the first law of Motion is no expression of the actual movements, but simply the ideal standard by which all movements may be measured.

The mathematician knows that when a point moves along a curve there is inaccuracy in saying that it moves in any one direction through any arc however small. But a straight line may be found at every point which more nearly than any other straight line represents the direction of the motion. In the same way no motion can be uniform, no velocity can be uniform, but we can at every instant assign an uniform velocity which shall more nearly than any other represent the rate at which the body is moving. This is obviously an ideal construction, not a real transcription. Assuming that if there were no force traversing the direction of a body, then the body would proceed in a straight line, we are enabled to estimate the forces in any *deviation* from that straight line. Rectilinear Motion, though never possible, is thus the ideal Type to which all actual motions are ideally made to conform. We must regard it purely in abstraction, — the ideal limit replacing the real limit, — otherwise the law is false.*

* "La direction d'une force est celle de la ligne suivant laquelle le point se mouvrait en vertu de son action, s'il était entièrement libre." — DUHAMEL, *Mécanique*, I. 28. But as the point never *is* entirely free,

71. Schelling well says * that "the necessary tendency of all Science is to pass from Nature to Intelligence. The highest perfection of research would be the thorough spiritualization of natural laws, reducing them to laws of Intuition and Thought. The material phenomena must give place to their laws. Optical phenomena are nothing but a geometry whose lines are drawn by light; and this light itself is of dubious materiality."

It may not at first be apparent why, since we have always to deal with concretes, we must always transform them into abstractions; why, having to understand the phenomena presented to Sense, we effect this through Laws that are intelligible but not sensible. An examination, however, of the conditions of Knowledge discloses that Science differs from Sensation in being indirect and constructive, — that Abstraction is a primary condition of Perception, — that Inference, or hypothesis, is largely mingled in what seems simple sensible experience. Thus it appears that among the preliminaries of exact knowledge there are two which have the paradoxical aspect of *looking away from* the data directly presented, and of *guessing* the presence of other data, — looking away from the particular object, to find some general object which includes this particular one without including its individual characters, seeking Man in Socrates and the Rodent in this rabbit. Instead, therefore, of vaguely warning Philosophy against the dangers of Abstraction and Hypothesis, — real as these dangers are, — we should openly avow them to be indispensable aids, and, by a clear recognition of the aid they furnish, learn wherein their dangers lurk.

the straight line is imaginary. Nevertheless, the admirable artifice which resolves all forces into two, and gives their resultant as the diagonal of the parallelogram formed by these components, presents the Calculus with a straight line never presented in Nature.

* SCHELLING, *Transcend. Idealismus*, p. 3.

72. Let us glance at one or two transcendental conceptions, and note the value of a purely imaginary Type. And first of the conception by which the great poet Goethe illuminated the whole of Vegetal Morphology, one of those germinal conceptions which change the state of a science. Amid all the diversities of sensible experience he saw the typical form of the Leaf present in every organ of the Plant, and conceived the Plant itself to be only a variously transformed Leaf, a Type which, developed in spirals in the stem, was also developed or aborted in calyx, stamen, and pistil, but always under every variety presenting constant relations, and preserving one typical order. Schiller's objection, which irritated him so much, that the Leaf was an idea, though true enough in fact, was irrelevant as an objection. The Leaf was an idea, but an idea which had sensibles for its concrete elements. A similar conception was applied by Goethe to the skeleton of vertebrates; and, in the hands of his successors, the Vertebral Type has been a potent instrument of morphological research. Of the same order is the conception of the Animal Series, first suggested by Aristotle, but brought into effective clearness by Lamarck, Geoffroy St. Hilaire, and still more luminously by Mr. Darwin.

73. It is, however, a profound mistake in regard to Nature, and no less in regard to Method, when such Types are wrested from their position among Ideals, and offered as Reals. There is not in Nature, there never was, a typical Leaf, a primitive Vertebra, or an existent Series, from which all plants, vertebræ, and animals have successively varied. There never was a Plan laid down, according to which the organic world was constructed, after the manner of a plan prearranged by an architect for the builder's guidance. On the contrary, this Plan and these Types are our after-thoughts, abstractions formed out of the sensible data presented by various plants, ver-

tebræ, and animals; they are ideal constructions from reals, obtained by the mind's grouping together the dominant resemblances, and setting aside all the many diversities. The theologian and metaphysician, by a procedure familiar to them, seize hold of these Types and present them as indices of a Plan in Creation. But this is the ὕστερον προτερον fallacy of supposing a *resultant* to have been the *determinant*. All that Experience warrants is the assertion that the original protoplasm, which was wholly destitute of plant-form, leaf or other, and the germinal membrane equally destitute of vertebral form, did, in the successive stages of evolution, pass through many forms, each new form being determined by that which preceded it, *and* by the external pressures of the medium in which it was evolved; consequently, in so far as these external influences had a general resemblance, the resultant forms were necessarily similar. The Type is an abstract expression of this general similarity.

Such is the positive doctrine of Morphology. The speculative doctrine which finds favor with theologians and metaphysicians teaches that the Type pre-existed in the Divine Mind, or at any rate in Nature; or teaches that somewhere there was a vertebra formed, and from this vertebra all the other bones were constructed by modification of its special parts, and so the skull was a modification of the spinal column, etc.*

* In the following passage Prof. Max Müller combats an analogous error: "There never was a common uniform Teutonic language; nor is there any evidence to show that there existed at any time a uniform High-German or Low-German language, from which all High-German and Low-German dialects respectively are derived. All we can say is, that these dialects passed at different times through the same stages of grammatical growth. We may add, that with every century that we go back the convergence of these dialects becomes more and more decided; but there is no evidence to justify us in admitting the historical reality of one primitive and uniform Low-German language, from which they were all derived. This is a mere creation of grammarians, who cannot

74. The scientific value of Types is that of being ideal guides, not real facts. They are standards by which deviations may be appreciated. It is because so few writers, even of those who adopt the Evolution Hypothesis, remember that it is only an hypothesis, and being an Ideal cannot be accepted as a Real, that opponents demand — and advocates endeavor to supply — evidence of its *reality*. The Animal Series is an ideal construction. Writers who forget this, not content with the inductive data for a speculative insight, demand — and evolutionists endeavor to supply — evidence which, could it be furnished, would at once transform the hypothesis into a demonstration, the problem into a theorem. Thus one of the commonest objections urged is, that were the hypothesis true we ought to find a gradual and continuous line of organic development, from one group to another, and one species to another; whereas, in point of fact, what we do find is group sharply demarcated from group, species separated by an unbridgeable gulf from species; and these gaps the imagination is baffled in attempting to fill up, so as to render the transition from one form to the other apparent to Sense. The objection is wholly irrelevant; and although one cannot but be grateful for the interesting researches of those zoölogists and paleontologists who endeavor to supply the evidence of "missing links," — grateful because all extensions of our knowledge of organic forms is valuable, — one cannot applaud them for thus attempting to answer the objection, or for evading it by refuge in our geological ignorance. The objection is based on a twofold misconception. Continuity of form — in the sense demanded — is *incompatible* with that variety of form which Evolution postulates and Observation discloses. Such continuity would make the whole

understand a multiplicity of dialects without a common type." — *Lectures on the Science of Language*, I. 205. 1871.

organic world one form. The Type would cease to be an abstraction, and degenerate into a concrete sensible. Between any two forms, however similar, short of identity, there must, *ex vi termini*, be a solution of continuity; if the incident forces which determine the form be unequal, the resultant must necessarily be a variation. Thus, suppose we have two samples of protoplasm identical in all respects, but subject to forces which vary in some respects, the resultant forms must be separated by a gap which is indefinite. It is an elementary deduction from mechanical principles, that when a body susceptible of various positions of stable equilibrium is moved in various directions on a plane, the changes from one position to another must be abrupt, without any *stable* intermediates. If two forms differ, and they must if they are two, then their difference is a solution of continuity, though it may be accompanied by resemblances. There can be no *stable* transition between an exogen and an endogen, between an animal with a shell and an animal without a shell, more than between a crystal and its solution, or between sugar and oil, both hydrocarbons. We may regard all sensations as modifications of Sensibility, but there is no transition between one sensation and another; and just as Sensibility is the abstract expression for all concrete sensations, and comes into existence with them, so Animal is the abstract expression for all concrete animals.

75. The distinction between Types and Reals was entirely overlooked in the famous controversy between Cuvier and Geoffroy St. Hilaire, and is equally so in the controversy now raging between the opponents and adherents of Darwinism. It will one day be likened to the controversy raised by the first promulgation of the Differential Calculus, the logical basis of which even Leibnitz himself very imperfectly conceived, and which even in our own day is generally acknowledged to be incomprehensi-

ble, because, as I hinted before, quantities are not discriminated from operations on quantity. Leibnitz when pressed by objections declared that he regarded infinitesimals as *incomparables* * which might be disregarded in reference to finite quantities as grains of sand in reference to the sea; a defence which Comte remarks completely vitiates the analysis reducing it to a mere calculus of approximation, "Qui sous ce rapport serait radicalement vicieux puisqu'il serait impossible de prévoir à quel point les opérations successives peuvent grossir ces erreurs premières, dont l'accroissement pourrait même évidemment devenir ainsi quelconque." †

Without pausing here to exhibit the logical justification, let us ask, how did mathematicians practically justify the new Calculus? By showing that it enabled them to solve problems hitherto insoluble. In like manner the adherents of the Evolution Hypothesis may answer the objections urged against it by showing — and they do show — the vast reach of organic phenomena, hitherto inexplicable, which are rendered intelligible by its aid. This will not prove the hypothesis to be *true;* but it proves it to be *effective,* which is all an hypothesis can pretend to be. Infinitesimals may not exist in Nature; the Animal Series may have no real correspondent; but the calculus and the evolution hypothesis are ideal constructions of vast power in scientific research.

MORAL TYPES.

76. As a final example let us not omit to mention the creation of Moral Types, the standards for our conduct in life. It is often made an objection against moral and religious conceptions of Duty that they demand for their realization a perfection which is not human. Certainly

* Leibnitz, *Opera, Ed. Dutens,* II. 370.

† Comte, *Philos. Positive,* I. 242.

no man ever did, or could, realize in conduct the exalted ideal of life which he may have formed, or accepted from others. "O, would that for one single day we had lived in this world as we ought!" is the passionate exclamation of A'Kempis (or whoever wrote the *Imitation*). It has been most keenly felt by those whose lives have been most free from reproach. The objection to ideals, on the ground of their surpassing human nature, is a misconception of their function. They are not the laws by which we live, or can live, but the types by which we measure all deviations from a perfect life. The mind which has once placed before it an ideal of life has a pole-star by which to steer, although his actual course will be determined by the winds and waves. The pole-star is not the helm, nor is the helm more than one of the active agents. Our passions and our ignorance constantly make us swerve from the path to which the pole-star points; and thus the ideal of a Christian life, or the ideal of Marriage, are never wholly to be realized, yet who denies that such ideals are very potent influences in every soul that has clearly conceived them? It is a truth, and not an idle phrase, that man does not live by bread alone; that it is his privilege to live by aspiration, hope, and love, to be moved by ideal impulses which cause him to check the impulses of a lower self, to forego the transient pleasure of Sense, and passionately strive after the nobler pleasures of heart and intellect. We all place before ourselves the ideal of a noble life, the type of a grander character than our infirmities enable us to realize; and we do not look on that ideal as a fiction, on that type of character as a falsehood, because we fail to realize it. Like the typical laws of physical processes, these conceptions are solid truths although they exist only as ideals; and he who imagines their validity impugned because human nature can but imperfectly realize them, is as ignorant of Life as he would be who should deny the validity of natural Laws, because of the perturbations observable in natural events.

The contrast between a real law and an ideal law, such as we find in the second law of Motion (formulated by Galileo in the parallelogram of forces) and the first law, which is only the formula of what would be the motion were all disturbing conditions absent, is equally exhibited in the moral law that "the habit of right action is the securest preparation for acting rightly under emergencies," — and the ideal law that "we should love our neighbors as ourselves." No moving body does move uniformly in a straight line; no man does love his neighbor as himself. All bodies do move in the diagonal of the parallelogram of two incident forces; and all men are trained to act rightly on emergencies by what is a kind of moral instinct, organized in previous habits of acting rightly.

77. It would be of eminent service if a classification of the Laws — real and ideal — were drawn up, so that in every case there might be distinct understanding whether we were dealing with a Type which pretended to no objective reality, or with a Notation of the real process observed, and only varying from observation as the general varies from the particular. To effect this it would be necessary first to settle the question mooted in the succeeding chapter.

CHAPTER VI.

WHAT ARE LAWS OF NATURE?

78. Referring to what was briefly stated in our Inroduction (*On the Method of Science*, § 70 *et seq.*), we there saw that Law was originally supposed to have not only an objective existence *in* the phenomena, but an objective existence independent of the phenomena; and this ancient error is still alive. By one of the illusions into which Philosophy easily glides, a Law of Nature is supposed to hold a position with respect to natural objects which is analogous to that held by a legislative enactment with respect to social life. Laws are a kind of wise police keeping Nature in order. How far the connotations of Language inevitably transfer this conception of the regulation of conduct to the regulation of Nature, it may be difficult to say; but the fact is that, having once named Process by the word Law, we have great difficulty in keeping the two conceptions distinct. Even careful writers are apt to express themselves ambiguously on this point;* and the majority of writers assuredly suppose that Law is independent of the phenomena which it rules. Strongly impressed with the mischievous tendency of its

* To give a single instance, Archdeacon Pratt in his important treatise *The Mathematical Principles of Mechanical Philosophy* (1836) opens with the following statement: "The uniformity which characterizes the operations of nature leads to the conjecture that the phenomena of the material world [not then the phenomena of the spiritual world?] are regulated by certain fixed laws. Numberless appearances strengthen the suspicion that they are the necessary consequences of some universal principles with which matter has been endowed by the Creator."

suggestions, I was many years ago led to propose the abandonment of the word Law in relation to physical phenomena; but I soon found that the reform was impracticable; the word is too deeply rooted. Instead, therefore, of attempting to get rid of it, we must be content with a recognition of its misleading connotations, and fix in our minds that Law is only one of two conceptions, 1°, a notation of the process observed in the phenomena, which process we mentally detach and generalize by extending it to all similar phenomena; 2°, an abstract Type, which although originally constructed from the observed Process, does nevertheless depart from what is really observed, and substitutes an Ideal Process, constructing what *would be* the course of the process were the conditions different from those actually present.

79. The first conception is so far real that it expresses the *observed series of positions.* It is the process of phenomena, not an agent apart from them, not an *agency determining them,* but simply the ideal *summation of their positions.* The story of a man's life is not a theorem which he has to work out, but a story which *we* elicit from all the events, and exhibit in its leading directions. Phenomena, in as far as they are ruled, — regulated, determined in this direction rather than in that, and necessarily determined in the direction taken, — are determined by no external agent corresponding to Law, but by their *co-operant factors internal and external:* alter one of these factors, and the product will be differently determined.

It is owing to the very general misconception of the nature of Law that there arise the misconception of Necessity; the fact that events arrive irresistibly whenever their conditions are present, is confounded with the conception that the events must arrive whether the conditions be present or not, being fatally predetermined. Necessity simply says that whatever is is, and will vary with varying conditions. Fatalism says that something *must be;* and this something cannot be modified by any modification of the conditions.

Every Law has two aspects, one concrete and experimental, the other abstract and theoretical. In the experimental department a Law is simply the notation of observed facts; in the theoretical department this is exhibited as the necessary consequence of certain other and more fundamental facts; and, as Prof. Challis reminds us, "every fact, every law which experiment makes known, is a problem for the theorist to solve by mathematical reasoning." Kepler discovered that the radius vector of each planet *would* describe round the sun equal areas in equal times, were there no perturbing conditions; and he grouped the observed facts under this Law. Then came Newton, who deduced this Law, not from the observed facts, but from the primary fact of which it was the necessary consequence, namely, the Law that gravitation is a force acting in the line of the attracting and attracted bodies.

80. A Real Law differs from an Ideal Law, or Type, not in being less of a subjective conception, but in being less of a *construction,* — not in having an existence independent of objects and of us, in contradistinction to the Ideal Law supposed to be entirely our own creation, but in expressing more rigorously the results of observation, and being thus reducible to sensible experience. It so far agrees with the Type that it is not any one series of observed positions, but a generalized series, — an abstract group of resemblances from which differences are rejected. By this generalization a particular series becomes a general Law, under which all resembling phenomena are classed, and the notation is made once and forever. We are said to have explained any particular fact when we have ranged it under the series to which it

belongs, in other words, assigned its Law. What is this? simply the series of positions which each phenomenon occupies under definite conditions. The position is not determined by the series; the phenomenon is not coerced by the Law, but each successive position is assumed because that, and no other, is the resultant of the co-operant forces. And when observation discloses a discrepancy between a fact and its Law, do we not at once declare this to be due to some difference in the factors? do we not preserve the integrity of the Law by invoking the presence of some *perturbation?* Now this is clearly the substitution of one series for another. Perturbations are mere figments of the mind, cloaks for ignorance, unless we acknowledge them to be positions which we do not observe, and which if observed would reveal that *this* series was not the series expressed in our Law. For in truth the so-called inviolability of Law is absolute only in so far as whatever is is, and cannot be otherwise. It declares the facts to be unchangeable so long as their factors are unchanged.

"Every process," we are told, "has laws known or unknown, according to which it must take place." I regard this as very inexact or very misleading. The law *is* the process; and there is no other *must* in the case than is involved in the identical proposition that the process must be the process. When comets are said to have laws in obedience to which they return at the times predicted, this obedience is metaphorical; the comets, in fact, sometimes do not "obey" the prescribed law, the prediction is falsified because the positions have been different. If it be replied that this only proves our conception of the process to have been inaccurate, and that we neglected in our formula certain elements which were co-operant, this, although perfectly true, only restates the argument that the real law of cometary movement is the series of cometary positions; and this must in each case *be* what it *is*.

81. But if in this sense the Real Law is inviolable because it is simply the expression of *what is*, and all the so-called perturbations are different Laws, the Ideal Law is of course inviolable, because it is abstracted not only from all perturbations but from all real processes. It expresses not *what is*, but what *would be* under other conditions. Motion never is uniform, never rectilinear; the stamen or pistil of a plant never is a leaf; the bones of a skull never are vertebræ; the planet never does describe an ellipse, — these and all other Ideal Laws are abstract truths; and they can only be applied in explanation of concrete facts by a constant rectification of our natural tendency to mistake abstractions for realities.

82. The distinction here established is not quite the same as that proposed by Mr. Mill, who divides laws into Ultimate and Derivative. He assigns inferior importance to the Derivative Laws, and will not allow them to be Laws of Nature. According to the views exposed in this chapter the Derivative Laws are those understood as Laws of Nature, while the Ultimate Laws are *not* Laws of Nature, but subjective constructions having no corresponding objects. Mr. Mill holds that the three laws, 1°, air has weight; 2°, pressure on a fluid is propagated equally in all directions; 3°, pressure in one direction not opposed by equal pressure in the contrary direction produces motion, — are three Laws of Nature. I agree; but cannot follow him when he adds that although from the combination of these Laws we can predict the rise of mercury in the barometer, this last is not a Law of Nature, but simply a derivation from three Laws, — a case in which all three co-operate. It seems to me that the law of atmospheric gravity is a case of the general law of gravitation, and the law of fluid pressure is not

less derivative than that of the rise of mercury in the barometer; the equal propagation of the pressure is a fact reducible to factors, namely, the uniform disposition of the molecules of the fluid and the laws of motion of those molecules. The only Laws that can with strictness be called ultimate, in Mr. Mill's sense, are those of Number, Position, and Force in the object-world, and those of Sensation and Grouping in the subject-world; all phenomena may be reduced to cases of these Laws.

83. This mode of regarding Laws, namely, as Processes briefly formulated in their essential characters, and as Types by which Observation may be guided, enables us to escape the fallacy of supposing phenomena to be *determined by their own resultants.*

Ideal Laws, or Types, stand somewhat in the relation to Real Laws, or Generalization, that Hypotheses do to Theories. There can be no doubt respecting their immense service in Research, and yet they wear the paradoxical aspect of assisting Observation by deliberately neglecting it in favor of Ideal Construction. Before considering the limitations which this employment of Ideal Construction demands, it will be needful here to come to a distinct understanding on the use of hypothesis.

CHAPTER VII.

THE USE AND ABUSE OF HYPOTHESIS.

84. COULD we *observe* the processes of nature we should need no Science to *explain* them: Perception would suffice. But we cannot observe them, or can observe them only in fragments; we must therefore imagine what we cannot see, and link the fragments into a whole. Explanation of phenomena is always a making visible to the mind's eye of what is invisible in the facts presented: it is the rendering conspicuous of those inconspicuous Relations of coexistence and succession through which one phenomenon co-operates with, and thus determines a change in, another. When this is seen, there is an intuition of the truth that *everywhere* a recurrence of these Relations, or of similar conditions, must be accompanied by this change, or a similar change. This is the intuition which rests on the assumption of homogeneity (Rule X.) and is justified by the logical principle of Equivalence (to be hereafter expounded).

85. Not only does Science pass from the consideration of isolated visible facts, to their co-ordination and consolidation in general, invisible facts; but it necessarily tends to generalize more and more, to become more and more abstract, less and less ocupied with concrete observation; and this because every concrete observation is limited, whereas the grasp of a few general facts enables us to anticipate an endless multitude of observations, and that in cases where Observation would be difficult, some-

times impossible. Science is fertile, not because it is a tank, but because it is a spring. The grandest discoveries, and the grandest applications to practice, have not only outstripped the slow march of Observation, but have revealed by the telescope of Imagination what the microscope of Observation could never have seen, although it may afterwards be employed to verify the vision.

No reader of these pages will misunderstand the reach of this remark, or suppose that it warrants any neglect of Observation through a too confident reliance on Imagination and Reason; for Imagination and Reason are only powerful as the organized results of previous Observation. If Types are to be valid they must be formed by abstraction from concrete experiences, thus enabling Prevision to be only an extension of Vision, and enabling Deduction to rest securely on a basis of Induction. It is the neglect of this single, but indispensable condition, that constitutes the danger of Hypothesis.

86. Certain facts are observed to coexist, or to succeed each other, but the process of their connection is hidden, and we seek to drag into light the facts which come *between* the facts which are seen. There is a gap to be filled up. How? Not by direct vision. Then by indirect vision. We guess, and our guess has a Greek name, Hypothesis, namely, that which is *placed under*, and supports the observed facts; it is the imaginative arch thrown over the gap which we may traverse as a bridge. Unless this arch rests on solid supports, it will not bear our weight; and many a visionary hypothesis turns out to be no better than the arch of the rainbow, beautiful to look upon, impossible to walk upon.

It is therefore of the utmost importance to ascertain the conditions of solid support. Guessing has a wide and capricious range; it is oftener wrong than right; but worse than all is the fatal facility with which the mind accepts a guess in lieu of vision, believing in the image it has formed out of materials from within, as if it were an image formed of materials from without; and thus, while the probabilities of error are enormous, the pertinacity with which error once formed on very slight evidence is held, resists all but demonstrative evidence against it. Hypothesis thus becomes pernicious. It retards Science by *arresting* inquiry; it quiets the unrest of the mind with the anodyne of a phrase, and seems to explain what it only rebaptizes. It also retards Science by *misdirecting* inquiry, stimulating the mind to seek direct relations where none exist.

87. These dangers have been eloquently exposed by many writers, and need not here be illustrated. Yet while it would be difficult to express too strong a condemnation of the lax unscientific use of Imagination, which has brought Hypothesis into disrepute, it would be difficult to exaggerate the immense, the indispensable service of Hypothesis in the construction and advancement of Science. How largely Newton availed himself of its aid, and how he reprobated it, have already been indicated (*Introd.*, § 49). When Newton said that Hypothesis had no place in experimental philosophy, he probably meant that we must not take fancies for facts, guesses for conclusions; which is a warning not the less needed because it seems so obvious. But if we regard Hypothesis in its true light, namely, that of ideal experiment,—the tentative process of trying which among many possible conceptions best accords with perceptions,—that experimental character will place it beside the tentative process of trying which among many physical conditions will determine a modification of the result.

Cuvier, in his dispute with Geoffroy St. Hilaire, was always insisting on the dangers of Hypothesis; and elsewhere proclaimed it his guiding principle to adhere simply to the "exposition of positive facts"; a declaration which occasionally meets with the fatal objection that what he expounds as facts have been proved to be fictions; and which may always be met by the undeniable statement of Laplace, that if men had limited their efforts to the collection of facts, Science would have been only a sterile nomenclature, and would never have revealed the great laws of Nature. Without Hypothesis no step could be taken. Our very perceptions involve it. Nay more, I venture to affirm that the wildest flights of Imagination consciously sweeping round the circle of Experience, and alighting where it pleases, are legitimate tentatives of scientific Research, if only they submit to the one indispensable condition (unhappily too often neglected) of ultimate verification. The profound remark of Copernicus,* that the value of an hypothesis consists in reconciling Calculation with Observation, has not been duly appreciated; so little has it been appreciated that most people would echo Bacon's sneer at Copernicus as "the man who thinks nothing of introducing fictions of any kind into Nature, provided his calculations turn out well." The answer to this sneer is the triumphant achievements which are effected by the introduction of avowed fictions among the artifices of Research.

88. It is not only in Algebra that in endeavoring to form an equation we often begin by assigning any value we please to the unknown quantity, and submit this to all the operations necessary for ascertaining whether it answers the conditions or not, so that the result is to the

* From Gassendi's work, *Nicolai Copernici Vita*, p. 319. 1655. I find that the remark to which reference is made in the text was perhaps only due to Copernicus in the sense that he countenanced its publication, for it was not written by him, but by his disciple Osiander in the preface which he added when he gave the work of Copernicus to the public. It may therefore have been simply *une précaution oratoire* to render the heretical doctrine of the earth's movement less offensive.

correct one as the assumed value is to the unknown one.* We may employ what materials we please for our scaffolding, on the sole proviso that since this scaffolding is not the house, it must be carefully taken away again, when the *house is constructed;* we must not allow the beams, ropes, and ladders, used as auxiliaries, to thrust themselves discordantly into the structure itself. No doubt great skill is needed in the selection of auxiliaries, and in avoiding the danger of thrusting parts of the scaffolding into the structure; and the formation of true hypotheses is the severest task for the scientific imagination; while the invention of false, or illusory, hypotheses is the sterile abundance of an untrained imagination. The principle here proclaimed is the absolute freedom of introducing any elements in the formation of an equation, on the understanding that *nothing which is introduced as an auxiliary be permitted to appear in the result.* On this principle we may admit the conception of Atoms, even if we regard them as pure fictions: and we may endow these Atoms with any shape, size, or qualities we please, if thereby calculation can be aided; provided always that we assume nothing absolutely contradictory of experience, but only what is in harmony with experience; that is to say, the Atoms must be Extra-sensible, not Supra-sensible. The truth, or falsity, of the existence of these Atoms is another question altogether; and need never be raised so long as we treat them purely as auxiliaries, not realities. Thus, suppose I assume the Atoms to have the shape of an ellipsoid, and to be capable of moving only in rotation about three fixed axes, but incapable of vibration or translation. The assumption is inadmissible, because

* "Personne ne révoque en doute l'exactitude des résultats qu'on obtient par le calcul des imaginaires, quoiqu'elles ne soient que des formes algébriques et des hieroglyphes des quantités absurdes." — CARNOT, *La Métaphysique du Calcul Infinitésimal*, p. 120. Compare also FECHNER, *Psychophysik*, II. 40.

it is contradictory of experience, which rejects the idea of rotation as an exclusive form of motion. If, however, I merely assume that under *given* conditions the only motion possible is that of rotation, and I deduce from this some exact results, not otherwise obtainable, my assumption is valid, since it is proved thereby to represent *some* relation of the real agents. But that this relation is only one among many is proved by the simple fact that bodies expand, which would be impossible unless there were internal motions, not necessarily of vibration.

89. Again, the hypothesis of an undulating Ether, so largely employed in modern inquiries, is perfectly legitimate, and is proved to be so by its results. The vast array of phenomena which it explains, and the striking anticipations of Observation which it has effected, do not indeed prove the reality of the Ether, though they render its existence highly probable. The hypothesis with its dependent calculations brings into view a larger number of conditions which must be accepted as true, even when the ether itself is rejected.

The controversy on this question is too often confused by the want of a clear recognition of the principle I am here expounding, namely, that the value of the hypothesis is one thing, its evidence for the reality of an Ether is another. We are not bound to prove the existence of the Agent, so long as we confine ourselves to the hypothesis of an Agency acting on hydrodynamic or molecular dynamic laws; and so long as we do not allow more than the demonstrated Agency to enter into the final equation; such as would be the case if from any assumed, but not demonstrated, properties of the Ether we deduced conclusions at variance with, or not verifiable by, experience. And the reason of this reliance on the Agency, irrespective of the reality of the Agent, is that at any rate what is thus demonstrable must be true of the relations of the

Agent, be that Agent what it may. Let this Ether be only an attenuated form of ponderable Matter, or a fluid, or a solid, *sui generis,* we know at least that its mode of action in certain phenomena is explicable on dynamic laws. But there are phenomena which these laws have hitherto failed to explain. Hence we conclude that the Agent has other modes of action besides those already revealed, that the dynamic laws require to be supplemented by some other laws of molecular movement.

90. Some years ago I suggested a course of inquiry which was unhappily beyond my own power, but which in the hands of a powerful analyst might resolve some of the difficulties at present attending the undulatory theory. That theory only regards the movements of *vibration,* leaving out of sight the movement of *rotation.* But if the Ether be assumed as atomic, these atoms must have form; their geometric properties entail corresponding dynamic properties; and they cannot have movements of translation without also having rotation. Now if the mathematical investigation of the movements of translation were supplemented by an investigation of the movements of rotation, it is eminently probable that this new analysis would disclose the equations necessary for the reduction of those phenomena which still resist mathematical analysis.*

91. Be this as it may, the achieved results are ample justification of the hypothesis of an Ether. I cannot, therefore, agree with Comte in his polemic against the hypothesis, a polemic which could only avail against those who proclaimed the reality of the Ether. But he will not allow it to have even an auxiliary value. "À la vérité les physiciens se défendent vivement aujourd'hui

* Prof. Tait informs me that some distinguished investigators, notably Professors Thomson, Rankine, and Clerk Maxwell, have been working at this subject for years. My absence from England during the printing of these sheets prevents my giving more precise information on this point.

d'attacher aucune réalité intrinsèque à ces hypothèses, qu'ils préconisent seulement comme des moyens indispensables pour faciliter la conception et la combinaison des phénomènes. Mais n'est ce point là l'illusion d'une positivité incomplète, qui sent la profonde inanité de tels systèmes et pourtant n'ose point encore s'en passer?" * To this question I answer, No; and in so answering it, believe I am standing strictly within the sphere of positive science. But as Comte's view is shared by some eminent writers, we are bound to consider it carefully and impartially.

Hypotheses relate either to the Agents, or the Agencies, which link together the observed phenomena, i. e. the qualitative or quantitative elements which are the determinants of the phenomena. Sometimes we know the determinant (Agent, or Substance), but are ignorant of its mode of operation in effecting the change observed. Sometimes we know this mode of operation, or Agency, but are ignorant of the Agent. Thus we know that oxygen is the agent in the transformation of venous into arterial blood, and in the decomposition of the tissues necessary to the liberation of organic force; but the mode in which this is effected, whether by direct or indirect oxidation, is still a mystery. On the other hand, we know that the agency of Light is that of wave-movement; but the moving agent is unknown. The mode of operation of what is called chemical Affinity is known, but Affinity itself is unknown. We know as an experimental fact that Heat is Motion, and therefore the laws of Motion are laws of Heat; but we are still unable to explain many of the phenomena, "because we do not know *what* is moving nor *how* it moves. Results of the theory *in which these are not involved* are experimentally verified." †

* *Philos. Positive*, II. 441.

† THOMPSON and TAIT, *Natural Philosophy*, I. 311.

92. Now, any hypothesis introduced either respecting the Agent or the Agency is justified if it facilitates Research and conforms to the test of Verification; and it can only be called upon to show evidence for its reality, when we declare it to be the *real* Agent, and when as such it enters into the final equation. Whether the Agent which determines the orbit of a planet be an Angel seated in the sun, or an Attraction issuing forth from the sun and the planet, is a matter of indifference, so long as we admit nothing but the law of the Agency into our final equation, and allow neither any assumed properties of Angels, nor any assumed properties of an occult Attraction, to find expression. Again, whatever hypothesis we form respecting the Agent of Heat will be indifferent, so long as we confine our equation to the Agency. Thus, while assuming Heat to be Motion, we only select from all the possible forms of Motion those of Vibration and Rotation, which constitute the known Agency; and since the results of calculation thus obtained agree rigorously with observation, we conclude that we have detected something at least of the real mode of operation, let the Agent be a peculiar substance moving amid the particles of the heated body, or simply the molecules of the body itself in a state of agitation. Comte is right in saying that it would be difficult to see how the dilatation of a body by heat is explained by the idea of an imaginary fluid interposed between its molecules, tending constantly to augment their intervals, since we should then have to inquire whence the fluid gained its elasticity, which is assuredly less intelligible than the primitive fact. But although the introduction of a fluid as an Agent explains nothing, the fluid as an Agency — i. e. its hydrodynamic laws — explains much. Of course, any other hypothesis — that, for instance, of expansion being due to the increased oscillation of the molecules — may take the place

of this hydrodynamic hypothesis; and it will remain for the advocates of each to justify the preference by the greater sum of verified results. The two hypotheses of Light both explained many of the phenomena; and the one was finally victorious only when it succeeded in explaining what its rival stumbled over as a contradiction. The undulatory hypothesis itself, as usually stated, may perhaps have to yield the place to another.

93. Let us never forget that the agreement of observation with calculation does not prove the reality of the Ether as an Agent; it only proves that the mode of operation of the real Agent (whatever that may be) is to some extent such as we assume; and it is only because we are in doubt of the reality that we call upon hypothesis to aid us. Were the reality proved, there would be no longer an hypothesis, the supposition would give place to a demonstration. To demand that what are avowedly fictions should be called to prove their reality, is inconsistent. Hypotheses are guesses, aids to research, and not to be treated like the results. There are good and bad guesses; and unhappily their inventors are generally careless in verifying them. Sometimes verification is, in the nature of the case, not attainable; we then rely on probability. Our guesses may be ranged under three classes: 1°, the Real Hypotheses, which being *intrinsic* are explicative; 2°, the Auxiliary Hypotheses, which being *extrinsic* are merely aids in construction; 3°, the Illusory Hypotheses.

94. *A Real Hypothesis* is one which explains observed phenomena, and anticipates the results of future observation, by means of some Agent or Agency *known* to be present among the elements of the observed phenomenon, the precise relations of which, however, as determinants, are not known. Thus the phenomenon of Expansion in gases and solids is explained as the wider sweep of the

oscillating molecules. That the molecules are in a state of oscillation is known; the laws of oscillation are sufficient to account for the phenomenon, without the intervention of any extrinsic agency. If a vibrating fluid be introduced to account for the oscillation of the particles, and be absolutely restricted to the simple office of transmitting vibrations, without any admixture of undemonstrable properties, the hypothesis still keeps within the sphere of the known; and all the demand we can make on it is that it shall explain what we observe.

95. When the x is obtained in an equation, what is known of it (its functions) must satisfy the equation, otherwise no step in advance is made. Thus, if we introduce a Spirit as the Agent in certain changes, how does this enlighten us, unless we know the *properties* of the Spirit and its *laws of action?* Whereas if instead of a Spirit we introduce Attraction, although we may be equally ignorant of this Agent, if we know the laws of its action, through these known laws the equation is satisfied. Newton's great hypothesis is a fine example. It was what I have called a Real Hypothesis, — what he would have put forward as legitimate because it was "deduced from the phenomena." He began by assuming that the force which at each instant deflects a planet from its tangent (the observed fact of deflection leading to the assumption of a deflecting force), and which causes the planet to move in a curve round the sun (another observation), is a force tending directly towards the sun. He then showed that, on such premises being granted, the conclusion follows that the planet will describe equal areas in equal times, — and this conclusion Kepler's first law had already established (subject to the qualification I have before noted, and accepting the law in its ideal aspect). Newton further showed that if the deflecting force did not tend towards the sun, the planet would not describe

equal areas in equal times. Having thus demonstrated that the hypothesis necessarily carried the conclusion which observation disclosed, and that a contradictory hypothesis would not carry such a conclusion, his assumption was established as a truth, his guess was "deduced from the phenomena."

96. It is characteristic of all Real Hypotheses that they pass by Verification into inductive truths. Since they admit nothing extrinsic to the phenomena, directly the right guess has been intuited the process of demonstration requires no elimination of auxiliary elements. Hence it is obvious that our first aim should be to frame hypotheses of this kind, and to seek for an explanation of phenomena in Agents or Agencies already known, or surmised to be present (Rule XV.). But it is no less obvious that were we to confine Inquiry to such a procedure, the advance of Science would be extremely slow, since it is seldom that we have this solid foundation to stand on, and it mostly happens that we do not know but are forced to guess, what is the Agent or Agency in operation. Hence the employment of Auxiliary Hypotheses.

An Auxiliary Hypothesis is a conscious fiction by which Imagination pictures what would be the effect of a given Agent, or Agency, *if present.* It is purely a tentative process, like that of assigning an arbitrary value to an unknown quantity. The advantage of such a tentative process will of course depend on the degree in which the imagined agency resembles the actual agency; and for this purpose it must be of a character strictly analogical with those of the elements known to be present in similar phenomena (Rule XV.) For example, the complications of the planetary movements would baffle all rational theory were it not for the various fictions by which astronomers turn the difficulty; and especially by that of the Type presented in the problem of two bodies, one of which is assumed to be fixed. It is to this Type, avowedly a fiction, that the real movements are reduced by successive approximations; and its completion is Lagrange's celebrated theory of the *variation of arbitrary constants,* which treats the effective movement of any planet as if it were really elliptical, but with variable elements instead of constant elements.

"So many of the properties of matter," says Professor Clerk Maxwell, "can be deduced from the hypothesis that their minute parts are in rapid motion, the velocity increasing with the temperature, that the precise nature of this motion becomes a subject of rational curiosity. Daniel Bernouilli, Herapath, Joule, Krönig, Clausius, etc., have shown that the relations between pressure, temperature, and density in a perfect gas can be explained by supposing the particles to move with uniform velocity in straight lines, striking against the sides of the containing vessel and thus producing pressure. It is not necessary to suppose each particle to travel to any great distance in the same straight line; for the effect in producing pressure will be the same if the particles strike against each other; so that the straight line described may be very short. Clausius has determined the mean length of path in terms of the average distance of the particles, and the distance between the centres of two particles when collision takes place. We have at present no means of ascertaining either of these distances; but certain phenomena such as the internal friction of gases, the conduction of heat through a gas, and the diffusion of one gas through another, seem to indicate the possibility of determining accurately the mean length of path which a particle describes between two successive collisions. In order to lay the foundation of such investigations on strict mechanical principles, I shall demonstrate the laws of motion of an indefinite number of small, hard, and perfectly elastic spheres acting on one another only during impact. If the properties of such a system of bodies *are found to correspond to those of gases, an important physical analogy will be established which may lead to more accurate knowledge of the properties of matter.* If experiments on gases are inconsistent with the hypothesis of these propositions, then our theory, though consistent in itself, is proved to be incapable of explaining the phenomena of gases. In either case it is necessary to follow out the consequences of the hypothesis.

"Instead of saying that the particles are hard, elastic, and spherical, we may, if we please, say that the particles are centres of force of which the action is insensible except at a certain small distance, when it suddenly appears as a repulsive force of very great intensity. It is evident that either assumption will lead to the same results." *

97. The freedom which Imagination is here allowed in the creation of conscious fictions does not prevent these guesses being submitted to the most rigorous tests; and the value of such fictions appears in the aid they furnish to calculation. We find Mr. Maxwell not only explaining the pressure of a gas by this assumption of elastic particles moving in straight lines, — the square of the velocity being proportional directly to the absolute temperature and inversely to the specific gravity of the gas at a constant temperature, — but also that the number of particles in a unit of volume is the same for all gases at the same pressure and temperature: a result in striking accordance with the chemical law that equal volumes of gases are chemically equivalent. Again, it is a pure fiction which transfers the circular nature of the Earth and all the geometrical properties of the circle to the Heavens. That the Earth is a sphere, or approxi-

* MAXWELL, *Illustrations of the Dynamical Theory of Gases. Philos. Mag.*, p. 19. 1860.

mates to one, is a fact; but that it is enclosed in a heavenly sphere is a sheer fiction; yet it is the celestial circles by which the terrestrial latitudes and longitudes are calculated; and were it not for this fiction, which connects Geography with Astronomy, our geographical science could not have been constructed.

98. It is necessary to insist on the strictly scientific use of the Imagination in constructing these auxiliaries, because Newton has in emphatic language condemned them, though his own practice we have seen to be a splendid vindication of them. He pronounced hypotheses illegitimate which were not deduced from the phenomena; in fact it was these only that he called hypotheses. "Whatever is not deduced from the phenomena," he says in the famous Scholium, "is to be called an hypothesis; and hypotheses, whether metaphysical or physical, have no place in experimental philosophy." The weight of his authority has pressed Hypothesis into the mire, where it is trodden on by the feet of writers who are by no means slow to profit by its services; and thus, in spite of its services, Hypothesis has become the pariah of research.

99. The rival hypotheses respecting Light are manifestly auxiliary. The corpuscular is now discredited, but it was once, if erroneous, effective. Some writers declare that there was this initial defect in it, that only on the supposition of a corpuscle being visible and tangible, could the hypothesis have been justifiable. This is precisely the objection urged by Comte, Mill, and others against the undulatory hypothesis. If the Ether be admissible, although no one has seen or could see it, then surely luminous corpuscles are admissible? Neither of these Agents is known to be present in luminous phenomena; neither is positively known to exist. But the valid ground for the rejection of the one hypothesis is not that the Agent is proved to be absent, but that the

Agency invoked as an auxiliary fails to explain the phenomena; whereas the Agency invoked in the other case, although still incompetent to explain *all* the phenomena, explains so many, that its aid is more effective, and therefore preferred.

The vortices of Descartes have long since passed into the rag-shop of worn-out finery; and those who see the hypothesis huddled among many others equally discarded, forget that it was once a part of the furniture of Science. In estimating an opinion we must always take the historical stand-point; for the suggestion which from a later stand-point appears inept, may be recognized as ingenious from the earlier. The vortices of Descartes thus viewed present an example of the three stages through which most hypotheses must pass, its stage of indispensable though temporary aid, its stage of application and verification, and its stage of final displacement in favor of some more successful rival. Placing ourselves for a moment at the point of view prevalent when Descartes devised the vortices, we at once see the enormous and indispensable aid it furnished, simply by the introduction of the idea of *mechanical law* where even the great Kepler could only conceive the *action of genii.* A philosophy which explained phenomena by the aid of such genii could only be set aside by a philosophy which explained the phenomena on mechanical grounds. And although when Celestial Mechanics had received a sure foundation by the discovery of gravitation, the hypothesis of Vortices was an obstruction, not an aid, its doom was not sealed until geometers and astronomers proved that it was in contradiction with known facts and known mechanical laws; * and

* "Rien ne serait plus satisfaisant pour l'esprit que la physique céleste de M. Descartes si elle eût pu soutenir l'épreuve de l'examen et de l' observation." — MONTUCLA, *Hist. des Mathématiques,* II. 537. Compare NEWTON, *Principia,* Book II., Sec. XI., Schol., to Prop. 411; and the general Scholium to Book III.

proved that another hypothesis accomplished all it pretended, and explained what it left inexplicable. Here, as elsewhere, those who declared that it was impossible to theorize without such an aid were answered by a more effectual theorizing with another.

100. Among auxiliaries a distinction is to be made between those which relate to Agencies and those which relate to Agents. In the first class are the quantitative hypotheses of mathematical physics, where, in entire ignorance of the Agents, we can, from mathematical laws, at least deduce their mode of operation. The nature of Heat, Electricity, or Magnetism may be unknown, but some of their quantitative laws are absolutely known. Yet auxiliary hypotheses have always to be treated as auxiliary, and, when applied to physical facts, require numerous modifying and limiting considerations, such as are always requisite in passing from the abstract to the concrete. Thus Newton says: "I use the words attraction and impulse not defining the species or physical qualities of forces, but investigating the quantities and mathematical proportions of them. In mathematics we are to investigate the quantities of forces with their proportions consequent upon any conditions supposed; then when we enter upon physics we compare those proportions with the phenomena of Nature, that we may know what conditions of those forces answer to the several kinds of attractive bodies. And this preparation being made we may agree more safely concerning the physical species, causes, and proportions of the forces.*

"The history of physical science," says Prof. Challis, "seems to show that theoretical investigation proceeds in but one course, that of deducing quantitative laws, by means of solutions of equation, from known or hypothetical principles."

* *Principia*, Book I., Section XI., Scholium.

101. The second class of hypotheses is of smaller value. Unless we already know the law of the Agency, our guess at the Agent is almost certain to be erroneous; a consideration which should make us particularly cautious. Even when we know the law, there is great danger of missing the one out of many possible Agents which may be involved. For example, the Electrodynamic theory of Ampère merely expresses the law of the Agency: the experimental data of the action of closed currents on each other give expressions for the mathematical law of the action which one element must exert on another. But Weber seeks the Agent, and his hypothesis is that of an electric current formed by the motion of particles of two kinds of electricity moving in opposite directions; an hypothesis which is open to many objections.*

102. Another example is the hypothesis propounded by Young, and adopted by Helmholtz, of three special retinal fibres for the three primary colors; or the kindred hypothesis of Helmholtz, that the auditory nerve has special fibres for notes of particular pitch. I shall examine this more in detail in a subsequent Problem. Enough for the present to remark that these different fibres are assumed Agents, and there must first be demonstrated the presence of fibres having different structure and properties; no attempt has been made to demonstrate this, and we cannot accept them merely on the ground of the Agency, i. e. merely because the known law of distinct primary colors suggests the presence of distinct fibres. The more so because the Agency may be otherwise interpreted. I shall hope to make clear that the Agency can be rigorously deduced from the general Law of Grouping which determines all sensitive phenomena, each color and each tone being simply a special group of neural units. We do not need three different fibres, since one fibre can

* See THOMSON and TAIT, *Natural Philosophy.*

readily be conceived vibrating with different *nodes*, like a rod or cord; and the principle of the superposition of small oscillations may be applied to nerves as to rods.

103. Whether an hypothesis refers to the Agent or the Agency, the one thing needful to be steadily borne in mind is the one thing commonly neglected, namely, that while *any* supposition which can furnish aid is justified by the assistance we derive from it, *no* supposition can be accepted for more than instrumental aid, no supposition can be allowed to take the place of a truth, until it has itself been submitted to the operations which establish a truth. An hypothesis may be false, yet help us to a truth; but no demonstration of the truth of any process proves that the hypothesis which explains the process is true. The existence of Ether is not demonstrated because the hypothesis of an Ether is the most satisfactory means we have at present of explaining luminous phenomena; all that is proved is that the hypothesis is effective. This caution is the more needful because of our tendency to consider the verification of a result as a proof of the independent truth of the hypothesis. Because the supposed Agency is adequate, is it therefore to be held as existent? Laplace mentions an example of the danger which besets auxiliary hypotheses, "quand on les réalise au lieu de les regarder comme des moyens de soumettre les observations au calcul." Dominic Cassini, he says, in forming a table of refraction, started from the simple supposition of a constant density in the atmosphere. This table was exact at the heights at which the stars are usually observed, and was adopted by astronomers; and the hypothesis that the refraction augments with the elevation gained universal acceptance until Bouger proved, by observations made at Quito, that the refraction at that height instead of being increased was diminished.*

* LAPLACE, *Exposition du Système du Monde*, I. 191.

104. Were Newton's *dictum* to be followed, no auxiliary hypothesis would be permitted. If, however, we clearly understand its nature, and do not confound an *instrument* of construction with an *element* of construction, we may allow Imagination unrestricted license. Any operation is legitimate by which we can submit observations to calculation, or by which new observations are rendered practicable. Suppose I am studying the evolution of an ovum, and unable by the microscope to see the mutual relations of its parts, which could be seen were a thin section made of it; the delicacy of the structure prevents my making such a section; I must therefore seek some external aid. A solution of chromic acid hardens the ovum sufficiently to enable a section to be made. Nothing can be more foreign to the organic tissue than this chromic acid; yet by its aid I am enabled to detect certain constituent elements in that tissue; and no one would object to my employing it, on the ground that it was extra-organic. But if, after employing chromic acid as an auxiliary, I allowed it to enter into the construction, i. e. if in treating of the chemical and physical composition of the tissue, I introduced among the constituents those results which were due to the agency of the acid, then, indeed, every one would rightly object to the procedure. And it is this error which is committed when hypotheses originally introduced as aids in bringing phenomena into appreciable relation, are finally allowed to appear in the result.*

* "L'objet de tout calcul se réduit à trouver les relations qui existent entre certaines quantités proposées, mais la difficulté de trouver immédiatement ces relations oblige souvent de recourir à l'entremise de quelques autres quantités qui ne font point partie du système proposé, mais qui par leur liaison avec les premières peuvent servir comme intermédiaires entre elles. On commence donc par exprimer les relations qu'elles ont toutes ensemble ; après quoi on élimine du calcul celles qui n'y sont entrées que comme auxiliaires afin d'obtenir entre les quantités

105. *The Illusory Hypothesis* must be broadly distinguished from the other two classes. It is not deduced from the phenomena; it is not an aid; it is simply a restatement of the observed facts in a compendious, and generally ambiguous phrase. It rebaptizes an observation. Yet such is the influence of mere naming, that the rebaptism of our ignorance seems to be an illumination, and exercises a charm that is all the more obstructive to Research, because we often find a positive advantage in a phrase which condenses a multitude of details; and the advantage of the formula leads us to confound it with a principle. To many minds the word Affinity is more than a term; and when chemists say that oxygen unites with hydrogen because these gases have a strong Affinity, many persons accept this as an explanation. In former days a multitude of phenomena were condensed in the formula of the *fuga vacui.* Nature was said to "abhor a vacuum." This phrase named, and by naming linked together, observed facts of suction, breathing, the rise of water in a tube, etc.; and had it been limited to the simple expression of the observed facts, it would, like the term Affinity, have been of unimpeachable advantage. The error lay in taking the formula for a principle, and supposing that it explained what it simply named. Believe to be a principle, its action was necessarily generaized beyond the sphere of observation; and thus Mersenne imagined a siphon which should go over a mountain; whereas the real law of suction, on which the siphon depends, is limted to drawing water to the height of 34 feet, — above that, the "horror of a vacuum" ceases.

106. In our own day writers who ridicule the *fuga vacui* are quite ready to invent or accept Illusory Hypotheses of the same calibre. They confidently assign

proposées seules les relations immédiates qu'on voulait découvrir." — CARNOT, *La Métaphysique du Calcul Infinitésimal*, p. 21.

phenomena to Electricity, Ozone, Polarity, Nervo-atmospheres, Repulsive atmospheres, Psychic force, Vital force, and the like. Nay, it is popularly supposed that the invention of such hypotheses is an exercise of the Imagination; and on this ground soberer thinkers are wont to decry Imagination, believing it to be the pest of Science. Such hypotheses are indeed a pest; but so far from their source being Imagination, it is precisely a defect of Imagination which forms their nidus. To imagine a natural process is to see the Agents or Agencies which are really operative, or which, if present, would act so as to produce the result observed. But this mental picture of the unseen process is given only to the highest minds equipped with exact knowledge. In Science, as in Art, any feeble mind can satisfy itself by vaguely supposing that something *may* in *some way or other* (not specified) determine the changes which take place; the difficulty is in precise vision. But precision is the one quality which impatient minds least appreciate; and therefore Illusory Hypotheses spring up like mushrooms in half-cultivated minds, and are readily accepted by the uncultivated, who see no difficulties because they have no vision of the requisites: marvels are not marvellous to them, for ignorance does not marvel.

107. Whenever an hypothesis suggests itself it should be submitted to the following conditions: first, the supposed Agent or Agency must be a *true cause.* This does not mean that it should be a cause already known to be in operation here, but one known to be in operation *somewhere,* so that from its known properties the phenomena may be deduced. "Nature's horror" and "Psychic Force" are clearly not brought from some other part of our experience to explain a present difficulty, but are invented for the nonce. "Nature's horror" and "Psychic Force" must first be made known to us by their properties in *other*

cases before we can explain any phenomena by their presence; or conversely, if we assume that the present phenomena clearly suggest the presence of these agents, we must show that these agents *are* operative elsewhere; and this must be done by direct demonstration of their existence, or by the indirect demonstration that no *other* agents will suffice. Having laid hold of a *vera causa*, we must next render intelligible how its known properties in action agree with the phenomena it is brought in to explain. That is to say, suppose Electricity be the Agent assumed, we must show how the known laws of electrical action lead deductively to the facts observed; or if any laws of electrical action be assumed for the nonce they must not be in contradiction with known laws, nor in contradiction with any of the observed facts. Having got thus far there remain two final conditions: it is not sufficient that the phenomena can be deduced from the hypothesis, there must be also a deduction of new phenomena not hitherto observed, or an extension of the hypothesis to other cases, thereby justifying the hypothesis as at least an aid in enlarging knowledge, and not simply a rebaptism of the known; and, secondly, there must be proof that no other hypothesis will at once explain the old observations and lead deductively to the new. Kepler's hypothesis of the elliptical orbit of the planets did not satisfy Dominic Cassini, who proposed to replace it by a curve of the fourth degree roughly resembling an ellipse in certain cases, and in which the product of the focal distances, instead of their sum, remained invariable. But why have astronomers rejected this *Cassinoïd*, and retained the ellipse? Simply because the one does not, and the other does, reconcile calculation with observation. Again, of the four hypotheses suggested to explain meteoric stones, some facts are explicable on all four; and by turns it may appear that the meteorites are products of volcanoes in the moon, volcanoes in our earth, or condensations of atmospheric particles; but a wide survey of the facts, and comparison with these three hypotheses in all their consequences, leaves each defective, and the fourth hypothesis (of the cosmical origin of these bodies) takes their place by right of conquest over the phenomena.

108. To conclude: all hypotheses are illusory which cannot justify themselves by enlarging knowledge; and if their inventors would hesitate to put them forth until they had submitted them to the requisite tests, or shown what *new* results are obtainable by the hypotheses, the amplest scope would be given to their inventive powers, without any evil accruing.

109. Having thus described the use and abuse of Hypothesis, I must, before quitting the subject, notice a restriction on its effective range, placed by Comte and Mill, which is a departure from the principle I have adopted from Copernicus. Mr. Mill considers it allowable to assume the law of what we already know to be the cause, but not to assume the cause itself. "It is allowable, useful, and even necessary to begin by asking ourselves what cause *may* have produced the effect, in order that we may know in what direction to look out for evidence to determine whether it actually *did*. The vortices of Descartes would have been a perfectly legitimate hypothesis, if it had been possible by any mode of explanation to bring the reality of the vortices as a fact in Nature conclusively to the test of observation. The hypothesis was vicious simply because it could not lead to any course of investigation capable of converting it from an hypothesis into a proved fact." *

This argument is equally destructive of the Nebular Hypothesis and the Evolution Hypothesis, both of which

* MILL, *Logic*, II. 19.

Mr. Mill regards in the light of genuine scientific procedures. Nay, it is destructive of the hypothesis of *universal* Gravitation (which, indeed, Mr. Mill hesitates to accept). No one of these is capable of being brought to the test of observation, of being converted into a proved fact. Indeed the restriction placed by Comte and Mill would interdict all speculation respecting geological and astronomical phenomena which, dependent on past causations, cannot receive verification except by reflection from present causation. If such indirect evidence be inadmissible, vainly will astronomers, geologists, and biologists accumulate evidence. The various phases of the earth's evolution, the various stages of animal evolution, are explained on the assumption that causes similar to those now observed in operation were formerly the agents in bringing about the evolution; and the assumption is admitted, but no one pretends that there is proof of the hypothesis. The Nebular Hypothesis and the Evolution Hypothesis have amply justified themselves by the aids they have furnished to Research; but few imagine them to be demonstrable; nor can we assert them to be final.

CHAPTER VIII.

THE PASSAGE FROM THE ABSTRACT TO THE CONCRETE.

110. THE recognition of the fact that Science is in no respect a plain transcript of Reality, in no respect a picture of the External Order, but wholly an ideal construction in which the manifold relations of Reals are taken up and assimilated by the mind, and there transformed into relations of ideas, so that the world of Sense is changed into the world of Thought, — this fact leads to the deeply interesting question, How can Science avail in our search after the External Order, and explain the real relations of Things? Its own domain is exclusively ideal. Yet it seeks to reveal the processes of Reals, the Laws of Things, that thereby we may so modify the conjunctures of events as to render events our servants; or so modify our attitude towards events as to reconcile us to the fatalities we cannot alter. Its vision is directed to processes rather than to objects, and it regards objects solely in the light of necessary materials for the construction of general conceptions which are to guide action. This comparative disregard of the concrete in favor of the abstract, this transformation of the particular into the general, of the sensible into the intelligible, is the necessary consequence of our mental limitation. Every Real is the complex of so many relations, a conjuncture of so many events, a synthesis of so many sensations, that to know one Real thoroughly would only be possible through an intuition embracing the universe. This being impos-

sible, we can only approach a knowledge of an object by separately studying its several relations, so far as each can be laid hold of by itself, i. e. by Abstraction. The nature of our organism prevents our having more than one aspect of an object at each instant present to Consciousness; so that relations which are objectively simultaneous are by us perceived successively. In succession we feel that a thing is visible, tangible, resistant, etc., and such successions are condensed into a single perception. Any one element of this group becomes the *sign* of all the rest. Every perception is also an act of judgment which classes the present feeling with past feelings, and assumes the presence of unfelt relations. The validity of the perception is the possibility of converting the unfelt into felt relations. A scientific conception differs from the simple perception mainly in its higher degree of abstraction and generality. It has constructed general formulas of the relations of visibility, tangibility, etc., which it extends to all similar cases, real or imaginary, and thus is furnished with the Law or condensed synthesis of experiences.

The Laws of Light, of Vision, of Motion, of Muscular Sensation, of Quantity, of Combination, etc., are all separately studied, — are abstractions from the processes actually observed. The mathematician keeps to Quantity, never allowing himself to be perplexed by considerations of Quality. The astronomer fixes attention on the movements of the planets without regarding the structure and composition of these masses. The physicist and chemist separate the molecular relations from all the phenomena of Life, and the biologist studies the phenomena of life apart from historical and social relations. In every science the concrete Real is stripped of all its qualities except those which the science specially needs for its construction. The actual sensible thing is set aside. Nor is this all. The substitution of an ideal object for a sensible object, an abstract for a concrete, is the substitution of a general relation for a particular relation. The relation of weight in *this* mass is the relation which will exist in *all* similar masses similarly placed; the resistance recognized in *this* body is seen to belong to *all* bodies. To the geometer a circle is not the round figure visible by his eye, but a figure visible by his mind, in which all the radii from the centre are absolutely equal; it is not this particular sensible circle, it is the ideal circle To the physicist Heat is not a sensation, but a vibration of molecules; to the physiologist it is not a vibration of molecules, but an affection of a sensory nerve. The sciences of Thermotics and Acoustics are not records of the actual phenomena observed in thermal and sonorous events, but general relations detached from them. The first effort of the physicist is not to enumerate all the facts, but to reduce the multiplicity to certain elementary relations of a mechanical kind; these are then translated into mathematical formulas, which are operated on as if *they* were Heat and Sound.

111. The universe presented to us is constituted by Elements, Groups of Elements, and Groups of Groups. The combinations being practically infinite we can never know them all, and being complex, we can only approximate to the knowledge of any. Imperfect as our knowledge is, it may be absolutely certain, to the extent of its own reach; and this certainty is secured whenever the boundaries are not overstepped. A particular relation is absolutely certain under the particular conditions; if we generalize it we must at the same time generalize the conditions, or else we are substituting a new proposition in place of the old one. "That I feel warm at this moment," is an irresistible truth, though not one valuable to science. "That I shall always feel warm," is equally certain, if I generalize the present conditions: but if I sim-

ply assert that I shall always feel warm irrespective of any change whatever in the conditions, it is clear that I violate the first principle of rational judgment, unless I have previously established the fact that warmth is wholly independent of conditions.

112. Now the power of Science consists in this: having seized upon the relations that are uniform amid the relations that are various, and having formulated the conditions under which phenomena occur, it is enabled to generalize these, and say "whenever such conditions are present such phenomena must be present," no matter how various may be the accompaniments. And observation having disclosed that some conditions are very general, others universal, these are formulated as Laws of Phenomena. But as all these must be first disclosed by observation before they are generalized, — as all deductions rest on inductions, and all inductions on sensible experiences, — Science, which seems to depart from Experience in its pursuit of abstractions, is only a reproduction of Experience, — a translation of the heterogeneous facts *observed*, into the homogeneous relations *thought*, — and it errs whenever its abstractions admit any elements not given in the concretes.

113. The passage from the abstract to the concrete can only be the inverse of the passage from the concrete to the abstract. What was dropped out of sight in establishing the ideal — namely, all the details which particularized the particular phenomena — must be restored in each particular case. The law of uniform Motion was reached by abstracting it from all the variations to which every moving body is subject; in applying this ideal law to any real case we must compound it with the observed variations. That all bodies fall to the earth in equal times is ideally true, but really false; to make it accord with fact, we must abstract the resistance of the air,

which, inappreciable in the fall of condensed masses, is appreciable in the fall of masses with surfaces which are broad compared with their thickness. And so with all other laws. Applied Mechanics presents us with the best illustration of ideal laws, true in their generality yet falsified in every particular case, which are nevertheless because of their ideal truth the most invaluable guides in practice.

CHAPTER IX.

IDEAL CONSTRUCTION IN METAPHYSICS.

114. In the foregoing exposition of the nature of Science, stress has been laid on its being ideal *construction* and not faithful *representation* of what is, has been, or could be presented to Sense. The philosopher looks away from the Visible and Actual, endeavoring to form a picture of the Invisible and Possible.* He strives to discover not what we should see with sharpened faculties, but what would be seen were the constitution of things different from that which it is. Philosophy is not an instrument like the telescope or microscope, intended only to magnify the powers of Sense, but an organon of Imagination by which to reconstruct an ideal world of Abstraction. The first operation of the scientific explorer, either through Speculation or Experiment, is to strip the phenomenon under investigation of every character which individualizes it, makes it the particular phenomenon it is, and to carry this residuum into the region of generalities, where it finds its place amid others of a similar order. The experimenter removes the object from its normal conditions, placing it under conditions unlike those in which it is naturally observed, sometimes under conditions which could not coexist in Nature, — as when elements are isolated (in retorts) which always rush into combination when such violent restriction to their

* "In der That ist das Denken wesentlich die Negation eines unmittelbar Vorhandenen." — Hegel, *Encyklopædie*, § 12.

movement is no longer present; and thus we see in the Laboratory of the Chemist what cannot be seen in the Laboratory of Nature.

115. It appears, then, that the search in all Science is never for the Visible which Sense reveals, but for the Invisible which Sense obscures. If, therefore, Truth is the conformity of Inferences with Sensation, all Science must be false. And yet we declare Science to be true; and moreover declare that its truth is only reached through the ministration of Sense. A paradox. Where is the issue? It has already been indicated with sufficient clearness. The truth of Science is the truth of ideal construction; and because its abstractions are formed out of sensible concretes, its truths are applicable to reality *in the precise degree to which the ideal constructions express the real facts.* Thus the truths of Dynamics are absolutely exact only in the ideal region, — in mathematical abstraction; and they would be rigorously true even if they were never applied to concrete cases, where they are necessarily always inexact. It is because in the difficult passage from the ideal to the real, from the abstract to the concrete, we reverse the process of ideal construction, and restore the elements which abstraction has let drop, that ideal truths become realized in observation. It is because we can show that the abstraction is only an abbreviated expression of what is constant in the concretes, that we declare it to be an expression of the real process of Nature.

116. When, therefore, the metempiricist proposes his ideal constructions as guides for Speculation, and asks us to accept his abstractions with the same reliance that we yield to those of the mathematician, or physicist, are we to deny him that license of Imagination so liberally accorded to the scientific seeker? and if so, on what grounds? Why may one seeker deliberately look away

from the plain and palpable order of things revealed to Sense, in favor of another order constructed by Imagination; whereas the metempiricist is told that his search is hopeless because he is wandering beyond the landmarks of Sense? The experimenter is suffered to wrest hydrogen from all its many compounds that it may be studied in itself; why may not the metaphysician strip an object of all its sensible qualities to study *it* in itself?

Whoever can satisfactorily answer this question has settled for himself the old dispute between Metaphysics and Science. It has already been answered implicitly in the preceding pages. An explicit answer may now be given. Let me premise that in what follows a metaphysician is considered to be one who pursues the metaphysical Method, and constructs his conceptions without regard to the control of objective verification, and is therefore willing to admit metempirical and empirical elements among his data. This Method would be justifiable if the problems mooted had no objective application. The ideal world of the metempiricist would be as valid as the ideal world of the empiricist, if by it no attempt were made to explain the real world. The conceptions of the theologian relating to a world beyond might be irresistibly consistent if confined to *that* world; but when he pretends by such conceptions to regulate our *conduct in this world*, we have to demand that he exhibit the necessary connection between the premises and consequences, and shows us the passage from his abstract conception to the concrete realities. If he gained his abstract conception by abstraction from real concretes, the reversal of the process will be a demonstration of the truth of his conclusion. If he gained it thus his Method was scientific, and his results must be tested by the canons of Science. But if he framed his conception on the subjective Method, and attempts to explain the External Order by laws not originally gathered from experience of it, we reject the validity of his procedure. What is here said of the theologian applies equally to the metaphysician.

117. The ideal constructions of Science are built up from the real elements of Experience. The abstractions are raised from verifiable facts. If the law of Motion is never actually presented in Nature, its elements are presented; and experiment can *demonstrate* — i. e. reduce to Intuition — what sensory organs can never see. The intuitions of Science are not gleams of Fantasy, not arbitrary assumptions, not traditional assents for which no better reason can be given than that they are in the mind and are held to be truths; they are *organized experiences,* which although often no longer decomposable into their elements, and therefore presenting themselves as instantaneous and indubitable acts of Thought, are nevertheless composite, and disclose to analysis the sensible elements from which they were constructed, — these elements can be recognized no less indubitably than the carbon and oxygen can be recognized in the carbonic acid which presents itself in chalk.* Inferences are only reproduced sensations; they become so welded with their sensible accompaniments that at length the groups are indissoluble; they are then known as intuitions, i. e. as instantaneous undecomposable acts of mental vision. Just as we have all an intuition of distance in every vision of an object, so we have an intuition of a mathematical, or of a causal, relation in every presentation of terms that are familiar. That $7 + 5 = 12$, or that central forces decrease according to the inverse squares, is seen with nearly the same rapidity, and with a certainty quite the same as that an object is distant. Remote as the intuition of central forces is from its sensible data, there is no doubt that it was originally constructed from such data; and only

* Compare here HEGEL, *Encyklopædie,* § 66.

by an inverse reduction to these data can it be demonstrated to one who disputes its validity.

118. The abstractions and intuitions of Science being always expressions of sensible Experience can always be verified; whereas the abstractions and intuitions which play a great part in Metaphysics often want this basis; and are seen, on analysis, to be traditional prejudices, or unverified assumptions,—**οὐκ ἐξ αἰσθητῶν,** as Aristotle says of the Pythagorean notions. Take an example: Science regards Motion as an ultimate, consequently declines to seek for its cause. Not so Metempirics: "Les philosophes," says Maupertius, "qui ont mis la cause du mouvement en Dieu, n'y ont été réduits que parcequ'il ne savoient où la mettre. Ne pouvant concevoir que la matière eût aucune efficace pour produire, distribuer, et détenir le mouvement, ils ont eu recours à un *Être immatériel.*" That is to say, dissatisfied with an ultimate, they had recourse to a fiction. . . . . "Mais lorsqu'on saura que toutes les loix du mouvement et du repos sont fondées sur le Principe du *Mieux,* on ne pourra plus douter qu'elles ne doivent leur établissement à un *Être tout puissant et tout sage. . . . . Ce n'est donc point dans la mécanique que je vais chercher ces loix; c'est dans la sagesse de l'Être suprême.*" * And it is on the strength of this principle that he deduces his famous "*principle of least action,* 'principe si sage, si digne de l'Être suprême.'" The intuition of a Supreme Being may indeed be advanced as a ground for the inference that he would act in the most intelligent manner; and Maupertius is strictly logical in assuming that since the principle of least action appears both wise and worthy of the Supreme Being, it may be accepted as the principle in operation. But who can fail to see that this Intuition, and the assumed wisdom of the principle, are altogether wanting in a sensible basis; and

* MAUPERTIUS, *Essai de Cosmologie; Œuvres,* p. 18. Dresden, 1752.

that a simple denial of the Being, or denial of the wisdom of this procedure, leaves the argument powerless? Nothing would then be left to Maupertius but to reiterate the assertion of his intuition. The fact that the "principle of least action" has been turned to account by mathematicians rests solely on the logical truth it involves, and not at all on its being the intuition of a Best.

119. By similar intuitions the Pythagoreans justified their doctrines. "Since ten appeared to them the perfect number, potentially containing all numbers, they declared that the moving celestial bodies were ten in number; and because only nine bodies are visible, they imagined a tenth, — the Antichthone." *

120. The metaphysician may object that I have here adduced exploded errors; I will therefore adduce one not open to this criticism, namely, the assumption — which is frequently passed off as an intuition not to be disputed — of the Soul being a simple substance because it is the opposite of Matter. That it is a substance at all ought first to be established; whether or not the substance is simple would be a subsequent point for research. But the assumption once made, there are deduced from it the necessary consequences of freedom and immortality, — which conclusions were in fact the grounds of the original assumption. I do not intend here to discuss this question,† I only wish to point out that we have no sensible data into which such an intuition can be resolved: we have no experience from which the simplicity of the

* ARISTOTLE, *Metaph.*, I. 5.

† Whether the soul is or is not a simple substance is of no consequence to us in the explanation of its phenomena. For we cannot render the notion of a simple being intelligible by any possible experience sensuously or *in concrete*. The notion is therefore quite void as regards all hoped-for insight into the cause of phenomena, and cannot at all serve as a principle of the explanation of that which internal or external experience supplies. — KANT, *Prolegomena*, § 44, trans. by *Mahaffy*, p. 129.

soul's substance can be a necessary conclusion analogous to the conclusions of Science. It is founded on the negation of Matter. We imagine that it must be whatever Matter is not. But negations furnish no positive data.*

121. Hegel saw that Philosophy is the transformation of sensations and perceptions into abstractions; yet in his own system it is obvious that abstractions are sometimes raised from concrete experiences, and sometimes from intuitions which are defective in their sensible basis. Although admitting Experience to be the sole foundation, he objects to the Empirical Method because, he says, it contains within it no unviersality, no necessity: it is occupied wholly with particulars and cannot rise to generals.

Were this objection true in fact, it would be fatal in effect. It is, however, false. Its plausibility is dependent on the unwarrantable restriction of Experience to Perception,— a restriction which is one of the commonest of philosophical mistakes. In virtue of this it appears that the Empirical Method can only deal with particulars, and can never reach universal and necessary truths. This is the *cheval de bataille* of Metempirics, and I shall presently devote a chapter to its refutation. If, however, the Empirical Method is incompetent, where are we to seek an explanation of universal and necessary conditions? In the laws of Thought, says Hegel; and these laws he admits belong to Experience, though he is not successful

* Exploded errors are instructive, we may therefore profit by such argument as Frascotorio advances in his once celebrated *Homocentria* to prove that the stars cannot have independent motion, this being "totally at variance with our notion of a simple and undecaying substance like the heavenly bodies. For that which is simple is altogether single, and singleness is only of one nature, and one nature can only be the cause of one effect." It had not occurred to him that before a fact could be discredited by its variance from our notion, the absolute accuracy of the notion itself needed demonstration.

in deducing them from it. What is the consequence? It is that the deductions drawn by him from these said laws of Thought are often found to be absurdly at variance with Experience; and that so far from his laws of Thought being in accordance with the laws of Things reached inductively, they are at times positively ridiculous in their misrepresentations. His mistake is that while avowing the origin of Knowledge to be sensible experiences, yet because Reason is a higher development of these experiences, he imagines that deductions from rational premises have a higher validity than the inductions from sensible premises; forgetting that these rational premises themselves receive their validity from the sensible inductions. The prejudice in favor of the higher validity of rational premises is very intelligible. We find that particular experiences have often little value because they are particular, whereas generalities include multitudes of experiences, and have a multiform value. Hence the philosopher takes his stand upon generalities as upon some sacred mount from whence are delivered the texts of a higher revelation. It is the purpose of his labors to apply these texts to the confused tumult of sensible experiences, interpreting the many-colored phenomena of the world by the pure light of reason.

122. To conclude: Science owes its certitude to the power of resolving its ideal constructions into elements of sensible experience; Metempirics owes its incessant incertitude to the Method on which it is pursued not requiring, and very often not being able to effect, the reduction of its intuitions to sensations, its abstractions to sensible concretes. Because it disdains the Empirical Method of construction and step-by-step verification, it is obliged to assume principles which no Experience has guaranteed and which none can confirm. The Supra-

sensible is got at analytically by analysis of analysis. Why may it not be as legitimate as analysis of sensibles? or as differentials of differentials? Because it cannot be sensibly integrated. No synthetic verification is possible, — no re-entrance from the abstract into the concrete.

CHAPTER X.

THE SEARCH AFTER CAUSES.

123. PHILOSOPHY is the generalization of Research. What is sought? The causes of visible appearances; not the appearances themselves, for they are already found. On this point there is unanimity. Yet observe the contradiction! Many philosophers, metaphysical and positive, declare that causes cannot be known. If beyond knowledge, why then are they sought? Comte is less paradoxical than those metaphysicians who hold causes to be inscrutable; for he consistently declares that the search after a cause is frivolous because futile; they admit it to be futile, yet pronounce it to be man's highest prerogative.

124. Here, as in so many other cases, the initial defect is in the presentation of the problem. The terms are used in fluctuating senses, the conclusions fluctuate with them. There has been a general outcry against Comte's condemnation of the search after causes; and it has been in so far merited that his polemic is rather against the term and its connotations than against the idea of Cause. In practice he is found introducing Law in the place of Cause; and what philosophers *denote* by Cause is simply what he denotes by Law. What many of them *connote* both by Cause and Law he rejects, and in this rejection he is supported by all scientific teachers. There is a metempirical conception of Law which is the precise equivalent of the metempirical conception of Cause. There is also an empirical conception of Cause which is

the precise equivalent of Law. We need not therefore adopt Comte's rejection of a term which is familiar, and may be made precise; we have only to make ourselves fully aware of its metempirical connotations, and eliminate them, as we eliminate all metempirical elements.

125. Phenomena present themselves in Experience as dependent on other phenomena which precede and coexist with them, — varying as these vary, being their *function* (to speak mathematically). We detach these dependencies and connections, and call the abstractions *causes*. Obviously the search after these is strictly scientific; Science has no other object. But metempirical philosophers have been dissatisfied with such results. Seeking for revelations of Existence which transcend the concrete revelations of Experience, they presuppose a mysterious something over and above the mere relation of dependence, a Power by which the connection is affected (the Efficient Cause), or a Purpose for which it was effected (the Final Cause). It is this conception of a transcendental Causality, efficient and final, which Comte condemns, and which must be condemned by all who recognize the fault against rational Method which transforms knowable dependencies into unknowable entities. I believe, however, that if we eliminate the metempirical elements from the conception of efficient causes, the search after efficient causes is not only justifiable, but may be successful.

126. The metaphysician who discards the Method of Science, and believes in the possibility of our knowing the Supra-sensible, will of course demur to such an elimination. His constant complaint against our Method is that its field of vision is too narrow. "Granting all you claim," he says, "you can only expound the How, and must ever remain silent respecting the Why. A miserable restriction! The impatience of the soul to apprehend the Why has urged in all past ages, and in all ages to

come will urge men to the noble study of Philosophy. It is this which inspires the divine desire to penetrate the secrets of the plan divine. It is restless until the causes have been found, and however baffled, it will not be appeased by an exposition of mere laws of connection and dependence. To know that the facts *are* thus or thus is useful, and by such knowledge Science subserves the uses of mankind. But utility is not Philosophy; and is far below the sublime aspiration of knowing *why* the facts are thus or thus, and knowing that the course of Nature *must* be what it is, and *why* it must be so."

A sublime aspiration, it may be, but it is *only* an aspiration, — a mere breath. This is evident when we come to learn the genesis of knowledge and its limitations. Then we see the Why resolved into the How; then we see that it is a verbal distinction, not a real distinction; and that it is only by an artifice that Cause can be separated from Conditions.

THE IDEAS OF CAUSE AND SUBSTANCE.

127. The investigation of any phenomenon, or group of phenomena, may be likened to the exploration of the sources of a river. The wanderer follows the river from the sea through valleys and watercourses till it is lost in a lake. The exploring mind is unsatisfied, and asks, Whence the lake? From streams that have their origin in rivulets, and these rivulets in water-threads oozing from the mountain-side. He ascends the steep sides, guided by the trickling brightness, till finally he arrives at the vast snow-fields of the summit. There, where earth ceases, he stands thrilled, awed, perplexed. Before him lies the wide expanse of snow, above him the wider sweep of sky. All traces of the river have vanished, and this mystery fronts him. The restless craving for a cause, or origin, is unappeased. The snow was the origin of the

river, but whence the snow? It must have a cause. It is not an origin, but a landing-place. The river was only the snow fluent. Onwards the exploring mind proceeds, following the snow into the clouds, where it appears as delicate vesicles of water enclosing air. This water, whence? It rose in exhalations from the sea. The explorer thus returns to his point of departure. And whence the sea? It is not the origin of the water, since it visibly receives the water from the land. Thus the circle of movement runs. Further examination discloses that every single particle of water persists unchanged through all its changing fellowships with other particles, and with changing Heat, Air, Salts, etc., as it successively forms an integer of rivulet and river, cloud and snow. It is these particles which alone are real. Rivulet or river, cloud or snow, is an abstraction, — a group of events. The form of the river, and its course through the land, give it individuality as a phenomenon; but these are obviously determined by the conjunture of external events. Its individuality at each stage expresses these conjunctures; and that which was a babbling brook is now a navigable river only by the co-operation of new conjunctures; the thread of light, the cloud of spray, the floating mist and leaping cataract, the snow-flake and the breaker, are embodied histories. Each successive form is a succession of events, each event having been determined by some prior group. This is the circulation of Cause. Causation is immanent Change.

128. Throughout these transformations there has been something persistent, something that has not changed, namely, the Existence we call Substance; and it is this persistent Value whose changing Positions have determined the events. If the *changes* are causes, the *changed* is substance. Cause and Substance, Force and Matter, are the indissoluble elements of every phenomenon.

129. Corresponding with these two divisions of the one Existence there are two lines of inquiry. Either we seek to know *what* is, or *how* it came to be what it is: the thing, or its history; Ontology or Ontogeny. The first goal is reached when we have defined the thing, and described the phenomenon under those aspects which it presents to Sense, or Intuition; with the implied understanding that under similar conditions it will present these to all minds. The second goal is reached when we have described the antecedent and coexistent conditions which determine the phenomenon to be what it is; and since each of these conditions is itself a phenomenon, having its history therefore, and being a complex of events, the pursuit must be interminable if not arbitrarily limited. This *arbitrariness* in the definition of Cause will have to be invoked by and by; enough for the present to have indicated it.

130. We conclude, then, that a thing *is* what it *appears*. It is the expression of a particular history of events, the group of conditions which are said to *determine* it. We may abstract these conditions, and consider each of them by itself, or two or more together; but in this abstraction the thing disappears, and we have only one or more of its causes. Again, we may consider the whole group of conditions, and then the thing reappears as the expression of this totality. There is nothing in the object that is not in the conditions, unless we artifically eliminate the conditional substance; there is nothing in the conditions — thus defined — that is not in the object. Our logical separation of a Thing from its Relations is only possible in so far as we can severally consider any one aspect of a Thing, without considering the Thing as a complex.

131. The search for a cause, origin, or history is a speculative instinct prompted by our needs and cherished

by constant experience of events depending on other events.* But this instinct, like most other instincts, is sometimes misleading, and is peculiarly so in Philosophy, where it manifests itself as a craving for double sight: dissatisfied with a vision of what the thing is, we desire to know what it is not and cannot be, — and we are under the strange hallucination that this imaginary state, this aspect which the thing does not and cannot present to us, is more real and enduring than the fleeting phenomenal aspect which alone it can present to us! Not content with a vision of the group of relations actually existing, and of those which preceded it, Speculation craves for a vision of the thing, or event, *in itself*, — i.e. *unrelated*: in other words, as it does not and cannot exist.†

THE HOW AND THE WHY.

132. Our restless impatience, dissatisfied with the How, demands a Why, and seeks a cause of the cause. We see that oxygen unites with hydrogen, the product being water. This is *how* water is formed; but this is not enough for us, and we ask, Why? And the question is answered when the chemist shows how certain conditions of motion, pressure, and temperature determine the result, — how the loss of a given amount of heat from the

* "Notre tendance intellectuelle à chercher les causes de tout objet qui frappe notre attention," says Sophie Germain, one of the few women who have been distinguished mathematicians, "me paraîtrait indiquer que nous n'aperçevons pas l'objet dans son entier. Il s'offre à nous avec le caractère fractionnaire; nous demandons quelle en est l'unité. Nous le voyons comme étant une partie; nous voulons connaître le tout auquel cette partie appartient." — *Considérations générales sur l'état des sciences*, p. 41. 1833.

† "Das Dingansich als solches," says Hegel, "ist nicht Anderes als die leere Abstraction von aller Bestimmtheit, von dem man allerdings *nichts wissen* kann, eben darum weil es die Abstraction von aller Bestimmung seyn soll." — *Logik*, II. 127.

two gases *causes* their condensation into water. The Why or How is simply the conditions under which the union takes place, or (as it is otherwise phrased) the conditions by which the effect is produced, caused. When these conditions are enumerated, the Why is given. There is no other Why in operation; — unless indeed we choose to consider as a part of the *operant* conditions any or all of the *antecedent* conditions which determine these. But as this would involve a regress of causation through the whole past history of the Cosmos, no one thinks of such an extension of the inquiry.

133. But while the positive thinker affixes these limits, and accepts the immediate conditions as the causal conditions, accepting these as full explanation of the Why, — since it is an explanation of the How, — the metaphysical thinker demands that the How of the How, or the Why of the How, should be explained; and is not satisfied by a regress to antecedent conditions; on the contrary, he demands a transcendental condition. Over and above those sensible conditions, which the physicist assigns, he believes there is an undefinable Something, named Power, which causes the oxygen to unite with hydrogen, — a something which gives these conditions their efficiency. This Power he either conceives to be external to the substances, or immanent in them; in the one case he regards it as the action of the Deity, operating on and through the gases; in the other case as the action of a Force, — Affinity; in both cases the Power is assumed to be the efficient Agent; and this Agent some thinkers believe to be knowable through an Intuition not dependent upon Experience; other thinkers declare to be unknowable, though undeniable.

134. The objection to both these views is that the assumed Power is wholly without a basis in sensible Experience, and must be excluded from the province of

Research, to be relegated to the province of the Suprasensible, which demands a special organ, and has no community with positive knowledge. Nor is this all. Granting the presence of such an Agent, it would be powerless in the absence of the substantial conditions, and would vary in its effect with every variation of these conditions. Since, therefore, the knowable effect depends on and varies with the known conditions, and since, moreover, nothing is given in Experience except the fact of the union, and the fact of the conditions, it is clear that the introduction of a Power, over and above these, is superfluous. If any one ask, Why is the planetary path elliptical? he is answered when the conditions are enumerated which determine that path to be elliptical, and not otherwise. If this How be further questioned, and a Why be sought, it again resolves itself into another How, and so on in endless regress of conditions, unfolding dependencies on dependencies, till the final pause: "This is so because Nature is so, or because God has willed it so."

135. No one asks for a Why in mathematics; to show the How, to demonstrate the proposition, is enough. No one asks why a circle has every point of its circumference equidistant from the centre, or why all its radii must be equal. But one may ask why it is impossible to draw such a circle on paper; and the question is answered by showing how from the necessary unevenness of the surface there must be unevenness in the tracing. So long as the circle was ideal it was perfect, for it depended solely on ideal conditions; directly it was dependent on real conditions it expressed those and their departures from the ideal definition. The ideal conditions are unalterable for they are self-contained; the real conditions are variable for they have varying dependencies on others.

136. Hence the distinction between the How and the Why expresses something like the distinction between a consideration of the object and a consideration of its history; and as the object is truly its *embodied history,* — it being simply the group of Relations, — the How and the Why are essentially one.

THE TWO CONCEPTIONS OF LAW.

137. I said there was a conception of Cause which was the precise equivalent of the conception of Law, whether the empirical or the metempirical point of view be taken; Comte's rejection of the term Cause and his substitution of Law, therefore, could only be justified on the ground of his understanding the one term in its metempirical, and the other in its empirical sense.

138. The metempirical conception of Law is that phenomena are *regulated,* determined by certain active Agencies, very much in the manner of passive bodies coerced to obey external forces. The Laws of Nature are regarded in the light of Statutes. These statutes men are said occasionaly to violate; and God is supposed to suspend their action in Miracles. Even minds of a less theological leaning regard the Laws of Nature as Powers attendant on, or immanent in, Matter.

139. The empirical conception of Law is that of an abstraction of observed dependencies. It is thus another term for Cause, another aspect of a Fact. It is a term for Cause when it expresses the process and the conditions of a change, — e. g. the law of Gravitation. It is a term for Fact when it expresses these conditions solely, without reference to change, — e. g. the fact of Gravitation, the fact that air has weight, or that pressure in a fluid is propagated equally in all directions. Since facts and causes are innumerable, and are of various degrees of importance and frequency, it is useful to have a term which

designates those facts or causes which have a special importance; the term selected has been Law.

140. Had the essential identity of Law, Cause, and Fact been duly apprehended, much misty speculation would have been dissipated. Men would have recognized that by Law or Cause, they were only expressing what had been observed, or inferred as Fact. The new term implied no addition to the old. But unhappily the tendency to suppose that a distinction in terms denotes a corresponding distinction in things early led men to suppose that Law really denoted something over and above Fact. A Law of Nature is not an Agent nor an Agency by which substances are coerced, but an abstract expression of the series of positions which substances assume under given conditions. It is not a creator of the phenomena, it is their *formula*. It does not precede and coerce them, it is evolved by them. No positive biologist imagines that the Laws of Life determine animal and vegetal forms; the metempirical biologist imagines this, and believes in the objective existence of Types. What Types are in Biology, Laws are in Philosophy: ideal constructions expressing the observed uniformities among phenomena. But these uniformities do not depend on some agency apart from the constituent integers of the phenomena, they are simply the expression of the Coexistent Values.*

141. That Law and Cause are the same, appears directly we restore the concretes from which they are abstracted. Thus the law of gravitation is the cause of gravitation, whether regarded as immanent or external, i. e. as the gravitating *process* of the bodies in motion towards each other, or as the external *pressures* moving the bodies. The cause of planetary motion — or its law — may be described as the motion determined by tan-

* See Prob. II. for a fuller elucidation of this term.

gential and centripetal motions, or as the motion due to the sun's position; in the one case the cause is regarded in its immanence, in the other case in its externality.

When thus we eliminate from the conception of Cause all its metempirical connotations, it becomes identical with the empirical conception of Law; and the search after causes — nay, after efficient causes — is strictly philosophical.

CHAPTER XI.

INTUITION AND DEMONSTRATION.

142. THE main positions occupied by those who defend the Metaphysical Method, and by those who believe in the possibility of Metempirics, are the evidences of a *source* of knowledge which is antecedent to and independent of Experience, and of a *kind* of knowledge which transcends Experience. We must have a higher organ, it is said, because we have the higher knowledge. That organ is Intuition, that knowledge is Necessary Truth.

All that has been written in the preceding pages would be either set aside as erroneous, or disregarded as irrelevant, if these two positions were left in the possession of our antagonists.

143. The ancient doctrine of Innate Ideas having been relinquished, or modified till it became ineffectual, the doctrine of Intellectual Intuition was put forward in its place. The most precise form this doctrine assumed was that given it by Jacobi, when he affirmed that over and above the intuitions of sensible objects, we had a special organ of rational intuition for the perception of supra-sensibles.* He admitted that its special intuitions are given in the overflow of feeling (*in überschwänglichen Gefühle*), but declared these to be nevertheless truly objective. It was this organ which Schelling christened the Intellectual Intuition, and to it assigned the principle of Demonstration and final ground of Certitude.

* JACOBI, *Werke*, II. 55. "Die Vernunft ist das unkörperliche Organ für die Warhnehmungen des Uebersinnlichen." Comp. also p. 59.

144. Jacobi was misled, I think, by an imperfect appreciation of the nature of Demonstration. He said that the conviction gained through demonstration is a certainty at second hand; it rests on comparison, and can never be perfectly secure. "If, then, every opinion is Faith, which does not issue from Reason, so must conviction from rational grounds issue from Faith, and owe its force to Faith alone."* There is an equivoque here. Conviction is assuredly a feeling, and Reason has only force in proportion to the feeling involved. But although the certainty of a demonstration may be reached by a comparison of feelings, and is thus second-hand, what is usually understood by Faith is not this comparison of feelings, not the reduction of inferences to sensations, but the reliance on unverified inferences. Granting that Feeling is the common basis of sensible and rational inference, we cannot admit that any unverified inferences are to be accepted as objective truths. My conviction that the object before me is an apple, and my conviction that the riots in Ireland are parts of a "providential scheme," may be equally true expressions of my state of feeling, — I who have these convictions cannot doubt that I have them, — but one or both may be absolutely false expressions of the objective realities; and their truth or falsehood can only be demonstrated by the reduction of what is inferential in each to its correspondent sensibles. In the case of the apple such a reduction may be easy. In the case of the providential scheme it is impossible, simply because the providential scheme is a conception framed out of data which never were and never could be sensible. And herein is displayed the futility of this pretended organ. It professes to deal with supra-sensibles, yet these can only be thought of under sensible forms. Nor let it be urged that precisely this is the course followed with

* JACOBI, *Werke*, IV. 210.

respect to extra-sensibles. The only test there admitted, namely, the reduction of the extra-sensibles to the sensible standard, is the very test which the theologian and metempiricist reject. For if that test be admitted, it brings the Supra-sensible within the range of Experience, and thus Religion and Metaphysics become amenable to the Method of Science; a Method which, by excluding whatever cannot be verified, at once sets aside a mass of speculations declared to be unverifiable, and a mass of dogmas declared to be absurd.

145. No reader firmly persuaded that the mind of man is endowed with the power of apprehending the Supra-sensible can be expected to relinquish that belief, coerced by the arguments here advanced; it is with him a question of Faith, and cannot be shaken by Logic. But in opposition we may say to him: "The existence of such a power requires proof, and when proven it can only serve to construct a system of conceptions which have *no* analogy, or point of intersection, with the conceptions constructed out of sensible experiences; this being so, whatever range it may have it must be excluded from all theories having reference to the sensible world."

Our Method does not exclude mystery from the Universe, it only excludes it from Science, and assigns it to the region of the Metempirical, "whose margin fades forever and forever as we move." The doctrine of Intellectual Intuition is not only disputable, it is futile. But while rejecting its pretensions we may with advantage accept and interpret the facts it improperly classifies, and admit the existence of Experiential Intuition. This we will here consider.

146. Demonstration is the *showing* to Sense or Intuition, in other words, the reduction of Inference to its corresponding sensations, either directly through Sense, or indirectly through Intuition.

If I wish to demonstrate that three objects added to three others will form a group numerically equivalent to another group, named six, this can be done by a direct appeal to Sense, placing the groups side by side; or, by an indirect appeal through Intuition, the ratio symbolized in $3 + 3 = 6$ being intuited with a certainty equal to that which accompanied the vision of the groups. For this intuition to be possible, the sensible experiences must have preceded it; but once formed, the sensible experiences pass into symbols and are intuited. Just as Algebra in virtue of its generality can effect operations which are difficult to Arithmetic, and operations which are impossible to Arithmetic, so Intuition can detect relations which are obscure to Sense, and relations inaccessible to Sense. Thus although it it easy to *see* that three objects placed beside three others form a group equivalent to a group of six, the acutest eye would fail to detect at a glance that sixty objects placed beside sixty others were equivalent to a group of one hundred and twenty; but where Sense is bewildered by the multiplicity of objects, Intuition sees at a glance the equivalence of their ratios. We may therefore define Intuition as Mental Vision, or as the Perception of Relations.* It is differenced from Sensation on the one hand in that it sees objects not only as they affect Sense, but also in their relations to each other, and sees these present as constituent elements of the group; so that the intuition of an object includes a much wider range of Experience than a perception of the

* "In English writers this term has of late been vaguely used to express all convictions which are arrived at without conscious reasoning, whether referring to relations among our primary perceptions or to conceptions of the most derivative and complex nature. But if we were allowed to restrict the use of this term we might conveniently confine it to those cases in which we necessarily apprehend relations of things truly as soon as we conceive the objects distinctly." — WHEWELL, *The Mechanical Euclid*, p. 182. 1849.

object. From Conception, on the other hand, it is differenced by its restriction to definite particular objects and relations, always therefore reproducing the forms of sensible experiences; whereas Conception never does this, being in its nature analytical, general, abstract.

It is often impossible to demonstrate (to Sense) what it is impossible to doubt when intuited. Thus after proving that the area of a spherical triangle depends on the sum of its angles, we cannot exhibit to Sense that *any* two spherical triangles which have their sides and angles equal, each to each, have equal areas; because if they are symmetrical angles they can no more be made to *coincide* than a right and left hand can get into the same glove.* But the intuition of equality is perfect in this case.

147. This perception of ratios or intuition of equality, that two things equal to a third must be equal to each other, is in constant requisition. If I have a vacant space, and a box which I wish to place in it, my sensible perception of the relation between the boundaries of the space and those of the box is too imperfect for guidance; I cannot *see* the equality, but I can measure with a foot-rule both the space and the box, and finding that each contains this measure the *same* number of times, I conclude that the box will not go into the space; or, if the space contains the measure and something over, I conclude the box will go into it.

148. Intuition under its ideal aspect is Judgment. Demonstration is the exhibition of the grounds. We call judgment, 1°, *intuitive*, when the relations seem to embody experiences which are not specified or cannot now be specified, although originally they were capable of being so; and, 2°, *discursive*, when many or all of the experiences are or can be specified. The conclusion which is seen so rapidly that its premises are but faintly or not

* Comp. on this point KANT, *Prolegomena*, § 13.

at all recognized is said to be seen intuitively: it is an organized judgment. Its rapidity and certainty, together with our reliance on all spontaneous actions, have led to the notion, that Intuition is a source of peculiar validity. But Intuition is ideal vision, and is no less liable to error than sensible vision. It also has its illusions, and needs the control of Verification. In the perception of an object we are unconscious of the many evanescent muscular feelings by which its distance is estimated and its shape inferred. These relations are intuited; and because the judgments are so rapid, and so inevitable, we regard the perception of distance and the shape of the object as given in an immediate apprehension. Analysis, however, discloses that the evanescent processes of which we are unconscious must have taken place; and in the early days of Experience the processes took place slowly, consciously. All our other intuitions are organized experiences, groups of neural processes which originally were isolated. They are to the mind what automatic actions are to the body. Their mechanism is concealed because their action is so easy and so rapid. Among the automatic actions there are tricks of Habit, peculiar to the individual, tricks peculiar to his family, and tricks peculiar to his race; these are all perfectly irresistible, although often serving no purpose, and representing no vital necessity. Among our intuitions there are likewise tricks of Thought and Feeling, i. e. some personal prejudices, or traditions of the family, sect, nation; and these are irresistible even when Reason sees them to be absurd. We have to be on our guard against illusory Perception, we must be equally on our guard against illusory Intuition. In both cases the illusion arises from accepting what is only *inferred* as if it were really *seen*.

149. I will select examples of illusory intuition not from Theology or Ethics, where some intuitions which

are demonstrable fallacies are often appealed to as final arbiters; but from Science, e. g. the once common, now exploded, induction of "Nature's horror of a vacuum," and the more common and still popular induction of weight being inherent in bodies: two judgments which had become so organized that they passed for intuitions. The first has long been recognized to be a fiction; the second, which seems like direct experience, is an illusion. When daily and hourly familiarity showed that bodies had weight, and that no alteration in their condition affected this weight, but that whether solid, liquid, or aeriform, the balance proved them to preserve this quality throughout these changes, experiment seemed to guarantee the intuitive judgment; and the most sceptical regarded weight as an absolute quality belonging to the very nature of bodies, since it was a quality which did not alter under changing conditions. Now as a judgment expressing the facts of experience this intuition of weight was exact; but as an inference respecting the absolute quality inherent in bodies, the intuition was illusory, that is to say, it was an induction, not a real intuition. It was proved to be illusory when Newton showed that gravity was a relation dependent on the position of bodies. The weight of a body was unaffected by any change in the condition of form, structure, or combination of that body, simply because these conditions were not co-operant factors; the phenomenon did not express *them*, did not depend on them, therefore it could not vary with their variations. No sooner were the real factors of gravity detected than weight was found to vary with them, and thus, like all other qualities, was seen to be variable and relative.* The illusion

* Comp. POISSON, *Traité de Mécanique*, I. 280. The attraction of gravity varies as the inverse square of the distance from the earth's centre, *if we disregard the flattening at the poles and the centrifugal force,* and

consisted in inferring that what was true of bodies under all changes which had been investigated, would be equally true of bodies under all changes whatever, and that no investigation of *other* relations would disclose a variation in weight. But this inference needed verification; and it needed it all the more because when men observed that bodies did not vary under certain varying conditions, they ought to have suspected that this constancy was an indication of the observed conditions *not* being factors, since the real factors could not vary without a corresponding variation in the phenomenon.

150. The reader has doubtless noticed with surprise and misgiving that in the foregoing passage the word Intuition has a wider range than usual, wider indeed than my own definition of it as the perception of relations. Not only does it there represent Judgment, but even Induction. My purpose was to fix attention on the possible illusions of Intuition, because so many writers regard it with a sort of superstitious reverence, as if coming from a supra-natural source; and further I wished to insist on the essential uniformity in all psychical processes. Intuition is beholding: *Anschauung*, the Germans call it. We have sensible intuitions, rational intuitions, and moral intuitions, each of which is liable to the same possibility of illusion. Our intuitions of Space, Time, Motion, Quantity, etc., are constructed out of sensible experiences which lie so far back in the dim past that the subtlest analysis is tasked to detect their elements, and therefore many philosophers regard these intuitions as anterior to all Experience, being original endowments of the organism. The sense in which this is acceptable is expounded in § 23. A similar remark applies to our rational intuitions, such as Substance, Cause, Equality,

conceive the earth to be, what it is not, a spherical mass. But in the interior of the earth gravity follows a new law. — II. 28.

etc., which, in the gratuitous and restricted meaning of the word Experience (that of sensible affection), never could have been experienced. In a less degree there is a similar difficulty with respect to such moral intuitions as Freedom, Responsibility, Duty, etc.

151. The validity of all these intuitions depends on their reduction to identical propositions; in other words, whether the relations *are* what we *see* them to be. The possibility of error lies in the possibility of our supposing that we see what we only infer. Intuition must therefore be distinguished from Induction as vision is from Inference. Intuition is the clear *vision* of relations; Induction is the *inference* that the phenomena now seen in this particular case, or these few cases, will be equally visible in many, or all, cases resembling these. That the angles at the base of an isosceles triangle are equal, or that the square of 5 is 25, are intuitions, and admit of no doubt when the relations are clearly seen. We then know that the relations are what they are seen to be: for we have before us all the elements expressed by the propositions. But "all crows are black" is an induction: it is an inference that whenever a bird is found presenting the general characters classified under crow, it will also present this one character of a black plumage. The uncertainty of this inference lies in our not having before us all the generating conditions, and therefore we cannot know that there are not birds possessing all the other characters of the crow, and with these a white or gray plumage. We cannot reduce our proposition to an identical proposition; although if we choose to throw it into that form and say "all black crows are and must everywhere be black," it has the same irresistible certainty that belongs to our propositions about angles and squares.

152. It is important to bear in mind the *grounds* on which we admit the validity of intuitions, because, as

was formerly hinted, there are judgments which have the characters of intuitions (namely, immediate apprehension and irresistible conviction) which are nevertheless illusions, — are spurious intuitions. On the other hand there are inductions which although formulated without a clear vision of the generating conditions, are nevertheless freed from all uncertainty by being *enunciated so as to include these, and to exclude all other conditions.* The uncertainty lies precisely in the ignorance of whether the cases to which our induction is extended are, or are not, legitimately classed with the cases which furnished the inference; and it would necessarily cease if this assumed homogeneity could be verified; or if the induction were converted into an identical equation. Thus although we do not know all the conditions which determine the death of animals, the induction that all animals must die is reducible to an identical proposition by the assumed homogeneity of the terms: we know that all animals must die if "all animals" include only animals precisely similar in nature to those that have died, and are placed under precisely similar conditions; and if with this intuition of known terms we exclude all unknown terms, our proposition becomes equally certain with a proposition about angles. Nor is this invalidated by the possibility that in other worlds or in other times there may be animals precisely resembling those known to us which will not die. That is to introduce the very element our proposition has excluded. In a space of two or of four dimensions many geometrical propositions which relate to a space of three dimensions would not be true. Who doubts it? Who expects that the same results can be the product of different factors?

153. "Our judgments," says Reid, "are distinguished into *intuitive*, which are not grounded upon any preceding judgment, and *discursive*, which are deduced from

some preceding judgment by reasoning." * In psychological strictness every intuition is grounded upon some preceding experience, and this may be either simple perception, or a group of complex judgments. The difference between the intuitive and discursive judgments lies in the different degrees of rapidity with which the constituent elements of the groups are apprehended. Suppose I see a glass accidentally swept from the table, I have an intuition of the consequences; this makes me snatch at the glass, to prevent its falling. The judgment and the action are instantaneous; and if I am asked why I exerted myself to catch the glass, I answer that I *knew* the brittle nature of glass, and *saw* that if it reached the ground it would be smashed. But these reasons which are furnished by Reflection were not distinctly present to my mind, although they were the organized experiences which determined my act. The proof that they were so is evident in the fact that if a child or savage had witnessed the fall no attempt would have been made to arrest it; or if instead of a brittle glass, a tin mug had fallen, I should have been impassive.* A discursive judgment is therefore what in its more exact and verifiable form is called a demonstration, namely, a judgment of which the constituent elements are *shown* instead of being simply *felt*.

154. Intuition is distinguished from Demonstration as an operation indicated but not performed. By an intuition the ratio of the square root of a to the square root of b may be seen to be identical with the fraction $\frac{2}{3}$. To demonstrate this is to perform the operation indicated, and to show that if the value of a is here 4 and the value of b is 9, while the square root of 4 is 2 and that of 9 is 3, the conclusion that $\frac{\sqrt{a}}{\sqrt{b}} = \frac{2}{3}$ is the identification of

* REID, *Essays on the Intellectual Powers*, Ess. VI. Chap. I.
† Comp. HELMHOLTZ, *Wissenschäftliche Vorträge*, II. 88.

the two expressions, since $\sqrt{a}$ is 2 and $\sqrt{b}$ is 3. Obviously the correctness of this operation, whether indicated or performed, whether intuited or demonstrated, depends on the correctness of the primary assumption that the values assigned to a and b are 4 and 9.

155. Intuition is of much greater range than Demonstration, because the greater fund of Experience on which we rely is too complex, and drawn too much from the forgotten past for us to be capable of showing all the successive steps which Demonstration requires. All the great discoveries were seen intuitively long before it was possible to exhibit the correctness of their grounds, and to disentangle the involved data.* But we must not on this account place unrestricted confidence in Intuition, for we know but too painfully how many absurd speculations have been propounded on "intuitive grounds." Demonstration is not an instrument of discovery, but a means of control. Intuition is seeing; Demonstration is showing. *What* is seen, and *what* is shown, may be illusory; they are only proved to be objectively valid when each inference has been reduced to its corresponding sensible.

156. "The method of demonstration in Mathematics," says Hutton,† "is the same with that of drawing conclusions from principles in Logic. Indeed the demonstrations of mathematicians are no other than a series of enthymemes; everything is concluded by force of syllo-

* "En réfléchissant sur les phénomènes les plus familiers il arrive souvent qu'on entrevoit certains principes auxquels sans doute il seroit dangereux de se livrer avant que d'être parvenu à leur donner la précision et la rigueur mathématiques . . . . ces principes ont été d'abord en quelque sorte aperçus dans le vague comme par instinct et appuyés plutôt sur leur conformité avec les résultats particuliers auxquels on arrivait par d'autres voies, que sur des démonstrations générales et rigoureuses." — CARNOT, *Principes de l'Équilibre et du Mouvement*, p. 89. 1803.

† *Mathematical Dictionary*, Art. *Demonstration.*

gism, only omitting the premises which occur either of their own accord or are collected by means of quotation." In other words, it is the exhibition of a necessary connection, or identification of the conclusion with its premises. Mathematical demonstration is the type of exactness because the validity of the premises is never questioned, they are either intuitively evident, or have been rendered irresistible by previous demonstration. When the premises are thus unquestioned the certainty of the result is necessary.

A demonstration is the exhibition of a necessary connection between the proposition to be demonstrated and one or more other propositions which have already been shown to be true, or may be *assumed* to be so. This assumption will not affect the rigor and consistency of the operation; but it may be wholly at variance with objective fact. The terms may be absurd, yet the form of the operation correct. The truth of a proposition is not given simply by showing that it is a necessary consequence from some preceding proposition; *that* is only showing the logical operation to have been irreproachable; and an operation may be accurately performed although its premises are inexact. A proposition is objectively true only in as far as it exhibits the *equivalence of inference and sensation;* and this equivalence may be exhibited directly or indirectly: an inference, or a demonstration, once verified, has all the value of the sensations by which it was verified; that the square root of 25 is 5, is not less absolutely certain than that 5 is 5.

157. Demonstration is the exhibition of the equivalence of propositions, the presentation of some object or property which is *not* apparent, through its equivalence with some object or property which *is* apparent. Since the presentation is thus always mediate, — always by means of something else seen by Intuition to be equiva-

lent, and therefore convertible, the mediation of Intuition may be effected by a succession of equations, or by one. But whether the demonstration depend on a succession of steps, or on only one step, it is always an intuition of equivalence.

158. Had this been clearly apprehended there would perhaps have been less misplaced ingenuity exerted by mathematicians in efforts to demonstrate, geometrically, propositions which are capable only of logical intuition, and for which geometric constructions are superfluous, the intuition being a mental construction. For example the proposition respecting parallel lines: attempts without number have been made to demonstrate it, and all attempts have failed; yet Laplace admits that the "enunciation alone carries along with it the fullest conviction"; why then seek for evidence of what is intuitively evident?* That a geometric proof is impossible, does not disturb the certainty that a line perpendicular to one parallel is perpendicular to the other,—a certainty which belongs to all identical propositions, and which cannot be increased by any geometric exhibition. Mr. De Morgan, indeed, denies that the definition of parallel lines—"lines which are equidistant from one another at every point"—gets rid of Euclid's postulate; for he says, "in this case before the name parallel can be allowed to belong to anything, it must be proved that there are lines such that perpendicular to one is always perpendicular to

* "Il ne faut que de médiocres connaissances en géométrie élémentaire, et un peu de réflexion, pour se convaincre que *l'imperfection* de la théorie des parallèles (pour employer le mot consacré) tient au refus d'admettre comme notion naturelle et primitive, la notion de la similitude, ou l'idée qu'une figure étant donnée, on peut toujours en imaginer une autre qui ne diffère de la figure primitive que parcequ'on a changé l'échelle de construction." — COURNOT, *Essai sur les fondements de nos connaissances*, II. 55. 1851. Aristotle justly comments on the absurdity of seeking a proof of that which is clearly seen, and for which all the conditions of a correct intuition are present. —*Physica*, VIII. 3; *Metap.*, IV. 4.

the other, and that the parts of these perpendiculars intercepted between the two are always equal." Mr. De Morgan thinks that in defining parallel straight lines to be such that any two points in the one are at equal distances from the other there is an assumption without proof, — since it cannot be stated *à priori* of two straight lines that more than two points of the one shall be at equal distances from the other. I admit that there is an assumption here, but it is the *assumption of homogeneity* which is fixed in the definition. Two equidistant points suffice, — and to prove that *they* are equidistant is to prove that A is A. What is meant by parallelism is equidistance; the two points are prolonged indefinitely, and as according to the assumption of homogeneity the lines are *nowhere changed,* nowhere cease to be parallel, what was true of the two points remains true of their infinite prolongation. The one act of Intuition by which the relation of two parallel lines, however small, is perceived, is the Intuition of the relation prolonged to infinity by universalizing the terms.

CHAPTER XII.

AXIOMS AND THEIR VALIDITY.

159. THE preceding considerations must be completed by an examination of Axioms, which, owing to a philosophical prejudice often greatly misleading, are supposed to have a higher validity than Theorems, all truths of a wide generality being held to be more certain than particular truths; and from this higher validity there is often deduced the conclusion of a deeper origin. Because an axiom expresses universal experience, is confirmed from all sides, and admits of no doubt whatever, it is said to be "self-evident," and because it is self-evident, self-luminous, needing no reflected light, it is held to be above Experience.

There are many conveniences in the separation of self-evident truths from reflected truths; unhappily, like most verbal distinctions, it has come to be regarded in the light of a real distinction; being classed apart, Axioms have come to be considered as due to another origin. This is untenable when we learn that Axioms have no such exclusive certainty, but arise from the general ground of Experience, out of which all truths arise. The logical processes which constitute the group in a general truth are precisely the processes which constitute a particular truth,—the difference lies in the terms, not in the forms; in the symbols, not in the operations. The widest of all axioms — "whatever is is" — cannot be more certain, more irresistible, than the most fleeting of particular truths, e. g. "I am sad." The axiom "If equals be taken from equals the remainders are equal," may indeed be more rapidly intuited than the particular truth respecting the square of the hypothenuse in the forty-seventh of Euclid, which can only be seen by a mind that has followed the steps of the demonstration; but this greater ease and rapidity of vision does not endow *the seen* with greater certitude; and the second truth is equally irresistible with the first, when once the relations are intuited.

160. Since, then, the characteristic of superior certitude must be given up, and the superiority rest upon the ease with which the conclusion is reached, shall we still adopt the common opinion that the distinguishing mark of an axiom is its self-evidence? Let us first understand what is affirmed. If a truth is self-evident only when it is self-luminous, i. e. when its luminosity is absolutely independent of *all* reflection from Experience whatever, being *à priori* not only to *this* experience and to *that*, but to *all*, — then I assert that the axiom of equality is not more self-evident than the 47th prop. of Euclid; for to the mind of the infant neither truth is evident. But if a truth is self-evident when the conclusion is evident in the premises, — self-luminous because its rays issue from within, and the mind in the very act of apprehending the terms apprehends the equation of those terms, — this definition may be accepted, and we should all agree to call a truth self-evident when no other evidence is needed outside the terms of its expression, because no other relations are implied beyond the relations specified. But this is no mark of *à priori* truths, as distinguished from demonstrated truths. To the mind which has once learned the properties of numbers, the proposition $2+2=4$ is self-evident. The terms mean that, and nothing else. But to the mind uninstructed in such properties, the proposition so far from being self-evident is not evident

at all; it may be made so, by placing a group of pebbles, naming it *four*, and then dividing it into two groups each of which is named *two*, when the mind sees that four is the group made by two and two.

161. Newton has been censured for the laxity with which he uses the term axiom. Technically his practice may be questionable, psychologically it is defensible. I think he is correct in applying the term to the fundamental principles of Dynamics: *axiomata sive leges*. The laws of Motion have the same certainty and self-evidence, when their terms are apprehended, as the axioms of Geometry; *neither* have these characters when the terms are imperfectly apprehended; both demand that the mind should already be in possession through Experience of the specified relations.

Is there, then, no distinction between axioms and particular propositions? Assuredly. Axioms express truths of universal application; and some of them inevitably arise in every man's experience, or may be extricated from it; whereas particular propositions are limited to special experiences. The former are self-evident, i. e. requiring no extraneous proof, because no doubt is suggested by contradictory experiences. Every instant of our lives we have evidence that a thing is what it is; and this evidence needs no confirmation, because we have never any experience that a thing can be and not be at the same instant. Every instant of our lives we see things change their positions in space after some other thing has been brought into new relations with them; and we express this constant experience in the axiom "Every effect has a cause." Such axioms obviously need no confirmation from particular experiences, because being expressions of universal experience they admit of no doubt. It is otherwise with particular propositions, in which the terms express inconspicuous relations, or relations that are hypothetical; though even particular propositions become irresistible when their terms are conspicuous and real. If the proposition be neither self-evident nor illuminated from general Experience, — as, for example, when first the proposition respecting the square of the hypothenuse is presented, — we have to ascertain what *are* the relations specified in its terms; these are shown to us, *demonstrated;* and from that moment the particular proposition is no less irresistible than an axiom. The relations *are* what they are, and cannot *be* other than what they are; and we have *ascertained* what they are. The contingency which existed at the outset has vanished forever. So long as these terms preserve their homogeneity, so long will the proposition preserve its necessity. Every school-boy who has learned his multiplication-table sees at once that 6 multiplied by 6 gives 36; this intuitive judgment is axiomatic; but although he may not see at once that the cube of 6 is 216, because he cannot at once intuite the relations, yet after rendering these inconspicuous relations conspicuous (after calculating), his discursive judgment becomes axiomatic: he is not less assured that the cube of 6 is 216, than he is that when equals are taken from equals the remainders are equal.

162. Our conclusion therefore is that axioms have a wider application than particular truths, but not a higher validity, not another origin. Having a wider application, they have a higher scientific value. But they had their origin *in* Experience, and cannot have a wider range than the inductions *from* Experience, which proceed on the assumed homogeneity of the unknown or unspecified relations with those that are specified.

I do not wish to be understood as adopting the view that Axioms are founded on Induction; on the contrary, I hold them to be founded on Intuition. They are founded on Experience, because Intuition is empirical. But it is a mistake to present them as founded on any *comparison* of instances, or as primarily established by Induction. Indeed the very conception of Induction is so far antagonistic to that of Axiom, that it includes the acknowledgment of a contingency which the Axiom excludes. There is an assumption of homogeneity underlying both. The assumption in the case of an intuition is that the relations *are* what they are *seen* to be; in the case of an induction it is that the relations *are* what they are *inferred* to be. Now the Axiom which universalizes an intuition assumes the homogeneity of the terms it formulates; and if these are invariant the conclusion is necessary. One act of Intuition establishes an Axiom, for the Axiom is simply the universalization of its terms. That the whole is greater than any one of its parts, is not indeed self-evident, in the rigorous sense of the words; but when its evidence has been seen, in the intuition of its relations,— when in any one case the meaning of the terms has been apprehended and the Logic of Feeling has passed into the Logic of Signs, so that a sensible mass is shown to be divisible into smaller masses, and the former is now understood to be what is called the *whole*, while the latter are called the *parts*, — the relations being intuited, the Axiom is complete, now and forever; and every future whole is seen to be greater than any of its parts, no other intuition being possible so long as the terms intuited are unchanged.

It is possible, indeed, to mistake inductions for intuitions and prejudices for axioms; but that is only when we fail to discriminate between what is seen and what is inferred. Hence the need of Verification.

163. Only one point more needs to be touched on here. Axioms are commonly said to be indemonstrable judgments. This theory of their lying outside Demon-

stration is another form of the theory of their being self-evident; but if the views respecting Demonstration put forward in the preceding chapter are corrcct, the theory is inadmissible. Admitting Demonstration to be the exhibition of the intuited equivalence, — the *showing* of what may be *seen in the terms,* — we must admit that it is even easier to demonstrate the axiom, "A whole is greater than any of its parts," than to demonstrate a particular proposition, "Water is composed of oxygen and hydrogen." Nay, even the axiom "Whatever is is" may be demonstrated, for we can exhibit the equivalence of each side of the equation; indeed the axiom only is irresistible on the assumption of this equivalence, i. e. that what we express by the word *is* on the one side, we also express by the same word on the other.

CHAPTER XIII.

NECESSARY TRUTHS.

164. Two errors have been rife in modern Philosophy: 1°, the reliance on Demonstration when the operation has been accurately performed, without regard to the intuitions, — in other words, whether the symbols operated on have, or have not, assignable values; 2°, the reliance on clear ideas as objectively axiomatic, and on axioms as objectively true. The first of these errors may be traced in Mathematics and in Metaphysics; the second is sometimes avowed, and always implied, in Metaphysics.

In the preceding chapters we have seen that axioms, intuitions, and demonstrations all need critical control, control not only of the operations but of the premises; verification of the premises consisting in the reduction of every inference to its corresponding sensation. A little reflection shows that clear ideas may be treacherous grounds of reliance, clearness of conception being no evidence of the existence of any corresponding perception. It is notorious that propositions may be perfectly clear, and even coercive, yet prove on inspection to be illusory. Nothing was clearer and for centuries nothing could be more irresistible, than the conception of the sun revolving round the earth; it is now rejected from Science. The proposition that mercury is lighter than water is clearer — more readily intelligible — than that two parallel lines cannot enclose space. The falsehood of the one, and truth of the other, must be proved on quite other grounds than that of clearness; although when proved the two propositions previously obscure will become transparent, and by this transparency the first proposition will be seen to want objective correspondence. No sooner are the properties of parallel lines and of mercury and water ascertained, than the truth and falsehood of the propositions which formulate these properties become evident.

165. Hume asserted that only the sciences of Quantity admit of demonstration; "all other inquiries regard only matters of fact and existence, and these are evidently incapable of demonstration. Whatever *is* may *not be*." This argument has been urged a thousand times, no one seeming to have suspected its paralogism, namely, that two *different* propositions are involved in the sentence, "Whatever is may not be." But of this anon. Hume continues: "No negation of a fact can involve a contradiction. The non-existence of any being, without exception, is as clear and distinct an idea as its existence. The proposition which affirms it not to be, however false, is no less conceivable and intelligible than that which affirms it to be. The case is different with the sciences properly so called. Every proposition which is not true is there confused and unintelligible." * This seems to me false in every respect. It is not true of any proposition; or is true only by a substitution of terms which would make it equally true of mathematical propositions. When Hume says that the proposition which affirms a thing not to be, however false, is as conceivable as the proposition which affirms it to be, he confounds a verbal with a real proposition. No one can conceive the thing now existing to be now not existing. He can state this verbally, he cannot realize the symbols. He can indeed conceive that, *under other conditions*, what is now exist-

* HUME, *Essay on the Academical Philosophy.*

ing might not exist, or might exist differently; but this change of terms substitutes in the place of the one proposition, "The thing exists," another wholly different proposition, "The thing no longer exists." Now by similar changes in the terms it is equally easy to conceive two parallel lines enclosing space, — the lines originally parallel are replaced by lines converging; and we, preserving the integrity of our proposition in spite of the change in the meaning of terms, say parallel lines may enclose space.

166. Here most of my readers will doubtless consider that I overlook the distinction between the contingency of the proposition in the one case, and the necessity in the other. It is not that I overlook, but that I deny, this celebrated distinction.

The position to be attacked is this: some truths, indeed most truths, are contingent, general or particular; others are necessary, and universal. The one class expresses facts which we easily conceive might have been otherwise, and for which there is no guaranty that in other times, or in other worlds, they would be what they are at this time, and under these conditions. They are therefore contingent. Contrasted with them are the truths that express facts which are not only seen to be facts now, and under the present conditions, but are seen to be facts which no effort of imagination can figure otherwise. Here and everywhere, now and always, they must preserve their unalterable characters. That acids redden vegetable blues, and that bodies unsupported must fall, are general truths, inductions contingent on certain conditions. We recognize in them no internal necessity why the facts must be so. We easily imagine a state of things in which the results would be different; nor indeed have we any guaranty that in other planets they are not different. But the truths that "Every effect must have a cause," and that "Two parallel lines cannot enclose space," have an internal necessity, — no intellectual ingenuity can conceive a variation in them.

167. Such is the thesis. First, remark the confusion of contingency in a proposition with contingency in a truth. Because there are propositions which express or imply contingency *outside* the conditions, the mind easily glides into the supposition that there is a contingency *inside* the conditions; because a group of phenomena may change, that group itself is held to be not what it is. A little reflection discloses that a proposition is either a true statement of the facts expressed in it, or a false statement of them; if true, it is necessarily true, and universally true, whenever and wherever those facts recur unchanged; but, of course, if anywhere, at any time, a change occurs in the facts expressed by the proposition, then the old proposition no longer truly expresses the new group of facts. That a body moving under certain conditions *as if* attracted by a force varying inversely with the square of the distance will describe an ellipse having the centre of attraction in one of the foci of the ellipse, is a proposition which when demonstrated — found to be a correct expression of the terms — is a truth having no contingency whatever: it is as necessarily true as the axiom respecting parallels. That the earth is a body under approximately similar conditions, and consequently describes what approximates to an ellipse, is also a proposition which having been verified is seen to be true, and will eternally be true so long as the conditions which are the terms of the proposition are unchanged. It is indeed conceivable that under other geometrical conditions — in a space of two, or of four dimensions — neither proposition may be true; or that even in our own space of three dimensions the second proposition may cease to be applicable because of some slight change in the co-operant

factors. But this contingency — that the factors *might* be otherwise — in no degree affects the necessity of the truths: that the facts *are* what they are. Ingenious geometers have of late years shown that even the much-relied-on axiom respecting parallels is affected with an analogous contingency; it would not be true in a space of four dimensions; while Mr. Mill and others have questioned the legitimacy of extending the axiom of causation beyond our world. I am unable to accept either of these positions; but I certainly admit that if the view of necessary truth which is current in Philosophy is to be accepted at all, it logically forces the acceptance of this contingency in the axioms. In other words, all truths are necessarily true, and all propositions are liable to a double contingency, — first, the *contingency of enumeration* (i. e. whether all the factors are, or are not, taken into account); secondly, the *contingency of application* (i. e. whether the old formula is applied to the old conditions, or to changed conditions, which would require a new formula). The only necessity is that a thing is what it is, and cannot be other than what it is; the only contingency is that our proposition may not state what the thing is.

168. The *à priori* doctrine maintains that only those truths are necessary which formulate facts transcending Experience by their universality, and are therefore incapable of direct verification; they are seen intuitively to be unchangeable. In opposition to this I maintain that all propositions are contingent which formulate anything transcending Experience, direct or indirect, — in which the co-operant factors cannot be enumerated and verified; whereas on the contrary, every verified proposition, whatever its nature, is necessarily true, and universally true, — *under the formulated conditions.*

Note this final clause. It is the pivot of the question. That a particular acid does redden this vegetable blue is a proposition in no respect contingent; that hitherto all known acids have been found to redden all vegetable blues, when applied under certain conditions, is also a proposition having no contingency; but if for these intuitions we substitute an induction, — if from these two necessary truths we infer that all acids will under all circumstances redden this or all vegetable blues, the proposition is contingent with a double contingency: it has not been and cannot be verified; the reddening depends on factors which may or may not be co-operant in any particular case; and because we are unable to enumerate what will be the factors, our proposition must be contingent; but if we could enumerate them the contingency would vanish. It is because we can be assured of our factors that most mathematical propositions have no other contingency than that of a possible miscalculation or uncertainty as to the condition. Thus if n be a whole number, the existence of the equivalent series for $(1 + x)^n$ is necessary, because the operation which gives it may be accurately defined. On the contrary, if n be not a whole number but a *general symbol*, then, because we cannot define the operation by which we pass from $(1 + x)^n$ to its equivalent series, a series which exists under such conditions only by virtue of the principle of the permanence of equivalent forms, the connection is contingent; the series becomes necessary when its existence is assumed; in other words, "if such an equivalent *does* exist it *must* be the series in question, and no other." *

169. The arguments which support the *à priori* view have been ingeniously thrown into this syllogism by Mr. Killick: The necessary truth of a proposition is a mark of its not being derived from Experience. (Experience cannot inform us of what *must* be:) The *inconceivability of the contradictory* is the mark of the necessary truth of

* PEACOCK, *Algebra, Preface* XIX. 1830.

a proposition: Therefore the *inconceivability of its contradictory is a mark of a proposition not being derived from Experience.**

This syllogism is perfect in form, but has a radical defect in its terms. The inconceivability of a contradictory results from the entire absence of experiences on which a contradiction could be grounded. If there were any truths independent of Experience, contradictions to them would be conceivable, since there would be no positive obstacle to the conception; but a contradiction is inconceivable only when all Experience opposes itself to the formation of the contradictory conception.

170. There are truths which can be intuited, seen at a glance, because they express relations simple, constant, familiar; there are other truths which cannot be seen until the complicated relations formulated are unfolded, and presented to Intuition: and there are truths which can be seen at a glance, but which, formulating particular relations seen to exist in the present conjuncture of events, but known *not* to be constant in recurrence, yield no assurance that they will not be contradicted to-morrow. There can be no objection against a classification of such truths into universal, general, and particular, or into necessary and contingent, if we mean no more by contingency than the impossibility of determining beforehand what will be the co-operant factors. When it is said that a necessary truth is one seen not only to be true, but one which there is no possibility of our conceiving otherwise; this can only be valid on the assumption that no change be made in the terms formulated: on this assumption, however, all truths are equally necessary; without this assumption no truth is so.

170*a*. What is Possibility? It is the ideal admission

* KILLICK, *The Student's Handbook, synoptical and explanatory of Mr. Mill's Logic*, p. 77. 1870.

as present of *absent* factors: it states what *would be* the fact, *if* the requisite factors were present. What is Contingency? It is the ideal admission that certain factors now present *may be* on any other occasion absent; and when they *are* absent the result must be different from what it is now. What is Necessity? It is the intuition of the actual factors, — the perception of adequate relations, — the recognition that what is, must be what it is. All inductions are contingent because they are generalizations of experience under the assumption of homogeneity; and the contingency lies in this, that the unknown cases which we assume to resemble the known cases in all the characters which constitute the terms of our proposition may not resemble them in some of these characters. All identical equations are necessary, and universal when we universalize the terms.

171. This understood, we may set aside the serious and very common error which asserts that an universal proposition is truer than a general proposition, a general proposition truer than a particular proposition. Nine philosophers in ten will declare the proposition "Every effect must have a cause," to be more certainly true than the proposition "Sugar is sweet." But the case is really this: the universality of a proposition carries with it the predicate of necessity in virtue of the assumed homogeneity of its terms; the generality of a proposition carries with it the predicate of constancy in virtue of the same assumption of homogeneity; the particularity of a proposition carries with it the predicate of contingency in virtue of an assumed *heterogeneity* in its terms: so long as its terms remain under the limitation of specified conditions, its truth remains unshakable.

In Rule X. attention is drawn to this assumption of homogeneity, which underlies all Inference, and all Generalization. We construct a triangle, or define its terms.

This done once is done forever. The truths respecting triangles are not generalizations but intuitions, universalized by universalizing the terms, not generalized by comparing all known triangles, and concluding from them to the unknown. We operate on *the* triangle, not on triangles. When any modification of the terms introduces a new kind, — as for instance a spherical triangle, — there comes a corresponding modification in our propositions, and some that are true of rectilinear triangles are no longer true of spherical triangles. It is here that Verification steps in. What we have to do in any particular case is not to ascertain whether a proposition is necessary or contingent, but whether it is true, expressing the actual factors of the fact; and what we have to do in any general case is to ascertain whether all the particulars thus generalized preserve that homogeneity which justifies the extension; and whenever an exception appears, we know that this must be due to some heterogeneity in the terms, — in other words, that for this case a new proposition is needed.*

172. It is one thing to state a proposition in terms which themselves involve no contradiction, another thing to state it in terms which correspond with fact. The objective truth must be verified, i. e. the conceptions must be reduced to perceptions, the inferences to sensations, and, when verified, its certainty is not deepened by assuming an universal expression, nor endangered by a particular expression. When we say that the proposition

* "Until very lately all analysts considered functions which vanish when $x = a$ as necessarily divisible by some positive power of $x - a$. This is only one of a great many too general assumptions which are disappearing one by one from the science. It appeared to be true from observation of functions, *and is so in fact for all the ordinary forms of algebra.* But observation at last detected a function for which it could not be true, as was shown by Professor Hamilton in the Transactions of the Irish Academy." — DE MORGAN, *Differential Calculus*, p. 176.

which is true now and here, may not be true to-morrow and elsewhere, we speak elliptically; written out in full, the statement would run thus: to-morrow and elsewhere the circumstances may be so far changed that the result now observable will no longer present itself; and it is because we do not know whether there will or will not be a change in the circumstances that we call our proposition contingent. There are indeed some propositions which exclude this possibility of change. That the whole is greater than any one of its parts, or that two things equal to a third are equal to each other: these are unassailable, because they are reducible to identical propositions. It is a mistake, however, to class these apart as necessary truths since all truths may be exhibited as propositions of identity; nor is *any* proposition verified until this has been effected. To make the argument plain consider the following contrasted propositions. "This bit of iron," says Prof. Bowen, "I find by direct observation melts at a certain temperature; but it may well happen that another piece of iron, quite similar to it in external appearance, may be fusible only at a much higher temperature, owing to the *unsuspected presence*" [Note this clause] "in it of a little more or less carbon in composition. But if the angles at the base of this triangle are equal to each other, I know that a corresponding equality must exist in *every figure which conforms to the definition of an isosceles triangle;* for that definition *excludes every disturbing element.*" *

Here we have a contingent and a necessary truth accurately indicated. Why is the first contingent? Simply because one bit of iron may structurally differ from another, although resembling it in external appearance; and the fusibility does not depend on the external ap-

* Quoted by Prof. Jevons in his suggestive work, *The Substitution of Similars.*

pearance, but on the molecular structure or composition of the iron, i. e. depends on that factor which is assumed to be the same in both, but may really be different in both. The "unsuspected presence of more carbon" is not excluded by the external resemblance. But the presence of any disturbing element *is* excluded from the isosceles triangle, by the definition of the triangle, and the conclusion that corresponding equality must exist in every figure which conforms to the definition is irresistible; but a similar conclusion may be established by a similar artifice with respect to the iron; and we may state the identical proposition that not only will this bit of iron always melt at this temperature under these conditions, but every piece of iron having a similar molecular structure and composition will melt at this temperature under these conditions. Our propositions respecting triangles will be not less contingent than our propositions about iron ores, if we admit the element of contingency (§ 170*a*) and leave undetermined whether the term "triangle" designates a scalene, isosceles, equilateral, or spherical triangle.

173. It was perhaps with surprise that the reader just now saw the statement that the proposition "Sugar is sweet" was a necessary truth; yet he may now be prepared to admit this, under the same limitations as apply to all necessary truths, namely, that no change be made in the terms. It simply formulates the fact that a given substance, A, in relation to a given organ of sense, B, has the sensation, C, for its product. We learn that in the many substances grouped under the general name "Sugar," and in the many sensory organs named "Taste," there are many variations, so that different sugars produce different sensations in the same organ of taste, and the same sugar will produce different sensations in different organs of taste. The formula "Sugar is sweet" is

independent of all these variations; it is wholly abstract, A + B = C, and is necessarily true in abstraction. If in particular concrete cases we find Ax or Bx we no longer conclude the product will be C, but Cx. This is equally necessary.

The proposition "Two parallel lines do not enclose space and would not meet were they produced indefinitely" is a necessary truth; but if any one alters the terms, and under the name of parallels includes two lines concave to each other; or if he admits the contingency that the straight lines may at any point alter their equidistance, then indeed the truth is no longer necessary,—or rather one necessary truth is displaced to make way for another.

174. Those ingenious geometers who have endeavored to show that *if* our bodies had no thickness and *if* we lived in the surface of a sphere, our Geometry would be very different from that now regarded as necessarily true,—that in such a world there would be an infinite number of curved lines between two points which would be shorter than a straight line, and that parallels would end by enclosing space,—may claim to have shaken the serenity of those who rely on the superior necessity of mathematical truths; since this imaginary geometry shows that the axioms are not true of every conceivable space, but only true of our known space; but so far as I understand the argument it fails altogether in throwing doubt on the only correct interpretation of an universal and necessary truth. Every truth is necessary; every truth is universal, when its conditions are universalized. When we assert that parallel lines *do* not meet, we stand upon our sensible intuition of the actual fact; when we assert that they *can never* meet, we stand on our rational intuition of the virtual fact; we assume that the lines will be what they are, and cannot be other than what

they are, so long as the identity of the terms is preserved. Any change in the conditions which would make the lines approach each other would require a new proposition to express the changed terms.

Is it not owing to neglect of the need of intuition of a figure that the geometers of fictitious space are able to argue that the angles of a triangle would always more or less exceed two right angles? Is not their whole argumentation based on the disregard of the psychological principle that symbols are only valid when their sensible values can be assigned?

175. In the next Problem we shall consider more at length the position already indicated that every truth is an identical proposition, or is capable of being reduced to one. A truth is the assertion that something is, and, being what it is, cannot be different, *unless* the conditions of its existence change. The proof of such an assertion in every particular case is direct, or dependent. The direct intuition of equality in A = A gives an identical proposition. The indirect demonstration of equality in A = C gives a dependent proposition which is established through two intuitions, — since A = B and B = C, then A = C. The conclusion here is necessary; yet there is a contingency, unless the homogeneity of the terms be assumed; for the equations A = B and B = C, although exact under the defined conditions, may be false under others; we must universalize the terms to make an universal truth.

176. Here one may remark how the common (and useful) distinction between necessary and contingent truths may take its place beside the algebraic distinction of *identical equations* and *equations of condition*. An identical equation is one of which the two sides are but different expressions of the same number, thus $\frac{a}{b} \times b = a$. This is true for any value whatever that

may be assigned to each symbol. An equation of condition is one which is true only in the case specified, there being but one assignable number which will satisfy the equation. Thus $a + 7 = 20$ is true only when the value of a is 13; no other value would satisfy the equation. Although this equation of condition is a new kind, and is particular because confined to the particular number which must be found in the equation itself, yet no sooner is the number found, than the identity is disclosed, and the truth $a + 7 = 20$ is necessary, and universal under the stated conditions.

177. Let us take a more familiar illustration. "Fire burns" would be called a contingent truth. It may be so; it may also be a necessary truth, — an identical proposition. The fact that the conception of Fire is the conception of something which burns combustible things is not rendered dubious, contingent, by the fact that we can conceive Fire placed in relations which would not be those of combustion. When we affirm that fire must burn combustible paper if the requisite conditions are present, our affirmation is simply the expression of certain verified facts; and *this* expression is not disturbed by the discovery of incombustible paper, is not affected by the substitution of new conditions requiring a new expression. That under particular conditions, the thing we designate Fire will burn the thing we designate Paper, is a contingent proposition, an equation of condition, which must be verified, i. e. the number found; when verified, it is not only a necessary truth from which all contingency has vanished, but easily assumes the universal form, namely, "Fire of this kind under these conditions will always and everywhere burn paper of this kind."

178. There are certain relations which are invariable in our experience, others which are variable. Identical equations, and equations of condition, comprise both

orders. Every proposition is contingent which in its expression *admits* the possibility of a variation in its terms; every proposition is necessary which *excludes* such variation; and whether the contingent or the necessary proposition be *true*, or not, depends on its being, or not being, reducible to an identical proposition. The square root of an unknown quantity may be *any* quantity so long as x has no value assigned; but given the value of x as a function of y, and the square root is determined forever. If only one black ball be placed in a box with a thousand white balls, there is very little probability of the black being withdrawn on a first trial; but though not probable the withdrawal is possible, — it is therefore, before trial, a contingency; after the trial there is no contingency whatever. From a box containing nothing but white balls it is absolutely certain that no black ball can be withdrawn. In the former case our ignorance of the position of the black ball and of the direction of the drawer's hand render the withdrawal of a black ball contingent; if we knew these the contingency would vanish. In the second case, in spite of our ignorance of the positions of the balls, and the direction in which the hand will move, there is no contingency whatever in the conclusion that no black ball will be drawn, for we know one condition which absolutely excludes it, namely, there is no black ball present. Apply this to parallels. That parallel straight lines can never meet, is a necessary truth; their meeting is excluded by the conditions of the problem, no less than the withdrawal of a black ball is excluded when no black ball is present. Should a black ball appear, we know that these conditions have been violated, and that in a box, assumed to be without a black ball, there was a black ball present. Should the parallel lines deviate in direction, the conditions of the problem have been violated.

179. It is a necessary truth that when several events are *equally* likely to happen, let one be proved to happen all the others must also happen; or if one be proved not to have happened this will be proof that none have. Obviously the cogency of this conclusion rests on the assumed homogeneity. Should one of the events happen, and any one of the others be shown not to happen, we conclude that there was some error in the original classification, and that the conditions present in all the other cases were not present in this one. Here as elsewhere it may be said that the necessity of a proposition depends on the transparency of its terms, the contingency on the opacity of the terms; in other words, whenever we have distinct intuition of *all* the generating conditions, we know the *only* possible result; whenever our vision of the generating conditions is obscure, we do not know the only possible result. In Mathematics we always have an intuition of the generating conditions, and hence the unalterable necessity of the conclusions.

180. It is because philosophers have failed steadily to bear in mind that the truth of a proposition subjectively is rigorously limited to the terms of the proposition, and objectively that the fixity of a result is coexistent with the fixity of its conditions, — that there has arisen this supposition of a class of truths, or class of results, essentially distinct in origin. What I have been in various ways endeavoring to make clear is that all true propositions are necessarily true, their truth when generalized depending on the generalization or assumed homogeneity of their terms; whereas, whenever a proposition admitted to be true under the defined conditions presents the character of contingency, and the mind recognizes the possibility of error in generalizing the proposition, and sees that the result now certain might have been uncer-

tain, there has been the *unconscious substitution of new terms in place of the old*, making in fact a proposition framed to express one set of conditions the expression of another set. This fallacy is common. When we say that what has occurred once will occur again, and will always recur, we mean (or ought to mean) that under precisely similar conditions there must always be similar results. If $A = B$, or fire burns paper, under *any* conjunctures, it must do so always under *these* conjunctures. When we say that what has occurred to-day may perhaps never recur, or will recur but seldom, we mean that the conditions are likely to be changed, and with any change in the conditions there must necessarily occur a change in the result: instead of $A = B$ there will be $A = C$ or $Ax = Bx$. This latter proposition is equally necessary with the former, but is obviously a *different* proposition.

Those who speak of the Laws of Nature being contingent truths, meaning that a modification or reversal of such Laws is conceivable, and that under changed conditions the propositions would be changed, seem not to be aware of the fallacy. A Law formulates certain specified conditions, and in itself is not at all contingent; it is either a true formula, or a false formula; by altering the conditions specified, substituting new conditions, and applying the old formula, we do not disturb the truth of the Law. The contingency lies elsewhere: it lies in our ignorance of the generating conditions.

181. "The belief in the uniformity of Nature," says Mr. Mansel, "is not a necessary truth, however constantly guaranteed by our actual experience. We are not compelled to believe that because A is ascertained to be the cause of B at a particular time, whatever may be meant by that relation, A must therefore inevitably be the cause

of B on all future occasions." * This is undeniable, but only by the concealed equivoque lying in the words "on all future occasions." If the co-operant conditions which now determine B to succeed A are preserved unaltered on all future occasions, the result must be then what it is now; but if we are at liberty to suppose, or have any reason to suspect, that on some future occasions the co-operant conditions will be altered, we conclude on the same principles that A will not be followed by B. Get rid of this equivoque by the phrase "on all similar occasions under similar conditions," and the truth that A is the antecedent of B becomes necessary. While every contingent proposition becomes necessary if its terms are made invariable every necessary proposition becomes contingent if its terms are contingent. If we define and thus *specify* the generating conditions of an equilateral triangle as a triangle having its three sides equal to each other, or define the growth of an organism by specifying the generating conditions, — the simultaneous process of molecular composition and decomposition, — the one proposition is not more necessary than the other; both express ideal constructions from real intuitions. The mathematician, indeed, who is occupied with ideal figures, is so far at an advantage that he is not like the biologist called upon to regard any possible variation in the objects of the terms of his propositions. The circles and angles of which he treats are not the figures drawn on paper, but the figures conceived in his mind. But this advantage ceases when he comes to apply his mathematical propositions to real figures. The biologist also when dealing with general principles disregards all variation: it is the ideal organism, the ideal tissue, not the real objects which his truths formulate. *The* organism is an abstraction. *The* tissue is an abstraction, — a group of organic elements which approximates

* MANSEL, *Metaphysics*, p. 267.

to the defined limit. But just as no mathematician ever saw a circle absolutely corresponding with his conception, so no biologist ever saw a tissue absolutely corresponding with the histological definition of it; but from the complex and variable group of organic elements, he extricates certain elements and names the abstraction, purified of all variation, a tissue. The ulterior questions whether there are in nature objects which approximate to the definition, circle and tissue, and whether these objects have the properties deduced from these definitions or seen by intuition, may be debated; but once demonstrated, there is no more contingency in a true biological proposition than in a true mathematical proposition. If we have shown to intuition that the circle has the property of comprising the maximum area with the minimum perimeter, or if we have shown that the nerve-tissue has the property of transmitting a stimulus from periphery to centre, from centre to centre, and from centre to periphery, — the certainty of the one is not less absolute than that of the other. Nor let it be urged that the property of the circle is necessarily universal, true of all circles and in all places; whereas the property of nerve-tissue is contingent, particular, subject to variation, being dependent on variable conditions: this is so; but the objection rests on a fallacy. The circle is no real figure, but the ideal figure defined by the geometer, and this ideal transported into distant times and places carries with it all its characters unchanged. The nerve-tissue similarly treated shows an equal constancy; and when we speak of its properties as variable, we draw on our experience of the variable conditions under which real tissues exist; we know that sometimes the nerve is exhausted by action, or by disease; we know that its properties depend on many complex conjunctures; and since we cannot at any moment be sure of knowing all the generating conditions, we say that the property is contingent. There would be the same contingency respecting circles were our propositions respecting them supposed to refer to real figures. I mean that if the necessity of a truth respecting nerves be denied because in reality nerves are observed under conditions which seem to contradict this truth, on such grounds the necessity of a truth about circles should be denied, since in reality it is never true that a real circle is a figure having every point in its circumference equidistant from the centre. If I define a nerve to be a part of a living organism capable of transmitting stimuli, and define a circle a plane figure having every point of its circumference equidistant from its centre, — the propositions which are true of either are true necessarily, universally; whereas if I displace this nerve and *substitute* for it something else which deviates from the terms of my definition of nerve, — or if I replace the circle by an ellipse, — the old propositions no longer apply, new propositions are needed to express the new terms. That equal forces perpendicularly applied at the opposite ends of equal arms of a straight lever will exactly balance each other, is an absolute truth, and is reducible to a series of identical equations. But that two particular objects, *supposed to be equal* in weight, will exactly balance each other on the arms, *supposed to be equal* of this particular lever, *supposed to be supported at its centre,* — this is a contingent truth, comparable to that which says that any given nerve when stimulated will excite the contractility of the muscle in which it terminates. The three suppositions here specified are of generating conditions; and it is only by assuming the presence of such conditions that we can apply our abstract proposition. Is it not obvious that if we are allowed to assume the presence of generating conditions in the case of nerve-action, our propositions will have equal necessity?

182. This will be disputed by the *à priorists.* They affirm that it is precisely the inability we are under of assuming the presence of the generating conditions which renders physical truths of inferior certainty to mathematical. We do not know, it is argued, why a nerve excites a muscle at all, and we can easily conceive a state of things in which such a property would not belong to nerves; whereas it is impossible to conceive a state of things wherein mathematical truths should not be precisely what we now know them to be.

I admit this fully; but reject the conclusion founded on it. I admit the contingency which hovers over our application to particular cases of general propositions respecting nerves; but while admitting the contingency in any particular case, — that is, while assuming the possibility or probability that in the particular case there will be *other* conditions present than those which the general proposition formulates, — I wholly deny that the general proposition is thereby invalidated *as* a general proposition. We do not indeed know why a nerve excites a muscle, as we know why the three angles of a triangle are equal to two right angles: we have not in the one case a clear intuition of all the generating conditions, as we have in the other. But if we know the fact that a nerve does excite a muscle, under certain conditions, we at the same time know that it will always and everywhere do so under the same conditions. We generalize the fact in generalizing the conditions. And this is all we are enabled to do in Mathematics. We do not there treat of variable but of invariable conditions: it is *the* triangle, in the abstract, of which we speak. And if we treat of *the* nerve acting on *the* muscle, there is a similar certainty. The abstract biological truth is not invalidated because of its failure to embrace all concrete cases, when these cases present relations not expressly included in it. The abstract mathematical truth is not invalidated because of its failure to embrace particular cases when these involve relations not formulated by it; and this is always observed in Applied Mathematics. Fix the terms, specify all the relations formulated, and a biological truth stands on the same level of certainty and universality as a mathematical truth. If nerve and muscle are terms which designate objects partly known, partly unknown, all propositions *which include the co-operation of the unknown factors* are of course hypothetical, contingent; but if the terms simply *designate the known factors,* and the propositions simply formulate these, the contingency vanishes, the propositions become identical; and having been verified once, are necessarily true in all identical cases.

183. The very great importance of the question here discussed must be my excuse for having, with perhaps wearisome iteration, presented my solution of it under various aspects. It is a fundamental question, and of late years all metaphysical discussion may be said to turn on it. More than twenty years have elapsed since I first suggested the solution here reproduced; but although it has been reargued in the second, third, and fourth editions of my History of Philosophy, I have not observed that any English writer has adopted or refuted it. This silence warrants the suspicion that I had not presented the arguments with sufficient clearness, or else that the view itself is radically defective. Naturally I prefer the former supposition; and I am confirmed in this conclusion by the gratifying fact that a distinguished foreign thinker, who shows no trace whatever of acquaintance with my writings, has put forth a view substantially similar, in two works * to which I wish to express many obligations. Believing, then, that the view

* DELBŒUF, *Prolégomènes philosophiques de la Géométrie,* Liège, 1860; and *Essai de Logique Scientifique,* Liège, 1865.

is a real contribution to the philosophy of the subject, I have endeavored by a fuller and more varied illustration to carry it home to the conviction of every reader. Those who still hesitate to accept it are referred to the further elucidation which will be reflected from the next chapter.

CHAPTER XIV.

MATHEMATICS AN EMPIRICAL SCIENCE.

184. BY a splendid *tour de force* Kant answered the question, How are Metaphysics possible ? He approached it through the more fundamental question, How are judgments independent of Experience possible ? Since Metaphysics claimed to solve problems which avowedly transcended the reach of Experience, it was indispensable to prove that the human mind was not restricted to experiential judgments, but was capable of forming judgments independently. Kant rightly saw that Metaphysics might be possible if Mathematics were possible ; but he failed, I think, in proving that *à priori* metempirical judgments were possible in Mathematics, and therefore were possible in Metaphysics. His conclusion is logical enough could we accept the premises ; but as these involve the fallacy of necessary truths having a metempirical character, the premises cannot be accepted.

Our purpose will be to reverse Kant's procedure, and show that mathematical judgments are absolutely and entirely dependent on Experience, and are limited to the range of Experience, sensible and extra-sensible. While, before Kant, the theory of Experience assumed that the Mind was a kind of mirror in which the *images of things* were reflected ; after Kant, it became the fashion to reverse this theory, and to assume that the unknown Existence (*Ding an sich*) was the darkened side of a mirror from whose bright surface were reflected the *forms of our minds*, the reflected images being the objective phenomena known to us. Both explanations were radically defective, since they both involved the fallacy *that a product could be the product of one factor*. The proof which Kant offered in support of his position was the existence of certain judgments which must have been anterior to all Experience, because from the nature of the case no Experience could furnish them, since they transcended its range. The proof that no Experience could furnish them was seen in the characters of Necessity and Universality which belonged to their essence; for as no Experience could be universal, none could exclude contingency.

185. But having seen the characters of Necessity and Universality to belong to all truths, or to none, we cannot accept those characters in proof of the existence of a particular class of truths independent of Experience; hence the conception of a Mind existing anterior to all sensible experiences, and capable of framing legitimate conceptions respecting supra-sensible existences, must be placed on another foundation, or given up altogether. I am as firmly convinced as Kant himself (and have argued it fully in Chap. II.), that every experience, and every judgment grouping experiences, must be referred back for one of its factors to a prior result, a judgment already organized, and in this sense *à priori*, since it is prior to and helps to form the latest experience; but I can see no tittle of evidence for an *à priori* in Kant's sense, i. e. of antecedence to all Experience; or that we bring with us at birth a Mind equipped with Forms and Faculties. But, if we do not bring with us this full-statured Mind, if the stature is acquired through growth and development, then the experiential origin and limitation of all knowledge follow irresistibly.

186. Should any of the truths of Mathematics be shown to have an origin lying beyond Experience, or a range

lying beyond the logical deductions from Experience, the claims of Metempirics will so far be made good that we shall be compelled to admit the possibility of metempirical knowledge. I purpose to show not only that the science of Mathematics has its origin in Experience, but that it differs from every other science only as each science differs from every other: it differs from Physics as Physics differs from Chemistry, or Chemistry from Biology, in the circumscription of its object, and the nature of its abstractions; but it has a similar origin, a similar Method, a similar validity, and similar limitations.

187. The majority of mathematicians and philosophers resist the notion of Mathematics being classed among the sciences of observation and experiment; a classification which is supposed to degrade Mathematics from its supreme position, and to introduce contingency into its results. Because it is with *intelligible* and not with *sensible* space that Geometry deals, and because its constructions are purely ideal, — because the line without breadth, and the surface without thickness, the perfect circle, or perfect parallels do not exist as reals, it is concluded that the science of these cannot be classed with sciences of Observation, Experiment, and Induction, which treat of real objects. The chapter on ideal construction in Science will have prepared us for an entire rejection of these positions (§ 110). The properties of Space and Number are assuredly discovered by Observation and Experiment, and their Laws are reached, like all others, through Intuition, Hypothesis, Induction, and Deduction being indeed simply formulæ of the conditions specified, and only true under such conditions. The primary facts, the sensible intuitions forming the basis of this great superstructure, are so general and familiar, are so inevitably given in Experience, that we cannot imagine a mind in which they should not be present, — implicitly or explicitly. Hence by an

easy transition they have come to be considered innate, antecedent to Experience. But they are no more innate than the primary facts of Chemistry or Biology. Although given in most sensible experiences they require to be observed, and reflected on, equally with less familiar facts.

188. A single body, seen and touched, presents Extension and Form; several bodies present Plurality,—Number. The bodies thus perceived are groups of sensibles, from which we abstract the qualities of Extension, Form, and Number. The bodies are also perceived in motion, i. e. changing their places without at the same time undergoing any change in their qualities. Place thus becomes detached from the bodies to be considered by itself; and the abstract of all places is Space. This Space, which is filled by all bodies,—occupied by their Extension,—is only sensible or intelligible as Extension: the characteristic quality of bodies has been transferred to this abstract Space, and as all places are extended, Space is Extension.

189. The science of Geometry may be defined,—the study of the properties of Extension; as Mathematics in general may be defined,—the study of the indirect measurement of magnitudes. Both Extension and Magnitude are qualities of reals. The properties of Space are observed, classified, reduced to Types and Standards, in precisely the same way as all other properties are observed, classified, idealized. They are first found in sensible intuitions of figures; and although rapidly carried up into the region of Conception, where they seem to depart from the reals of Perception, this is equally the case in all other sciences. The ideal constructions of Biology are never found realized in Nature. It is no more the sheer observations of the biologist than it is those of the mathematician which constitute the *material* of construction;

nevertheless without the observations no science would be possible. The mind intuites what the eye cannot see. Not — as is generally supposed — because the mind is independent of sense ; it is dependent on sense as Algebra is on Arithmetic ; and we could never *intuite* the mathematical and biological Types, had we not *seen* the real objects of which these Types are the ideal forms. So far from the mathematical intuitions being *innate*, the majority of mankind pass to the grave without a suspicion of them, — without making explicit to their Consciousness what, as elements of the Logic of Feeling, are implicitly present there. No one supposes biological intuitions to be innate ; yet the majority of philosophers hold that mathematical truths carry with them, in the characters of necessity and universality, evidence of their metempirical origin. How comes it, then, that the savage arrives at explicit biological truths long before he arrives at mathematical truths ; knows, and can state his reasons for knowing, that air is necessary to respiration, and food to growth, long before he has any suspicion that two things equal to a third must be equal to each other, or that parallel lines if prolonged would not meet ?

190. The objects of mathematical study are reals, in the same degree as that in which the objects of any other science are reals. Although they are abstractions, we must not suppose them to be imaginary, if by imaginary be meant unreal, not objective. They are intelligibles of sensibles : abstractions which have their concretes in real objects. The line and surface exist, and have real properties, just as the planet, the crystal, the plant, and the animal exist, and have real properties. It is often said, that "the point without length or breadth, the line without breadth, and the surface without thickness, are imaginary : they are fictions ; no such things exist in reality." This is true, but misleading. These things are fictions, but

they have a real existence, though not in their insulation of ideal form, for no idea exists out of the mind. These abstractions are the limits of concretes. Every time we look on a pool of water we see a surface without thickness; every time we look on a party-colored surface we see a line without breadth as the limit of each color. Both surface and line as mathematically defined are unimaginable, for we cannot form images of them, cannot picture them detached; but that which is unpicturable may be conceivable; and the abstraction which is impossible to Perception and Imagination is easy to Conception. It is thus that sensibles are raised into intelligibles, and, in the constructions of science, conceptions take the place of perceptions. But the hold on Reality is not loosened by this process. When we consider solely the direction of a line, we are dealing with a fact of Nature, just as we are dealing with a fact of Nature when we perform the abstraction of considering the movement of a body, irrespective of any other relations. We no more think that the line is unreal, than that motion is unreal; we no more believe that a surface can exist without an under surface, than we think that a movement can take place without a moving body. M. Delbœuf pertinently remarks that if Mathematics be called imaginary, there would be equal justice in our saying to Newton and Laplace: "Your celestial mechanics is false, for there are not in Nature bodies which are only heavy." *

191. Not only is it misleading to call the objects of Mathematics imaginary, it is also incorrect to call them generalizations. They are abstractions and intuitions. Any particular line that we can draw, or imagine, has breadth; any particular circle is imperfect; consequently generalized lines and circles must have breadth and imperfection. Whereas the line, or circle, which we intuite

* DELBŒUF, *Prolégomènes de la Géométrie*, p. 16.

mathematically is an abstraction, from which breadth or imperfection has been drop ed, and the figures we intuite are these figures under the form of the limit.

192. Unless the objects of Mathematics were real, in the sense just explained, it would be absurd to suppose that the relations intuited could be applied to the discovery of other real relations. A moment's inspection shows that the properties of angles and circles are discovered and demonstrated by the same principles that are applied to the discovery of gases or organic processes. Gauss, whose authority on such a subject weighs against a whole academy, declared Geometry to be the "science of the eye"; and Prof. Sylvester, also a very considerable authority, declares that most if not all the great ideas of modern Mathematics had their origin in Observation. Among the surprising examples cited by him may be named Sturm's theorems on the roots of equations "which stared him in the face in the midst of some mechanical investigations connected with the motion of compound pendulums," and the discovery of the method of continued fractions by Huyghens, "to which he was led by the construction of his planetary automaton." *

Hence it is that most of the difficulties in this science are difficulties rather of Intuition than of Reasoning; and most of the "vexed questions" which have occupied geometers — notably that respecting parallels and that respecting a fourth dimension in space — have arisen from neglect of Intuition. Because analysts are accustomed to operate on symbols they at last begin to assign a sort of talismanic virtue to symbols which will evoke results in defiance of intuitions. But here the words of the illustrious Poinsot deserve attention: "Ce n'est donc pas dans le calcul que réside cet art qui nous fait décou-

* *Address to the Mathematical Section of the Brit. Association*, 1869. Reprinted in *Nature*, I. 238.

vrir; mais dans cette considération attentive des choses où l'esprit cherche avant tout à s'en faire une idée, en essayant, par l'analyse proprement dite, de les décomposer en d'autres plus simples, afin de les revoir ensuite comme si elles étaient formées par la réunion de ces choses simples dont il a une pleine connaissance." *

193. Even in the higher developments of the Calculus, where sensible experiences seem most widely departed from, it is easy to trace a sensible origin for the extra-sensible intuitions; precisely as in Dynamics and Physics we detect the sensible origin of intuitions which transcend Sense, e. g. uniform rectilinear Motion and Atoms. If there is one conception which might be supposed to justify a metempirical origin, it is that of infinitesimals. Now we have this conception, it seems that it might have been evolved *à priori*, and that the active intellect of the Greeks might have reached it through their Method of Exhaustions. What is the fact, however? It is that the ingenious Greeks were arrested in their course by the impossibility of reaching a conclusion now seen to lie so near at hand. Nor was it until Mathematicians had mastered the theory of the composition of motions, by which the path of a projectile was seen to be compounded of two straight lines in different and unceasingly *changing* directions, that the conception of infinitesimals arose.

194. Enough has been said, some will think more than enough, to establish the first part of our thesis, that Mathematics is a science of Observation, dealing with reals, precisely as all other sciences deal with reals. It would be easy to show that its Method is the same; that, like other sciences, having observed or discovered properties, which it classifies, generalizes, co-ordinates, and subordinates, it proceeds to extend discoveries by means of Hypothesis, Induction, Experiment, and Deduction. On

* POINSOT, *Théorie nouvelle de la rotation des corps*, p. 78.

the large use of Hypothesis and Deduction there need be nothing said here, since no one disputes their importance. Induction and Experiment, however, demand consideration.

195. By some minds the very suggestion of mathematical truths being reached by Induction is resisted; yet it is certain that not only does Induction play a part, but according to some writers that part is very considerable. "Induction and analogy," says Professor Sylvester, "are the special characteristics of modern Mathematics in which theorems give place to theories, and no truth is regarded otherwise than as a link in the infinite chain." Some of the divergence on this point must be attributed to the divergent conceptions of what constitutes Induction, much that is even by Mr. Mill included under that head being either Intuition or Description. No one can refuse to recognize it as purely inductive when having calculated a number of terms of a series, and ascertained the law of the series, we fill up the succeeding terms without calculating them; the induction here consisting in our inference that the succeeding terms will conform to the law of the calculated terms; an inference which may be false in special cases. It was assuredly an induction by which Fermat concluded that $2^n + 1$ is always a prime number when n has the form 2^m, i. e. is 2, 4, 8, 16 . . .; but Euler showed that the induction was erroneous when n was 32; for $2^{32} + 1$ is not prime.

196. If these are pure inductions, the same cannot be said of numerous other examples, also classed under this head. Thus it is no induction by which we conclude that two straight lines having once met do not meet again, but continue divergent; we do not *infer* this truth from comparison of instances, we *intuite* it. Axioms are not inductions, nor can they have been inductively

reached; they are intuitions universalized. I should therefore propose to qualify Mr. Mill's statement "that every induction which suffices to prove one fact proves an indefinite multitude of facts"; the ambiguity which lies in the word "multitude" renders this proposition misleading. An induction cannot prove an indefinite multitude of facts, unless the facts be all *repetitions* of the one first proved; if the multitude include any facts having other relations than those proved, the inference is erroneous. On this ground it is misleading to call axioms inductions. Let us take a case selected by Mr. Mill.* He says that when we have to determine whether the angles at the base of an isosceles triangle are equal or unequal, our first consideration is, what are the *inductions* from which we can infer equality, or inequality? He specifies eight axioms. Recourse to inductions is necessitated because "the angles cannot be perceived intuitively to have any of the marks" specified in the axioms, although on examination it appears that they have such marks. I agree with him in considering this a case of discursive, and not of intuitive judgment (§ 153), and that the relations of equality are not immediately presented, but have to be *sought* and *compared.* But I cannot consider that the axioms, "Things which being applied to each other coincide are equals," or "The whole and the sum of its parts are equals," have the characters of Induction; they are *identical equations,* — propositions which exclude all contingency by excluding all inference. No one has more clearly shown than Mr. Mill the distinction between inductions properly so called, and "generalization in which there is no induction because there is no inference; the conclusion is merely a summing up of what was

* See also on this question a paper by Professor Robertson Smith in the *Proceedings of the Royal Society of Edinburgh,* translated in the *Revue des Cours Scientifiques,* VII. 190.

asserted in the various propositions from which it was drawn" (I. 324). On this ground we must refuse the character of Induction to those axioms which are simply intuitions generalized. With reference to the particular case chosen, instead of the roundabout demonstration of Euclid, or that proposed by Mr. Mill, we might reduce it to two intuitions: 1°, The isosceles triangle has equal legs; this equality is intuited in the terms defined; 2°, The legs being equal, what is seen of the one is seen of the other, i. e. the angle formed by one leg with the base will be equal to the angle formed by the other.

197. Were Mathematics founded on induction there would be contingency in all its propositions which extend beyond particular cases; and each conclusion would require experimental verification, direct or indirect. But this is true only of portions of the science. The greater part is founded on Intuition, and its conclusions are universal. We are not, however, to suppose that Experiment has little to do here. "A science is experimental," says Mr. Mill, "in proportion as every new case which presents any peculiar features stands in need of a new set of observations and experiments, and a fresh induction." Mathematics is experimental therefore in this, that for every step in advance, as Professor Robertson Smith has well said, everything not the result of calculation or deduction, there is needed a new figure and a new intuition. The experimentation is easier, less complicated, than in Physics or Chemistry, the elements are more manageable, because more sharply defined, and we are under no misgiving in dealing with them lest they should include any unknown elements which could affect the result. We are perfectly sure that in bringing a right line into relation with another, it is only *this* relation we have to deal with; whereas in bringing a gas into relation with a solid we do not know all the co-operant factors; and our experiment

reveals only some of the actual results.* But although easier, the procedure is similar. The necessity for a new figure, and a new intuition, is shown at every step. We could not reach the simplest proposition without these. Ask any one, not already instructed, whether it is possible to let fall from a point more than one perpendicular on a straight line; or whether all parallelograms between the same parallels are equal when their bases are equal. These propositions are so far from being self-evident, or capable of being deduced from the axioms and definitions, that he cannot answer until he has seen the figures and intuited the relations. It is by experiment alone that he can determine the equality of spaces included in figures so unequal as an oblique and a perpendicular parallelogram on similar bases. The chemist has his elements, or what he regards as such, and these he combines and recombines, in various ways, to watch the reactions, and detect the constant results. The geometer has his elements (points, lines, planes) which he combines and recombines, watching the results. He draws a circle, and divides it by a straight line into equal halves. This straight line he again divides by another, and thus forms four right angles which fill the space circumscribed by the circle. He goes on adding figure by figure and detecting new relations. Like the chemist he gets at constant results, which enable him to foresee what will be the effect of new combinations: he can *calculate* as well as *count*. But although Deduction will carry him much further than it will the chemist, because of the greater homogeneity of the elements he deals with, it will not suffice without

* Kant remarks that philosophy is occupied with clearing up the obscure and complicated Notions which it finds in the mind, whereas Mathematics starts from clearly defined Notions and sees what will issue from their combination. — *Ueber die Deutlichkeit der Grundsätze*, *Werke*, I. 68.

Experiment, Verification. The man who first discovered that $7 + 5 = 12$, did so by a synthesis, which was experimental, not less than that by which the chemist discovered that two volumes of hydrogen and one volume of oxygen constituted water.

198. If in cases so simple Experiment is needed, it may readily be understood how in more complex cases the mathematician essays the demonstration of a problem through a series of tentatives, till he hits upon the construction which discloses the solution, or finds that no solution is possible under the given conditions. Suppose, for example, he asks himself whether there may not be a quadrilateral figure having equal sides, and having two of its angles equal to three right angles: he cannot construct such a figure; the attempt would at once disclose that such a figure was inconsistent with the properties of quadrilaterals.

Kant has shown that even identical propositions such as $a=a$, or the axiom "The whole is greater than its part," are admissible only because they can be presented in Intuition; and we formerly saw that even these are demonstrable, and demonstrable only on the assumption of homogeneity. Whence we conclude that Mathematics must be dependent on and limited by Experience, which furnishes intuitions.

199. There has been much dispute as to whether Mathematics is founded on Axioms or on Definitions. This dispute may be cleared up by a more rigorous interpretation of the terms. In the sense commonly assigned, it is neither to Axioms nor to Definitions that the foundation can be ascribed, but to Intuitions; and to Axioms and Definitions only in virtue of their expressing Intuitions. Nor let this be considered idle cavilling. For those who take their stand on the Axioms, hold that the whole science is nothing but the analytical unfolding of

the few Axioms placed at the opening of each treatise; and this seems to be doubly erroneous; first, because those Axioms are too few for the purpose, — each step requiring a new intuition, which, when generalized, becomes a new Axiom; secondly, because *they* derive their whole validity from Intuitions. Both objections may be condensed in one: the science is synthetical and not analytical.

Take the Axioms of Euclid and try by them alone to deduce the Pythagorean theorem, and it will be found as idle as the attempt to deduce the action of a poison from the axiom "Every effect has its cause." Dugald Stewart, fully alive to the barrenness of Axioms, sought in Definitions for the real foundation. But the same argument applies here. Unless the Definitions are intuitions of the figures and relations defined, they are also barren.* Definitions, moreover, must not be arbitrary, if they are to lead to other than arbitrary conclusions. We may, if we please, define parallel lines, lines concave to each other; or define 5 to be the sum 2 + 2. But in this case all our deductions must be consistent with these assumptions; and we cannot then say that two parallel lines will never meet when prolonged, nor that 5 is 3 + 2 or 10 ÷ 2. The mathematician does not begin by assuming the properties of figures, and after defining them proceed to ascertain whether such figures exist; he begins by ascertaining that such figures and such relations do exist, and then defines them as he finds them. In other words, Definitions are the expressions of the figures, not their founda-

* Thus, from the definition of a cycloid, "the curve described by a point in the circumference of a circle while the circle itself rolls in a straight line on a plane," we may intuite the truth of Roberval's discovery that its area is equal to thrice that of the generating circle; but we require this to be shown to us through other intuitions, we cannot see it in the definition.

tions. With Definitions we can take no step in advance, we can only analyze *them.**

200. In the Imaginary Geometry of Lobatschewsky and Beltrami we have indeed a theory of parallels founded on Definitions. Instead of the intuitions *really* presented to us by the figures, the definitions are made to express relations different from those intuited; they are arbitrary, and although the deductions from them are *consistent* with these arbitrary premises, and are therefore logically accurate, they are *inapplicable* to the real objects given in our Experience. Lobatschewsky's arbitrary definition of parallelism † is as wide a departure from the real intuition expressed in Euclid's definition, as the definition of $5 = 2 + 2$ is from our definition of that number.

201. Not only do we find Observation, Hypothesis, Induction, and Experiment everywhere underlying the constructions of Mathematics, as in any other science, we also find that in both the abstractions are all raised from sensibles and extra-sensibles by a similar process. The argument that they cannot have been derived from sensi-

* "De la définition du triangle et de la définition de la bissectrice d'un angle, vous ne tirerez pas que les trois bissectrices des angles d'un triangle se coupent au même point ; *il faut une construction.* Le raisonnement, si raisonnement il y a, consiste toujours dans l'énumération des parties de la figure ; ceci est un angle, cela une bissectrice, c'est-à-dire une ligne équidistante des côtés, etc. De même le chimiste se dit : j'ai mis là autant d'oxygène, le double d'hydrogène ; j'ai maintenant de l'eau, donc," etc. — DELBŒUF, *Préliminaires de la Géométrie*, p. 79.

† "Toutes les droites tracées par un même point dans un plan peuvent se distribuer, par rapport à une droite donnée dans ce plan en deux classes, savoir : endroites *qui coupent* la droite donnée, et en droites *qui ne la coupent pas.* La droite qui forme la *limite* commune de ces deux classes est dite *parallèle* à la droite donnée." — LOBATSCHEWSKY, *Études Géométriques sur la théorie des parallèles ; traduit par* Houel, p. 3. Paris, 1866. In a subsequent work M. Houel admits that the conclusions of Lobatschewsky are in contradiction of Experience but not of Logic. — *Essai critique sur les principes fondamentaux de la Géométrie Élémentaire*, p. 77. 1867.

ble concretes, because our senses never present them under the forms dealt with by mathematicians, may equally be applied to other sciences: the heavens show no elliptical orbits; our laboratories show no perfect gases; our islands and continents show no species. And there is good reason why this must be so. Science deals with conceptions, not with perceptions; with ideal not real figures. Its laboratory is not the outer world of Nature, but the inner sanctuary of Mind. It draws indeed its material from Nature, but fashions this anew according to its own laws; and having thus constructed a microcosm, half objective, half subjective, it is enabled to enlarge its construction by taking in more and more of the macrocosm.

Science everywhere aims at transforming isolated perceptions into connected conceptions, — facts into laws. Out of the manifold irregularities presented to Sense it abstracts an ideal regularity; out of the chaos, order. The imperfectly straight real lines give place to lines ideally straight. Having to introduce Likeness (equations) amid a manifold Unlikeness, we begin by reducing to a first Likeness all the diversities of spaces and numbers presented to Sense, and thus get ideal Space everywhere homogeneous, and ideal Number. And so with the rest. But this recognition of the ideality of Mathematics must not cause us to overlook the fundamental fact that only in so far as the ideals are constructed from reals can they have any validity in reference to reals. Kant teaches that objects conform themselves to our modes of Sensibility, and that it is we who invest them with our forms, which is all we know of them; and he denies that the things themselves determine our forms. I have already stated in what sense I regard this as true, and in what as false; it is irreconcilable with the ideality of Science; for were it true that objects received their forms entirely from us, we should find in Nature those very forms which we do *not* find there, — the perfect circle, the pure gas, the defined species, the histological tissue. These exist, but they exist in our conceptions, not in our perceptions. How they arise in conception, as abstractions from perceptions, we know very well; whereas, if we only *saw* in Nature what the Mind *brought* with it, and *reflected* on objects, we should see the perfect abstractions, and not the imperfect concretes: and we should see these unaided by Science.

202. Having pointed out the cardinal characters in which Mathematics resembles other sciences, we have finally to inquire if there are any other essential characters which would suffice for a genuine difference. There is one character which will be considered decisive, and that is the apodictic certainty belonging to mathematical conclusions. Kant in the preface to his *Practical Reason* declares that we might as well attempt to squeeze water from pumice-stone, *ex pumice aquam*, as to get at necessary and universal truth through experience.* We, on the contrary, have seen that all truth is necessarily true, under the specified conditions; all truth is universally true if the conditions be universalized; and in these respects Mathematics has no superiority over Biology. But, it may be argued, mathematical truths have an universality denied to all other scientific truths, in that they relate to fundamental aspects under which all things are perceived by us, — thus all things whatever are numerable, and all things are extended. But mathematical truths are not true irrespective of conditions; and their universality is restricted to our universe. The space of geometers is a space of three dimensions; and many of their truths would cease to be necessary and universal in a space of two or four dimensions. We must say, therefore, that the truths of Mathematics, like all other truths,

* KANT, *Kritik der prakticshen Vernunft.* Vorrepe, d. 107. *Werke,* IV.

have their origin in Experience, and are true only of the universe known through Experience.

203. The superior certainty of Mathematics arises from the superior facility with which certainty is reached and exhibited to others. There can be but one certainty, — that of an identical equation, or identical proposition, — and this admits of no degrees; it is, or is not. Nor does the *equation of condition* admit uncertainty, directly the condition which satisfies the equation has been found.

The laws of Motion, Affinity, Life, and Mind, although in successive degrees less general than the laws of Quantity, are not less exact, less certain. The terms in which they are expressed may be less exact, and their application to particular cases may be far more contingent, than is the application of the laws of Quantity; but when the laws formulate real relations, and are true, their certainty is unaffected by contingencies of expression and application. A general law is raised by abstracting the constants from the variables, — out of many particular cases we let drop all the special circumstances which individualize each case, and the residuum is the generalized law. When this law has to be applied to some new case, we have to modify it by the reintroduction of such special circumstances as will individualize the case: unless we do this, the law will not hold good, the case will not fall under it. Now it is our very uncertainty respecting these special circumstances which constitutes the contingency of the law. Could we be assured, as in mathematical questions we commonly are, of having all the co-operant factors within our grasp, contingency would vanish. In many scientific propositions this condition is fulfilled; the abstract truth in Biology is as absolute as the abstract truth in Geometry. If this condition is rarely or never fulfilled in concrete Biology, the same must be said of Applied Mathematics. The proposition: "Water is indispensable to the vitality of a tissue," is not less exact, not less certain, than the proposition: "In a right-angled triangle the square of the hypothenuse is equal to the squares of the two other sides." Neither proposition is self-evident; both have to be shown by experiment; and when shown, each is seen to be an identical proposition. The intermediate steps through which it is shown that Vitality is never found without chemical change, and that water is necessary for such change, may pair off with the steps by which it is shown that in the parallelograms on equal bases, between parallels, the triangles are equal. In both cases a series of identical propositions forms the substance of the conclusions, and the conclusions therefore are equally identical propositions.

But now observe: although it is indisputable that alcohol in sufficient quantity, or concentration, will withdraw from a tissue in contact with it so much water as to destroy the vitality of the tissue, — and although it is an indisputable corollary that drinking alcohol in such quantity must cause a man's death, — the inference, which to many seems logical, that any quantity of alcohol must, if not destroy, at least diminish, Vitality, is an inference wholly contingent. Every one knows that quantitative differences must have corresponding functional differences. Because a certain quantity of alcohol will destroy a tissue, we are not to conclude that any smaller quantity will do more than disturb its molecular equilibrium, which temporary disturbance may be a positive advantage to the organism. We are here in the midst of indeterminate quantitative relations, and must call in the aid of experiment to determine whether certain quantities are or are not injurious. Could we once ascertain the precise quantities which had precise functional consequences, our treatment of the alcoholic question would be rigorously exact. But at present it is no more capable of a solution than an equation of the sixth degree.

CHAPTER XV.

SOME OBSERVATIONS ON KANT.

204. Our survey of the Limitations of Knowledge may end here, since to carry it further we should have to invoke the results of an examination into the psychological mechanism, which must be reserved for future Problems. All that now remains is to point out the radical difference between the empirical and metempirical philosophies; and since all modern Metempirics is either Kantian, or founded upon Kantian principles, we shall best achieve our purpose by confining our criticism to Kant's fundamental positions. No attempt to estimate Kant's work, his position in the history of speculation, can be thought of here. I have attempted this elsewhere; and any reader who considers that in the following remarks the constant antagonism seems to imply an undervaluing of Kant's greatness, may be referred to the more general estimate in the second volume of the fourth edition of my History of Philosophy.

205. Noticeable at the outset is the great general resemblance between the outcome of Kant's argumentation and the outcome of our own; whence it may at first appear that Kant, having fought our fight, should be welcomed as a powerful ally. But it turns out otherwise. He is claimed by our antagonists. The reason of this contradiction it will be profitable to ascertain.

First of the agreement: It was his purpose to define the Limitations of Knowledge, and to prove the relativity of all human conceptions. In strict logical result, the Supra-sensible was thus excluded from his philosophy no less than from ours. He did exclude it from the Speculative, but opened a back entrance for it in the Practical. He taught that our faculties are unable to transcend the limits of possible Experience, and that we only cognize in things, *à priori,* what we ourselves have placed there.

His aim, like our own, he declares to be to revolutionize Metaphysics by applying to it the Method of mathematicians and physicists. He affirms, as we do, that intuitions and conceptions make up the sum of Knowledge; and Intuition is the function of the Mind in the sphere of Sense, while Conception is the function of Mind in the Sphere of Understanding, or Judgment. The first has the power of receiving sensuous impressions, the second of knowing by means of these. He shows that " although our pure concepts of the understanding and our principles are independent of Experience, and despite of the apparently greater sphere of their use, still nothing whatever can be thought by them beyond the field of Experience, because they can do nothing but merely determine the logical form of the judgment relatively to given intuitions. But as there is no intuition at all beyond the field of the sensibility, these pure concepts, as they cannot possibly be exhibited *in concreto,* are then totally without meaning." And later on he says: " After all the very cogent proofs already adduced, it were absurd in us to hope to know more of an object than belongs to the possible experience of it, or to lay claim to the least atom of knowledge about anything not assumed to be an object of possible experience which would determine it according to the constitution it has in itself. . . . . And a still greater absurdity if we wished to have the principles of the possibility of experience considered universal conditions of things in themselves." * Not only does he thus clearly formulate the conclusions of the Experiential Philosophy, he no less clearly marks the illusions of Speculation when it passes beyond. "It first separates the elementary cognitions which inhere in the understanding prior to all experience, but yet must always have their application in experience. It gradually drops these limits; and what is there to prevent it, as it has quite freely derived its principles from itself? And then it proceeds first to newly imagined powers in nature, then to beings outside nature, — in short, to a world for whose construction the materials cannot be wanting, because fertile fiction furnishes them abundantly, and though not confirmed is never refuted by experience." †

206. Now as to differences: In spite of all this, and so much more to the same effect, Kant not only sustained the old metempirical tradition, but by his supposed discovery of the *à priori* elements in knowledge furnished the ground for subsequent speculators. Fries, Fichte, Schelling, Hegel, Schopenhauer, and the rest, founded their systems on this. In the great debate respecting the origin of Knowledge, whether it is wholly due to Experience, or partly due to Experience and partly to a higher source, Kant adopted the ambiguous position of declaring that we *have* a source of Knowledge which is independent of Experience, but that all such knowledge is illusory beyond the range of Experience. His successors fastened on the positive part of his teaching, and rejected the negative. I accept the negative, and reject the positive; or to speak more precisely, I interpret the positive in another way. In what sense we can be said to bring with us *à priori* conditions of Knowledge, and even *à priori* Experience (paradoxical as the phrase may

* *Prolegomena*, §§ 35, 37 (Mahaffy's translation, p. 96, 150).
† *Ibid.*, § 36.

sound) which must determine the result of our individual *à posteriori* experiences, has already been shown (§ 22). Kant could not have so interpreted the facts, simply because Biology and Psychology were not sufficiently advanced in his day to suggest such an interpretation. He was hampered by two traditional conceptions, which to his mind were irresistible, namely, the conception of Mind as an entity, and the conception of Necessity and Universality as tests of a truth transcending Experience.

207. The reader must be reminded that the important point in the following discussion is not whether *à priori* elements can be detected in knowledge, but whether those elements were or were not originally formed out of ancestral sensible experiences; because it is on the decision of this point that the conclusion will rest whether *à priori* elements prove a supra-sensible origin, and carry a higher validity.

208. Since Kant undertakes to show that the Mind brings with it a fund of *à priori* knowledge in which *no* empirical influence, personal or ancestral, is traceable, we must first see what it is he means by Experience. On this, and indeed on most points, his language is very contradictory. The following passages are, however, such as will generally represent his position: —

"Experience consists of intuitions which pertain to the Sensibility, and of judgments which are entirely the work of the Understanding." "Experience consists in the synthetical connections of phenomena (perceptions) in consciousness, so far as this connection is necessary." (*Prolegomena*, I. §§ 22, 23.) "The reader has probably been long accustomed to consider experience a mere empirical synthesis of perception, and hence not to reflect that it goes much further than these extend, as *it gives empirical judgments universal validity* [let this be noted] and for that presupposes a pure unity of the understanding which precedes *à priori*." (*Ibid.*, § 26, p. 87, of Mahaffey's translation, which occupies the third volume of his *Critical Philosophy for English Readers*, 1872.) Thus when defending Experience he is careful to separate it from "a mere aggregate of perceptions" on the one hand, and from a mere sensuous impression on the other. But in the course of his argument he is frequently found using the term Experience simply for sensuous impression: and much of his argument depends on this restriction of the term.

209. Observe the contradiction into which he is led. First, he declares that Experience demands the combination of sensitive receptivity with logical spontaneity: the one giving the objective *matter*, the other the subjective *form*. "It is the matter of all phenomena that is given to us *à posteriori*; the form must lie ready *à priori* for them in the mind." Having thus emphatically stated the two requisites of all Experience, — the *à priori* condition and the *à posteriori* condition, — he nevertheless presents us with this paradoxical statement, that although *all* knowledge begins with Experience (as just defined), *some* knowledge is antecedent to and independent of Experience. I do not mean to say that this contradiction is expressly stated by him; but I do say that such is the plain interpretation of his confused statements. I believe that he unwittingly confounded one factor with the product of two factors, so that after first defining knowledge to be the product of a subjective element and an objective element, calling the one *à priori* and the other *à posteriori*, he henceforward treated the subjective element as if it alone constituted a peculiar *kind of knowledge*, and not simply one of the factors of all knowledge. It was open to him to call the *à priori* condition of Experience Knowledge, if he wished it; but it was not open to him to do this without due warning; and, above all, it was

not open to him after he had expressly defined all knowledge as arising in Experience. The *à posteriori* factor is not less indispensable than the *à priori* factor.

210. Let me first exhibit the evidence on which Kant is arraigned; the explanation of how he came to fall into the contradiction may then be suggested. The asserted contradiction is that of concluding the existence of *à priori* knowledge, because Knowledge presupposes an *à priori* Faculty of Knowing; in other words, when he argues that before sensuous impressions can be transformed into Experience they must be moulded by the Mental Forms of sensible Intuition and logical Conception, he does indeed assert the existence of an *à priori* element, a *condition* rendering Experience possible; but in flagrant contradiction with his own principles he concludes from this that this element is *Knowledge.* Granting (what indeed must be rejected) the rationality of supposing a Faculty to exist independent of and anterior to its active realization, — granting this *potential* existence of a Cognitive Faculty before there is any Cognition, and of Laws, or Forms, of Experience, before there is Experience, — we must still separate what he confounds, namely, the Faculty of Knowing, or Laws of the mental organism, from the Knowledge which is the *product of those Laws, under objective stimulus.* On his own showing it is not the Knowledge which is *à priori,* antecedent to all Experience, but the element added to sensuous impression, supplied from the Mind itself. He has expressly told us that Experience is much more than sensuous impression, more even than an aggregate of perceptions. It is a synthesis, "a mode of cognition which requires the co-operation of the Understanding." He says: "Before objects are given to me, that is *à priori,* I must presuppose in myself laws of the Understanding which are expressed in conceptions *à priori.* To these conceptions all objects of

Experience must necessarily conform." (*Preface to second ed. of Kritik.*) Still this is only presupposing one of the two conditions of Knowledge.* But having identified the product with one of its factors, he grounds on it a further distinction. "Knowledge of this kind," he says, "is called *à priori* in contradistinction to empirical knowledge which has its source *à posteriori*, that is, in experience." He confounds *à priori knowledge* with an *à priori condition* of knowledge, and sets apart this *à priori* knowledge as something radically distinguished from *à posteriori* knowledge, — although his own definition of the *à posteriori* declared it to be empirical, and he assumed knowledge to be possible only through the co-operation of this *à priori* and *à posteriori*.

211. Many more passages might be given; they would be superfluous. It only now remains to suggest the explanation of how so great a thinker came to commit so great an oversight. We must try and place ourselves in his position. The question in the schools had been that of innate ideas. Unless the existence of such ideas could be established, the whole range of Metempirics would of course prove to be a dream. To prove that we have any knowledge not ultimately reducible to sensible experience, it was necessary to prove the existence of data inaccessible to Experience. The school of Locke had indeed presupposed the existence of the Faculty of Knowing, and only asserted that what was Known had an external origin, — that is to say, the Faculty was called into ac-

* "Our nature is so constituted that intuition with us can never be other than sensuous, that is, it contains the only mode in which we are affected by objects. On the other hand, the faculty of thinking the object of sensuous intuition is the understanding. Understanding cannot intuite, the sensibility cannot think. *In no other way than from the united operation of both can knowledge arise.* But we must not on this account overlook the difference of the elements constituted by each." — *Kritik, Transc. Logik*, I. 88.

tivity through Sensible Experience. What Locke vaguely presupposed, was definitely and expressly brought forward by Leibnitz. This was an important step. "The senses," he said, "although *necessary* for all actual knowledge, are not sufficient to *give* us all of it." This is also Kant's fundamental position. That which the senses do not give is the character of necessity. "Mathematics must have principles of which the proof does not depend upon examples, nor consequently upon the senses, although without the senses one would never have thought of them. So also Logic, Metaphysics, and Morals are full of such truths, and consequently their proofs can only come from those internal principles which are called *innate*."

212. Let me pause a moment here to remark that there is a fallacy in saying the proof of a mathematical truth does not depend upon examples; it does not depend on any number of repetitions, or any variation of the examples, but it does depend on the intuition of the example intuited. Thus $2+2=4$ is not proved by repeating the formula, or varying the numbered objects; but is proved by intuition of the numerical relations. When Leibnitz says that without the senses we should never have thought of such a truth as $2+2=4$, he might have added, nor would the truth itself have been demonstrable.

All that Leibnitz effected was therefore to render explicit what had been implicit in the argument of Locke. He vindicated the active co-operation of the subjective factor. Kant came, and by his theory of the Mental Forms gave greater precision to this factor. Following Leibnitz he assumed, as incontestable, that the characters of universality and necessity proved the non-experiential nature of every truth which contained them. This position I have argued against at great length, and,

I trust, to the reader's satisfaction; but of course since Kant adopted it we must allow him all that he can deduce from it. I think his deduction faulty in this respect: granting their *à priori* character, this does not, by his own showing, establish more than that certain cognitions, derived through Experience, are distinguishable from others by subjective conditions not traceable in the others. Whether any cognition has or has not these characters, it is always the product of two factors, objective stimulus and subjective reaction, the matter and the form.

213. There are three meanings to be assigned to *à priori* knowledge. First, there is that which belongs to all Deduction, — i. e. we have already established by Induction a general principle, from which *à priori* we conclude some particular result. This meaning Kant explicitly sets aside. He will only recognize as pure *à priori* that which is absolutely independent of all experience whatever.

Secondly, there is the meaning I have already considered (§ 22), namely, the organized experience usually termed Instinct which we inherit from our ancestors, and which forms, so to speak, part of our mental structure. In this sense we may be said to be born with a knowledge of Space, with a knowledge of Causality, etc., because although these registered tendencies were originally framed out of sensible experiences, we who inherit the structure so modified only need the external stimulus, and forthwith the action of that structure produces the predetermined result. The chicken, which two or three hours after escaping from the shell captures an insect, puts in action the organized experiences of space, food, etc., which were acquired by remote ancestors.

This meaning Kant also rejects, and indeed it would not have served his purpose. "It is quite possible," he says, "that some may propose a kind of pre-formation system of Pure Reason in which the Categories are neither self-conceived *à priori* first principles of Knowledge, nor derived from Experience; but are merely aptitudes for thought implanted in us contemporaneously with our existence." And this, which would reconcile his doctrine of Mental Forms with psychological facts, is rejected, because "the Categories thereby lose their character of objective necessity. Nor would there be wanting persons to deny their subjective necessity, though compelled to feel it. Certainly we could never dispute with any one about that which merely depended on the manner in which he was organized."

214. Having thus excluded the only two meanings of *à priori* knowledge which embrace Experience, he is forced to fix on that which is altogether aloof from every empirical element. Only thus indeed could he carry on the traditional doctrine which held Mind to be an entity, mysteriously inhabiting the organism, looking at the external world through the organism, but with visions also of an existence not included in this sublunary sphere. Plato and Leibnitz were consistent in holding this opinion, but Kant was not consistent; for he had expressly declared that *all* knowledge had its *rise* in Experience, although it was not all *constituted* by Experience, since for Experience itself there was needed an *à priori* no less than an *à posteriori* condition; in other words, all knowledge depends upon material furnished in Sensation, and on form furnished by the Knowing Faculty. Now observe two points: first, the union of *à priori* and *à posteriori* is necessary for every cognition; secondly, and as a corollary, no cognition can be furnished by the Knowing Faculty alone, since Knowing involves a Known. It is because Kant forgets his own definitions, and speaks of Experience as if it were sensuous impression without

the co-operation of the *à priori* element, that he is led to regard what is logically separable from this *à priori* condition as if it were really separable, and thus to speak of the Knowing Faculty as pure *à priori* cognition.

215. Taking his analysis, and accepting Space and Time as the forms of Sensibility, and the Categories as the forms of the Understanding, these forms are only *à priori conditions* of knowledge, and cannot *of themselves* constitute a cognition. By themselves they are as powerless as the external conditions. There never was, and never could be, a cognition constituted out of the forms alone.*

That my interpretation is exact may be seen in Kant's letter to Eberhard (*Werke,* ed. Rosenkrantz I. 444), wherein he says that the *Kritik* "allows of no innate or unacquired (*unerschaffene*) representations, all of them, intuitions and conceptions, are acquired. But there is, to speak with jurists, a *primitive acquisition or inheritance,* consequently of that also which previously did not exist, and hence belonged to nothing before this act. Such are the form of things in Space and Time, and the synthetic unity of the manifold in conceptions, for neither of these are drawn from objects, as given to our cognitive faculty, but are brought *à priori* by that faculty out of itself. The first *formal condition* of the possibility of an intuition of Space is innate, but not the representation of Space itself."

Nothing can be plainer; yet because in the course of his argument he frequently employs the term Experience in the restricted meaning of sensuous impression, and the *à priori* formal condition in the improperly extended meaning of *à priori* knowledge, he is led to maintain that the Mind brings with it *knowledge* wholly destitute of empirical elements. By a similar substitution he some-

* Compare *Kritik, Transc. Analytik,* § 13.

times speaks of Intuition and Conception as pure forms, formal conditions; and at others treats them as the products of the forms *and* the matter, namely, as intuitions and conceptions. Only thus can he instance Mathematics in illustration of pure *à priori* knowledge. It is obviously nothing of the kind, in his meaning of *à priori*. The pure formal *condition* of Space is not, he admits, the *representation* of Space; the pure formal condition of Quantity is not any representation of Quantity. Although these forms may accompany, *as conditions*, every particular experience of space relations, and every particular judgment of quantitative relations, they cannot in themselves be other than pure forms. The conception of causality may be a condition of our judgment, may necessitate the conclusion that every change we observe must have had an antecedent cause; but it can tell us nothing more, it can throw no light on any particular cause in any particular change. Manipulate the conceptions of Space and Magnitude in the abstract how you will, you cannot get out of them any geometrical *knowledge*, simply because knowledge, geometrical and other, needs sensuous intuition, needs particular experiences to which the *à priori* forms can be applied. Has not Kant laid it down at the very outset of his exposition that the only mode by which our knowledge can relate to objects is by intuition? "To this as the indispensable groundwork all thought points. *But an intuition can take place only in so far as the object is given to us.* This again is only possible, to man at least, on condition that the object affect the mind in a certain manner. . . . . By means of sensibility objects are given to us, and it alone furnishes us with intuitions; by the understanding they are *thought*, and from it arise conceptions. But all thought must directly or indirectly by means of certain signs relate ultimately to intuitions; consequently to sensibility, because in no other way can an object be given to us." (Meiklejohn's trans., p. 21.) Again: "Pure intuition contains merely the form under which something is intuited, and pure conception only the form of the thought of an object. Only pure intuitions and pure conceptions are possible *à priori;* the empirical or *à posteriori*" (p. 45).

216. How in the face of declarations so explicit is he enabled to propound the hypothesis that we have pure *à priori* knowledge? It is that besides the unconscious substitution of one meaning for another in the terms employed, he fixes on the characters of necessity and universality as infallible tests of *à priori* knowledge. At all points this argument meets us.

He divides judgments into those which are subjectively valid, and those which are objectively valid. The first are judgments of Perception (*Wahrnehmungsurtheile*); the second are judgments of Experience (*Erfahrungsurtheile*). Although all judgments of Experience are empirical, i. e. have their ground in the immediate sensuous perception, all empirical judgments, he says, are not judgments of Experience. Does this seem contradictory? It is explained thus: over and above the empirical element given in sensuous Intuition there is required the additional element of conceptions (*Begriffe*), which have their origin, *à priori,* in the pure Understanding; and under these every perception has to be subsumed before it can be changed into experience. All our judgments are at first judgments of Perception; they are simply the logical connection of perceptions in Thought, and are consequently only valid for the thinker at that particular moment. But afterwards we place them in a new relation, namely, to a world outside the thinker, and insist on their validity for all thinkers and for all time. Hence objective validity and necessary universality are reciprocal notions. "Judgments of experience take their objective validity not from the immediate knowledge of the object (for this is impossible), but from the *condition of universal validity in empirical judgments*, which rest not on empirical or sensuous conditions, but on pure conceptions" (*Proleg.*, § 19; Mahaffy, p. 70). He illustrates the two judgments thus: When I say the room is warm, I by no means require that every one shall always find this true as I do now. I only express the relations of two sensations to my present self; consequently my judgment is not valid for the object: it is simply a judgment of Perception. Very different is the other kind, which teaches me that whatever Experience reveals under certain circumstances, it must always reveal to me and to every one; its validity is not confined to the subject, nor to the particular moment, but to the object for all time. Before a judgment of Perception can become a judgment of Experience, it must be subsumed under a Conception. For example, "When the sun shines on the stone, the stone grows warm," is a judgment of Perception. No matter how often it may have been perceived by me and others, it contains within it no necessity. But if I say, "The sun warms the stone," I add to my perception of the effect the conception of cause which *necessarily* connects the conception of sunshine with that of heat. The judgment then becomes universally valid, and is converted into experience.

"But how," he asks, "does this proposition, that judgments of Experience contain necessity in the synthesis of perception, agree with my statement, that Experience as knowledge *à posteriori* can give only contingent judgments? When I say Experience teaches me something, I only mean the perception which lies in it: for example, that warming of the stone always follows the shining of the sun on it, and thus the *proposition of Experience* is always so far contingent. That this warming necessarily follows from the shining is indeed contained in the *judgment of Experience* (by means of the conception of cause); but *I do not learn that through Experience;* on the contrary, *Experience is first constituted by* this addition to perception of this conception of cause" (*Proleg.*, § 24, *note.*)

217. Without pausing to inquire how far he has resolved the contradiction here indicated, we may simply note the reappearance of the old confusion of Experience as constituted by an *à priori* and an *à posteriori* element, with Experience as only *à posteriori*. He argues that wherever we find the characters of necessity and universality, there we have pure *à priori* knowledge. Merely noting that on his own explicit statement, constantly repeated, this would only show an *element* of knowledge, let us ask what proof he offers in support of this argument? It is the old assertion: "Experience never gives us strict and absolute, but only comparative universality gained by induction, and which asserts that so far we have found no exception. Empirical universality is, then, but an arbitrary or contingent exaggeration from the cases we and others know to all cases; whereas *strict universality is essential to the judgment in which it is found,* and points to a peculiar source of knowledge which we have designated *à priori*." But if universality is essential to the judgment in which it is found, and if, as he asserts, it is always found in a judgment of Experience (for without the *à priori* addition Experience cannot be constituted), how in the name of all Logic can he pretend to show that Experience never gives universality, and that the presence of universality is a proof of *à priori* knowledge? It is like saying that the working of a steam-engine is effected by the steam and the engine, and then arguing that because the engine is powerless without the steam, this proves another source of the power that is to

be found in the steam and the engine. By dropping out of consideration the agency of steam, it is easy to show that the engine cannot be the source of steam-engine operation. By restricting Experience to the mere external action of objects on Sense, dropping out of consideration the reaction of the mental organism, it is easy to show that Experience will not suffice.

218. The truth is, Kant tried to hold contradictory positions. The whole drift of his polemic against the ontologists was to show that knowledge was limited, relative, and could not extend beyond the sphere of possible Experience; but while thus cutting the ground from under the ontologists, he was also anxious to cut the ground from the sensationalists and sceptics, and therefore tried to prove that the Mind brought with it an *à priori* fund of knowledge. Nay, so resolute was he to break away from the experiential doctrine in respect of the origin of knowledge, that he refused to accept the very explanation which was at hand to reconcile his insistance on the *à priori* element, and his insistance on the limitations of experience, — I mean the recognition of the Laws of Thought as Laws of the Organism.

219. It is unnecessary to prolong this discussion and to show that when he attempts to prove Mathematics to be *à priori* because founded on the pure *à priori* intuition of Space, his argument rests on the confusion of the two meanings of the word "intuition," one in which it stands for the primary condition, the Form of Sensibility, and the other in which it stands for the product of that Form and sensible excitation. Blank Space, the pure form, can never generate geometrical figures; and without the intuition of figures there can be no geometrical propositions.

220. Rejecting Kant's arguments in favor of a source

of Knowledge not directly dependent on the Organism and its relations to the Cosmos, and not evolved through Experience which condenses these relations, we need not here pause to consider the arguments of any other thinker, but may be content with the manifold evidence brought forward in the preceding chapters respecting the range and limitations of Research.

CHAPTER XVI.

THE PLACE OF SENTIMENT IN PHILOSOPHY.

221. OUR survey of the sources and limitations of Knowledge would be manifestly incomplete if it omitted the element of Sentiment, or Emotion, which obviously plays a considerable part in the construction of social and religious theories, and less obviously, but yet demonstrably, in the construction of even common perceptions. It cannot therefore be excluded from the data of a Philosophy which aims at explaining the World, Man, and Society. The *purpose* of Knowledge being to regulate Conduct, and the *nature* of Knowledge being that of virtual Feeling, the importance of Sentiment both as regulative and representative is indisputable. None but shrivelled souls with narrow vision of the facts of life can entertain the notion that Philosophy ought to be restricted within the limits of the Logic of Signs; it has roots in the Logic of Feeling, and many of its products which cannot emerge into the air of exact science nevertheless give the impulse to theories, and regulate conduct.

222. While thus proclaiming the necessity of its inclusion, we must be careful to assign the limits of its range. Appeals are often made to Sentiment, and questions peremptorily decided by it, which are wholly beyond its proper jurisdiction. Rhetoric and Prejudice are thus called upon to do the work of Reason and Demonstration, in cases where Verification, and not Conviction, is the immediate object of research, — where we are not inquiring into the fact of whether a certain conviction exists,

but into the ponderable evidence for its truth,—not whether some men or many men feel disgust or admiration, wrath or compassion, but whether this sentiment which has its personal grounds has also impersonal and rational grounds, such as must coerce every impartial mind desirous of ascertaining the truth. Hence the facts of Sentiment need to be interpreted with the same caution as the facts of the External Order; and this interpretation is never complete until we reach those limits which are the ultimates of all research.

223. We live encompassed by mysteries; we are flooded by influences of awe, tenderness, and sympathy which no words can adequately express, no theories thoroughly explain. These are ultimate facts of Feeling which we simply accept. For instance, we have Moral Instincts and Æsthetic Instincts which determine conduct and magnify existence; but of these desires for the welfare of others, and this enjoyment of Beauty, we can give no better account than that we find them as facts of human nature; and no better justification, when questioned, than that their influences are beneficial. We can give no better reason why we ought to care for the welfare of others,—suffering from their sufferings and rejoicing in their joys,—than why sugar is sweet to the taste: they are facts of the human organism; which facts Psychology and Physiology may approximately explain by exhibiting the factors, pointing out the observed reactions of the organism under certain conditions; but which in a last resort can only be justified by asserting that the facts are so. To use Cicero's pregnant phrase, "Nature has inclined us to love men; and this is the foundation of the Law." * If a man is insensible to the welfare of

* "Ubi enim liberalitas, ubi patriæ caritas, ubi pietas, ubi aut bene merendi de altero, aut referendæ gratiæ voluntas poterit existere? nam hæc nascuntur ex eo quod natura propensi sumus ad diligendos homines; quod fundamentum juris est."—CICERO, *De Legibus*, I. 15.

others, we can no more convince him that he ought to feel for them, than we can convince the blind man that he ought to see the glories of color. If a man is insensible to the mystery of the universe; if his soul, like that of an animal, is unvisited by any suggestions of a life larger than his own, and of any existence where his feelings have no home; if he is blind to the visible facts of evolution manifest in the history of the world and the progress of his race, deaf to the cries of pain and struggle which deeply move his fellows, dead to the stirring impulses of pity which move others to remedy the sorrows and enlarge the pleasures of mankind, — by what array of argument could we hope to make him feel what his nature does not feel?

Happily there is no such man. There are only men who feel less vividly than others; none are wholly without the feelings. And it is on this foundation that a Moral Science is possible; which proceeds like Physical Science by an exact classification of the observed facts, and their co-ordination. The facts are more complex, the co-ordination is more delicate and difficult; but their analysis and synthesis, if accurately performed, must yield results of equal validity.

224. All depends therefore on the interpretation of the facts. The inconsiderate way in which Sentiment is suffered to mingle with and pervert rational research, in matters beyond its jurisdiction (as when geological or biological inquiries have been arrested or perverted by alarmed Theology or national Prejudice), has given rise to an impatient distrust of its admission anywhere in Philosophy. Not only is the physicist justifiably indignant at the idea of his procedures being controlled by appeals to feelings which are not directly implicated in his researches, not only does he reject all personal considerations as irrelevant to the impersonal relations he is

considering, but by the violence of reaction against this foolish interference he is swung into the opposite foolishness of altogether denying a place to Sentiment in Philosophy. He insists that Sentiment be excluded from the Laboratory; and this is wise. But he also often insists that it be excluded from the teacher's chair: and this is unwise. Limiting his conception of Science to its procedures, and not taking into account its social inspiration and its social purpose, he divorces it from Religion, and from all connection with Sentiment; although such a divorce at once abdicates the highest position, converting Science into the sheer occupation of an unsocial curiosity, and leaving Religion to teachers who pretend to explain the universe without the aid of positive knowledge.

225. No reader of this work will, I presume, so far misunderstand this protest as to suppose that it implies the slightest approval of the appeals to Sentiment in inquiries which directly concern the objective relations of things, and makes personal feelings or traditional dogmas the arbiters of facts. The investigation of fact is one thing; the interpretation of the significance of this fact in the general system of things is another. Sentiment is only admissible when the relations investigated are relations of Feeling; as, for instance, when doctrines of Political Economy are considered in their social, not in their purely commercial aspects; the law of supply and demand, being one or the other, according to the indirect or direct point of view. This will become clearer when we appreciate the psychological principle which necessitates the admission of Sentiment.

226. We have already seen that everywhere the final test of philosophical interpretation is Feeling. Every demonstration rests on the reduction of inference to sensation or intuition. We have also seen that what is perceived, whether outward or inward, depends for one of

its factors on the psychostatical condition of the percipient,—what is felt and thought being felt and thought thus, and not otherwise, in consequence of the mental state, and this mental state being itself a product of historical evolution. The light of the past mingles with the light of the present. This being the case even with simple perceptions, how much more must it be the case with complex conceptions compounded out of simple feelings; and still more with those larger conceptions which constitute Philosophy.

227. If we desire to see the part played by Preconception in the construction of conceptions we may advantageously contemplate its action in the abnormal cases of Insanity, which are only exaggerations of normal processes. Cervantes, who has admirably painted the wayward logic of the insane, makes Don Quixote fashion a pasteboard helmet, and test its strength by a blow with his sword. The helmet is smashed, and the Don is much displeased at this fragility of a defence on which he had counted. He thereupon makes another helmet, and remains so perfectly satisfied with its strength that instead of once more putting it to the test he regards it as a helmet of the finest temper.* Again, when he has assumed that Haldudo is a knight, he meets the contradiction that the man is a shopkeeper by asking, What does that matter? There may be Haldudos who are knights.†

228. To descend from Fiction to Fact, M. Trélat had a patient firmly convinced that he had discovered perpetual motion. All reasoning of an adverse order left him unshaken; but he was at last brought to confess that if Arago declared him to be mistaken he would bow to that

* "El quedó satisfecto de su fortaleza, y sin querer hacer nueva experiencia della la diputó, y tuvo por celada finísima de encoje." — *Don Quijote*, Cap. I.

† "Importa poco eso respondió D. Quijote, que Haldudos puede haber caballeros." — Cap. IV.

authority. An interview was arranged. Arago, Humboldt, and some others listened with patience to the arguments by which he pretended to demonstrate the possibility of his machine. Arago then explained the mechanical impossibility, and thus concluded: "You were good enough to say you would accept my verdict. I give it you, and believe me that all present think as I do, that you are in error." The patient was for a moment as if stunned, and then burst into tears. Arago and Humboldt were much affected at the sight, and Trélat had strong hopes that the hallucination was dispelled. But they had not left the house many minutes before the patient's eyes were dry again, and raising his head proudly he exclaimed: "No matter. Arago is wrong. I have no need of a motor power: *my* wheel turns of itself!" *

229. M. Despine had a patient who fancied that poison was constantly mingled with her food. In vain he argued with her, in vain he accumulated proof on proof, her quiet answer was: "You may be right, but I feel that it is as I say, and nothing will ever remove that idea or prove the contrary." Her language accurately expressed the fact; she did not say "I know," but "I feel." She did not invoke material or rational evidence, but the evidence of her feelings.†

230. Examples of this order abound in medical literature; but we need not seek them there, for our daily experience furnishes an ample supply. No one can have argued against a superstition without noticing an entire insensibility to the plainest evidence when it opposes a conviction. Usually even an exposure of imposture, or the plainest contradiction, has but a temporary effect. The staggered believer quickly recovers his old position, and snatches at some suggestion which will explain the

* TRÉLAT, *La Folie Lucide*, p. 116. 1861.

† DESPINE, *Psychologie Naturelle*, II. 43. 1868.

contradiction. He may admit imposture in this particular case, but "is sure" there was none in the undetected cases. He cheerfully admits that the facts asserted are in contradiction with all recorded experience, but he is sure that there "is more between heaven and earth than is dreamt of in our philosophy,"—and these facts are precisely of this mysterious class. In truth his mind has received a deep impression; a conception has been fixed there, and his feelings keep it supplied with energy sufficient to bear down any opposing conception.

231. The doctrine which to one mind seems transparently absurd, because it is opposed to the mass of conceptions which have previously been formed, is not absurd, it is simply mysterious, to another mind, and although mysterious is eagerly welcomed because it is in harmony with some conceptions already formed. The mind which to-day sees the absurdity of the doctrine, may hereafter come to proclaim its truth. The conversion may be either due to intellectual readjustment, through the gradual infusion of new conceptions, or to emotional influence gradually changing the attitude of the mind, and its consequent receptivity. When we see men holding certain theological opinions which are flatly contradictory of their scientific opinions, we are not, on this ground alone, to conclude them to be hypocrites. Each position may be held in perfect sincerity, though not with perfect logicality. The one set of conceptions being in a great measure the expression of their emotions, Sentiment not Reason weaves the web of argument. The other set of conceptions being impersonal, objective, unconnected with emotions, Reason is left free to estimate the objective relations.*

* Steinthal mentions the case of a distinguished anatomist who made a pilgrimage to the relics of a saint, and whose edification at the sight of the sacred bones was not in the least disturbed by the fact that he recog-

232. A conviction having once been formed, no matter on what evidence, the strength of this conviction is derived from the amount of Feeling it engages, and not at all from the ponderable evidence; so that evidence which to other minds seems overwhelming will be set aside impatiently with some such remark as this: "That is all very well, but I *feel* I am right. I can't pretend to answer your arguments, but somehow I am convinced that the case is what I state." Although such declarations often betray profound irrationality, the speaker not seeing that the fact of his conviction is one thing and its truth another, while the point in question is not the state of his feeling but the state of the case on which he passes judgment, still such a position is less discredited and less discreditable than it would otherwise be, owing to our general recognition of the truth that many of our judgments were formed upon evidence so complex and evanescent that we cannot now recall it. When conclusions have become organized in our minds the data are usually quite irrecoverable; yet we may be fully assured that originally the evidence was present, and could be again produced were ample time and opportunity allowed us. If we have a rational conviction, although we cannot produce the grounds on which it rested, and cannot therefore force it upon others, why are we to scout the declaration of the man who relies on a conviction for which he can assign no reasons? Why do we treat our conviction as rational, and his conviction as irrational? It is because we assume that our forgotten evidence, if produced, would not simply justify our conviction, but would har-

nized them as the bones of an animal. — *Abriss du Sprachwissenschaft*, p. 228. 1871. It seems difficult not to suspect the sincerity of this; and yet not only is there psychological ground for accepting such a duality of conception, but a similar contradiction, on a smaller scale, is incessantly brought under our observation.

monize with the evidence which is now present; whereas he *resists the evidence produced,* and relies on evidence which is not producible. Every investigator may have the consciousness of having carefully examined facts before he adopted their results; and suspects, generally with justice, that those who manifestly disregard the evidence *now* before them, because it contradicts their conclusions, were not very scrutinizing in their examination of the facts on which their conclusions were originally formed. No one who has been long occupied with investigating a subject is unaware of the growth of convictions stronger than the available evidence seems to warrant. It is this experience which cannot find its accurate expression that justly endows an investigator with authority. But no worker hopes to impose his conviction on his contemporaries in the face of available evidence which contradicts it; and all sincere minds are alive to the human infirmity of grasping at evidence which harmonizes with our views, rejecting those which oppose it, or seeking to nullify their force by extraneous considerations, — an infirmity not less chargeable on philosophers than on ordinary men.

233. Here again we see how needful it is to make clear to ourselves the kind of evidence on which we rely. People will oppose the rational interpretation of admitted facts on the ground that such an interpretation is in "contradiction to their holiest instincts." This rejection or instinctive repulsion may be eminently wise, or eminently foolish. It is foolish when in the hardihood of ignorance men rely on Instinct as necessarily unerring, having a higher source than Reason; for the fact is that instincts are variable, and often fatally misguided. The instinct which urges the moth into the flame, or which makes the insect deposit its eggs in a fetid plant when that plant has the odor of putrid meat (whereby the eggs are hatched in a nidus where they perish from want of

food), these are but two of the many examples of Instinct fatally misleading.* Nor are *our* instinctive judgments to be trusted. The judgment of the child that the moon may be grasped by its tiny outstretched hand, — the judgment of the ordinary man that the redness of the rose is a part of the rose, and present in the darkness where there is no light reflected from it, no eye to see it, — these and other judgments teach us how little we can rely on Instinct, even in simple cases.

To any one who objects to some social change, not because it is demonstrably inconsistent with social welfare, but because he infers that it is so "since it excites his instinctive repulsion," we may justly ask, What are the experiences organized in that repulsion? You *feel* that the proposed change will be injurious, — it excites images of alarm; but what is the origin of your feeling? upon what social induction does it rest? what guaranty have you that the images of alarm are not unreasonably excited. When he can state the grounds of his repulsion as we can state the grounds of our proposal, there is a

* "I one day met with a curious example of failure of instinct, which, by showing it to be fallible, renders it very doubtful whether it is anything more than hereditary habit dependent on delicate modification of sensation. Some sailors cut down a good-sized tree, and, as is always my practice, I visited it daily in search of insects. Among other beetles came swarms of the little cylindrical wood-borers and commenced making holes in the bark. After a day or two I was surprised to find hundreds of them sticking in the holes they had bored, and on examination discovered that the milky sap of the tree was of the nature of gutta-percha, hardening rapidly on exposure to the air, and gluing the little animals in self-dug graves. The habit of boring holes in trees in which to deposit their eggs was not accompanied by a sufficient instinctive knowledge of trees which were suitable or trees which were destructive. If, as is very probable, these trees have an odor attractive to certain species of borers, it might very likely lead to their becoming extinct; while other species to whom the same odor was disagreeable would avoid the dangerous trees, and would survive and be credited by us with an instinct, whereas they would really be guided by a simple sensation." — WALLACE, *The Malay Archipelago*, II. 275. 1869.

weighing of evidence possible. But the mere repulsion, though not to be disregarded, is only a warning, it is not evidence. It may indicate the presence of some condition which ought to be taken into account; but unless it spring from one of the deep-seated instincts which express the moral experiences of the community, it is no more than an indication; and even then, we must bear in mind that our moral experiences widen with advancing civilization, the deep-seated instinct of the community of to-day will not correspond with the enlarged social experiences of to-morrow, for there is evolution of the Moral Instincts no less than of the Rational Judgments: we learn to feel differently respecting social relations, as we learn to think differently of the cosmical relations. The boast of one age may become the infamy of another.

Granting, therefore, its due weight to Sentiment and to Conviction irrespective of producible evidence, we must still say that any proposition opposed by these ought not to be rejected until their sources and range have been scrutinized. Scrutiny will often detect that the repulsion is due to some unconscious desire to preserve the existing order, because agreeable to our prejudices or interests; sometimes it is due to confidence in an old custom, or a venerated teacher; and then we may ask: On what was the custom founded? What means of knowing the truth had the venerated teacher? and what part did *his* feelings play in interpreting the evidence?

234. The legitimate influence of Sentiment in determining Belief, and thus regulating conduct, is a delicate question. Theologians have not been wrong in ascribing Faith and Incredulity to moral predispositions, and in affirming that religious conviction mainly depends upon religious feeling. But they have been wrong in assuming that religious feeling can be reached by argument, or created, where it is absent, by an effort of the will. It is

not true that a man can believe or disbelieve what he will. But it is certain that an active desire to find any proposition true will unconsciously tend to that result, by dismissing importunate suggestions which run counter to the belief, and welcoming those which favor it. The psychological law that we only see what interests us, and only assimilate what is adapted to our condition, causes the mind to *select* its evidence.

235. Further, in respect of religious convictions we must distinguish between the personal or subjective aspect, and the impersonal or social aspect, — between the truth which is a law to the man himself, and the truth which is a law for the community. The feeling which determines the actions of the man is valid for him: what he feels, he feels; what he thinks, he thinks. But this may not be communicable to others, cannot be made guides for them. For communicable truths, two things are requisite, — the possibility of showing them in their objective relations, or by intelligible symbols, and the mental state ready to grasp these. The beauty of a statue is felt by twenty spectators in a somewhat similar manner, owing to a similarity in their minds, and for all these it would be a true proposition to affirm "This statue is beautiful." It would not be true for other spectators, insensible to the æsthetic charm. Here is a truth which in the nature of things is limited: we may generalize it, and affirm that many minds, perhaps the majority, will feel this pleasurable emotion; but we never assume that the truth represents an invariable relation for all minds, like that of parallel lines, or the composition of water, which express objective relations that are invariable and undisturbed by any subjective variations; these latter are communicable truths which all minds must apprehend when the terms are distinctly presented. No one will say that a personal incommunicable truth is less cer-

tain than an impersonal communicable truth. If I say, "There I see an apple," this expression of a subjective fact requires no evidence; but if it be affirmed as an objective fact affirming the present existence of the apple and not merely my present feeling, evidence is needful. I can communicate to others the fact of my feeling, but I can only communicate to them the fact of the existence by placing their senses in relation to the object. What I see may be no apple, but an imitation in stone. My inference from the visual sensation may have been false, and my affirmation in such a case would be subjectively true, objectively false: true in that I had the visible feeling which an apple would excite; false in that I concluded from this to the existence of an apple there present. Nor would the testimony of fifty thousand people all affirming that they saw the same apple, all declaring that what they saw really *was* an apple, add one tittle of objective validity to my assertion. This is a paradox only to those who do not appreciate the nature of evidence. Because we habitually find our inferences confirmed, or corrected, by the testimony of others, we fall into the mistake of counting testimony instead of weighing it, and suppose that many spectators are more to be trusted than one; whereas it is not the multitude of observers but the variety of the means of observation which gives value to their testimony. The concurrent testimony of fifty thousand persons would only prove that they were visually affected in the same way, and had inferred the same thing; and unless these observers were placed under different conditions, fifty thousand observations are no better than five. A miracle performed in the presence of a multitude has no greater credibility than the same miracle performed in the lonely chamber of a solitary,—unless some among the multitude have sources of experience on which to ground their inferences, which were not open to the solitary. When wonder-workers ask for our belief because their assertions are certified by hundreds of respectable witnesses, they should be told that neither numbers nor respectability have scientific weight, when all the witnesses are under the same disadvantages respecting the reduction of their inferences to sensations; the same assertion repeated many times, however varied its expression, is not made more credible by repetition. All that the testimony of a multitude of witnesses really amounts to is that they had certain sensations, from which they inferred certain corresponding events.

236. During M'Clure's Polar Expedition the watch one night *saw* a bear on an iceberg. He called to his mates, and they having armed themselves cautiously approached the spot where the bear stood. To the astonishment of all, this visible bear rose in the air and flew away. They had mistaken an eagle for a bear; yet not one of them had doubted his inference from the optical sensation common to them all. Had they not alarmed the eagle, or had the spot been inaccessible, they would all have sworn sincerely that they had *seen* a bear. Would a million of such witnesses have rendered this statement more credible? But now suppose the sailors to have returned to the ship because they found it difficult to approach this bear, and only two of them had remained behind hoping to find a more accessible path; one of these remaining on the watch while the other seeks a path, presently the watcher *sees* the eagle rise and fly away; and on his return to the ship he tells his companions what he saw. They may or may not believe his statement, according to their trust in his veracity or the intensity of their previous conviction; and if now the other sailor returns with the eagle which he has just shot, the conviction is complete.

237. All Knowledge, being virtual Feeling, is only

communicable through Feeling. A man may communicate to me the fact that he has a sensation, a perception, or an emotion, but he can only awaken similar sensation, perception, or emotion in me by placing me in similar conditions, objective and subjective. He may tell me that a certain fruit has a sweet taste, and I may believe this statement to be objectively valid; but I must myself taste the fruit before I can share his feeling. He may tell me that he has a misgiving, but that misgiving can only be awakened in me by a presentation of its grounds. There are degrees of communicability. If I am told by some one that he has seen a dog, I have so distinct an image raised by that word that I can understand his feeling, and in a sense share it. If I am told by the same person that he has seen a gangrened limb, the absence of experience will make me very imperfectly understand him. If he tells me he has had a bilious attack, my apprehension is vague. If he tells me that the summer dawn fills him with religious joy, and an autumnal evening with religious awe, my apprehension is still more vague. I too may have many times been touched by the tender lights of a summer dawn, but unless there is some communicable mark by which these reactions of feeling can be seen to resemble those reactions in him, our two experiences remain personal, subjective, incommunicable. Hence it is that Sentiment only passes into Science when it is capable of being *translated into objective signs.* The sensations of color and sound must be translated into vibrations, and then the reactions of Feeling are measured with reference to their objective vibrations. Every variety of tone, however distinct to Feeling, was a personal fact of no value to exact Science, until it thus became interpretable through its objective sign. This connection once established, Science had its instrument. Every single tone had its dynamical sign, — every subjective fact its correlative external fact, — and then whatever could be deduced from dynamical laws of vibration was inferable of Sound; thus were discoveries made by mathematical analysis which could never have been approached through analysis of Feeling.

238. In conclusion, we may say that the part played by Sentiment in Philosophy is very large, and is admirable, or the reverse, according to circumstances. It is necessary and admirable as an inspiration, when duly controlled by verification. It is admirable, and its jurisdiction is final, when feelings form the subject-matter of the debate. It is disastrous when it takes the place of verification and substitutes personal for impersonal relations.

Among the curious features of our mental organization must be noted that by which on all subjects of immediate practical importance we always proceed at once to verify any conjecture we may have formed, whereas on subjects of speculative importance we are too impatient to await this control, and in our eagerness for an explanation readily accept conjectures as truths. The anticipatory rush of thought prefigures qualities and foresees consequences; instead of pausing to ascertain whether our anticipations do or do not correspond with fact, we proceed to argue and to act on them as if this mental vision were final. Native indolence unchastened by repeated failure, and native impatience unchecked by caution, are sustained by the energy of our confidence in what we think. Even a false explanation is preferred to the unrest of doubt; and a plausible explanation is so gratifying to the feelings by quieting this agitation of unrest, that we cling to it in spite of adverse evidence. Who has not observed, even in himself, the eagerness with which some argument is snatched at, and some statement credited, when these seem to confirm his own view of the case? To submit our conclusions to the rigorous test of evidence, and to seek the truth irrespective of our preconceptions, is the rarest and most difficult of intellectual virtues.

How then can truth be decided? What are the tests of certitude? These questions must be examined in the next Problem. Hitherto we have examined the range and limitations of Knowledge, and have only touched incidentally on the nature of Certitude; henceforward we shall have to apply the principles here expounded.

END OF VOLUME I.

Cambridge: Electrotyped and Printed by Welch, Bigelow, & Co.